Trade Unionism since 1945

Trade Unions Past, Present and Future

Edited by Craig Phelan

Volume 1

PETER LANG
Oxford • Bern • Berlin • Bruxelles • Frankfurt am Main • New York • Wien

Trade Unionism since 1945

Towards a Global History. Volume 1: Western Europe, Eastern Europe, Africa and the Middle East

Craig Phelan (ed.)

PETER LANG
Oxford • Bern • Berlin • Bruxelles • Frankfurt am Main • New York • Wien

Bibliographic information published by Die Deutsche Bibliothek
Die Deutsche Bibliothek lists this publication in the Deutsche National-bibliografie; detailed bibliographic data is available on the Internet at <http://dnb.ddb.de>.

A catalogue record for this book is available from The British Library.

Library of Congress Cataloging-in-Publication Data:

Phelan, Craig, 1958-
Trade unionism since 1945 : towards a global history / Craig Phelan.
v. cm.
Includes bibliographical references and index.
Contents: v.1. Western Europe, Eastern Europe, Africa, and the Middle East.
ISBN 978-3-03911-410-8 (alk. paper)
1. Labor unions--History. 2. Industrial relations--History. I. Title.
HD6483.P45 2009
331.88--dc22
2009012916

ISSN 1662-7784
ISBN 978-3-03911-410-8

Je dédie ce livre à Sibye Placca

Contents

Introduction ix
CRAIG PHELAN

Western Europe

Belgian Trade Unions:
Between Social Movement and Service Centre 3
PATRICK PASTURE

France: The State, Trade Unions, and
Collective Bargaining – Reform or Impasse? 37
GUY GROUX

German Trade Unionism in the Postwar Years:
The Third and Fourth Movements 65
STEPHEN J. SILVIA

An Historical Analysis of Trade Unionism in Italy:
Between Pluralism of Ideas and Unity of Action 97
VALERIA PULIGNANO

Trade Unions and the Politics of Renewal in Spain in Historical
Context: Making and Enacting Regulation and Representation 121
MIGUEL MARTÍNEZ LUCIO AND KERSTIN HAMANN

The Swedish Model of Industrial Relations:
Self-Regulation and Combined Centralisation-Decentralisation 155
ANDERS KJELLBERG

Trade Unionism in Britain since 1945 199
KEITH LAYBOURN

Eastern Europe

The History of Trade Unionism in Hungary, 1945–2002 231
LÁSZLÓ NEUMANN

Trade Unionism in Poland since 1945 261
DAVID OST AND MICHAL WENZEL

Ukrainian Trade Unions since 1945 291
PAUL KUBICEK

Africa and Middle East

The History of Trade Unionism in Cameroon 315
PIET KONINGS

Trade Unionism in Israel since 1945: Its Origins and Functions 343
ITZHAK HARPAZ

Trade Unions in Nigeria since 1945 363
IFEANYI P. ONYEONORU AND JIMI O. ADESINA

Workers Divided, Workers Uniting:
South African Unions since 1945 387
SAKHELA BUHLUNGU AND EDWARD WEBSTER

Zimbabwe Congress of Trade Unions 413
FREEK SCHIPHORST

Notes on Contributors 437

Index 443

Introduction

CRAIG PHELAN

For two centuries trade unions have led the struggle to achieve a more equitable distribution of the world's wealth and power. In virtually every country trade unions have battled at the workplace and in the community, in law courts and legislatures, at the bargaining table and in the streets to improve the living and working conditions of their members. As the principal institutions for the defence of workers' rights, they have played many roles and assumed many guises, at times operating as little more than lethargic bureaucracies on behalf of a minority of workers with leverage at the workplace, and at other times at the forefront of dynamic social movements for radical change. At their best, trade unions have championed campaigns for social justice and participatory democracy that have fundamentally altered national histories by giving voice to disenfranchised majorities. Whether as narrow vested interest for a privileged minority or the embodiment of the hopes for all workers, trade unionism has been a major feature of the modern world.

In the advanced capitalist economies, trade unions reached the pinnacle of their influence during the three decades following World War II. Work and labour relations during this so-called 'golden age' of capitalism were built upon the three pillars of Fordist manufacturing, Keynesian economic policies and what are often referred to as labour-capital accords. Despite wide variation the postwar accords represented an often tacit understanding between trade unions, employers' associations and the state that benefited all three and buttressed the unparalleled economic growth of these years. The accords were based on trade union acceptance of managerial prerogatives over questions of investment and the organisation of production, while employers and the state recognised that trade unions had a legitimate role to play in matters of wages, hours and working conditions. Beyond this understanding, the labour-capital accords differed widely, reflecting the enduring economic and social diversity of the countries themselves. For example, in many European countries, including West Germany, Austria and Sweden, accords took the form of national social pacts that elevated trade unions to the level of social partner. In France and Italy, where communists dominated the labour movement and where the state assumed a more interventionist role in the economy, labour-capital accords legitimised and strengthened trade unionism by institutionalising their role in the factories. Accords even took root where decentralised collective bargaining was the norm, such as in Britain and the US, although in these cases the supporting institutional framework was not as deeply embedded and the accords therefore proved far more fragile.

Whatever the specific arrangements, the postwar accords offered trade unions unprecedented power and influence, and they provided a degree of institutional stability beyond the imagination of prewar trade unionists. By 1950 trade unions wielded considerable clout in national politics in the democracies of Europe, North America and Japan, and they became a bulwark in the pursuit of economic growth and social improvement. Relative stability ushered in a long period of growth in union density rates, and in every advanced industrial economy unions organised between one-third and two-thirds of all workers. In most cases workers outside the mass production sector did not share equitably in this system. The high wage and secure job contracts were usually reserved for those fortunate enough to work for profitable firms in mass production. But trade union influence in the political arena led to the erection of expansive welfare provisions, such as national health and unemployment insurance, which benefited the entire working class.

The generally labour-friendly industrial relations systems of the postwar years were unable to withstand the economic shocks of the 1970s and 1980s. The oil crises of the 1970s, the slowing of economic growth coupled with high inflation and rising unemployment, ultimately proved fatal for the economic system built on the pillars of Keynesianism, Fordism and labour-capital accords. In the 1980s leading firms in all advanced economies evidenced a determination to restructure in order to compete in the new economic environment, although the pace and nature of restructuring was often dependent on the institutional power of unions in their respective industries and national settings. Except in those countries where trade unionism remained deeply embedded in the institutional framework of national decision-making, such as Sweden and Belgium, the labour accords were placed under enormous strain and trade unionism declined. Increased capital mobility and international economic competition, profound corporate restructuring, the long-term shift of employment from manufacturing to the service sector, the rise of neo-liberal politics and the abandonment of Keynesianism have all undermined the industrial relations systems that characterised the thirty years following World War II. Trade union movements in most advanced economies have seen their memberships plummet, their power on the shopfloor and in legislatures sapped, and their bargaining coverage substantially reduced. The buoyancy and confidence that exuded trade unionism after 1945 have given way to pessimism and a sense of desperation.

Although rarely as large as its counterpart in the advanced economies, and often operating under the thumb of repressive regimes, trade unionism in developing and transitional economies has nevertheless played an equally important historical role. The 'golden age' of capital in the developed North following World War II was matched by an almost simultaneous and equally impressive 'golden age' of development in the world's poorer nations. Colonialism had long imposed a division of labour in which, by and large, raw materials from the colonies were exploited to sustain the industrial development of the imperial powers. With successful independence movements in the late 1950s and early 1960s, however, a 'new international division of labour' took shape, marked by the rapid expansion of the world market for industrial production sites and cheap labour. International firms led the way in industrialising significant areas of the global South, often transplanting mass production techniques to sites in the developing world (peripheral Fordism) in order to escape the heavy labour costs of the advanced economies. And it was under the new international division of labour that trade unionism, already with long-established roots in certain pockets of the global South, began to prosper.

Latin American trade unionism experienced substantial growth under state-directed, import-substitution industrialisation. The often vicious repression by dictatorial regimes gave rise to highly politicised trade union movements that fought for better wages and conditions in state-owned factories and at the same time championed movements for workers' rights and welfare systems at the national level. The powerful connection between trade unionism and Juan Domingo Perón in Argentina and Luiz Inácio 'Lula' da Silva in Brazil illustrates the politicised nature of Latin American trade unionism. This region is covered in depth in Volume 2. While never representing more than a fraction of the working population, trade unions in sub-Saharan Africa have at times exercised considerable economic and political influence. Often at the forefront of nationalist movements against colonial rule, African trade unions struggled to retain their independence under authoritarian post-colonial regimes, and as key civil society actors they have been indispensable in campaigns for justice and democracy. Trade unionism's leading role in the overthrow of apartheid in South Africa, and its creation of Zimbabwe's Movement for Democratic Change in opposition to Robert Mugabe testify to its importance as an agent of change. In the transitional Asian economies, autonomous trade unionism has long been hindered by various forms of state authoritarianism. While some regimes sanctioned official trade unions and others chose to exclude worker organisations of all stripes, harsh repression long precluded the possibility of powerful, independent union movements that exercised significant influence in the political or economic arenas. The vanguard role played by Korean trade unions in the 1987 democracy movement, however, signalled a decisive breakthrough for trade union rights.

With the broadening of democracy, however, the independent trade unions in Latin America, Asia and Africa encountered difficulties every bit as severe as those faced by trade unions in the advanced economies. Democratic governments, under pressure and encouragement from the World Bank and International Monetary Fund, have pursued policies that have led to the same spiral of declining union membership and loss of trade union political influence faced by unions elsewhere. The Latin American debt crisis of 1982 signalled the end of state-led development based on import substitution and ushered in the era of neo-liberalism. Throughout the developing world, states began opening their economies to foreign competition, slashing social welfare budgets, privatising state-owned companies, and legislating labour market flexibility. Structural adjustment programmes have had a devastating impact on the fortunes of most trade union movements in the developing world. New private sector labour legislation and massive public sector layoffs have resulted in heavy membership losses. High unemployment and declining real wages have forced many former and would-be trade unionists into the informal labour market, which remains largely impervious to union organising drives. Moreover, in many parts of the developing world, trade unionists continue to face dismissal and discrimination, even imprisonment, while obstacles to organising and collective bargaining mount in the increasingly competitive global marketplace.

Trade unionism in communist bloc countries was in many ways unique. Under state socialism trade unions were expected, as Lenin famously put it, to assume the role of 'transmission belts', meaning that they served to implement party goals at the workplace and to mobilise workers in pursuit of those goals. Lacking autonomy, communist trade unions assisted management in achieving state-dictated production goals, encouraged high production levels through various forms of 'labour competition', and administered the wide array of social welfare services provided by the state. As an appendage of the party, trade unionism rarely defended workers against management. This form of trade unionism persists today in China, explored in detail in Volume 2. The All China Federation of Trade Unions, with its nearly 170 million members, is larger than all other trade unions in the world combined. It remains the only legally sanctioned trade union organisation, yet even here the advent of capitalism in China has left its future role in doubt. With the collapse of state socialism in the former Soviet Union and the eastern bloc countries, most of the old official bodies have either withered or disappeared, and the new independent trade unions have struggled to cope with the harsh economic and political environment of post-communism. Large state-owned firms have collapsed or have been privatised, often replaced by numerous smaller ones that are generally hostile to unions. New political parties are often eager to attract foreign investment by liberalising labour laws, and public payrolls have been slashed as many eastern bloc countries sought (or are seeking) to meet the monetary requirements for entry into the European Union. Lacking an autonomous trade union tradition, and still hampered by the legacy of the communist era, when trade unionism embodied state rather than worker interests, trade unions in the post-communist world have generally found it exceedingly difficult to establish a foothold in the new market economies or the new democratic political scene.

In all parts of the world, therefore, trade unionism is in peril. Whether defined by falling union densities, declining strike levels, or the diminution of political clout, there is no doubt that there is a crisis facing trade unionism, that is a crisis of long standing, and that it is being felt in every part of the globe. Trade unionism worldwide is losing influence in areas of traditional concern (wages, hours and working conditions), and it is also losing its capacity to promote the broader aims of political democracy, civil liberties and redistributive justice. Some observers have been quick to suggest that trade unionism will never again achieve the influence it exercised in the three decades after World War II, that the era of 'big labour' is gone forever. Other observers recognise that trade unionism has always had to struggle and adapt to ever-changing environments, and that it tends to grow in great bursts rather than incrementally; they watch for signs in the economy and the body politic, and especially in the revitalisation efforts of unions themselves, that trade unionism will rebound.

This book and its sister volume are intended to shed light on contemporary trade union problems by offering accessible yet sophisticated historical overviews of trade union development in a total of 26 countries, 15 of which are included here, representing Eastern and Western Europe, Africa and the Middle East. Countries were selected on the basis of geography, with an attempt made to cover each region of the globe, and on the basis of diversity, with an attempt to reveal the rich variety of trade union experience worldwide. Leading authorities from each country were asked to contribute chapters that illuminate the key characteristics of trade unionism as they developed over time, to place trade union histories in political and economic context, to describe the present health of trade unionism in that country, and to reveal the historical roots of problems faced today.

The organisation and approach of this two-volume project is based on the premise that the first step towards a world history is recognition that trade unions are the products of national systems of interlocking political and economic institutions. The structure, strategies and even the goals of trade unions are products of the unique historical development of the countries in which they operate. Each country's trade union movement represents a distinctive accommodation to a nation's industrial relations system and labour market, its legal and political and traditions, and therefore each national trade union movement is faced with discrete sets of opportunities and challenges. It is this national diversity that makes understanding worldwide trade union trends so difficult and why any world history of trade unionism must be based on an understanding of the national movements that comprise it. By providing a total of 26 such national histories, it is hoped that these volumes begin the process whereby scholars begin to come to grips with the enduring differences as well as the similarities that has marked trade unionism from its inception.

Western Europe

Belgian Trade Unions: Between Social Movement and Service Centre

PATRICK PASTURE[1]

1. Introduction

While the Belgian labour movement offered one of the most important models for the organisation of the late-nineteenth-century working class, Belgium seldom figures in overviews of contemporary trade unionism and industrial relations. That is a pity, since the country in many respects constitutes a European microcosm in which very different European traditions and features coexist; it really is the 'quintessential European state' (Carl Strikwerda). But as regards trade unions, Belgium is an exception. Belgian unions, unlike those in most other Western countries, have experienced an almost uninterrupted growth since 1945, maintaining one of the highest density rates in the world even throughout the 1980s and 1990s up to the present day. It made unions a formidable actor on the Belgian socio-political scene.

That situation, however, was not written in the stars from the very beginning. Even if it was one of the earliest industrial nations, indeed the first on the European continent, organised labour developed late and working conditions throughout the nineteenth century were notoriously bad. Moreover, from a more structural point of view, the development of Belgian trade unions was closely related to the political struggles of the nineteenth century. The predecessor of the socialist confederation even

1 I wish to thank Guy Van Gyes for comments on an earlier version of this chapter and Craig Phelan for editing it.

originated from within the Belgian Labour Party. Until today, trade unions remain divided between socialist, Christian (Catholic) and liberal unions that, notwithstanding claims for political independence, retain ties to the respective political parties. In the late 1930s, extreme right Flemish nationalists also created unions, called Autonomous Unions, although these did not gain much of a foothold. Independent unions for white-collar workers and teachers in the interwar period were largely incorporated into the major confederations. The post-World War II social consultation system made it very difficult, if not impossible, for newcomers to be recognised. Nevertheless, in the 1980s some local autonomous unions did manage to carve out a niche for autonomous syndicalist action.

While generally trade union pluralism is associated with trade union weakness, it seems not to have hampered trade union growth and power in Belgium, not even at the end of the second millennium. Remarkably, while the socialist unions dominated by one-third in 1900, the Christian unions have continuously expanded their share and surpassed their socialist competitors in the 1950s. This unique situation can only be explained by observing the largely non-confessional, open stance of these unions, which could never be considered a Catholic association obedient to clerical authorities and therefore deliberately called themselves 'Christian', and by the regional dynamics and the 'pillarised' nature of Belgian society. The latter means that society to a large extent (of course never totally) became divided into different 'pillars', networks of ideological-political associations, among which trade unions, covering (nearly) all aspects of daily life. The regional factor was especially important, although it was not the only one (on the regional dimension see Pasture 2000). Due to their earlier development, the socialist unions had a decisive advantage in the heavy industries of the Walloon region. However, they were never able to escape their association with the francophone workers' aristocracy, not even when the traditional industries in the old industrial basins declined after World War II. This, including the francophone dominance as well as their neglect of the language issue, hampered their development in Flanders. By contrast, the Christian unions originated mainly in Flanders, where Catholicism remained strong until the 1960s. However, here they had the advantage as major parts of Flanders industrialised in the 1960s. They also succeeded in appealing to newcomers on the labour market by particularly targeting them, including Islamic migrant workers, also in Wallonia. They also appeared more open with regard to Flemish demands, if only because their leaders spoke Dutch. Liberal unions progressed slowly as an alternative to both major confederations (on the evolution of unionisation see Vandaele 2005; Ebbinghaus et al. 2000).

Table 1. Union density rates 1945–2000

	Socialist	Christian	Liberal	(a)	(b)	(c)
1945	14.1	9.4	1.6	26.3		
1950	19.4	18.5	2.3	43.3		
1955	21.7	20.9	3.0	47.8		
1960	22.4	23.8	3.1	51.6	40.7	41.5
1965	21.9	24.6	3.0	50.5	40.0	39.9
1970	23.5	27.1	3.0	54.9	42.3	42.1
1975	28.6	32.3	4.3	69.0	53.3	51.9
1980	29.2	34.1	5.2	75.7	56.6	53.4
1985	28.2	35.1	5.4	80.9	56.5	50.7
1990	27.4	36.5	5.4	77.6	56.7	53.9
1995	28.8	38.7	5.3	85.0	59.5	55.7
2000				86.1	61.1	55.6

Data corrected for propaganda inflation.
(a) Gross density: Rate of the major confederations' union members/gainfully employed.
(b) Net density 1: Rate of the major confederations' union members, excluding retired members / gainfully employed.
(c) Net density 2: Rate of the major confederations' union members, excluding retired and unemployed / gainfully employed.
Source: 1945–90: Ebbinghaus et al. 2000; 1995–2000: Dorssemont et al. 2005 (there is a slight difference between both calculations <1 per cent point); (c): 1990–2002: Visser 2006, 45, table 3. According to recent calculations by Guy Van Gyes the latter figures for net density 2 grossly underestimate the number of unemployed union members. The actual net density rate would not exceed 50 per cent.

The following chapter charts the development of Belgian trade unions since World War II, and in particular assesses the factors that constitute their uniqueness and may explain the particular development and strength of Belgian trade unions in a society renowned for its complexity and divisions. It argues that its originality lies in a unique combination of service provision and militancy proper of a social movement. To understand this evolution, however, one should also have some notion of the structural features of Belgian trade unionism.

When unions finally developed on a national scale, which was not before 1894, they quickly centralised. As the socialist unions were the first ones established, the socialist confederation's traditional base is with the industrial unions, which organise blue-collar workers in certain industries, as well as white collar workers and employees in the public sector. The Christian confederation, which originated in the anti-socialist unions of the 1880s, more clearly rests upon a double structure of industrial unions and district unions. Also the confederal authority is more important; for example, it holds a central strike fund. The liberal confederation is only subdivided into a general union for the private sector, and an all grades union for the public sector (Ebbinghaus and Visser 2000).

2. Restoration and Renewal of Trade Union Structures

While there is much to say for a narrative that stresses the continuity between 1950 and the 1920s and 1930s, World War II and its aftermath posed a tremendous challenge for unions, and hence offers a convenient starting point for an analysis of postwar trade unionism in Belgium. The German occupiers introduced the Nazi system of industrial relations, with a Labour Front and corporatist unions (Luyten and Hemmerijckx 2000). To the astonishment of many, the socialist party leader and renowned theoretician Hendrik De Man supported the New Order, hoping to play a major role in it. He was the main architect of the new industrial relations scheme which introduced obligatory unitary unionism, the *Union des Travailleurs Manuels et Intellectuels* (UTMI). While the prewar leadership of the (socialist) General Labour Confederation of Belgium opposed the UTMI, many socialist unions did join. Under the influence of its Flemish affiliates, the Christian confederation CSC (*Confédération des Syndicats Chrétiens*), in contrast to earlier decisions and contrary to the French-speaking unions, initially agreed to participate in the UTMI, hoping that it could dominate it and that it would safeguard some basic trade union liberties. Notwithstanding that the confederation ended its collaboration in the summer of 1941, the split between Flemish and Walloons took many years to heal (Mampuys 1994).

In the meantime, while free trade union activities remained prohibited and the major union confederations opted for a cautious, clandestine stance in order to safeguard their position after the war, on the shopfloor new radical unions took root, particularly in the Walloon industrial basins and the public administration in Brussels. The communists benefited from the opportunity by setting up very active trade union 'fighting committees', organising labour resistance against the Occupation, and promoting trade union unity. So too did André Renard, a young dynamic socialist trade union leader of the metalworkers of Liège who created a new syndicalist movement, the *Mouvement Syndical Unifié* (MSU), arguing for political autonomy, trade union unity, and workers' control. In the other major Walloon industrial city, Charleroi, similar initiatives saw the light of day. A noteworthy movement also arose in the public services, in opposition to the majority of the socialist public sector union which, together with the textiles union, had joined the UTMI. Although they appealed to Christian workers (and some indeed felt attracted), all these new initiatives posed a challenge primarily to the socialist unions (Hemmerijckx 2003).

The leaders of the prewar confederations focused rather on preparing for the aftermath of war. They were divided between those in exile and those living in occupied Belgium. Those exiled in France, and later in London, being well informed on new ideas and confronted with alternative traditions and influences, dreamt about radical changes once the war was over. In contrast, those in occupied Belgium cautiously negotiated with industrialists and businessmen about what could be done. Several, often rather isolated, made plans and conducted secret talks. It became increasingly obvious that labour and capital, workers and employers, would somehow cooperate in corporatist structures. What remained unclear was what role the state would play, how powerful employers would be, and the degree of trade union liberty that would be allowed. Negotiations between leaders of the socialist trade unions and some particularly influential employers and civil servants led to the achievement of a so-called Social Pact, followed by the drafting of the postwar social order (Luyten and Vanthemsche 1995; Pasture 1993).

After the war the immediate task was to reconstruct democratic trade unionism so that it could help tackle the immense problems that workers faced, not least of which the restoration of purchasing power. But as the trade union landscape had been modified, and the power balance between labour and capital altered, this reconstruction raised some fundamental questions. Labour unity stood at the top of the agenda of renewal. 'A real hurricane in favour of unity blew through the ranks of the working class', one Christian trade unionist testified in 1944 (quoted in Pasture 2004: 27). But appearances are often misleading, and circumstances proved not to be in favour of labour unity at all. While experiences during the war, particularly amongst those in the resistance and those who were imprisoned, had often united people and helped to bring down the ideological walls separating them (which is what most scholars emphasise), the occupation had also deepened divisions and created new ones. Belgian society as a whole was ripped apart in the first postwar years and on the brink of civil war, brought about by conflicts originating in World War II. Moreover, then as much as later, views on what unity should entail diverged considerably. As some are more equal than others, so it is with unity as well. Pleas for unity usually include arguments for primordiality and leadership: who would lead the unified workers? Regarding themselves as the only legitimate representative of the working class, socialist unions aimed at becoming the linchpin of the new unitary trade union. The Christian unions, well aware of that situation, could therefore only conceive of joint action with the socialists, but not a merger. Moreover, they in any case refused any association with the communists and resisted pressure, including from the US in the framework of its attempts to neutralise the communists, to join an all-encompassing unitary confederation (Mampuys 1994; Pasture 1992). Which objectives the Fighting Committees pursued by proclaiming unity remains a matter of debate, but there is reason to believe, controlled as they were by the Communist Party, that they wanted simply to dominate and control the union movement in order to achieve the broader communist goal.

Perhaps more importantly, the unions found themselves trapped in a competitive struggle with the dawn of the new postwar social order. The Christian trade unions in particular remembered how they had been overtaken by the socialists in 1918; they did not want to make the same mistake twice. They had carefully prepared for Liberation and immediately went on the offensive. They knew all too well that in the new social order, power and representation, and the distribution of seats in corporatist institutions, would be determined by numbers. Very soon they bypassed the socialist membership in Flanders, a success that would be repeated in Wallonia. The socialist unions, notwithstanding their unitary claims, responded in kind and gave priority to the building up of a trade union apparatus. The policy of the old reformist Belgian Trade Union Federation, which experienced dramatic membership losses in Wallonia and Brussels (up to more than −80 per cent in Liège and Verviers), in certain Flemish areas (−57 per cent in total), and in certain sectors (−71 per cent of white collar workers), constituted a case in point of the ambiguous policy pursued: its leaders restored the trade union apparatus while they appealed to all other unions to join them, and at the same time they engaged with the Christian unions, the employers and the government in collective negotiations for obtaining substantial benefits and pay rise for the workers, excluding newcomers. Likewise, the Communist Fighting Committees, transformed into the Unitary Trade Unions, argued for political independence which strongly appealed to many workers, including Catholics, while at the same time remaining firmly under control of the Communist Party (Hemmerijckx 2003). Nevertheless, all leftist unions did merge into a new confederation in April 1945, the General Labour Federation of Belgium (*Fédération Générale du Travail de Belgique* FGTB). Though all factions were represented in the confederation's governing bodies, the reformist leaders of the prewar federation dominated. By able manoeuvring and, paradoxically, helped by the polarised national political context and later also the Cold War, they succeeded in sidelining the communists. One of the leftist militants nevertheless managed to advance himself up the confederation's leadership structures and put his mark on it, André Renard.

In one respect at least, trade union renewal did take place. All unions emphasised their political autonomy. While in the interwar period unions were still integrated into the political party structures, parties abolished collective membership after 1945. This did not mean, however, that trade union leaders had cut all their ties with political parties and hence lost all ability to influence them. The political ties would even be considerably strengthened in the following years as a result of the political tensions which increasingly tended to replicate the prewar political cleavage between Catholics and anti-clericals. But the unions were no longer structurally part of the parties as had been the case before World War II.

3. Unions in the Unfinished Consultation Economy

After the war, Belgian society entered a long period of sharp political tension which lasted until the late 1950s–early 1960s (a general political overview in English is Witte, Craeybeckx and Meynen 2001). The first divisive issue was how to deal with collaborators, particularly the political collaboration of Flemish nationalists. This issue was closely connected with the position of King Leopold III, who was absent at Liberation and had been discredited in the eyes of many during the Occupation, as well as after Liberation by refusing to recognise the legitimacy of the government in exile and by still expressing sympathy for an authoritarian regime. These painful questions impacted trade unions, but rather indirectly; they too had some interest in not dwelling too much on their role during the war. Unions excluded collaborators from their ranks and emphasised their roles as victims and as members of the resistance. While in 1945 this was not yet the case, increasingly the position adopted in the political conflicts duplicated prewar divisions. Socialists and liberals for example most strongly opposed the return of Leopold III, particularly in the French-speaking part, while Catholics, predominantly in Flanders, supported his return to the throne. Political tension continued after the abdication of King Leopold in 1950 and his succession by Baudouin I, mainly concerning the role of the state and of the church in society. Socialists argued for a greater role for the state, while Christian democrats – who manifested themselves as a new political movement rather than just a restoration of political Catholicism aiming at safeguarding the interests of the Roman Catholic Church – emphasised the social responsibilities of civil society. Liberals to a certain extent defended the interests of industry and capital, but shared with the socialists the ambition to roll back the influence of the Catholic Church, which came to the fore in the so-called 'school war' concerning the organisation and financing of public and private (largely Catholic) education.

Generally speaking, the trade unions were not prime actors in these political struggles, but were forced to largely abandon their claim for political independence in practice and to enhance their political solidarity, leading to the re-establishment of opposing Catholic (or rather Christian democratic), socialist and liberal 'pillars'. During the debate over the role of the state in social security, socialist and Christian unions stood in opposite camps. Nevertheless, in collective negotiations, political opposition was put aside as much as possible. There were, nevertheless, moments when labour relations also suffered from these inter-union conflicts.

The establishment of the new postwar socio-economic order did not, however, follow this oppositional logic. Neither were revolutionary changes introduced. Some left-wing politicians and intellectuals, particularly if they had spent the war in Britain or the US, had found inspiration in foreign plans for social restructuring, such as Keynes, Beveridge and Roosevelt, but, like the blueprints of other more reactionary think tanks and pressure groups, their plans were largely ignored by the political elite in 1945. Elites favoured social progress along the lines of the prewar development, which recognised the role of established social organisations alongside the State. This most clearly came to the fore with regard to the introduction of a new social security scheme. It was the socialist Minister of Labour, Achille Van Acker, who initiated a major reorganisation of social insurance in December 1944, largely following the conclusions of the Social Pact of

April 1944. The principal innovations were the introduction of a general scheme of social security for the private sector, and the generalisation of compulsory unemployment and health insurance for employees. In comparison with other social security programmes, these innovations were actually quite modest and indeed show continuity with prewar practices and plans, although Van Acker had resolved the most contentious issues. The basic principles were the joint administration of social insurance, which would gradually be extended into 'social security', by employers' and workers' associations, the deduction at source of contributions from employers and employees, and the payment of benefits by social organisations, in the case of unemployment insurance, mainly by the trade unions (Vanthemsche 1995).

The importance of the latter decision, incidentally, can hardly be underestimated. It compelled unions to set up an extensive and effective bureaucracy, which had been the reason why in other countries, such as the Netherlands, unions often willingly abandoned organising unemployment insurance. Doing so, however, robbed them of a valuable asset, as it provided Belgian unions with a large and stable membership. In a pluralistic trade union landscape it also offered unions a tool to compete with other unions. Belgian unions would therefore regularly extend the services provided to members. While it certainly increased the unions' administrative burden, it also created communication channels through which the leadership, to some extent at least, remained in touch with the aspirations of ordinary members.

The social insurance scheme proved very effective and stable. Nevertheless, social security became the field of a fierce political battle over the role and responsibility of the state in the late 1940s and 1950s. This mainly saw the Christian-democrats in direct opposition to the socialists. Broadly speaking, the socialists, and certainly the Minister of Labour Léonce-Eli Troclet, argued for a public organisation of social security, or at least one in which the state determined policy, while the Christian-democrats adopted the 'subsidiary' principle and believed social insurance must respect the individual's responsibility. The Christian unions recognised the necessity for state intervention but insisted on joint organisation. Likewise, the socialist unions accepted that social organisations could organise social security, in particular unemployment insurance, more effectively than the state, a position sometimes at odds with the Socialist Party members and certainly that of minister Troclet, who was responsible for the 'social security war'. The conflict did not lead to a fundamental revision of the system, but it did allow the state to increase its financial responsibility (Pasture 1992; Vanthemsche 1995).

With regards to industrial organisation, the unitary trade union movements demanded economic democracy, which they interpreted in quite different ways. For the FGTB, which followed the views of André Renard in this respect, it meant workers' control as the primary objective, and co-determination as some vague long-term goal. The Christian unions, however, argued for immediate co-determination at every level of the economy, in particular within companies. This implied essentially that workers would co-manage the economy jointly with the employers. This was unacceptable both for the latter and for the socialists, who refuted the idea of workers 'collaborating' with capital. The stand-off delayed a prompt reform.

In the first months after the war the government tried to control prices and wages, and tripartite national labour conferences sought to unite the unions behind that policy. However, authoritarian corporatist views had not disappeared. A proposal to organise the economy by the Liberal Minister of the Economy Jules Delruelle in November 1944, would have given industrial councils complete authority over industrial policy; strikes would have been prohibited and there was no mention of trade union participation in the industrial councils. Yet Delruelle's proposal never materialised. The initiative to reorganise the economy shifted to the Minister of Labour, Van Acker, who recognised the established trade unions, sidelining the leftist newcomers, as joint 'partners' alongside the employers. Van Acker also reinforced the role of the state by organising tripartite labour conferences and by taking some particular measures to facilitate working in certain sectors such as mining, including the right of civil mobilisation and to impose temporary restrictions on the right to strike, by giving the state the authority in principle to declare collective labour agreements legally binding – the actual execution of this would only follow in 1968 – and by introducing civil servant 'mediators' in case of social conflict (Vercauteren 2007a).

The unions, strongly opposed to such civil mobilisation and the temporary restrictions on the right to strike but accepting them given the need for economic recovery, took the initiative in restoring collective bargaining in 1948. They allied with employers in a multi-industrial General Joint Commission and in the industrial Joint Committees. A more elaborate industrial organisation scheme was introduced in 1948, the result of complex and difficult negotiations. Employers were very reluctant to allow unions any sort of co-determination in the economy. But the unions themselves were divided on this question and to what extent social and economic competence should be unified in different bargaining and consultation institutions. The law finally restored the joint committees as the cornerstone of collective bargaining, with the general joint commission – in 1952 transformed into the National Labour Council – as an umbrella association mainly for social consultation. In March 1948, a final national labour conference was held, after which the government retreated and wage setting was left to the collective bargaining process in the joint committees, which in 1950 re-introduced the practice of automatically adjusting wages to prices (Vercauteren 2007a: 138–53). The law also provided for joint works councils in large and medium-sized companies, where workers and employers would negotiate on working conditions, as well as joint Committees for Health and Safety at Work. There was no mention of workers' representation in the Board of Directors, for which the Christian unions had argued. But the law did recognise trade union delegates in the companies. These delegates became a figure of trust and mediation in the company, and hence also an invaluable asset of the unions. In addition, it should also be mentioned that unions and employers each appointed assistant judges in the labour courts to rule over individual labour conflicts under the presidency of a 'professional' judge.

This elaborate framework related only to social issues. As the unions insisted on dissociating social and economic competence – in order to avoid social progress being subjected to economic considerations – and *de facto* accepted the basic principles of the capitalist free market (including the authority of the employer on production), economic policy remained largely an industrialists' affair. Also the government did not seek to develop an active interventionist policy. Yet industrial councils were erected in several industries, though their actual authority was rather limited, as well as a Central Council for the Economy in which unions, employers and government consulted on major issues of economic policy.

This elaborate consultation scheme nevertheless offered unions a voice in the economy, from the individual company to the industrial and multi-industrial level, which no doubt gave them a semblance of power and authority. This system had other consequences. It demanded professionals as well as militants. The professionalism of trade unionism – which one should not overestimate, as even the officials of the study departments did not yet have university degrees – most obviously comes to the fore as a result of the consultation system. This incidentally also required a large cadre of trade union militants to fill the many representations and functions (Georgi et al. 2005) which gave the Belgian unions a strong popular base. Becoming a trade union militant, for example in a works council, was not without personal risk. Therefore, trade union militants could count on the protection of the unions and the law. This nevertheless represented a different kind of activism from the one cherished by the advocates of direct syndicalist action. Another consequence of the new social order is that it enhanced competition between the unions of different political orientation. Indeed, representation in the industrial and multi-industrial councils was established on the basis of membership – in 1953 the Christian and socialist unions concluded a secret pact on the subject, agreeing also to inflate their published membership figures by a fixed percentage – and in the companies on the basis of four-annual elections, which were always marked by intense competition. Competition induced unions to develop propaganda capacities and expand their services to members. Many unions for example offered cheap holidays to members and militants, but by far the most important service consisted of legal advice and assistance in the case of labour conflicts (Van Gyes et al. 2000; Pigenet et al. 2005; Pasture 1992). Liberal unions, which because of their marginal character before the war had been excluded from most joint committees, benefited from their alliance with the Liberal Party by increasing their presence in the joint committees and other consultation bodies (Vercauteren 2007a: 129–34).

As the institutional framework for collective bargaining was set in place, the country was being ripped apart by political struggles. These indirectly impacted labour relations, increasing competition between unions and the political constellation partly determined the unions' general political stance: when the Christian democrats ruled (1950–4), the FGTB adopted an aggressive stance and the Christian unions showed far more accommodating. Roles were reversed in 1954 when an anti-clerical coalition was formed: the Christian unions then took the lead in social protest. The action for a reduction of working time and a minimum weekly income, for example, clearly had not only social but also political motives. But that industrial relations remained far from pacified was also due to the spirit of opposition which motivated both many employers and particularly the socialist unions. While the FGTB still had to digest the merger with the communist and syndicalist factions that continued to exercise a radicalising influence, important employers, particularly in the export oriented heavy industries, wanted to keep wages low and objected to union recognition. Moreover, the Christian unions felt compelled not to appear as 'employer friendly' compared to their competitors on the shopfloor. Hence strike activity remained high.

Notwithstanding the tense political and social climate, leading unionists and employers remained on speaking terms, not least because all feared too much government interference in industrial relations. In May 1954 unions and employers even reached an important collaborative agreement in order to increase productivity: this Productivity Protocol, heralded by the Christian unions as a 'new social pact', anticipated the 'Fordist compromise' of the 1960s by which productivity gains would be exchanged for social benefits. In practice, the Protocol changed little. The Christian unions even mobilised massively against the anticlerical government coalition and its '*etatist*' policy. The socialist unions could not remain lagging behind. Only at the end of the decade, when the political struggle exhausted and economic conditions worsened, did things start to change.

4. The 'Golden Sixties'

In many ways, the year 1958 was pivotal. The ideological 'school war' had ended, the World Exhibition in Brussels heralded a new era of progress and affluence, and the Walloon mining industry entered a steep decline. The latter event may sound odd in an overall narrative of progress, affluence and hope, but it was no less real, and it provoked some important changes in economic policy.

The Walloon industries were already aging in the 1950s but continued to produce while Flanders remained largely rural, poor and unemployed. Flemish economists for years pleaded for regional economic policies, but always found their demands unheeded. With the collapse of the mining industry, all that changed: Flemish economists and (mainly Christian democratic) politicians, and Walloon 'regionalist' socialists such as André Renard, temporarily found common ground. Several national and regional expansion acts resulted, providing for direct state intervention in the financing of investments. A Bureau for Economic Programming (1959) was set up along with a National Committee for Economic Expansion (1960), in which trade unions, employers and state officials would deliberate, and not merely consult, about regularising and accelerating economic expansion, creating additional employment and increasing the standard of living. Industrial relations were finally pacified and after several years of informal negotiations, leading entrepreneurs and trade union leaders signed up to a first two-year multi-industry 'social programming' agreement in May 1960, which cleared the way for more coordinated collective bargaining based on mutual trust and productivity gains. However, the new liberal-Christian democratic government (1958–61) needed resources to combat economic depression and the unexpected de-colonisation of the Belgian Congo, which lead to a broad package of public savings in December 1960, the so-called 'Unitary Law'. This provoked a huge wave of protest and a general strike led by André Renard.

The strike against the Unitary Law again divided the unions, but perhaps more importantly it put the Flemish workers at odds with their

French-speaking counterparts, and this had an effect on the unions (on the regional divisions and the trade unions see Pasture 2000; on the strike and its consequences Neuville and Yerna 1990). The strike was widely supported in Wallonia and Brussels, while the Flemish proved far more hesitant. The issue divided both major confederations, but as the Flemish constituted a wide majority in the Christian confederation and the socialist confederation was dominated by Francophones – although in membership terms Francophones and the Flemish matched each other – it appeared that both unions stood against each other. Nevertheless the FGTB opposed a revolutionary general strike during which the blast furnaces would be stopped. Frustrated because the Flemish refused to follow him, Renard created a Walloon-regionalist political movement, the *Mouvement Populaire Wallon* (MPW). It would never recover from the untimely death of its leader in 1963 but Renard had been able to infuse the Walloon socialists with a regionalist perspective. Whether the strike affected the popularity of the unions, either positively or negatively, is doubtful: the slight decline of unionisation rates was due to a correction after the rapid growth of the Christian miners' unions during previous years (Pasture and Mampuys 1990: 100–1). The strike had, however, exhausted the socialist strike funds.

A new Christian democratic-socialist coalition (1961–5), benefiting from overwhelming public support and a favourable economic climate, introduced Keynesian employment policies and economic planning, although the implementation of the plans remained inadequate, and by the end of the decade interest in it had waned (Wijnens 2007). Even though the strike against the Unitary Law had interrupted the first Social Programming Agreement, the employers, who looked for the means to stabilise industrial relations, finally recognised the unions as genuine partners. The unions, for their part, considered full employment a greater goal than wage increases. Both found common ground in social programming, in which social progress was connected to productivity increases and social peace. The 1960 multi-industrial agreement was but one of many to follow. Multi-industrial programming agreements were complemented by industrial agreements or, in some sectors with decentralised bargaining traditions (such as electronics), in companies. All agreements included some sort of 'social peace' paragraph, although its concrete content varied widely. In

1968 another major step was taken with the introduction of a law giving the government authority to declare collective labour agreements legally binding (Vercauteren 2007b). This law illustrated the strength of the 'social partners' and of the neo-corporatist compromise, although neither the unions nor the employers realised that this procedure gave the state a tool to play a greater role in industrial relations.

In the meantime, social programming had a pacifying impact on industrial relations, positively impacting the economy. It also changed the function of the unions which found themselves in the role of 'pacifiers' rather than initiators of social action. As social advantages followed, productivity increased almost automatically. Unions were wary of 'free riders' and feared membership losses. As trade union liberty remained a contentious issue in a pluralistic trade union context, the confederations' leaders blocked suggestions by their rank and file to impose closed shop practices or compulsory unionisation. They did come up with an alternative, however, providing substantial additional benefits and premiums for trade union members in the collective labour agreements (Pasture and Mampuys 1993). Indeed, such premiums were introduced on a large scale, particularly in the industrial sector. Unions moreover provided information about professional matters such as labour law, health and safety and also more general issues, as well as professional training and education for militants. In several industries, unions and employers also set up special industrial funds for education and training. All these measures explain why trade union membership remained high notwithstanding some years of minor decline (see Vandaele 2005 for a detailed analysis in English of unionisation in Belgium). For several reasons, including growth in a now booming Flanders and also their predilection for targeting 'new' workers (women, white collar workers, workers in the new industries and high-tech enterprises, and Islamic immigrants), addressing them on their own terms, the Christian unions benefited most from the recovery and surpassed their socialist competitors. While they profited from the Catholic networks, they emphasised their trade union character and demonstrated an extraordinary ideological flexibility, which immunised them against the dramatic de-Christianisation and from tensions between progressive and conservative Catholics. By contrast the socialist unions largely remained stuck, geographically and ideologically, with the traditional workers' aristocracy of the stagnating Walloon heavy industries and barely differentiated between different workers. Both socialist and Christian unions lost ideological clout, however, and many hoped the rapprochement and neo-corporatist collaboration would result in a merger. By the end of the decade, the unions effectively constituted a unified 'trade union front'. Yet, in contrast to the Netherlands, competition continued to keep both apart.

Increasingly, the disadvantages of the highly institutionalised social system came to the fore. Several leftist groups, some of which had roots in the socialist movement, some with Left Catholic antecedents, developed bitter critiques of a society in which economic rationality dominated, critiques which did not spare the unions. The Christian workers' associations – the socio-cultural branch of the Christian labour movement – for example, argued for a fundamental reform of the company, which should become a 'human enterprise' instead of a capitalist instrument. They compelled the reluctant Christian unions to question their view on co-determination. These at a major congress in 1968 pleaded for 'an economy at the service of man'. One of the original ideas advanced was the suggestion to create alternative employment in social care and culture and so to transform the capitalist economy; this idea would later be picked up in a different context, to combat unemployment. A number of traditionally socialist concepts such as 'planning' and 'worker control' found their way into the Christian trade unions' programme. An economic setback in 1967–8, minor perhaps in hindsight but at the time considered serious and effectively demonstrating the obsolescence of some heavy industries such as metalworking in Wallonia and the coalmines in Flemish Limburg, reminded workers of the economy's vulnerability. When the economic growth resumed, the inflexibility of the social programming agreements created tension on the labour market. Workers also suffered from high productivity demands and began to pay more attention to qualitative demands and working conditions instead of higher premiums. More generally, one realised that the existing welfare system did not automatically eradicate poverty nor, less still, all social problems.

Nevertheless, no one anticipated the wave of social conflict that wracked the country between 1969 and 1976 (Hemmerijckx 2007b; Vandaele 2007).

The number of strikes grew rapidly, with many of strikes spontaneous, particularly in relatively young industries without strong trade union traditions. Often new groups of workers initiated the action, such as young people and migrants. New forms of protest appeared, such as sit-ins and factory occupations, particularly in the wake of French examples such as Lipp (1973). Apart from higher wages, particularly nominal increases for all categories of workers, there were more qualitative demands formulated regarding actual working conditions on the shopfloor. The unions were criticised for being estranged from the workers and too integrated into the system. Of interest was the presence of leftist students, grouped either in independent socialist associations such as the Socialist Young Guards (in 1965 they split from the Socialist Party) or groups originating from Catholic student organisations, many of which joined a Maoist political movement AMADA (All Power to the People). The latter developed an especially radical anti-trade union discourse, but their impact on the workers was far less than their presence in the media suggested. Nevertheless, for a moment unions seemed lost. They soon regained control though, following a double strategy: isolating and repressing the most radical militants, but also trying to recuperate the dynamics of the moment and radicalising their discourse. The socialist unions re-discovered the class struggle and workers' control, the Christian unions abandoned their ideal of co-determination or co-management, and put forward 'self-management' (*autogestion*) as their final goal in a true democratic society (Pasture 1996). Working class unity was strongly put forward once more (*travaillisme*), but again appearances were deceptive: the ideological emphasis actually distanced socialists and Christians. Moreover, since the state subsidised new initiatives in response to welfare demands, competition between the 'pillars' for these subsidies increased substantially (Pasture 1992; 1998). Unions also benefited from new opportunities to receive subsidies, for example for training organisers.

Perhaps surprisingly, the unions emerged strengthened from this period; the Christian unions in particular achieved a breakthrough amongst women, migrants and above all white collar workers, and so unionisation reached new peaks. Moreover, by radicalising their doctrine, the unions managed to attract new militants, some of whom came from the student movement, and these strengthened the links with new social movements, such as the feminist, consumer and peace movements. Some of these radicals would pursue important careers within the trade unions. Partly as an unexpected result of the democratisation, fewer and fewer workers worked themselves up from the shopfloor to the higher trade union positions. This meant that there was a need for highly qualified militants with academic degrees, not only for staff functions, but also as leaders. This paradoxically contributed to the unions reaffirming themselves as social actors in a broad sense. Yet collective bargaining and social and economic consultation suffered from the new militancy (Vercauteren 2007a).

5. Crisis, Restructuring and Regionalisation

The so-called first oil crisis did not immediately provoke a fundamental change in trade union policy. To be sure, unemployment skyrocketed, but at first the unions feared overreaction as in 1967–9. When it gradually dawned that the crisis would last and had structural causes, the unions continued to stress for Keynesian public interventionism consisting of more planning and state support for declining industries in order to maintain employment and purchasing power, while arguing that unemployment should be combated by a reduction of working time and the creation of an alternative labour circuit by the state. They forcefully rejected new economic theories such as neo-liberalism and supply side economics, as advanced by contemporary economists and adopted by the major employers' associations. The consultation mechanisms, already under pressure because of union radicalisation and the strike waves, became stuck. Between 1975 and 1981, no multi-industrial programming agreement was reached at all. Collective bargaining, within narrow boundaries imposed by the government, shifted towards sectors and increasingly companies. In these circumstances, the unions, paradoxically, benefited from rising unemployment, as they paid out benefits much more efficiently than the public institution. However, results from social elections show that workers also put their trust in the unions, particularly in the Christian ones.

The inability of the social partners to agree upon socio-economic policy – they called themselves 'social discussion partners' now – allowed the government to step in. Indeed, the government used the consultation instruments to impose wage restraints. Hence, it only asked advice of the National Labour Council for its own policies, and only declared legally binding those collective labour agreements containing wage restraint measures. Despite all the difficulties, including the disappearance of the National Committee for Economic Expansion and the suspension of multi-industrial agreements, unions, employers and the ministry and the Minister of Labour maintained contact and continued to consult, particularly in the National Labour Council and in more informal places, such as the Regency Council of the National Bank (Vercauteren 2007a).

By the end of the 1970s, Belgium was in deep economic trouble. Public debt was spiralling out of control, one factory after another closed or went bankrupt and unemployment peaked, while the political system was paralyzed by communal disputes. Attempts to control budgets had not prevented an extremely pernicious mechanism of industrial support for the so-called 'national sectors in difficulty' from developing. This safeguarded employment in the short term, as well as political stability, but (together with the extremely costly employment policies) derailed the state budget and, moreover, prevented a much needed fundamental reorganisation of obsolete industries. Even if there was a pronounced sense of urgency from the late 1970s onwards, the communal divergences between Flemish and Francophones, *inter alia* about the policies to be developed, and the ensuing political instability made it extremely difficult to change tack, as there was no consensus on the exact remedy. The unions recognised that the problems were structural, but saw a solution in a guided economy for which finances were lacking.

The implementation of a new constitutional revision in 1980, which largely regionalised economic policy, although industrial relations and wage policy remained federal competences, actually cleared the way for much needed political stability and radical economic policy change initiated by 'Roman-blue' coalitions (Christian democrats and liberals, 1981–8). Priority went to the reorganisation of public finances and the restoration of competitiveness. The turning point was the devaluation of the Belgian frank in 1982. This quite radical policy change put the unions on the defensive. The workforce split over the best strategy to pursue. While the socialist unions strongly opposed the new policies, the Christian confederation supported the reforms in return for employment measures, although the costly programs of the previous decade were abandoned. After the coalition change of 1988 and the restoration of coalitions of Christian-democrats and socialists under leadership of Jean-Luc Dehaene which continued to focus on economic recovery and downsizing public debt, the main confederations remained divided. Hence, the attempt to organise a general strike against the government's Social Plan in 1993 failed (Van Gyes et al. 2000; Vilrockx and Van Leemput 1998; Vandaele 2007).

The crisis had almost bankrupted the state's finances and threatened the fundamentals of the public system. Since the social partners remained utterly divided and incapable of agreeing on the basic orientation of the economy, the governments in the 1980s and 1990s expanded their competency at the expense of the social partners, particularly the unions. A key instrument in this operation was the 1989 Law on the competitiveness of Belgian Industry, which allowed the government, albeit after consultation with the Central Council for the Economy, to intervene directly in the economy if the competitiveness of Belgian companies and industries was under threat. As unions and employers in practice refused to agree upon the fundamentals of social and economic policy within the limitations the government imposed, in particular after the Treaty of Maastricht (1992), and after the so-called 'shadow of hierarchy' (Fritz Scharpf) had proved ineffective, the government simply did without them and even created new institutions without the support and participation of the unions. The Global Plan of 1993, including a three year wage increase ban, is a case in point, as it was imposed after failure to agree upon a negotiated Global Social Pact. The government also increased its grip on the social security institution and undermined automatic wage indexation – without being able to break it altogether, notwithstanding some temporary suspensions. Moreover, it established expert committees, such as the High Council for

Employment (1995), composed of academics appointed by the government instead of representatives of the social partners.

Unions in these circumstances were under threat. They also suffered from heavy criticism from both left-wing intellectuals and neo-liberal hardliners, including the flamboyant Guy Verhofstadt, who was to become Prime Minister in 1999. In a tight labour market labour militancy also flagged. Due to the high number of plant closures a great deal of local labour conflict still occurred, although it was short lived and rarely resulted in success for the workers. In the meantime, the conciliatory attitude of the Christian union leadership provoked serious internal tension and disaffiliation. Christian unions suffered heavy defeat in the social elections (held in large companies) of 1983 and 1987. The socialists also lost out, but to a lesser degree. Unionisation stagnated and declined for some years, though not to the extent seen elsewhere in the Western world. Actually, while the socialists declined, the Christian unions continued to gain new members, especially among the non-economic sector and (but not exclusively) the unemployed, considerably increasing the gap between both confederations. Since the late 1970s the liberal unions, which portrayed themselves as a 'third' force between the 'political' unions and which, like the Christian unions, subscribed to a policy of economic restructuring, increased their number of votes and membership. Due to declining incomes and high expenses, the unions also experienced financial problems. They were even granted a special status as 'company in difficulty', which gave them some protection against creditors and allowed them to propose early retirement to their employees in order to avoid redundancies. However, as contemporary opinion polls show, notwithstanding these difficulties, Belgian trade unions could still count on popular support and esteem (see Van Gyes et al. 2000: 122–4), in sharp contrast to political parties.

This may explain why the successive governments in the 1980s and 1990s, including those headed by the Guy Verhofstadt, continued to try to reactivate corporatist practices. The basic framework of the welfare state remained intact and the social consultation structure, though ineffective, were not actually dismantled.[2] Even though automatic wage indexation was severed, it was not abolished as the employers insistently demanded. The Central Council for the Economy was even given new competency. The governments tried to win over the support of the social partners, if only to seek legitimacy for their policy – the importance of which should not be underestimated, as it safeguarded the tools for its reactivation at a later stage. This explains why at regional level an institutional framework could be established for tripartite social consultation.

In the last quarter of the twentieth century Belgium became increasingly a federal country, largely against the will of the unions which emphasised national solidarity. The unions had to adapt their decision-making structure, which they did very reluctantly, following the transfer of legal competency. Regional competency was quite limited in the 1970s, but the institutional revision of 1980 gave the regions (Flanders, Wallonia and Brussels) important powers, *inter al.* regarding employment policy, regional economic and industrial policy, energy policy, public works, and transport (industrial relations, incl. wage stetting, and social security remain federal competencies). A regional consultative framework was established that soon became an important actor in the development of socio-economic policy. In Flanders, the social partners established the Flanders Social-Economic Council (SERV). This institution offered the administrative backing for a new tripartite consultation committee, the Flemish Economic and Social Consultative Committee (Vlaams Economisch Sociaal Overlegcomité, VESOC). If a consensus is reached within this body, the Flemish government commits to carrying out its resolutions. In the other regions, Wallonia and Brussels, a similar development took place, although somewhat less successfully. The new institutions in Flanders benefited from particular circumstances, in particular the weakness of the young regional administration and the inexperience of policy making at regional level as well as, from 1986 onwards, more favourable economic conditions. The difference with

2 On this point I disagree with prominent scholars such as Vilrockx and Van Leemput 1998, who argue that 'the state' completely altered the power relations to its advantage from the end of the 1980s onwards.

the national or federal level is nevertheless remarkable. The constitutional revision of 1992–3 which transformed Belgium into a federal state with even greater autonomy for the regions incited some Flemish to dream about regional collective labour agreements. While the Christian unions, which in the past had backed the Flemish demands for regional autonomy and the 'Dutchification' of Flanders (i.e. the use of Dutch not only as an official language but also in the companies in Flanders), initially supported the idea, they opposed the proposal of the Flemish government in 2002 not only to allow regional collective labour agreements (which theoretically as private agreements are legal) but also to make them legally binding. The unions argued that this would further undermine federal solidarity and create confusion over working conditions, particularly in Brussels.

6. A New Equilibrium?

In the meantime, the general climate in Belgium had been altered as the economy recovered. The amelioration of the economy resulted in a rise of employment, but Wallonia, particularly the old industrial basins, was not able to recover and structural unemployment remained high. However, even in Flanders, industry experienced difficulties, even those that had underpinned its rise in the 1960s. This provoked several major conflicts, such as the closure of the Renault car assembly in Vilvoorde in 1998. The latter resulted in new social legislation to protect workers in the case of collective dismissals.

The Law on the Promotion of Employment and Preventive Safeguarding of Competition of 26 July 1996 illustrated a change in federal policy: it imposed a 'wage norm' preventing wage increases superior to those in neighbouring countries. This wage-norm disconnected wages from productivity, a fundamental break with postwar Fordist wage formation. But the law recognised the social partners as important participants in designing wage policy and offered them new competency, in particular with regards to socio-economic policy. Suggestions about a 'new social pact' appeared; they soon disappeared when the anti-union Guy Verhofstadt became Prime Minister of the first ever 'purple' coalition consisting of liberals, socialists and greens in 1999 (the greens until 2003). However, the Dehaene government (1992–5; 1995–9) hoped to gain greater support for its policies in return and, moreover, retained the possibility of imposing its own measures if an agreement was not reached within a certain time, which is what effectively happened in 1996. Since 1998 the practice of multi-industrial agreements resumed, although their content remained meagre, in particular in the case of the 2002 agreement which was labelled a 'non-agreement' or *standstill* (Vandaele 2004: 128; Arcq and Pochet 2000; Van Gyes et al. 2000).

The background of this relative change is complex. Arcq and Pochet have argued that the unions realised that resistance to the principle of wage-coordination was futile (Arcq and Pochet 2000: 130). It also seems that the EMU (in contrast to initial fears) enhanced consultation and offered a framework for more complex exchanges and compromise building (Arcq and Pochet 2000; Hemerijck 2007). Nevertheless, employers continued their harsh anti-union discourse. They even tried to push their objectives through using courts, for example to break strikes, completely ignoring traditional bargaining practices (Van Gyes et al. 2000). In a different context, the public sector, increasingly under stress as a result of public savings on the one hand and increased demands on the other hand, became a focus of militant action. In particular, the non-profit sector reacted by way of a large and sustained action (the 'white anger').

The improving labour market, at least in Flanders, finally blew some wind in the sails of the unions and, after a period of stagnation and decline, unionisation picked up again in the 1990s. Nevertheless the unions still found themselves in a state of ideological and financial disarray. In the public sector some particularly militant professional unions (train drivers and pilots) challenged their monopoly of representation. Additionally, the socialist unions suffered from some scandals when trade union professionals were involved in fraudulent practices. This did not harm them too much; Belgians are extremely tolerant towards tax fraud. Yet unions adapted. Both the socialist and the Christian confederation tried to centralise. A number of national unions merged, creating larger and, more especially, all grades unions. White-collar workers' and public sector unions eclipsed the metalworkers unions as the largest affiliated unions in both confederations, signifying that the membership of Belgian unions more or less follows the changing social composition of society. All confederations now focus on particular groups such as women, youth, job-seekers or ethnic minorities (women constitute more than 40 per cent of trade union membership). This renewed emphasis is often seen as a way of increasing trade union participation and creating a new dynamic, although the effect appears less than convincing and, to the outsider at least, the unions seem unable to formulate a highly motivating discourse. Trade union training has expanded thanks to state subsidies for professional training and 'socio-cultural' work, which of course further integrated the unions into the system. Unions also extended their services, such as introducing tax advice to members. All these activities demanded more and more professional staff with degrees in social work and even university degrees (quite a number of historians populate the training offices). Also the outlook of union offices and buildings changed accordingly: the local trade union house, once a dingy room annex in a smoky café, has become a clean modern office that is hardly distinguishable from the local bank (Van Gyes et al. 2000). Relations with political parties degrade with ups and downs, but still remain important.

Both the socialist and the Christian unions loosely subscribe to the objectives of the new social movements with whom they entertain friendly relations, and devote attention to the principles of sustainable development. They even position themselves at the forefront of the anti-globalisation movement. They are systematically present at international demonstrations and in their publications demand attention to the negative consequences of globalisation, of industrial relations in 'third world' countries (particularly child labour) and even climate change. To which extent this openness for world problems is translated to the shopfloor remains open for debate, however. As an open, export oriented economy, Belgium experienced first hand the negative effects of delocalisation. In the 1990s, restructuring and delocalisation occurred in sectors on which the economic success of the 'golden '60s' was built. The dramatic downsizing operations in the Belgian automobile industry were key events in this regard: starting with Renault Vilvoorde in 1997 and followed by Ford Genk (2003), Volkswagen Vorst

(2006), and Opel Antwerp (2007). Appeals for real international solidarity resulted in some symbolic action but with little effect.

7. Conclusion

Belgian society was transformed in the half century after 1950. From a relatively closed, pillarised and low wage society, it became an open, secular consumer economy in which, according to Belgian political scientists, the impact of the main traditional cleavages of Belgian society – at least those between Catholics and secularists and between labour and capital – largely evaporated (it is hard to maintain that the third major cleavage, between Flemish and Walloons, diminished) and replaced by a 'postmodern' cleavage between authoritarian conservatives and 'left libertarians' (Hellemans and Hooghe 1995). The trade unions in contrast at first sight appear beacons of stability. They remained politically divided, federal, and buttresses of the social order – a function, however, that they had only obtained since the 1950s. Their almost uninterrupted expansion, admittedly following waves of intense growth, alternated with more modest increases (Vandaele 2005), can also be viewed as an element of continuity. Yet since the late 1970s Belgian unions appear on the defensive: it is no longer they who decide the agenda. Indeed, the perspective of realising social progress coupled to economic growth, the goal of the first postwar decades, seems to have vanished (Vercauteren 2007a). Being able to hold on seems a victory.

Nevertheless, Belgian unions never considered themselves as just an interest group for the defence of the collective labour interests of workers. They believed they were part of a socio-political movement. That was even the case for the liberal unions, but particularly of socialists and Christian-democrats. Their overall aims changed over time, however. The political goal of social transformation slowly evaporated, even if the unions regularly reformulated their ideological position. Such statements mainly illustrate the gap between rhetoric and actual practice. A new orientation comes to the fore in their declarations on broad social issues typical of the sensitivities that developed from the 1960s, in the connection with new social movements. This orientation sometimes creates tension as workers' interests and broader perspectives do not coincide, for example with regards to environmental issues, or in the case of arms' production (unions for example support the peace movement's objective of preventing arms sales to 'conflict areas' or immoral regimes, which is not always appreciated by workers in Belgium's important arms factories). Hence, such broader objectives remain largely formulated by the confederation as general policy issues; actual labour relations remain the task of the industrial unions. Somewhat surprisingly this orientation did not hamper their relations with political parties, even if the privileged connections diluted somewhat, mainly because of the different economic perspectives.

Paradoxically, the orientation towards new social movements has not led to a rapprochement between different unions. It even fuelled mutual competition, which on the one hand reinforces the increasing similarities between the union practices, but on the other hand also keeps them sufficiently apart to prevent mergers, and will probably continue to do so as long as no union finds itself in great financial difficulty. This competition largely underpins the service-like character of Belgian unions, which is its strength as well as its weakness. It is often considered in the latter perspective, as it is said to hamper union militancy: unions are often depicted as giants with feet of clay. But no doubt these services are much appreciated by members. Moreover, they create communication channels between leaders, professionals and ordinary members. Notwithstanding the pillarised character of Belgian society, unions always had to compete for members, and dissatisfaction with services provided could effectively lead to disaffiliation, which has increased since the 1950s. Complaints about the lack of trade union militancy are a recurrent theme and there are some indications that the problem was aggravated in the 1980s and 1990s, although one should bear in mind that Belgian unions, because of their extensive representation within companies, actually appeal to militants.

In conclusion, Belgian unions show a remarkable and paradoxical mix of features, as they are strongly integrated within the socio-political system, reminiscent of Dutch or Austrian neo-corporatism, but also influenced by syndicalist traditions (particularly in Wallonia) and to some extent at least oriented towards new social movements. There is no trade union crisis in Belgium, but one may well question the ability of unions to change the way thins are.

Suggested Reading[3]

Arcq, E. and Pochet, P. (2000) 'UNICE and CEEP in 1999: Social Policy Perspectives' in Gabaglio, E. and Hoffman, R. (eds) *European Trade Union Yearbook 1999*, Brussels: ETUI.

Devolder, C. (2005) 'To Innovate or Not to Innovate: De bedrijfswereld en de productiviteitsopvoering, een opportuniteit voor het ondernemingssyndicalisme? (1944–1980)', unpublished PhD thesis in History, University of Ghent.

Dorssemont, F., Cox, G. and Rombouts, J. (2005) *The Evolving Structure of Collective Bargaining in Europe 1990–2004: National Report, Belgium*, 'The Evolving Structure of Collective Bargaining. A Comparative Analysis Based on National Reports in the Countries of the European Union', Research Project Co-financed by the European Commission and the University of Florence (VS/2003/0219–SI2.359910), University of Florence: European Commission.

Ebbinghaus, B., Visser, J., Slomp, H. and Pasture, P. (2000) 'Belgium' in Ebbinghaus, B. and Visser, J. (eds) *Trade Unions in Western Europe since 1945*, Basingstoke: Macmillan.

Georgi, F., Bolle, F., Pennetier, C. and Puissant, J. (2005) 'Être militant syndical des années 1960 aux années 1980, en France et en Belgique. Pour une histoire compare des militantismes européens' in Pigenet, P.,

3 Hemmerijckx 2007a contains a recent overview of the historiography of Belgian trade unionism.

Pasture, P. and Robert, J.-L. (eds) *L'apogée des syndicalismes en Europe*, Paris: Publications de la Sorbonne.

Hellemans, S. and Hooghe, M. (1995) *Van Mei '68 tot Hand in Hand. Nieuwe sociale bewegingen in België*, Leuven: Garant.

Hemerijck, A. (2007) 'Corporatist Governance, the Welfare State, and European Integration' in Davids, K., Devos, G. and Pasture, P. (eds) *'Changing Liaisons': The Dynamics of Social Partnership in 20th Century West-European Democracies*, Aldershot: Ashgate.

Hemmerijckx, R. (2003) *Van verzet tot koude oorlog, 1940–1949: machtsstrijd om het ABVV*, Brussels: VUB Press.

—— (2007a) 'De historiografie van de Belgische vakbeweging' in Vanthemsche, G., De Metsenaere, M. and Burgelman, J.-C. (eds) *De tuin van heden. Dertig jaar wetenschappelijk onderzoek over de hedendaagse Belgische samenleving*, Brussels: VUB Press.

—— (2007b) 'In de geest van mei 1968. Arbeidersprotest en radical militantisme in België', *Bijdragen tot de Eigentijdse Geschiedenis/ Cahiers d'histoire des temps présents*, 18: 162–78.

Luyten, D. (1996) *Sociaal-economisch overleg sedert 1918*, Brussels: VUB Press.

—— and Hemmerijckx, R. (2000) 'Belgian labour in World War II: strategies of survival, organisations and labour relations', *European Review of History*, 7(2): 207–27.

—— and Vanthemsche, G. (eds) (1995) *Het Sociaal Pact van 1944. Oorsprong, betekenis en gevolgen*, Brussels: VUB Press.

Mampuys, J. (1994) 'Le syndicalisme chrétien' in Gerard, E. and Wynants, P. (eds) *Histoire du mouvement ouvrier chrétien en Belgique*, Leuven: Leuven University Press.

Neuville, J. and Yerna, Y. (1990) *Le choc de l'hiver 1960–61. Les grèves contre la loi unique*, Brussels: De Boeck.

Pasture, P. (1992) *Kerk, politiek en sociale actie. De unieke positie van de christelijke arbeidersbeweging in België (1944–1973)*, Leuven: Garant.

—— (1993) 'The April 1944 "Social Pact" in Belgium and its Significance for the Post-War Welfare State', *Journal of Contemporary History* 28: 697–713.

——(1996) 'Belgium: Pragmatism in Pluralism' in Pasture, P., Verberckmoes, J. and De Witte, H. (eds) *The Lost Perspective? Trade Unions between Ideology and Social Action in the New Europe*, Aldershot: Avebury.

——(2000) 'Divergent Developments, Regional Alliances and the Need for National Solidarity in Belgium' in Wets, J. (ed.) *Cultural Diversity in Trade Unions: A Challenge to Class Identity?*, Aldershot: Ashgate.

——(2004) 'Window of Opportunities or *trompe l'œil*? The Myth of Labour Unity in Western Europe after 1944' in Horn, G.-R. and Kenney, P. (eds) *Transnational Moments of Change: Europe 1945, 1968, 1989*, Lanham, MD: Rowman and Littlefield.

——and Mampuys, J. (1990) *In de ban van het getal. Ledenanalyse van het ACV 1900–1990*, Leuven: HIVA.

Peiren, L. and Messiaen, J.-J. (1997) *Un siècle de solidarité. Histoire du syndicat socialiste*, Brussels: FGTB / Ludion / AMSAB / Institut Emile Vandervelde.

Pigenet, M., Tartakowsky, D., Deneckere, D., François, P. and Wrigley, C. (2005) 'Expression et mise en scène syndicales à l'heure de la communication: une mutation delicate' in Pigenet, P., Pasture, P. and Robert, J.-L. (eds) *L'apogée des syndicalismes en Europe*, Paris: Publications de la Sorbonne.

Vandaele, K. (2004) 'Op weg naar een nieuw machtsevenwicht? Een kijk op de Belgische arbeidsverhoudingen in de Janusperiode van de jaren negentig' in Devos, C. and Gaus, H. (eds) *Schijn of scharnier? Politieke trendbreuken in de jaren 90*, Gent: Academia Press.

——(2005) 'A Half Century of Trade Union Membership: The Cyclical Macro-Determinants of Postwar Union Growth in Belgium', *World Political Science Review* 1(2): Article 3. http://World Warw.bepress.com/wpsr/vol1/iss2/art3

——(2007) 'From the 70s Strike Wave to the First Cyber-Strike in the 21st Century: strike activity and labour unrest in Belgium' in van der Velden, S., Dribbusch, H., Lyddon, D., and Vandaele, K. (eds) *Strikes around the World, 1968–2005: Case Studies of 15 Countries*, Amsterdam: Aksant.

Van Gyes, G., De Witte, H. and Van der Hallen, P. (2000) 'Belgian Trade Unions in the 1990s: Does Strong Today Mean Strong Tomorrow?'

in Waddington, J. and Hoffmann, R. (eds) *Trade Unions in Europe: Facing Challenges and Searching for Solutions*, Brussels: ETUI.

Vanthemsche, G. (1995) *De beginjaren van de sociale zekerheid in België 1944–1963*, Brussels: VUB Press.

Vercauteren, G. (2007a) *In naam van de sociale vooruitgang. De rol van de overheid in het sociaal overleg in België (1944–1981)*, Leuven: Acco.

——(2007b) 'Fixed by Law. The Significance of the Legislation on Collective Labour Agreements in Belgium and the Netherlands (1945–1980)' in Devos, G., Davids, K. and Pasture, P. (eds) *'Changing Liaisons': The Dynamics of Social Partnership in 20th Century West-European Democracies*, Brussels: PIE-Peter Lang.

Visser, J. (2006) 'Union Membership Statistics in 24 Countries', *Monthly Labor Review*, 129(1): 38–49.

Wijnens, I. (2007) 'Between Planning and Muddling Through: Institutional Change and Economic Growth in Belgium (1945–1961)' in Devos, G., Davids, K. and Pasture, P. (eds) *'Changing Liaisons': The Dynamics of Social Partnership in 20th Century West-European Democracies*, Brussels: PIE-Peter Lang.

Witte, E., Craeybeckx, J. and Meynen, A. (2001) *Political History of Belgium from 1830 Onwards*, Brussels: VUB Press.

France: The State, Trade Unions, and Collective Bargaining – Reform or Impasse?[1]

GUY GROUX

1. Introduction

In many countries, histories of trade unionism mainly concern themselves with the place and role of trade unions in the workplace. In France, relations between unions and business have always been problematic. The high level of State involvement in the economy, and the influence of legislation on collective bargaining both played key roles in industrial relations over a long period, often inspiring, and even guiding, union action. Today, government has become far less interventionist, and the unions themselves have become progressively weaker. Their presence in the workplace is often under threat, particularly in medium-sized companies. Is the declining influence of trade unions one of the reasons for the state of French labour relations, which many observers consider to be in crisis? An examination of relations between the State, unions and business since the end of World War II would be useful to understand the different aspects of this question. 1945 is a good place to start, as this was when the foundations of the trade union movement were laid, foundations which greatly influenced the subsequent development of trade unionism.

1 Translated by Richard Jemmett, assisted by Chantal Barry (CEVIPOF, Paris).

2. After World War II: The Post-Liberation Years

In the immediate postwar period, unions and the State had a special and close relationship. The French trade union movement had already split into three main branches. This division endures to the present day.[2] Some trade unionists were close to the French Communist Party (PCF); a second group was reformist or social democratic, and a third was inspired by social Catholic thinking. Until 1947 membership of the CGT (*Confédération Générale du Travail*) included not only communists but also social democratic reformists. Then, as the Cold War began to take hold, and in a context of long-running, often violent, mass strikes, the confederation split. The reformist unionists, who left the CGT to found FO (*Force ouvrière*), accused PCF (*Parti communist français*) sympathisers in the CGT of creating a movement bent on revolt, and of following the lead of their alleged political masters on issues which had nothing to do with the interests of the membership (Lefranc 1969). Christian union activists formed the CFTC (*Confédération française des travailleurs chrétiens*) from which, in 1964, the CFDT (*Confédération française et démocratique du travail*) emerged.

An Exceptional Moment in Trade Union History

Another feature of the period immediately after Liberation was the unusually high rates of union membership for a country whose union movement has historically been weak, or even, as is the case today, very weak. The CGT was at that time the largest trade union organisation by far, claiming to have six million members. Although this is undoubtedly an inflated figure, it was certainly the case that membership had reached record levels, as had the electoral influence of the CGT: it won 80 per cent of the votes cast in the first professional elections at the company-level after the war. The

2 See appendix at end of this chapter on the main French trade unions and their histories from 1895 to 2007.

CFTC had almost 600,000 members and obtained nearly 20 per cent of the votes cast in the in-company elections (see table 2 below).

Nevertheless, the most characteristic feature of the immediate post-war period was its politics. The political context was greatly influenced by the programme of the *Conseil National de la Résistance* (CNR), which was formed during the German occupation of France. The CNR was an umbrella organisation which included a wide variety of political and social movements, drawn together in opposition to the collaborationist Vichy government headed by Philippe Pétain. This coalition grouped together the followers of Général de Gaulle (the Gaullists), communists, Christian democrats and socialists, as well as the trade unionists banned in October 1940 by the Vichy regime: the CGT and the CFTC unions.

The Legacy of the Conseil National de la Résistance (CNR)

It was in this context that several of the political parties which would govern the newly liberated France established close and lasting ties with the trade unions. These ties grew stronger during this period when employers adopted a low profile; in fact, employer organisations were conspicuous by their absence, not only from the main national resistance movements during the occupation, but also from social and political life after Liberation. In August 1944 the main trade unions re-formed, but the French Employers' Confederation did not. Some authors argue that the low profile of many employers was motivated by a desire to avoid scrutiny of their conduct between 1940 and 1944 (Lefranc 1969). Be that as it may, after Liberation employers were far from the centre of social and political decision-making, at a time when many features of the landscape of labour and contractual relations were taking shape, features which would endure throughout the *Trente Glorieuses* and beyond. In fact, the links between the political parties and unions involved in the CNR were not broken when the period of resistance to the German occupiers and the Vichy government came to a close. These ties survived into the 1950s, and for good reason. The CNR had outlined a programme of economic and social projects which would have a lasting impact on French society, on both sides of the political divide.

The programme was built around three main principles which united political and trade union movements. These consisted of, first, the establishment of 'genuine economic and industrial democracy'; second, the development of a body of effective employment law which would oversee relations between employers and employees within companies; and finally the prioritisation of the 'public interest' over the interests of private individuals or organisations.

Both in practice as well as in principle, the concept of the public interest provided a philosophical framework for the social and political coalition established after the Liberation. It was implicit in the values associated with both economic and industrial democracy, as well as employment law. On 12 September 1944, shortly after the liberation of Paris, General de Gaulle, in a speech to the CNR at the Palais de Chaillot, laid great emphasis on the public interest (see box), and it is this concept which would provide the justification for the hegemony of the State in labour relations for the best part of four decades. In other words, by advocating the establishment of economic and labour democracy, and the pre-eminence of employment law in the name of the public interest, the CNR's programme, put in place just after the Liberation, put the State at the very heart of labour relations.

1944, The affirmation of a principle: the public interest

To sum up the principles that will underlie the policies of France as a nation, we would say that while guaranteeing the maximum amount of liberty for all, and seeking always to nurture the spirit of free enterprise, our country will ensure that private interest always be required to give way to the public interest, that the great sources of common wealth be exploited and managed not for the benefit of a few, but for all, and that the coalitions of interest, which have had such a negative influence on the lives of individuals and even of the State, shall be abolished once and for all.

Source: Speech of General de Gaulle to the *Conseil National de la Résistance*, at the Palais de Chaillot, 12 September 1944, in *L'année politique et sociale, 1944–1945*. Preface by André Siegfried, 1946, Paris, Editions du Grand Siècle, p. 441.

3. The 1950s to the 1980s: State Hegemony

After Liberation, the State began to exert a great deal of influence on industrial relations. This was inspired by the economic and social programme of the CNR which called for deep, ambitious and radical reform. At the time there were those, Christian democrats in particular, who spoke of a 'legislative revolution'. Legislation quickly became the preferred tool for implementing reforms, as opposed to agreements and collective bargaining between unions and management.

Legislation: An Essential Tool for Meeting Trade Union Demands

Immediately after Liberation, one of the key reforms the government wanted to introduce was to give the unions a more important role in public and social life, and to strengthen their bargaining position during industrial disputes with employers. The pursuit of these objectives continued from the 1940s to the 1980s, producing a great deal of wide-ranging legislation. In the second half of the 1940s and in the 1950s, laws were enacted which stipulated the following: workers were to have representation in firms (works committees, staff representatives); new systems of social solidarity regarding health cover and pensions were created and run by employers and unions; collective bargaining procedures by category of employee were established; and the State was to fix a minimum wage. Later, in the 1960s and 1970s, further legislation was enacted to introduce workers' sharing of company profits and unemployment benefit systems, as well as the creation of unions within private firms. In the 1980s the existence and content of firms' obligations regarding collective bargaining were enshrined in legislation and voted by members of the National Assembly. These obligations included, for example, the requirement to negotiate salaries on an annual basis; the involvement of trade unions when new production technologies are introduced; the right to consultation by employees concerning working conditions and the way work is organised; consultation between management and unions regarding the professional training of employees; and successive reductions in the length of the working week, first to 39 hours, then to 35 hours.

State intervention in the field of legal regulation had a number of consequences. Firstly, the institutionalisation of unions in firms was directly imposed by the State, whereas in other countries it evolved out of negotiations and prior agreements between employers and employees' representatives. Secondly, the State initiated legislation regarding all aspects of working life and work relations within companies (social welfare, technological changes, and salaries). Furthermore, it had a special relationship with the unions: a great deal of legislation was largely inspired by demands made by the unions; this was the case, for example, with the 35-hour week and the lowering of the retirement age to 60. Finally, this policy of intervention, which continued uninterrupted until well after the end of the *Trente Glorieuses*, was implemented by right and left-wing governments alike, under the influence of political philosophies – Gaullism or socialism – which both advocated state hegemony.

Nationalisations, State-Owned Companies, and the Foundations of Trade Unionism

The continuous hegemony of the State over labour relations derives not only from its power to legislate and its legitimacy in the domain of employment rights and social protection. To the juridical legitimacy of the State, grounded in universal suffrage and the State's role as the defender of the public interest, another kind of legitimacy needed to be added; an economic legitimacy which widens the scope of State intervention in the domain of labour and social security law, as well as in union-management relations. In France, the State is not only a legislator, but it also runs a lot of very large companies. Its legal legitimacy in the field of employment law has been strengthened by the very real economic legitimacy and power it wielded as a result of nationalisation campaigns carried out from the 1940s to the early 1980s, by which time the left was in power.

From 1945 onwards, a wave of nationalisations placed the State at the centre of the French economy. The State came to own and had direct control over key sectors of the economy such as energy (mines, coal mines, gas, oil, electricity and later nuclear power), the aviation industry, transportation (airline and shipping companies, the railways, the Paris metro), the car industry (Renault), the biggest banks and insurance companies, media (TV, radio), etc. In 1982, following the election of President François Mitterrand, there was a new wave of nationalisations. By transferring into public ownership thirty-nine banks, two financial houses (Paribas, Suez), five new industrial groups (CGE, Pechiney, Rhône-Poulenc, Saint-Gobain, Thomson), as well as the control of other firms in the steel, electronics and information technology industries, the left took state involvement in the economy to unprecedented levels. 32 per cent of industrial production was brought under state supervision, compared to 20 per cent in 1981.

Nevertheless, the extent of the State's influence and its hegemony in the field of labour relations went beyond administrative supervision of key sectors of the economy. The State, by virtue of the fact that it ran a large number of nationalised companies, was a powerful player in negotiations between unions and management, sponsoring collective agreements which were often exemplary and later came to be used in the private sector. Collective agreements, produced by the collective bargaining process initiated by trade unions and the representatives of nationalised industries, introduced important changes in the workplace. These changes included the first worker in-house training programmes; the linking of salaries to productivity levels and technological innovations; the abolition of the least acceptable features of Taylorism (by varying the tasks allotted to the least skilled workers, for example); the creation of more opportunities for career development, which closed the gap between blue-collar and white-collar workers; the increase in annual paid holidays; the setting up of collective bargaining procedures with a view to the avoidance of industrial disputes, etc. (Groux 1998: 48–51). Modifications to employment contracts, initiated by the State and public sector unions, were innovative. On the one hand, they aimed at either making qualitative changes, or modernising working methods (training for workers, abandoning Taylorist practices), in contrast to collective bargaining in the 1960s where the agenda would be dominated by purely quantitative and material aspects of working conditions, such as wages and bonuses. Furthermore, these contractual initiatives were often applied in the private sector by government or administrative authorities, or through legislation. There they contributed to major changes regarding negotiating, the management of the workforce, and human resource management. In this way contractual conditions used in the nationalised sector of the economy were also extended to the private sector, increasing State influence in the workplace.

In industrial relations, therefore, State hegemony operated in two domains: firstly through legislation, and secondly through new contractual arrangements initially introduced in the state sector, and subsequently applied throughout the economy as a whole. Until the 1980s, the fact that collective agreements at company level were little used also increased the importance of the role played by the State. As Jean-Daniel Reynaud noted at the end of the 1970s, 'the use of collective agreements is not common, and certainly not the norm' (Reynaud 1978: 132). There were a number of reasons for the relative absence of collective bargaining in the private sector. Within such organisations conservative managers, resistant to social innovation, would often find themselves in a confrontational relationship with a trade union movement dominated by the CGT, which espoused a radical ideology, denounced capitalist exploitation, and favoured the use of industrial disputes and strikes over collective bargaining. Labour relations therefore tended to be carried out in an atmosphere characterised by a high level of mutual suspicion, which militated against the formation of real, lasting contractual arrangements, and peaceful relations built on trust (Rosanvallon 2006). Another factor was the relatively late institutionalisation of trade unions in the private sector, in contrast to the UK and other parts of northern Europe, where there has long been a union presence in private companies. In France, unions in the private sector were only legally recognised in the aftermath of the May 1968 strikes, in the Grenelle agreement and in a legislation passed in December of that year. Therefore, it seemed to be the case that the private sector gave the State free rein regarding both contractual and legislative labour regulation. When there were negotiations in the private sector they generally, if not always, amounted to arranging for the application of new legislation or agreements which had been initiated by either the State, or by the social partners in nationalised industries.

In another domain – that of the unions – State hegemony had other consequences. The unions fully approved of the State's interventionist approach to industrial relations, and for good reason. The interests of the unions and the State coincided, leading them to form an unusual alliance. While the State certainly relied on the law and nationalised industries to enable it to have a controlling influence over relations between the social partners, the unions themselves built their influence on the very same foundations. They too relied heavily on legislation and the nationalised sector, the two sources of the 'power of the unions'; firstly the law, because the legislators were often influenced by union demands when drafting bills, and secondly the nationalised industries, not only because this was the power base of the union movement where membership levels were particularly high, but also because, as we have seen, innovative agreements originating in public companies frequently spread throughout the private sector. This situation prevailed until the beginning of the 1980s, when the historic foundations of French trade unionism began to be seriously undermined.

4. The 1980s and 1990s: A Break with the Past

The 1980s was a paradoxical time. On the one hand, it was a decade when the left came to power, committed to a programme of state intervention. In 1981, in an atmosphere which was in some respects similar to that which prevailed at the end of World War II, the government, made up of socialists and communists and led by Pierre Mauroy, set out to radically transform French society. Inspired by socialist and Keynesian ideology, its aim was to drastically change France's market economy by turning over key parts of it to the public and nationalised sectors, as well as radically reform social legislation, and ensure that labour law defend the interests of labour (Kesselman and Groux 1984). So was revolution in the air? Yes it was, but not for long.

The Left-Wing Government Changes Tack

Before long, State interventionism and radical reformism, with which the left intended to transform the workplace, was called into question. In the mid-1980s the economic and social situation continued to deteriorate, with unemployment, inflation, public-sector debt and trade deficit statistics reaching alarming levels. The government of Laurent Fabius decided to drop the reflationary policies, followed since 1981, which had been intended to boost consumption and wages. 'Left-wing Keynesianism' was quickly abandoned, to be replaced by strict austerity measures regarding pay awards, and new policies which aimed to create an environment in which the economy and business were freed of some of the legal and regulatory constraints which had hitherto been imposed upon them. When the left came to power, talk of the workplace and the role of the unions were central to their political rhetoric. Now, in their speeches, the socialist leadership often referred to the importance of industrialists and the business world. Economic growth and investment were given priority over consumption and wage increases. In fact the new direction taken by the Fabius government was in many respects similar to that of the Barre government of the late 1970s, during the presidency of Valéry Giscard d'Estaing: 'the jobs of the future will be created by investment in business, not by putting up wages to boost consumption'. The new policies, which amounted to a kind of 'left-wing Barrism', would have important repercussions on trade unionism and collective bargaining.

The Private Company: A New Place for Negotiations

One consequence of the left's new policies was greater use of collective bargaining within private companies. This increase in company-level bargaining constituted a break with established practice. As we have seen, during the *Trente Glorieuses* there was little bargaining within private companies and it was uncommon for management and unions to strike local-level collective agreements. From the beginning of the 1990s there was an unprecedented increase in the number of such agreements. In 1970 there were 658 local collective agreements, 6,198 in 1992, 9,109 in 1996, 11,849 in 1998 and 13,635 in 2001. The numbers continued to rise, to 19,324 in 2004, and 20,178 in 2006. Furthermore, the content of particular agreements had greatly changed. Previously in France, as in many other countries, agreements – and industrial disputes – between management and workers were usually about wages, a state of affairs characteristic of Fordist industrial relations. At the end of the 1980s, wage settlements still made up 56.4 per cent of agreements signed in France but by the first decade of the twenty-first century this percentage had dropped, fluctuating in the region of 30 to 35 per cent: 29.7 per cent in 2004 and 36.9 per cent in 2006. Contractual negotiations in companies now focus less on wages and more on a wide range of other issues, such as the length of the working week, the sharing of company profits by employees, vocational training, stress at work, occupational mobility, etc. Finally it is becoming more common for collective agreements to be arrived at by the offer and acceptance of mutual concessions. Examples of this kind of *quid pro quo* arrangement include the insertion of clauses requiring workers to be flexible and to adapt to the needs of the employer in agreements concerning the number of hours to be worked. The decision to calculate working hours on a yearly basis rather than on a statutorily defined weekly basis provides an example of such clauses. Clearly, the change in contractual relations between unions and employers is linked to the state of French society which, for more than twenty years, has been characterised by high unemployment and falling job security. In France in 1981, unemployment stood at 1.5 million. In the middle of the 1990s this figure had risen to 3 million, which does not include the almost 2 million people receiving social benefits (income support, professional training courses etc.). Today the situation is still critical; this state of affairs has led, as in other countries, to a paradigm shift in collective bargaining within private companies. The wages paradigm which used to dominate the content of negotiations, following a Fordist, redistributive logic, has been replaced by a new paradigm which aims to preserve and protect jobs, and results in greater flexibility, even individualisation, as regards both the content of agreements and their application in the workplace (Gazier 2003; Groux and Pernot 2008).

Quite apart from the changes in union-management relations within companies, economic policy changes made by the Fabius government in the mid-1980s initiated other deep trends. These trends included the emergence of two processes which have continued to the present day, sponsored by both the left and the right, unperturbed by changes of governments. Both of them involve the rolling back of the State, firstly in the economic sphere leading to massive rounds of denationalisation, and secondly in the legislative sphere, resulting in the establishment of new relations between the law and collective bargaining.

The Rolling Back of the State

The reduction of State involvement in the economy was a blow to the trade union movement and reduced the leverage it derived from its power base in the nationalised sector. The first denationalisations were implemented during the 1986–8 premiership of Jacques Chirac and have continued from 1993 to the present day under both left- and right-wing governments. Indeed, the Socialist government under Lionel Jospin (1997–2001) implemented its denationalisation programme every bit as thoroughly as governments led by right of centre politicians such as Alain Juppé, Jean-Pierre Raffarin or François Fillon. The effect of successive waves of denationalisation is clear. With very few exceptions – notably in the public transport sector, the French national railway company (the SNCF) and the Paris City Transport Authority (the RATP) – from 1986 to the present day practically every nationalised industry has been returned, partly or entirely, to the private sector.

The law is the second domain in which there has been a reduction of State involvement, in particular in its role of legislator in labour law. As we have seen, in the past, the procedural and substantive rules governing collective bargaining were enshrined in the law. Many improvements in conditions of employment were introduced by legislation, rather than by means of a contractual agreement on foot of negotiations between management and labour. In the past, legislation imposed itself on negotiations by the 'letter and spirit' of the law. Mandatory and prescriptive, the law also greatly influenced contractual arrangements.

Today, collective bargaining has become far less regulated. Legislation no longer imposes itself as such on the social partners. This is the case at the company level, where agreements reached using the employment paradigm (which makes the avoidance of job losses of paramount importance) lead to ever greater flexibility and, increasingly, are not covered by legislation. These changes also apply to higher-level agreements. In 1986, the 'Delebarre law' – named after the Employment Minister in the Fabius government – modified the law on employee working hours. Departing from French tradition, this piece of legislation, known as an incitative law, did not impose its provisions; it was for unions and employers to negotiate agreements, which would determine how it would be applied. If no such agreements were reached, the law would become a 'dead letter'. At the beginning of the twenty-first century, laws which related to night work for women and vocational training drew heavily for inspiration on a large number of special agreements, which had been made at a local level in industry and the service sector throughout the 1990s.[3] In the same way, company-level agreements regarding the application of the 'Aubry laws', which set the weekly amount of working time at 35 hours, have made a significant contribution to modifications of the legislator's intentions, not only with regard to the amount of working time but also to more general labour law provisions (see box).

Finally, in January 2007, a law on the 'modernisation of social dialogue' was adopted which required any modification of the labour code, or adoption of a law relating to industrial relations to be preceded by consultations between employers and unions; only if the social partners fail

3 By company special agreements we mean agreements which are not covered by existing labour law, and so do not fall within the prescriptions and obligations laid out in public and employment legislation. These types of agreement do, however, require the approval of the public authorities or the department of labour and social affairs.

to negotiate a collective agreement can the government intervene to apply the legal and legislative modifications proposed. Thus, relations between collective bargaining and the law have been profoundly transformed. Collective bargaining is no longer necessarily dependent on the law. On the contrary, it is part of the process by which laws are developed. In other words, collective bargaining has not just become more autonomous, but can now even be said to exercise a certain amount of hegemony over the law. This occurs in two ways: firstly, when the drafting of bills is directly influenced by collective bargaining agreements, and secondly, when the formulation of new legislation is only undertaken after prior consultation with the social partners. Under such circumstances, the normative function of the law is to supplement collective bargaining agreements; the role of the law is to put the finishing touches to the provisions of agreements rather than override them (Supiot 1999). Therefore, the rolling back of the state in the legislation reflects the primacy of collective bargaining in the formulation of common rules governing relationships in the workplace. In this way, France's labour relations system is now coming to more closely resemble those of its European neighbours.

A Critical Moment for Trade Unions?

For the trade unions, the current state of affairs is ambiguous, even contradictory. On the one hand, as has also happened in other countries – in particular in the majority of capitalist economies – the growth of collective bargaining can be regarded as presenting the trade union movement with opportunities: more negotiating could lead to an increase in the influence of unions in the workplace, and in society at large. Nevertheless, these opportunities are presenting themselves at a time when trade unions are in no position to take advantage of them. In fact, and this is a major paradox, the expansion in collective bargaining in France occurred at the same time as the collapse of what had been, between 1945 and 1980, the main sources of French trade union power, namely the unions' ability to influence the law, and their close links with the nationalised sector. To make matters worse, the contradictory trends of a boom in collective bargaining

A particular case. The Aubry laws on the 35-hour week or the negotiation of the law

In the past, the authority of laws relating to the length of the working week, notably those passed in 1936 and 1968, was clearly non-negotiable. A law was passed, and the measures set out in the legislation were directly enforced. Today, the implementation of laws takes place within an increasingly fluid and flexible market, and this context has transformed the way in which laws are applied. The evolution of the Aubry laws on the 35-hour week is a case in point. The CFDT and the CGT had been demanding the introduction of a 35-hour week since the 1970s. When, in June 1998, the Jospin government, and its Employment Minister Martine Aubry, introduced the first piece of legislation to implement this demand, the law had two particular characteristics: firstly it was to remain provisional until a final version of the bill was passed; secondly, the way it was applied could be influenced by company-level bargaining between the social partners. In the period between the two laws – the second law was passed in 2000 – 45,000 company-level agreements were signed. Under the influence of these agreements, certain rules of labour law and parts of the new legislation were amended, and sometimes even transformed. This was the case for the following measures: the status of overtime, the calculation of working hours over a 12-month period (*annualisation*), the representativeness of the collective agreements and the use of referenda, and the calculation of working time for professional staff. Furthermore, one of the key clauses in the first version of the Aubry law required agreements regarding the 35-hour week to include provisions for the creation of new jobs or the protection of old ones. After the period of company-level bargaining, when the adaptation of working practices was given priority over job creation or protection, the second law dropped any mention of the latter objective.

Bibliographical reference: Groux, G. (ed.) (2002) *L'action publique négociée. Approches à partir des '35 heures'. France-Europe*, Paris: L'Harmattan, Collection Logiques politiques.

and the breaking up of the foundations of trade unionism occurred at a time when support for trade unionism was in a period of unprecedented decline. Consequently, the decline in the power base of the unions meant that the potential offered by the boom in collective bargaining at various levels in French society could not be fully exploited. This situation is all the more worrying as it will handicap reform projects for the working world, including those currently envisaged by the government.

5. Reform or Deadlock?

In the run-up to the last French Presidential elections, all the main candidates – Nicolas Sarkozy, the Socialist Party candidate Ségolène Royal, and the centrist François Bayrou – were united in proclaiming the need to reform French society, a society which seems to see itself as a *société bloquée* (a society in deadlock), to quote sociologist Michel Crozier's well-known phrase (Crozier 1994). Since coming to power in May 2007, the new President of the Republic, Nicolas Sarkozy, has re-stated his commitment to reform, and announced a programme of measures which, in the breadth of its ambition, recalls two other moments in French history: the return to power of General de Gaulle in 1958, and the election to the presidency of François Mitterrand in 1981. The current programme of reforms outlined by the government covers many aspects of labour law: employment contracts, conditions of recruitment, health insurance schemes and retirement plans, the handling of unemployment, working hours, Sunday work, the status of public employees, the representativeness of trade unions, the new procedures for the validation of collective agreements, professional elections in companies, the financing of unions, and the status of certain state-owned companies, are just some of the raft of large-scale reforms on the government's agenda.

2007: On the Eve of Major Social Reforms

Clearly, the reforms being proposed would have an impact on the social partners, and the trade unions in particular, in two ways. On the one hand, they call into question the role of the social partners in the formulation of employee demands and job contracts, at company and other levels. On the other hand, they require the involvement of unions in consultation processes. This requirement applied, for example, to the negotiations about the modernisation of the job market which began in September 2007. Bringing together all the trade unions and employer organisations, the aim of these negotiations was to reach an agreement regarding the transformation of social legislation on, among other matters, work contracts. Beyond a few immediate agreements, questions about the long-term future remain. How will trade unions respond to the challenges which arise under such circumstances? Will they maintain positions of entrenched opposition, or can they become active participants in the processes of reform, in particular regarding labour law modifications, which seem likely to result in a weakening of their own position?

The Current Trade Union Crisis: A Major Handicap

In order to reply to these questions, it is necessary to closely examine the current state of trade unionism in France, with a view to the role unions might play in future reforms. It is certainly the case that the content, scope and application of forthcoming reforms will be greatly influenced by the current state of French trade unions. In fact, analysis of future prospects for the trade union movement gives few grounds for optimism. French trade unions, without exception, are in crisis and face an uncertain future. The crisis, which has lasted for over 20 years, and has been of quite unprecedented severity and duration, has various causes, some of which affect the majority of union organisations throughout the capitalist economies of the EU and the US, others being more specific to France. Developments which contribute to the general crisis in trade unionism include the transformation of the productive apparatus, the disappearance of many categories of worker, the rise in importance of the service sector and white collar jobs, increasing individualism in modern societies, as well as the crisis of Fordism and the contractual redistribution logics it entailed, etc. (Andolfatto and Labbé 2000). In France's case other factors, discussed above, such as the breaking of the ties which enabled trade unions to exert particular influence over the nationalised sector and social legislation, largely account for the fact that trade unions in France experienced a more dramatic decline than their counterparts in other countries.

The clearest manifestation of the decline in French trade unionism has been the fall in its membership. In 2003 only 8 per cent of French workers belonged to a trade union (see table); this figure represents the lowest rate of union membership of any European or OECD country, and is dwarfed by the corresponding figures in Sweden (78 per cent), Italy (34 per cent), the United Kingdom (29 per cent), Germany (23 per cent), the Netherlands (22 per cent), and even Spain (16 per cent) (Visser 2006). France also experienced a particularly sharp fall in union membership: 47 per cent between 1970 and 2003. The only country which witnessed a comparable decline in union membership over the same period was the UK where, in a difficult time for the TUC, characterised by economic crises and the anti-union offensives of Thatcher's governments and their successors, the number of trade unionists fell by 35 per cent; certainly a dramatic drop, but still less, percentage-wise, than in France. Lastly, it should be noted that all French trade unions, irrespective of their strategic line and sectoral distribution, experienced rapid decline. Militant unions, espousing confrontational even revolutionary approaches, as well as more reformist organisations, suffered a decline in membership. The same trend could be observed in both the public sector – where employees enjoyed a 'job for life' – and the private sector.

Table 1. Membership figures for the main union organisations in 2007

	Membership claimed by the organisation itself	Estimated membership
CGT	729,000	530,000
CFDT	803,000	450,000
FO	800,000	310,000
CFTC	141,000	111,000
CGC	160,000	80,000

Source: La Documentation française.

The significant fall in union membership is an undeniable fact. Nevertheless, this trend has sometimes been overlooked in France, and for good reason. Compared to trade union movements in other countries, membership of trade unions in France has generally been relatively low. The period immediately after World War II was exceptional in this respect. In the early 1970s, in an unusually favourable context of full employment combined with a large collective mobilisation post-May 1968, the five representative organisations still struggled to recruit between 22 and 25 per cent of employees. Consequently, for trade union activists and observers alike, the legitimacy of the unions derived in the main from in-company elections.

How well do the trade unions perform in company elections? In fact, once again, they now find themselves in a distinctly unenviable position. Generally, such elections attract a turn-out of around 60 per cent of employees, and the vote is shared by numerous trade union organisations. In large companies in particular, the vote is frequently divided up between a large number of candidates, and turn-out is relatively low. Not only is the vote for union organisations fragmented, but it has also been affected by other, more important long-term trends. After the Liberation the situation was clear: voters opted for one of two organisations, with the CGT alone receiving 80 per cent of the votes. From this peak, the CGT's share of the votes has fallen considerably (see table). Since 1946 it has fallen by almost 60 percentage points. For a while some, though not all, of these votes went to other union organisations, notably the CGT's main rivals, the CFDT and FO. Nevertheless, other unions ceased to benefit from the CGT's declining fortunes over twenty years ago, and their share of the vote has remained more or less stable, notwithstanding minor fluctuations. In sharp contrast, 'non-unionised' candidates, – namely those candidates who were not affiliated to the officially recognised unions – have captured a steadily growing proportion of the votes polled. Between 1966 and 2003, this is the only group of candidates whose share of the vote has risen significantly, by over ten percentage points; they now consistently come out top in works council elections. Clearly, this state of affairs leads the legitimacy of the major French trade union organisations to be brought into question. Currently, the organisations which are officially recognised have their legitimacy conferred upon them by the law and not the electorate, whereas those whose legitimacy is solely based on members' votes find themselves marginalised. Is an electoral system which produces such an anomalous situation not ripe for reform? This is an important question which is part of the debate about trade union representativeness, an issue which, as we have already noted, is on the government's reform agenda.

Table 2. Results of works council elections: in % 1946–2003: four selected years

	1946	1976	1986	2003
CGT	81.1	39.8	27.0	22.1
CFDT	(1)	19.6	21.3	22.6
FO	(2)	9.2	12.8	12.7
CFTC	17.2	2.9	4.3	6.7
CGC	1.7	5.4	6.7	6.6
Non-unionised	(3)	16.5	22.5	23.2

1. The CFDT did not yet exist as such. It was part of the CFTC.
2. FO did not exist in 1946.
3. Numbers not recorded at that time.
Source: Ministry of Employment, France.

The crisis in French trade unionism is not just a matter of falling membership and electoral decline. It also has to do with collective mobilisation. It is worth noting that foreigners tend to think of France as a country where strikes occur relatively frequently, and where unions have formidable powers of collective mobilisation; several large-scale movements over the last decade – in 1995, 2003, 2006 and 2007 – which brought sections of the French economy to a standstill, are seen as evidence of the power of the union movement. Nevertheless, the impressive scale of these social movements may have been misleading; they are best seen as outbursts of frustration with little long-term impact. In fact, analysis of long term trends regarding industrial action shows that the frequency of strikes has fallen considerably from the 1950s to the present day, revealing a kind of 'relative pacification of industrial relations'. Between 1947 and 1958 an average of 6,734,600 working days was lost annually as a result of strike action. In spite of the impact of May 1968 and its aftermath, the first significant drop came in the 1970s: in the first half of that decade an average of 4,000,000 working days were lost each year. In the 1980s, the trend became more pronounced. Between 1981 and 1985 the average figure dropped to 1,500,000 and finally, between 1996 and the beginning of the following decade, the average annual total had fallen to 540,000. Although this decline in strike action is part of a general trend which has been observed in practically every country in the world, in France the decline in the number of days lost to strikes has been particularly rapid.[4]

The movements of social protest which have periodically shaken French society over the last ten years or so were outbursts which never gathered any long-lasting momentum. They were also purely defensive, in that they arose out of opposition to reforms of already existing employment conditions or pensions, and it is not clear how much they achieved. This may be contrasted with movements in the past: the strikes of 1936 and 1968, for example, led to a series of reforms entailing new rights for workers. Paid holidays, the introduction of staff representatives and then unions in private companies, extended union rights as well as other reforms transformed not only the workplace, but also the wider society. Clearly the same cannot be said for the mass mobilisations of the last decade, since they resulted in no significant new rights for workers. In fact, in the history of industrial action, the current situation is quite unprecedented. Even when they are part of massive social protest movements – 1995, 2003, etc. – strikes now occur less frequently and, when they do, they are much more often of a defensive nature than they were in the past (Sirot 2002; Groux and Pernot 2008). Strikers nowadays rarely make demands for new rights to be adopted or created. When they strike it is usually to engage in 'rearguard industrial action', in defence of rights that already exist, but which are threatened, by the government or others, with modification or reform. From 2003 to 2007, despite high levels of mobilisation, major industrial disputes have, obtained little or nothing for the strikers and generally seem to operate

4 Source: 'Labour Disputes', *The Economist*, The Economist Group, 2004.

purely as protest. Basically, since 1995, the French trade union movement has appeared to be exhausted by its 'confrontations with the government and employers' (Pernot 2005). The unions can still mobilise and be disruptive but, considering the scale of mobilisations, the concessions obtained are generally meagre. In fact, the activism and determination of French unions is more often a sign of weakness than strength.

French trade unionism is clearly in a critical condition. To summarise, there are three main aspects to the crisis: very low union membership, the fragmentation of the vote in works council elections, and the purely defensive, protest nature of mobilisations. The crisis is further exacerbated by the fact that unions are no longer close to the changing realities of the world of work. Already in the 1970s the CFDT leader Edmond Maire, a leading trade union reformist, commented that trade union activists are increasingly out of touch with the grass roots. In his opinion, the most vulnerable categories of worker – the young, immigrants, and women – particularly those in the private sector, were too often neglected by the union movement.[5] In the intervening years this situation has continue to deteriorate. In France, the workers hardest hit by the competitive nature of capitalist markets are increasingly unlikely to be members of a trade union. The crisis in the job market, linked to the transformation of the industrial and productive apparatus, has also led to the union movement playing a less integral part in the working world. Nowadays, in France as in other countries, the main stronghold of the trade unions is the civil service, where employees enjoy guaranteed job security. On the other hand, unions are conspicuous by their absence from those industries which are in the process of transforming the working world and society at large, and where most new jobs are being created, namely the world of immaterial production, trade, tourism and service industries, etc. (see box).

5 Source: Maire (ed.) (1986), 'Interrogations sur l'entreprise et l'anticapitalisme: l'individu et l'action syndicale', *CFDT Aujourd'hui*, March–April 1986.

The CGT. A union 'out of touch' with the working world?

According to a report on past activities presented at the last CGT conference in June 2006, almost 50 per cent of CGT members belong to one of nine federations, which themselves represent no more than 16 per cent of French workers. Four federations – railway workers, the energy sector, postal and telecommunications workers, and State employees – make up almost one third of CGT membership, although these sectors employ only 5 per cent of the working population. On the other hand, the CGT claims to have only 26,000 members who work in trade and related activities, despite the fact that this category of worker accounts for almost one third of private sector employees. It should also be noted that the average age of trade unionists, 48, is high, whereas the new and expanding sectors of the economy – call centres, the knowledge economy, etc – employ workers who tend to be much younger. In the 1990s Louis Viannet, the Secretary General of the CGT, referred to PME (Small and Medium-Sized Companies) who employ less than 50 workers and collectively employ more than half the French workforce, as a 'desert for trade unions'. That diagnosis could equally apply today. In fact, as Jean-Pierre Basilien and Denis Monneuse explain: 'How can employees in the private sector identify with an organisation whose demands and way of operating appear to be essentially geared to the concerns of public sector employees? (...). This private/public rift puts the organisation at risk'.

Sources: Report on recent activities, CGT conference, Lille, April 2006.
Basilien, J.-P. and Monneuse, D. (2007), 'Les transformations du paysage syndical en France. Etats des lieux: crise du syndicalisme, de la représentativité et recomposition', Paris: Entreprise & Personnel, p. 27.

Are Trade Unions in the Process of Being Marginalised?

In the context described above, what role can French trade unions play in the formulation of the major reforms which have been placed on the agenda by the government? The crisis in the union movement has made unions weak and chronically vulnerable: they are in no position to effectively influence the processes of change which are already underway. How can the crisis be handled? In fact, the weakness of French trade unions is due, in part, to divisions and fragmentation within the union movement. Unsurprisingly, the leader of the CGT, Bernard Thibaut, has for the last few years been calling for trade unions to rally round and unite. But how can divisions within the movement be fully healed, given the depth of the historical, cultural and organisational differences between the different parts of the movement (see appendix at the end of the chapter)?

Basically, if no solution to the crisis is found, there is a distinct possibility that French unions will find themselves effectively sidelined. If this turns out to be the case, two possible scenarios can be sketched, one played out on the company level, the other at the national level. As regards the business world, in industrial relations and collective bargaining within companies, the employers' representatives – the board of directors – could find themselves centre stage, having a hegemonic influence: their influence, wishes, projects and strategy would determine the procedural and substantive aspects of collective bargaining. In such a scenario, which is not dissimilar to that described by Kochan, Katz and McKersie, the role of the unions in processes of change and reform would be more or less reduced to that of a facilitator (Kochan et al. 1986; Pernot 2005). Is this scenario farfetched? Not according to many trade unionists, who oppose and condemn the fact that bargaining agendas are increasingly set by the employers.

At a national level, government-sponsored reforms already frequently enjoy the support of employers. In view of this, what role remains for unions to play, given that they are in crisis? Once again, the risk is that they will be sidelined and deprived of a role in the reform process. So the second scenario – played out at the national level – would involve an inversion of the situation in 1945. After the Liberation, the economic and social reconstruction of France was largely built on a particular alliance, between the State and the trade unions, which left the employers temporarily sidelined (see above). Now, at the beginning of the twenty-first century, the arrival of a cycle of reforms which will break with the legacy of the *Trente glorieuses* is imminent. Other coalitions are now emerging, including a special alliance between the State on one side, and the employers and key economic players on the other. This time it is the trade unions that are being marginalised, and left powerless to influence the social and political handling of the changes taking place.

Suggested Reading

Andolfatto, D. and Labbé, D. (2000) *Sociologie des syndicats*, Paris: La Découverte, Collection Repères.

Crozier, M. (1994) *La société bloquée*, Paris: Seuil, première édition: 1971.

Gazier, B. (2003) *Tous sublimes: vers un nouveau plein-emploi*, Paris: Flammarion.

Groux, G. (1998) *Vers un renouveau du conflit social?*, Paris: Bayard, Collection Société.

—— and Pernot, J.-M. (2008) *La Grève*, Paris: Presses de Sciences Po, Collection Contester.

Kesselman, M. and Groux, G. (eds) (1984) *The French Workers Movement, Economic Crisis and Political Change*, London: Allen and Unwin.

Kochan, T.A., Katz, H.C. and McKersie, R.B. (1986) *The Transformation of American Industrial Relations*, New York: Basic Books.

Lefranc, G. (1969) *Le mouvement syndical. De la Libération aux événements de mai-juin 1968*, Paris: Payot, Collection Bibliothèque historique.

Pernot, J.-M. (2005) *Syndicats: lendemains de crise?*, Paris: Gallimard, Collection Actuel.

Reynaud, J.-D. (1978) *Les syndicats, les patrons et l'État*, Paris: Éditions ouvrières.

Rosanvallon, P. (2006) *La contre-démocratie. La politique à l'âge de la défiance*, Paris: Gallimard.

Sirot, S. (2002) *La grève en France. Une histoire sociale (XIXe–XXe siècle)*, Paris: Odile Jacob, Collection Histoire.

Supiot, A. (ed.) (1999) *Au-delà de l'emploi. Transformations du travail et devenir du travail en Europe, Rapport pour la Commission européenne*, Paris: Flammarion.

Visser, J. (2006) 'Union Membership Statistics in 24 Countries', *Monthly Labor Review*, January: 38–49.

Weber, H. (1986) *Le parti des patrons. Le CNPF–1946–1986*, Paris: Seuil.

Appendix

National Level Representative Trade Union Organisations: A Brief History, 1895–2007

For employees, there are five large trade union organisations which are recognised as being representative at a national level.

The CGT. *The Confédération générale du travail* (CGT) remains to this day the most active and influential trade union organisation. Although it was close to the French Communist Party (PCF) for many years, the CGT began to distance itself from the communists in the mid-1990s. Created in 1895, it constitutes one of the historic branches of the French workers' movement. It now tries, not always successfully, to follow a line midway between 'radical protest' and 'reformist' positions. After its split with the PCF, there has been a great deal of debate between partisans of the organisation's traditional, 'hard line', protest stance and those who favour a reformist overhaul of the organisation. Some regard this debate as a sign that internal union democracy is in good health. Others see it as symptomatic of both deep divisions within the movement, and the complete lack of a clear strategy.

FO. *Force ouvrière* represents the reformist, socialist and secular branch of the French trade union movement. It was founded in 1947, at the beginning of the Cold War, as a result of a split in the CGT. It immediately joined the ranks of the International Confederation of Free Trade Unions (ICFTU), which had been founded by the TUC and American unions in opposition to the pro-Moscow stance of the World Federation of Trade Unions (WFTU), which is based in Prague. Since 1990, and the disappearance of the Eastern bloc, FO's demands tend to be along similar lines to those of the CGT.

The CFTC and the CFDT. In 1919, alongside the socialist workers' movement, another union movement appeared: Christian trade unionism. The CFTC (*Confédération française des travailleurs chrétiens*) represents a very small minority of French workers. In 1964, the movement experienced an identity crisis, out of which emerged a new organisation which broke away from its Catholic roots: this new organisation was the CFDT (Confederation française et démocratique du travail). The CFDT, which is the most powerful union organisation in France after the CGT, has had an eventful history. It had its origins in social Catholicism, and in 1966 entered into an alliance with the CGT, which at that time still had very close ties with the PCF. Post-May 1968, the CFDT adopted a radical, even revolutionary, line and proclaimed its support for socialist self-management, anti-capitalism and class struggle. In the late 1970s, partly as a result of the economic crisis, the CFDT took up more reformist positions. Today, its principal concerns are the promotion of collective bargaining, the construction of a social Europe, and ensuring that major market economy reforms include a social element.

The CGC. The *Confédération générale des cadres* is an organisation which has no real equivalent in other countries. It represents all managerial staff, from supervisors to engineers. Although it was corporatist, the CGC obtained official recognition in 1946, and was endowed with a status analogous to that of the other big inter-professional trade union organisations, like the CGT and the CFDT, allowing it to participate in all national-level and company-level negotiations, in the same way as the other confederations do.

German Trade Unionism in the Postwar Years: The Third and Fourth Movements

STEPHEN J. SILVIA

1. Introduction

Germany's particularly painful path to representative democracy, mass prosperity and political unity has shaped the contours of trade unionism in the country. Most historians and German trade unionists emphasised the continuities in the movement dating back to the mid-nineteenth century. Yet the experience of Germany's trade unions can best be understood as a succession of four movements that coincide with Germany's political regimes: the Second Empire from the expiration of the final anti-socialist law to the abdication of the *Kaiser* (1890–1918), the Weimar Republic (1919–33), the Bonn Republic (1949–90), and the current Berlin Republic. German trade unionism has also been disrupted by Hitler's National Socialism and the Communist German Democratic Republic (GDR). Neither of these regimes contained authentic trade union movements because of their totalitarian character, but they have left marks on German trade unionism that are still discernable today. This chapter focuses on the 'third' and 'fourth' German trade union movements, that is, those of the Bonn and Berlin Republics. It discusses the achievements and shortcomings of each and concludes with a modest assessment of the prospects for German trade unionism in the twenty-first century.

2. The Postwar Restoration of German Trade Unionism

The collapse of the Nazi regime on 8 May 1945 left Germany with a ravaged economy, society and polity. Over the course of the 1930s, the Nazis had either subordinated or liquidated all social and political organisations except their own. As a result, rebuilding civil society in postwar Germany was a huge and uncertain undertaking. Deep divisions among the four powers occupying Germany – France, Britain, the Soviet Union and the United States – made the task even more difficult.

Differences arose almost immediately between the Soviet Union and the other occupying powers in the area of industrial relations. The Soviet authorities were interested in re-establishing trade unions, but they wanted a subservient movement that would serve as a 'transmission belt', relaying and enforcing in the workplace orders from central political and planning authorities. The Soviets acted fast. Within a month after the war's end, they gave substantial direct assistance to pro-Communist trade unionists to organise in the Soviet occupation zone. Trade unionists of other political persuasions could not keep pace because they lacked comparable support. In early February 1946, Soviet authorities took advantage of their organisational lead by facilitating a meeting in eastern Berlin of trade unionists predominantly from their zone to create a full set of trade-union institutions. The gathering formed the Free German Trade Union Federation (*Freier Deutscher Gewerkschaftsbund*, FDGB). The FDGB was a unitary, centralised labour organisation to which members belonged directly. Within a few months the FDGB was subordinated to the new Socialist Unity Party (*Sozialistische Einheitspartei*, SED), which was the product of a forced merger in the Soviet occupation zone between the Social Democratic Party of Germany (*Sozialdemokratische Partei Deutschlands*, SPD) and the Communist Party of Germany (*Kommunistische Partei Deutschlands*, KPD) (Schneider 2000: 240–1).

The growth of trade unions in the western occupation zones followed a markedly different trajectory. Britain led by Clement Attlee's Labour government and the United States under Democratic President Harry S.

Truman were keen on re-establishing representative trade unions and collective bargaining as essential components of a re-democratisation of German society. The western allies nonetheless took a more gradual approach. Given the legacy of centralised fascist institutions under Nazism, the western allies shied away from quickly creating a comprehensive organisation with little local legitimacy, preferring that trade unionism begin at the local level and only be allowed to expand further once healthy and democratic grass roots had been established. The British preference for expansion in three steps – local, zonal and national – carried the day (Fichter 1982: 44–7).

Opinions differed widely among both the western allies and German trade union officials over the best structure for the postwar German labour movement. All involved save for the French authorities agreed that 'unitary non-partisan unionism' (*Einheitsgewerkschaft*) was preferable to the sectarianism of the past. Most German trade unionists who had survived Nazi rule were of the opinion that the Weimar Republic fell because the labour movement – which was divided along Christian, liberal and socialist lines – was unable to organise a general strike against Adolf Hitler when he first came to power in 1933. Postwar unionists also recognised that the adoption of unitary non-partisan unionism would end organised labour's structural disadvantage vis-à-vis unitary employers associations that had handicapped previous German trade union movements (Eley 1989: 658).

Unitary non-partisan unionism has always been a somewhat narrower construction than its ideological proponents made it out to be. *Einheitsgewerkschaft* was in practice an ideological melding of the Christian and social democratic traditions around a corporatist conceptualisation of the relationship between trade unions and the state. Social democrats supported unitary non-partisan unionism as 'the logical counterpart to the statist conception of socialist politics'. Christian unionists favoured it because it meshed well with Roman Catholic social teaching. Adherence to democracy defined the borders of *Einheitsgewerkschaft*. The nascent unions banned former officials of the Nazi party and the Nazis' supplicant workers organisation, the *Deutscher Arbeiterfront* (DAF, German Labour Front). Communists were also banned in 1956 after the German Constitutional Court (*Bundesverfassungsgericht*) ruled that the Communist Party of Germany was an undemocratic organisation (Pirker 1979: 259–60).

The adoption of the principle of unitary non-partisan unionism substantially enhanced the position of organised labour within postwar German society because it provided the labour movement with a widespread legitimacy that it had previously lacked. *Einheitsgewerkschaft* has resulted in one major political drawback for organised labour. The absence of an explicitly partisan bond between the trade unions and their strongest postwar political supporter, the Social Democratic Party of Germany, has at times impaired union efforts to achieve political ends.

Despite the widespread embrace of unitary non-partisan unionism, creating the structures of postwar trade unionism in Germany proved difficult in two respects. The first was setting the degree of centralisation for the new movement. Left-wing and centrist unionists preferred the creation of a single, general union for all German employees, whereas the traditionalist wing of the labour movement favoured a decentralised model comprised of a set of independent sectoral unions, which in turn would all be members of a single peak confederation. In the latter model, the individual unions would be the strongest organisations because only they would be allowed to have members, to collect dues, to maintain a strike fund and to call strikes. The confederation's roles would be to act as the political voice of the movement domestically, to represent the movement internationally and to provide a small set of common services for which there are significant economies of scale (Schmidt 1977: 41–5).

Hans Böckler, the influential trade unionist who eventually became the first president of the postwar German Trade Union Federation (*Deutscher Gewerkschaftsbund*, DGB), and most of his colleagues supported centralisation, but this position did not carry the day because both the British and American occupying authorities rejected it. The British and Americans feared that a single general union would give western German labour far too much power within a still underdeveloped and fragile civil society. The American authorities were particularly concerned that a highly centralised labour movement could fall under Communist control far too easily, just as it had in the Soviet zone. The British and Americans also preferred that German unionists adhere more closely to the decentralised Anglo-Saxon model of trade unionism. After some resistance, most western German trade unionists relented and accepted a decentralised structure as the model for the postwar labour movement (Markovits 1986: 65).

Once centralisation was foreclosed as an option, most trade unionists overwhelmingly embraced industrial unionism (*Industriegewerkschaft*) over craft unionism as an organising principle. The British and Americans had no objection to that choice. By late 1947 the American and British authorities were satisfied that most local trade unions had sufficiently strong roots, so they lifted the ban on mergers across zones. In May 1948 trade union representatives from the British and American zones formed a trade union council to plan bizonal mergers and the creation of a peak confederation. Later that year union representatives from the French zone joined the council. The council's deliberations produced a structure comprised of sixteen industrial unions that covered the whole economy, using the jurisdictions of the industrial unions from the Weimar Republic's old socialist trade union confederation as a starting point.

Five of the new unions covered manufacturing: the dominant union of the postwar German movement, *Industriegewerkschaft Metall* (IG Metall, Industrial Union of Metalworkers); the influential *Industriegewerkschaft Chemie-Papier-Keramik* (IG Chemie or IG ChPK, Industrial Union of Chemical, Paper and Ceramic Workers); *Industriegewerkschaft Druck und Papier* (IG DruPa, Industrial Union of Printing and Paper Workers); *Gewerkschaft Leder* (GL, Union of Leather Workers); and *Gewerkschaft Textil-Bekleidung* (GTB, Union of Textile and Clothing Workers).

Four unions had jurisdictions in the primary and construction sectors. The most important was *Industriegewerkschaft Bau-Steine-Erden* (IG BSE or IG Bau, Industrial Union of Construction Workers). The others were *Industriegewerkschaft Bergbau und Energie* (IG BE, Industrial Union of Mining and Energy Workers), *Gewerkschaft Holz und Kunststoff* (GHK, Union of Wood and Plastic Workers) and *Gewerkschaft Garten, Land- und Forstwirtschaft* (GGLF, Union of Horticulture, Agriculture and Forestry Workers).

Three unions organised workers principally in the private service sector: *Gewerkschaft Handel, Banken und Versicherungen* (HBV, Union of Retail, Banking and Insurance Workers), *Gewerkschaft Nahrung-Genuss-Gaststätten* (NGG, Union of Food, Hotel and Restaurant Workers) and

Gewerkschaft Kunst (GK, Union of Artists and Musicians), which actually was a federation of seven smaller unions and professional associations.

Four unions covered the public sector: *Gewerkschaft Öffentliche Dienste, Transport und Verkehr* (ÖTV, Union of Public Services and Transportation Employees), which was the second largest DGB union; *Deutsche Postgewerkschaft* (DPG, German Postal Workers Union); *Gewerkschaft der Eisenbahner Deutschlands* (GdED, Railroad Workers Union of Germany); and *Gewerkschaft Erziehung und Wissenschaft* (GEW, Union of Education and Science Workers).

The second major difficulty in creating the structures of postwar trade unionism in western Germany arose over the treatment of white-collar employees (*Angestellte*). The logic of industrial unionism (i.e. one workplace, one union, regardless of occupation) had its shortcomings when applied to white-collar employees. For example, a payroll clerk in the chemical industry would fall under the jurisdiction of the chemical employees union, whereas a payroll clerk doing the same job in the metalworking sector would fall under the jurisdiction of the metalworkers union. In 1945 white-collar employees formed their own organisation, the German White-Collar Employees Union (*Deutsche Angestellten–Gewerkschaft*, DAG). The DAG met the criteria of *Einheitsgewerkschaft* – that is, it was unitary and non-partisan – but it was not compatible with the concept of industrial unionism. As a result, debate broke out over the advantages and disadvantages of a separate white-collar employees union within a labour movement structured along industrial lines (Schneider 2000: 41–6; Mielke 1990: 254–5).

DAG officials argued that a separate white-collar union would be far more successful in recruiting that segment of the labour force and asserted that there would always be a bias against white-collar employees in industrial unions since in most instances they would be a minority of the membership. Trade union officials from blue-collar unions countered that solidarity among all employees within a firm mattered most in confrontations with employers. The dispute over industrial unionism continued until April 1949 when the DAG declared that it would remain a single independent union for public and private white-collar employees in the three western zones with no affiliation to any peak confederation. As a result, both the DAG and the individual industrial unions claimed jurisdiction over white-collar employees (Weber and Mielke 1989: 32–40).

Western German unionists completed the construction of the postwar labour movement in mid-October 1949, some five months after the establishment of the Federal Republic of Germany in the west and less than a week after the creation of the German Democratic Republic in the east. Representatives of the sixteen unions met in Munich to create the *Deutscher Gewerkschaftsbund* to serve as their peak confederation. The DGB has always been postwar Germany's predominant labour confederation. Throughout the history of the Federal Republic at least 80 per cent of all organised employees have belonged to unions that are DGG affiliates (Müller 1990: 87–93). The largest group of unions not affiliated to the DGB were those that focused on organising civil servants. These unions belonged to a separate confederation, the *Deutscher Beamtenbund* (DBB, German Civil Servants Federation). There also exists an extremely small dissident Christian trade union movement, which was established in the mid-1950s and has its own confederation, the *Christlicher Gewerkschaftsbund Deutschlands* (CGB, Christian Trade Union Federation of Germany). It has never posed a serious threat to the influence of the DGB and its affiliates.

During the first forty years of the postwar German labour movement, the organisational structure only changed at the margins. A police officers union, *Gewerkschaft der Polizei* (GdP), became the seventeenth DGB affiliate in 1978. In 1989 the printers union merged with the artists union to form the Industrial Union of Media Workers (*Industriegewerkschaft Medien*, IG Medien), which brought the number of DGB affiliates back down to sixteen.

Employee representation in Germany consists of more than collective bargaining. One of the most distinctive and well-known elements of German industrial relations is 'codetermination' (*Mitbestimmung*). Codetermination provides employees with limited influence over decision-making in their enterprises. Codetermination has roots dating back to the close of World War I, but its current form was largely codified in the early 1950s and expanded moderately in the 1970s. Codetermination has two components: the statutory right of employees to form works councils (*Betriebsräte*) to represent their collective interests in the workplace, and employee representation on the supervisory boards (*Aufsichtsräte*) of medium and large-sized firms (Schneider 2000: 260–72 and 366–70).

The benefits of codetermination widely outweigh the costs. Employee participation on corporate boards has helped employees gain a greater understanding of business objectives and has contributed to Germany avoiding the worst of corporate excess found in many Anglo-Saxon countries. Still, the practice has not prevented major corporate scandals and has sometimes even implicated employee representatives in them (e.g. Mannesmann and Volkswagen). Works councils, which are statutory bodies formally distinct from unions that do not have the right to strike, have posed their own set of opportunities and risks. The Works Constitution Act (*Betriebsverfassungsgesetz*) governing works councils provides access to internal company information, material support and legal protections that rank among the most extensive in the world. Unions quickly learned that by getting local union officials elected to the councils, the unions had *de facto* agents in the workplace with far greater capacities and protections than a shop steward would ever have. The law, however, draws a sharp distinction between unions and works councils. It requires works councillors to keep certain types of corporate information confidential and forbids works councils from calling strikes. At times the divergent constituencies and concerns of trade unions and works councils generate a certain degree of tension and rivalry between them, but over the years, trade union officials and works councillors at most workplaces have learned how to maintain a constructive relationship (Thelen 1991: 2–5).

Still, it must be said that the postwar reconstruction of the German economy did not follow the path preferred by trade unionists. Union leaders wanted to socialise the commanding heights of the economy, in particular, heavy industry and finance. They were dismayed when Germany's postwar government, dominated by conservative Christian Democrats, restored capitalism and private property with only a few exceptions (e.g. Volkswagen), and permitted some captains of industry and state officials to return to positions of prominence despite dubious records from the National Socialist era. When trade unionists failed to achieve their initial postwar objective of moving the economy beyond capitalism, they focused their energies primarily on the areas where they could make concrete progress for German workers: collective bargaining and political advocacy.

3. The Third German Trade Union Movement: Trends and Performance, 1949–89

Major measures of both the trade union movement and the economy as a whole indicate that the postwar German industrial relations system performed well in the Bonn Republic. Trends in trade union membership can be divided into three phases (see Figure 1).[1] The first phase, which spans the initial reconstruction years and the famous German 'economic miracle' that ran well into the 1960s, is marked by a combination of nominal success and consolidation of union membership, but a shrinking relative position in a robust economy. After an initial surge in unionisation in the early 1950s, trade union rolls continued to expand steadily, albeit modestly, until the first postwar recession of 1966–7. Between 1950 and 1966, unions increased total membership by more than one third, from fewer than six million to just over eight million members. The recession subsequently shaved 178,000 (2.2 per cent) off the union rolls. Despite the significant membership expansion for the period, unions were unable to keep pace with rapid job growth. Union density reached an all-time postwar peak of 37.9 per cent in 1952, but then declined thereafter, bottoming out in 1969 at 31 per cent (see Figure 2).[2]

1 Total union membership for Germany consists of the sum of the total memberships of all of the trade unions in Germany. Specifically, the data include the memberships of the affiliate unions of the DGB, DBB, DAG, CGB and a handful of independent unions. This chapter uses the data reported by the trade unions themselves and the *Statistisches Bundesamt*. It also uses the estimates by Ebbinghaus (2003) of independent trade union membership.

2 Trade union density (a.k.a. unionisation rate) in this chapter is calculated by dividing the number of *actively employed* union members by the number of 'economically

The second phase of organisational development covers the late 1960s to the early 1980s; these were in many ways golden years. Political trends shifted favourably from the perspective of most trade unionists. The Social Democratic Party came to power, first as a junior partner with the Christian Democrats from 1967 to 1971 and then as a senior partner with the liberal Free Democratic Party from 1971 to 1982. A surge in labour militancy throughout Europe in the late 1960s and early 1970s made unions more attractive, particularly to younger and more educated workers.

The SPD spearheaded the passage of legislation expanding codetermination rights in 1971 and 1976, and expanded the welfare state in several respects, including improved dismissal protection, unemployment insurance, and pensions (Herbig 1980: 238–43; Silvia 2007: 33). The new laws indirectly strengthened the unions' hand. Between 1968 and 1981, total union membership rose by 23 per cent to reach 9.7 million. Job growth was not nearly as robust in the 1970s as it had been during the economic miracle. As a result, German trade unions were able to improve the unionisation rate. After a brief dip at the start of the 1970s, density peaked at 33.3 per cent for both 1978 and 1979.

During the third phase, which coincided with the 1980s, trade union membership reached its apogee in the Bonn Republic, but the environment in which unions operated became more difficult. The political constellation shifted against the trade unions in 1982 when a centre-right coalition led by Christian Democrat Helmut Kohl came to power, remaining until 1998. The German economy put in a poor performance, growing at a modest annual average of 2 per cent during the 1980s. The entrance of the German baby-boom generation into the labour market (which came a decade later than its American and British counterparts) added extra strains, ending the era of full employment. A recession, which began in late 1981, reduced

active employees in the domestic labour market' (*erwerbstätige Arbeitnehmer Inland*) as reported in Bundesministerium für Arbeit und Soziales, *Statistisches Taschenbuch* (Berlin: BMAS, 2007), series StTb 2.5 and StTb 2.10. Labour market data for Saar from 1957 to 1959 and West Berlin from 1950 to 1959 are from various issues of the *Statistisches Jahrbuch für die Bundesrepublik Deutschland* (Wiesbaden: Kohlhammer, various years).

employment by 586,000 (2.4 per cent). Job losses were disproportionately severe in manufacturing and cut significantly into union ranks. Membership fell by over 300,000 (3.1 per cent) between 1981 and 1984. It recovered thereafter, albeit slowly. It took nine years for German trade-union membership to exceed the previous postwar peak. Membership topped 9.75 million in 1990. Density fared worse than membership. From 1979 to 1990, the unionisation rate edged downward. In 1986, it dipped below the 30 per cent threshold for the first time in the postwar era; by 1990 it had fallen to 28 per cent.

The performance of the wider economy in the Bonn Republic is marked by three strong decades followed by a weak final one. German growth rates, compensation gains and productivity improvements were consistently robust from the 1950s through the 1970s, and unemployment and inflation rates remained low (see Table 1). From the 1950s through the 1970s, real compensation increased between four and five per cent annually on average (see Table 2). As a result, distribution shifted in favour of employees; the labour share of national income exceeded 70 per cent throughout the 1970s and early 1980s, peaking at 73.2 per cent in 1974 (see Figure 3). The price of success at the bargaining table was not burdensome for trade unions. Despite the occasional large strike, Germany remained at the lower end of the international tables in terms of participants and days lost owing to industrial disputes. Germany's relative economic performance was so good during the 1970s that academics and even German Federal Chancellor Helmut Schmidt (SPD) proclaimed Germany an economic 'model' (Markovits 1982).

Signs of stress, however, did begin to manifest in the 1980s. Growth and productivity slowed markedly, which generated higher unemployment and contributed to reducing real increases in annual compensation to 0.8 per cent during the 1980s (see Table 1). Labour's share of national income began to slide in the early 1980s and fell to 67.1 per cent by the end of the decade. Trade unions attempted to combat rising unemployment by using collective bargaining to fight for weekly working time reduction from 40 to 35 hours. Employers resisted fiercely, but the trade unions broke through the 40-hour barrier in 1984 as a result of strikes by the metalworking and printers' unions. Over the next decade, trade unionists across the economy pursued weekly working time reduction, with varying degrees of success. Unfortunately, working time reduction proved ineffective at reducing unemployment. The campaigns for a shorter workweek did provide organisational focus for the trade unions, which helped to attract and to retain membership in the short run. The drive to cut the workweek also reduced firms' propensity to belong to employers' associations, which proved terribly costly for trade unions in subsequent years because it eroded the capacity to enforce region wide collective bargaining agreements (*Flächentarifverträge*) as the norm throughout each sector (Schroeder and Silvia 2003; and Silvia 1997).

In sum, the institutions and practices of the third German trade union movement performed remarkably well for three decades, but they had already begun to fray in the decade before the sudden and unexpected events that culminated in German unification on 3 October 1990.

4. The Fourth German Trade Union Movement: Trends and Performance, 1990 to the Present

The impact of German unification on the trade union movement has been substantial. Unification has been the catalyst and a prime factor shaping what in many ways can best be understood as Germany's fourth trade union movement. This may seem hardly surprising, given the enormity of the event. Unification abruptly changed the economic, political, social and geographic contours of the Federal Republic of Germany. The extent of the rupture can easily escape notice, however, because of the way Germany unified. The legacy of four failed political regimes on German soil during the twentieth century made most Germans east and west reluctant to tinker with the only regime that had worked, namely the Federal Republic. Consequently, the dominant political view in 1990 was that the most prudent way to unify the country was simply to transfer to the east without amendment all of the Federal Republic's institutions, laws and practices, including the entire industrial relations system (Bundesvereinigung der Deutschen Arbeitgeberverbände and Deutscher Gewerkschaftsbund 1990).

Simply absorbing eastern Germany into the Federal Republic avoided experimentation and averted the need to revise the elaborate economic, political and social arrangements that were the product of forty years of incremental conflict and compromise in western German industrial relations. In practice, however, the simple institutional transfer has proved extremely problematic. Many western institutions and practices, some of which had already demonstrated significant shortcomings before unification, proved ill-suited to the new, far more heterogeneous Berlin Republic.

At first, some western labour leaders considered merging their unions with their eastern counterparts, which in all but a few cases had very similar jurisdictional boundaries. Ultimately, however, only one DGB union, the chemical workers, actually did. The other fifteen rejected that option out of fear that a merger would designate their organisations as the legal, moral and political successors of the eastern labour movement, which could have exposed them to unknown liabilities. These fifteen DGB unions instead orchestrated the liquidation of the GDR unions and then extended their geographic boundaries to cover the east. This means of expansion, although prudent, did have costs. It deprived these unions of the ownership of the property of the former eastern labour movement, much of which had belonged to the prewar Christian and Social Democratic trade unions. It also swept away the entire leadership of the old eastern German unions, which removed some potentially 'tainted' individuals, but made establishing roots and legitimacy in eastern Germany much more difficult.

Union membership developments in the 1990s resembled those of the 1950s, but in an exaggerated form. Initially, the western German trade unions had great success recruiting new members in the former German Democratic Republic. By the end of 1991, over 4.5 million easterners joined unions, which increased total German union membership by over 40 per cent to reach a postwar high of 13.9 million (see Figure 1). Many easterners initially joined unions because in the GDR union membership had been a prerequisite for access to a wide spectrum of benefits (e.g. pensions and vacation homes) and because they hoped that being union members would provide greater job security. This was not to be, however. The Kohl government pursued an aggressive introduction of market mechanisms and privatisation that triggered a collapse in the eastern labour market. Eastern German union membership tumbled precipitously as a result, falling by over one-half to 2.2 million in 1998, which is the last year for which separate statistics were compiled. Total union membership in western Germany also declined. It dropped from 9.4 to 8.2 million (13 per cent) between 1991 and 1998. Between 1991 and 2007, total union membership for all of Germany fell by 5.75 million (41 per cent) to 8.2 million, which is over 1.5 million lower than western German union membership alone had been in 1990.

Unionisation rates gyrated as a result of the rapid shifts in membership. The sharpest change came in eastern Germany. The eastern unionisation rate was 51.3 per cent in 1991; it comfortably exceeded the western rate of 25.5 per cent for the same year (see Figure 2). By 1998 eastern German union density had plummeted to 23.3 per cent, which was barely above the western rate of 20.7 per cent for the same year. Survey data show that by 2000, the eastern German unionisation rate had fallen below the western rate. For all of Germany, the unionisation rate fell by over half between 1991 and 2007, from 32.1 per cent to 15.7 per cent.

The collapse in the membership ranks had institutional consequences for the trade union movement. Even before unification, pressure to restructure the trade union movement had been rising. Underlying changes in the economy (e.g. Europeanisation, globalisation and the shift from manufacturing to services), which the German trade union leadership dealt with reluctantly at best before unification, had a substantial impact on the trade union movement. The top three unions represented 59 per cent of total DGB membership, whereas the six smallest DGB unions comprised less than 10 per cent. These asymmetries caused governance problems. The leadership of small DGB unions often complained that the big unions – in particular, IG Metall – arrogantly used their preponderant size and vast wealth to dominate the trade union movement (Köbele 1994: 13). Officials from the larger unions responded that their actions simply reflected the democratic principle of proportional representation and that the smaller unions were often free riders, because they were unable to fulfil all the financial and organisational obligations required of a DGB affiliate (Lang 1994: 9). Jurisdictional disputes among affiliates had also begun to proliferate as new sectors arose that did not obviously fit into the divisions drawn up in the late 1940s (e.g. software production).

Recognising the urgent needs to reconceptualise the role of trade unions in the German economy and society, and to restructure the institutional architecture of the trade union movement, union leaders embarked on a reform effort in the early 1990s. The intellectual discussion of the future of the labour movement was at times vigorous, but it produced meagre results. The DGB spoke positively of Germany's famed 'social market economy' for the first time in its 1996 Basic Programme, but it contained several qualifiers, reflecting a hesitation among many in the movement to embrace capitalism unconditionally. The Programme as a whole broke little new conceptual ground (*Deutscher Gewerkschaftsbund* 1996; Silvia 1999: 107–8). Financial exigency in the wake of precipitous membership declines led to institutional reform crowding out intellectual and conceptual considerations. Calculations of narrow advantage by individual union leaders ultimately shaped the specifics of the institutional reform.

Among the distinguishing characteristics of the fourth German trade union movement have been the significant reduction of the number of individual unions as a result of mergers and a diminution of the relative importance of the DGB. Trade unions and the DGB spent substantial sums extending their organisations eastward in 1990 and 1991. At first labour leaders hoped that these expenditures would pay off by expanding the size of their organisations. It soon became apparent, however, that these hopes would not be realised. By the mid-1990s, eastern job losses far outstripped even the most pessimistic estimates from the early days of unification and all unions suddenly found it difficult to sustain their eastern offices.

Large DGB unions quickly began to absorb the small unions that were in financial distress. In some instances, the unions were in related sectors, but in others, they were not. The construction workers' union, IG BSE, and the Agricultural, Forest and Garden Employees' Union, GGLF, were the first to complete a merger in the 1990s, forming the *Industriegewerkschaft Bauen-Agrar-Umwelt* (IG BAU, Industrial Union of Construction, Agricultural and Environmental Employees) in 1995. In 1997, after several years of discussions, the chemical workers union engineered a merger with the mining and leather workers unions to create *Industriegewerkschaft Bergbau, Chemie, Energie* (IG BCE, Industrial Union of Mining, Chemical and Energy Employees). IG Metall merged with the clothing and textile workers union in 1998, and the wood and plastic workers union in 2000. One merger during these years was like no other. It combined five heterogeneous public and private service-sector unions – including the huge ÖTV public-sector union and the DAG, which had been outside the DGB – to form the *vereinigte Dienstleistungsgewerkschaft* (ver.di, United Service Employees Union).

The spate of mergers came to an end in 2001, six years after it had begun, leaving a radically changed institutional landscape. The mergers reduced the number of DGB affiliates from seventeen to eight, but the disproportionate influence of the largest unions, if anything, was accentuated. The biggest unions, IG Metall (2.3 million) and ver.di (2.2 million), continue to dominate, with the metalworkers playing the pre-eminent role. Ver.di has been less effectual than its size would indicate because the 2001 merger created a highly balkanised union that generated few budgetary or political economies of scale. The third-largest union, IG BCE (713,000), has remained an influential player, both within the DGB and German politics more broadly. The IG BCE's combination of efficient organisation, close partnership with employers and centrist politics has enabled its leaders to maximise the union's impact. IG BAU (352,000), the fourth-largest union, has seen its influence wane as it has been buffeted in recent years by a sharp contraction in the construction sector. The four small unions – GEW (249,000), GdP (168,000), NGG (209,000) and the recently renamed 'Transnet' railworkers union (239,000) – are not very influential, but they have been able to hang on as independent organisations. Of these four, only the GdP has a secure financial and membership base. The fate of the others remains an open question.

All the pressures that precipitated the dramatic institutional changes among the individual unions in Germany also affected the DGB as an organisation. Declining membership rolls and the resulting dues shortfall hit the DGB, because it depends on the affiliated unions for about 90 per cent of its funds. Individual union leaders, under extreme duress and looking for places to cut costs, quickly turned their gaze to the DGB. Although critics had attacked the DGB as ineffectual for decades (Pirker 1979; Hattinger Kreis 1992), the initial reforms focused narrowly on cost cutting rather than improving the performance of the peak confederation. The 1994 Berlin DGB convention amended DGB statutes an unprecedented 42 times. The changes reduced the size of the Managing Federal Executive Board (*Geschäftsführender Bundesvorstand*) from seven to five, the quadrennial federal convention (*Bundeskongress*) from approximately 600 to 400, and pared back the number of local DGB offices. It also cut the size and authority of the DGB departments for collective bargaining, education, foreign employees, handicrafts and technology, and eliminated DGB departments for civil servants, white-collar employees and blue-collar workers. The convention did spare the DGB women and youth departments, in large part out of fear of sending the wrong signal regarding labour's commitment to these groups.

Falling revenue forced the DGB to cut its operating budget by 17 per cent between 1992 and 1997. Over the same period, the DGB trimmed total staff by 625 to 2075, and headquarters personnel from 330 to 210. The 1997 decisions to move the provision of legal services for members out of the DGB and into a separate entity, and to cap total outlays for these services ended the DGB's financial free fall. It is important to note that all the cuts that took place within the DGB during the mid-1990s were ad hoc reactions to financial and organisational crises. In the end, however, they did amount to a *de facto* organisational reform. Their impact was to reduce the presence and importance of the DGB 'out in the field' and within the labour movement.

At the 1998 DGB convention, the leadership and the affiliated unions were determined to improve the coherence of the DGB's organisational restructuring and to bring closure to the reform process that had begun in the early 1990s. Specifically the leadership and the affiliates asked the delegates to approve granting the authority to complete the DGB's organisational reform to the Federal Executive Board and to approve transferring the headquarters of the DGB from Düsseldorf to Berlin by the year 2002. The delegates, protective of the status quo and still smarting from the most recent round of cutbacks, were wary of both proposals. Vague compromise language in resolutions that the convention eventually passed allowed the leadership to claim it had a mandate to proceed.

After the 1998 convention, a consensus formed that the DGB needed to shift focus from service provision (which included the production of seldom-read social and economic analyses) to political work. The leadership of the DGB and the individual unions agreed to assign to the DGB three 'central tasks': (1) 'act as "the union voice" vis-à-vis the state, business, organisations, parties, etc; ... (2) competently influence the political and in particular the legislative decision-making process at all levels, and (3) ... strengthen its capacity to mobilise and stage campaigns'. The larger objective behind these central tasks is to ensure that the DGB be 'permanently present in the political decision-making centres and competently be a part of the process' (Deutscher Gewerkschaftsbund 2002: 109–10). The tasks guided the subsequent reorganisation of the DGB. Individual unions took over the political education of the membership. Lobbying and monitoring government activities at all levels became the job of the DGB. The DGB changed its regional structures accordingly. It established lobbying offices in all but two *Land* capitals, closed its lobbying offices in Bonn and Kassel because of the moves of the federal government and the Federal Labour Court, and opened a new office in Erfurt, the new location of the Federal Labour Court.

By establishing the principal task of the DGB as political lobbying (broadly defined), the trade union leadership brought purpose and direction to the peak confederation, something that had been noticeably absent for many years. The transition to lobbying permitted the DGB to make substantial savings on its largest single cost: personnel. The decision to move the DGB headquarters to Berlin also furthered both dimensions of the organisational reform. It facilitated political monitoring and lobbying at the federal level. It also enabled the DGB to reduce operating costs further by shedding employees who were reluctant to make the move. As a result, by December 2005, the DGB headquarters employed 168 and only 84 of those were actual union officials. Total DGB employment had fallen to 860, down from over 2,000 a decade earlier.

The DGB simultaneously undertook an expansion at the European level to extend its monitoring and lobbying activities, which was in keeping with both the extension of European competencies and the logic behind the organisational reform. The DGB had already established an office in Brussels in 1997 to monitor and to lobby the European Commission. In 2000, it added an office in Strasbourg and expanded its Brussels office to cover the European Parliament.

Individual German unions also increased their activities in Brussels. German union officials rarely miss an opportunity to embrace Europe rhetorically because it resonates well with the post-nationalistic leanings of the German left. In practice, however, most German union leaders have repeatedly tried to use the European trade union apparatus simply to pressure unions in other countries into adopting German trade-union priorities.

The smaller, more focused DGB has produced at best mixed results in its new role as the lobbying arm of the trade union movement. Why? First, the DGB has continued to staff its offices largely with personnel from before the narrowing of the confederation's mission. New hires have mostly been mid-range officials from the member unions. Unfortunately, few have demonstrated the skills and experience needed to be effective lobbyists. Second, the DGB has not in practice shed some tasks. DGB officials still consume too much of their time organising educational seminars and producing mountains of brochures, pamphlets and reports of questionable value. Third, individual unions – particularly the larger ones – have not been able to resist the temptation to engage directly in lobbying themselves, which effectively elbows out the DGB. The DGB remains only a peak confederation. It has a budget and personnel that are only a small fraction of one of the bigger unions. In the real world of politics, this is not much to put on the table. Disagreements over political strategy and tactics have also prompted the leaderships of individual unions to distance themselves at times from the DGB, undercutting the confederation's effectiveness.

Continuing cost pressures in the wake of shrinking membership and the DGB's lacklustre record as a lobbying arm led the IG Metall leadership in 2008 to discuss openly the possibility of undertaking a new round of DGB reforms. High on the agenda have been suggestions to streamline further the tasks of the DGB and to reduce from the current 12 per cent the share of gross dues that each affiliate must pay to the DGB. It is therefore a real possibility that the duties and relative importance of the DGB will continue to diminish in coming years.

Economic conditions and trade union performance served as both backdrop and catalyst for the most recent round of institutional reform. The Berlin Republic has proved to be a challenging environment for the fourth German labour movement. Real per capita GDP growth has been modest. In the 1990s, it increased by 2.3 per cent a year on average; from 2000 to 2007, it rose by only 1.4 per cent (see Table 1). The unemployment rate jumped in the wake of soft economic performance and the structural fallout of German unification. The average annual joblessness rate reached 6.9 per cent during the 1990s and 9.4 per cent from 2000 to 2007. In eastern Germany, the unemployment rate exceeded 15 per cent for more than a decade. Hourly productivity grew at a moderate annual pace of 2.4 per cent on average during the 1990s, but then slowed to 1.5 per cent between 2000 and 2007. Slow growth, high unemployment and a weak productivity performance combined to make collective bargaining particularly challenging for trade unions. Real compensation improved on average by 0.8 per cent per year in the 1990s and actually fell by 0.5 per cent per year from 2000 to 2007. As a result, by 2006 labour's adjusted share of national income had sunk to 62.4 per cent, which is the lowest level since the end of World War II (see Figure 3). The decade of the 1990s ranked highest in terms of the number of employees involved in industrial disputes, but it placed only fourth out of the most recent five full decades in terms of working days lost owing to industrial action (see Table 2). In other words, more employees struck during the 1990s than ever before, but the duration of the strikes was shorter. The pattern can be explained in the main by a surge of short walkouts in the mid-1990s that were largely vain efforts to save jobs during the privatisation of the eastern German economy (Silvia 1999: 92).

Two challenges stand out as the most pressing for German trade unionists today: reversing declines in both membership and collective bargaining power. German trade unions have traditionally relied on a combination of social tradition, workplace pressure, ideological conviction, and in some instances material benefit to recruit members. The rise of individualism over more collective understandings of identity, the breakdown of class milieu, and economic shifts toward service employment and smaller firms have made union recruiting more challenging in recent decades. A few trade unions have begun experimenting with new approaches toward recruitment. In recent years, IG Metall in the state of North Rhine-Westphalia has led the way in placing greater emphasis on providing more and better services to its members, and experimenting with a combination of savvy public relations and more activist, 'social movement' unionism. The North Rhine-Westphalian metalworkers mobilised members through campaigns designed to achieve specific objectives, for example, the 'better not cheaper' (*besser statt billiger*) campaign to curtail the use of outsourcing. These efforts contributed to curbing membership decline in IG Metall's North Rhine-Westphalia district and were instrumental in the advancement of IG Metall's North Rhine-Westphalian chief Detlef Wetzel to the post of vice-chair of IG Metall in 2007. It remains to be seen whether a more activist approach pursued more broadly will be effective in reversing more than a decade of declines in membership and political influence for IG Metall and the German trade union movement as a whole.

More alarming for the trade union movement has been the erosion of its impact in the labour market. As recently as the mid-1990s, collective bargaining contracts directly determined compensation for 82.6 per cent of employees in western Germany and 73.4 per cent in eastern Germany. By 2006, these numbers had slipped to 65 per cent and 54 per cent, respectively (Institut für Arbeitsmarkt- und Berufsforschung 1993–2007). The principal explanation for these declines lies not in the declines in the union ranks, but in the increasing propensity of firms to eschew membership in employers associations. Employers associations have been more important than trade unions in extending the reach of collective bargaining because employers associations have traditionally had far higher densities than trade unions. In the metalworking sector, for example, employer association density was stable at approximately 75 per cent in terms of employment for several decades until the mid-1980s. It declined steadily thereafter, falling by almost twenty percentage points to 56.5 per cent in 2006. Employer association density fell far more precipitously in eastern Germany. In 1991, it stood at 65.7 per cent in terms of employment largely because the German government paid membership dues for state-owned firms, but by 2006 it had fallen to 17.4 per cent (Gesamtmetall 2007).

Cost concerns in increasingly competitive markets, a decline in the size of the median firm, a drop in peer pressure to join and poor provision of services account for the drop in employer-association membership (Silvia and Schroeder 2007: 1440–8). The landscape of social partnership is particularly desolate in eastern Germany. Densities for both unions and employers associations remain far below that found in western Germany. Three factors explain the difference. The first is structural. Eastern Germany has far fewer large plants and a smaller percentage of manufacturing employment than does western German. The second is sociological. Western Germans rebuilt a network of social partners starting immediately after World War II. Consequently, there were many trade unionists from the Weimar Republic who were still alive and able to draw on their experience to re-establish trade unions in the immediate postwar years. Re-establishing trade unions was also relatively easy in the West Germany of the latter half of the 1940s because collective identity grounded in class and community was still very important. Eastern Germans, in contrast, spent more than fifty years under totalitarian regimes. Institutional or individual links to the Weimar years no longer existed in the early 1990s when eastern Germans got their first opportunity to build an autonomous trade union movement and contemporary German society is far more individualistic than it was in the 1950s. The third is political. The legacy of privileged political parties and associations in the German Democratic Republic has made many easterners hesitant to join any mass organisations (Schroeder and Silvia 2003: 260–3).

The impact of the east-west gap on German industrial relations has been enormous. In many sectors, eastern Germany has become virtually 'union free', which has added labour costs as a new dimension for competition among firms. The greater heterogeneity has made it much harder for unions and employers associations in individual sectors to continue the practice of producing collective agreements that can be used throughout the country. Employers associations have responded to intensified wage competition by introducing a set of parallel organisations that offer personnel consulting and legal services, but do not include participation in the region wide collective agreements or in strike insurance schemes. These so-called 'no contract' (*Ohne Tarif*, or OT) associations enable employers associations to keep as paying members (at a reduced rate) firms dissatisfied with collective agreements. OT associations have been growing rapidly. In 2006, 9.4 per cent of the western firms that were affiliated to any type of metal industry employers association were in OT associations, up 2.2 percentage points from the previous year. These firms contain 6.9 per cent of all employees of member firms, a 1.8 percentage-point increase in one year. OT associations have been serving largely as way stations for disgruntled employers. It is too soon to tell whether these alternative associations are ultimately viable and what their impact will be on membership in traditional employers associations.

Trade union leaders all wish to prevent inter-firm and interregional wage competition from becoming a permanent reality, especially in eastern Germany. German unions are pursuing different strategies to achieve this end. Both the chemical and metalworkers unions have accepted a degree of controlled decentralisation in the determination of compensation. In 2004, for example, IG Metall and the employers associations in the metal industry codified in the 'Pforzheim Agreement' the practice of allowing firms experiencing temporary economic distress to negotiate 'hardship clauses' with their works councils. A hardship clause sets compensation below that of the standard collective agreement. In most instances, both the union and regional employers association must approve the hardship clause before it can go into effect. Since German unification, IG Metall has approved approximately one thousand hardship clauses. Hardship clauses have added a new degree of flexibility to German collective bargaining. They may have contributed to the slowdown in the decline of employers' association density in both eastern and western Germany since 2004. Hardship clauses have also at times even helped to boost union membership in the workplaces where they have been negotiated, because many employees wish to have influence on the union's decision whether to approve or to reject a draft agreement (Frankfurter Rundschau: 3 September 2007; Silvia and Schroeder 2007: 1451–2).

Not all German trade unions have adopted the use of hardship clauses as a means to reform the current collective bargaining regime. Ver.di, the union with jurisdiction over most of the private service sectors, has led a push for a statist solution. Ver.di, the NGG food and restaurant employees union, and the DGB have demanded the introduction of a national minimum wage set at 7.50 euros per hour. The proposal for a single minimum wage has its critics even within trade union circles. The construction workers union has taken the position that a national minimum wage could have the unintended consequence of depressing the wage rates of skilled workers. This union would prefer using a system of prevailing wages in sectors experiencing aggressive wage-competition. For each of these sectors, the government would decree a mandatory minimum compensation package for all firms that would match the existing collective agreement. For some time the construction industry has been using prevailing-wage contracts to set minima for a small number of occupational categories and for foreign workers posted in Germany by foreign based construction firms. IG Metall and the chemical workers union officials have maintained a low profile in this debate, but have expressed sympathy with the approach of the construction workers union. IG Metall has been pursuing a prevailing wage for workers at temporary employment agencies.

In summary, retrenchment has been the hallmark of the fourth German trade union movement. Sharp membership declines precipitated a thoroughgoing institutional consolidation that was driven largely by a scramble among the largest unions to be the first to snap up the weakest. The effort to refocus the DGB proved disappointing. Sharp declines in density for both unions and employers associations owing to economic and social change, and the failure of the social partners to establish a firm footing east of the Elbe have opened substantial holes in the coverage of collective bargaining for the first time since World War II. The collective bargaining muscle of the German trade unions has weakened considerably. Labour's share of national income has declined to unprecedented lows. The German trade union movement still retains its legitimacy in politics and society as the representative of working people, but if membership declines persist, it is by no means clear how long this will last.

5. Conclusion

Once re-established in 1949, the German trade union movement staged a slow but steady climb over three decades to a position of unprecedented power and prominence as one of the most powerful and effective trade union movements in the world. This third German trade union movement was instrumental in bringing about not only an unprecedented level of affluence for workers, but also political stability in a country for which such an achievement was by no means a simple affair. The trade union movement began to exhibit signs of stress during the 1980s when European integration, globalisation and social change made its work far more challenging. German unification punctured the postwar equilibrium and precipitated the creation of a fourth movement that is far more concentrated, has a weaker peak confederation and has significant holes in its collective bargaining coverage for the first time since World War II.

Germany's trade union movement is battered, but not beaten. Symphonies also have four movements. Whether the fourth German trade union movement can still produce a progression that will bring it back to resounding tones rather than a fadeout into silence remains to be seen. The task is daunting, but the German trade union movement still has significant assets. It remains among the richest movements in the world, and its leadership ranks among the best educated and the most sophisticated. German trade unions will only retain significance throughout the remainder of the twenty-first century if their leaders use these resources adroitly.

Table 1. Economic Performance: Germany*

	Mean Real Annual Change				
Period	GDP per capita	Compensation per Employee (Private Sector)	Productivity (GDP per hour worked)	Consumer Price Index (Mean Annual Change)	Unemployment (Mean Annual Rate)
1951–9	8.1%	5.4%	5.6%	1.9%	5.1%
1960–9	4.8%	5.3%	4.8%	2.5%	0.9%
1970–9	3.3%	4.4%	4.1%	4.9%	2.0%
1980–9	2.0%	0.8%	2.1%	2.9%	5.4%
1990–9	2.3%	0.8%	2.4%	2.5%	6.9%
2000–7	1.4%	–0.5%	1.5%	1.6%	9.4%

* Federal Republic of Germany, 1951–90; united Germany as of 1991.
Sources: OECD Main Economic Indicators, and OECD Productivity Base.

Table 2. Strikes and Lockouts in Germany*

Period	Mean Annual Striking and Locked out Employees	Locked Out as a Percentage of Total Striking and Locked Out Employees	Mean Annual Working Days Lost due to Strikes and Lockouts	Mean Annual Lockout Days as a Percentage of Total Days Lost
1950–9	139,590	2.7%	983,108	8.1%
1960–9	81,597	37.8%	315,725	43.4%
1970–9	198,278	34.3%	1,164,775	53.4%
1980–9	139,590	12.3%	609,841	44.3%
1990–9	215,151	0.01%	337,827	0.1%
2000–7	117,327**	N.A.	198,636	N.A.

* Federal Republic of Germany, 1951–90; united Germany as of 1991.
** Data for 2000–6.
Source: International Labour Organisation.

Figure 1

German Trade Union Membership, 1950–2007

Deutscher Gewerkschaftsbund (DGB), Deutscher Beamtenbund (DBB), and other trade unions
(Sources: DGB, DBB, CGB, and statistisches Bundesamt)

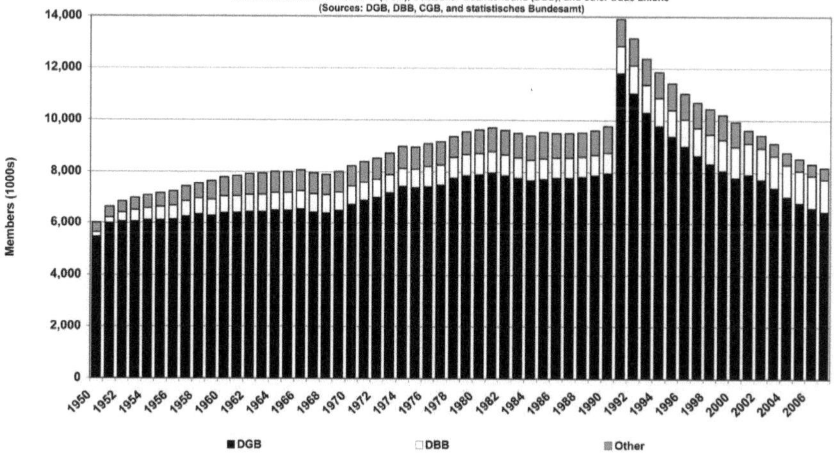

Figure 2

German Unionisation Rate, 1950–2007

Employed Union Members as a Percentage of Employees (Sources: DGB and Statistisches Bundesamt)

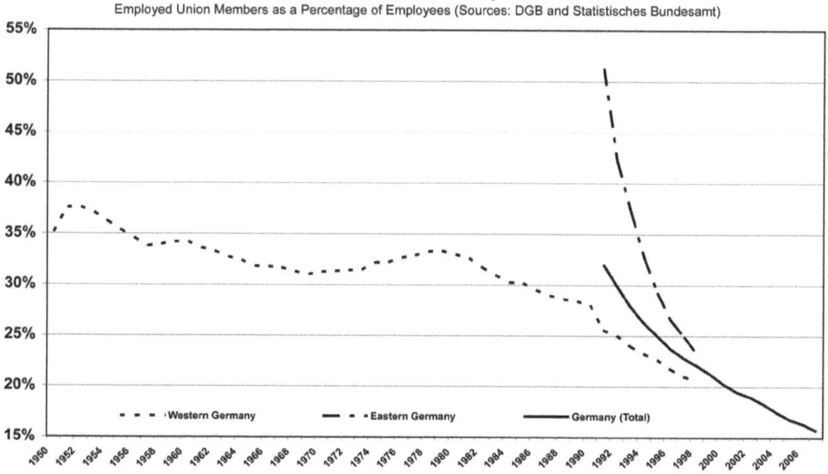

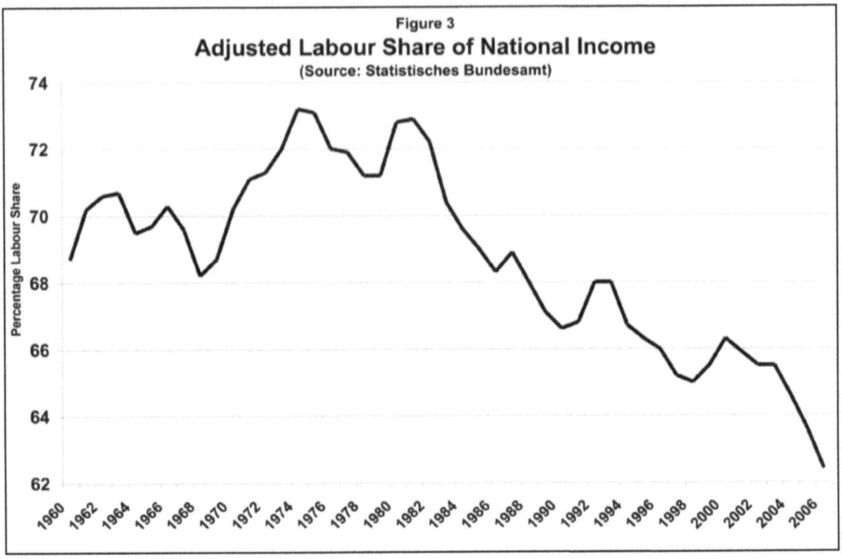

Suggested Reading

Bundesvereinigung der Deutschen Arbeitgeberverbände and Deutscher Gewerkschaftsbund (1990) 'Gemeinsame Erklärung zur Wirtschaft der Deutschen Demokratischen Republik', 9 March.

Deutscher Gewerkschaftsbund (1996) *Die Zukunft gestalten. Grundsatzprogramm des Deutschen Gewerkschaftsbundes*, Berlin: DGB.

——(2002) *Geschäftsbericht 1998–2001*, Berlin: Oktoberdruck.

Ebbinghaus, B. (2003) 'Die Mitgliederentwicklung deutscher Gewerkschaften im historischen and internationalen Vergleich' in Schroeder, W. and Wessels, B. (eds) *Die Gewerkschaften in Politik and Gesellschaft der Bundesrepublik Deutschland*, Wiesbaden: Westdeutscher Verlag.

Eley, G. (1989) 'Labor History, Social History, *Alltagsgeschichte*: Experience, Culture, and the Politics of Everyday: A New Direction for German Social History?', *Journal of Modern History* 61(2): 297–343.

Fichter, M. (1982) *Besatzungsmacht und Gewerkschaften. Zur Entwicklung und Anwendung der US-Gewerkschaftspolitik in Deutschland 1944–1948,* Opladen: Westdeutscher Verlag.

Gesamtmetall (2007) *Die Metall- und Elektro-Industrie in der Bundesrepublik Deutschland in Zahlen, Ausgabe 2007*, Cologne: Gesamtmetall.

Hattinger Kreis (1992) 'Schafft den DGB ab!', *Gewerkschaftliche Monatshefte* 43.

Herbig, R. (1980) *Notizen. Aus der Sozial-, Wirtschafts- und Gewerkschaftsgeschichte vom 14. Jahrhundert bis zur Gegenwart*, Frankfurt: Union, 1980.

Institut für Arbeitsmarkt- und Berufsforschung (1993–2007) *IAB-Betriebspanel*, Nürnberg: IAB.

Köbele, B. (1994) 'Interview: "Das Stimmrecht ist keine Geldfrage"', *Quelle* 45.

Lang, K. (1994) 'Das wäre das Ende des DGB', *Quelle* 45.

Markovits, A.S. (1982) 'Introduction: Model Germany: A Cursory Overview of a Complex Construct' in Markovits. A.S. (ed.) *The Political Economy of West Germany: Modell Deutschland*, New York: Praeger.

——(1986) *The Politics of West German Trade Unions: Strategies of Interest Representation in Growth and Crisis*, Cambridge: Cambridge University Press.

Mielke, S. (1990) 'Die Neugründung der Gewerkschaften in den westlichen Besatzungszonen – 1945–1949' in Hemmer, H.-O. and Schmitz, K.T. (eds) *Geschichte der Gewerkschaften in der Bundesrepublik Deutschland*, Cologne: Bund.

Müller, W. (1990) 'Die Gründung des DGB, der Kampf um die Mitbestimmung, programmatisches Scheitern und der Übergang zum gewerkschaftlichen Pragmatismus' in Hemmer, H.-O. and Schmitz, K.T. (eds) *Geschichte der Gewerkschaften in der Bundesrepublik Deutschland*, Cologne: Bund.

Müller-Jentsch, W. (ed.) (1993) *Konfliktpartnerschaft. Akteure und Institutionen der industriellen Beziehungen*, München-Mering: Hampp.
—— (2007) *Strukturwandel der industriellen Beziehungen: 'Industrial Citizenship' zwischen Markt und Regulierung*, Wiesbaden: VS.
Pirker, T. (1979) *Die blinde Macht. Die Gewerkschaftsbewegung in der Bundesrepublik*, vol. 1, *Vom 'Ende des Kapitalismus' zur Zähmung der Gewerkschaften*, Berlin: Olle und Wolter.
Schmidt, E. (1977) *Die verhinderte Neuordnung 1945–1952*, Frankfurt: Europäische Verlagsanstalt.
Schneider, M. (2000) *Kleine Geschichte der Gewerkschaften. Ihre Entwicklung in Deutschland von den Anfängen bis heute*, Bonn: J.H.W. Dietz.
—— (2005) *History of the German Trade Unions*, 2nd ed., Bonn: J.H.W. Dietz.
Schroeder, W. (2000) *Das Modell Deutschland auf dem Prüfstand. Zur Entwicklung der industriellen Beziehungen in Ostdeutschland*, Wiesbaden: Westdeutscher Verlag.
—— and Wessels, B. (eds) (2003) *Gewerkschaften in Politik und Gesellschaft der Bundesrepublik*, Opladen: Westdeutscher Verlag.
—— and Silvia, S.J. (2003) 'Gewerkschaften und Arbeitgeberverbände', in Schroeder, W. and Wessels, B. (eds) *Gewerkschaften in Politik und Gesellschaft der Bundesrepublik*, Opladen: Westdeutscher Verlag.
Silvia, S.J. (1997) 'German Unification and Emerging Divisions within German Employers' Associations: Cause or Catalyst?' *Comparative Politics* 29: 187–208.
—— (1999) 'Every which Way but Loose: German Industrial Relations since 1980', Martin, A. and Ross, G. (eds) *The Brave New World of European Labor: European Trade Unions at the Millennium*, New York: Berghahn.
—— (2007) 'Public Pension Reform in Germany and the United States', in AICGS (ed.) *Healthcare and Pension Reform*, Washington D.C.: AICGS, The Johns Hopkins University.
—— and Schroeder, W. (2007) 'Why are German Employers Associations Declining? Arguments and Evidence', *Comparative Political Studies* 40: 1433–59.

Thelen, K.A. (1991) *A Union of Parts: Labor and Politics in Postwar Germany*, Ithaca, NY: Cornell University Press.

Turner, L. (1999) *Fighting for Partnership: Labor and Politics in Unified Germany*, Ithaca, NY: Cornell University Press.

Weber, H. and Mielke, S. (1989) 'Einleitung', in Weber, H. and Mielke, S. (eds) *Die Gewerkschaften und die Angestelltenfrage 1945–1949. Quellen zur Geschichte der deutschen Gewerkschaftsbewegung im 20. Jahrhundert*, vol. 8, Cologne: Bund.

An Historical Analysis of Trade Unionism in Italy: Between Pluralism of Ideas and Unity of Action

VALERIA PULIGNANO

1. Introduction

In its short but rich history, Italian trade unionism (*sindacalismo*) exhibited several particular features, which combined to make it unique in comparison to trade unionism in the rest of Europe. A movement rooted in the nineteenth century, Italian trade unionism was severely impacted by the emergence of Mussolini's fascist state. Fascism contributed significantly to a weakening of the organisational strength of trade unions. On the other hand, it can be argued that the fascist state reinforced the politics and capacity of trade union mobilisation and their politics of opposition. As a result, in 1945 trade unionism emerged as a vital new force representing working-class interests, with restored links to society as a whole. Gramsci described the rise of Italian postwar trade unionism as the re-establishment of a 'missing link' between the union movement and both civil and political society.

Generally speaking, we can distinguish three discrete historical phases of development of Italian *sindacalismo*: the pluralistic phase (from the end of the nineteenth century to the corporatist period in 1922–6); the unitarist phase (1944–8) and, finally, the postwar phase (since 1948–50), when moments of pluralism and unity were accompanied by the trade unions' engagement in social reforms and social change. What are the patterns which have driven unity and division in Italian unionism? Are unity and division mutually exclusive forces in its history? And if so, why? In his analysis of Italian trade unionism, Hyman points to the complexity which accompanied the historical development of Italian unions. He argues that the Pact of Rome in 1944–8 signalled an artificial unity among Italian trade unions, and that the ideological edge of Italian unionism during the 1960s and the 1970s was clearly blunted by its encounter with the hard economic and political realities of the 1980s (Hyman 2001: 143–65). This means that as organisations representing the collective interests of the workers, Italian trade unions at certain times in their history have overcome their diverse ideological orientations while engaging in 'political' action and fashioning compromises with employers' organisations and the government for the enactment of important social reforms. What factors explain the capacity of the Italian unions to cross the boundaries of pluralism and ideology? Is union unity a genuine expression of the historical trends in Italian trade unionism?

The chapter will address these questions by examining the historical roots of contemporary issues in postwar Italian trade unionism. The argument put forward is that although the nature of *sindacalismo* has been pluralistic by tradition, Italian trade unions have historically been able to accommodate ideological division with unity of action. Union pluralism never excluded unity of action in Italy. As Couffignal (1979: 52) observed: 'Unity but ideological divisions, autonomy but intervention in the political sphere with (or without) the political parties have permanently characterised the dynamics of trade unionism in Italy.' Therefore any definition of Italian *sindacalismo* based on a singular theme would be inaccurate. On one hand, pluralism likely reflects the intrinsic nature of Italian unionism as traditional protagonist in 'political exchange' (Pizzorno 1978). On the other hand, it is evident that different socio-economic, political and international emergencies stimulated unity of action in the trade union movement. For example, the pressing need for economic recovery in 1944 and the atmosphere of social discontent in 1969–73 prompted calls for unity of union action. Moreover, privatisation, increasing competitiveness in external product markets, the emergence of new political and institutional forces (e.g. the necessity to join the Euro-zone) as well as neo-liberal efforts to expose the employment relationship to increased market forces emerged in 1980s and 1990s, all enforced union unity while prompting negotiation of important national social reforms in tripartite agreements. Interestingly, however, in some cases social reforms were also accompanied by separate negotiation of collective agreements by the three main union confederations, negotiations which reflected the enduring diverse ideological orientations of Italian trade unionism even in times of unity.

The chapter begins by presenting the re-emergence of *sindacalismo* in the postwar period. The aim is to examine the resurgence of the Italian trade union movement since 1945 in light of the structural socio-economic and political factors which contributed to shape its origins at the end of the nineteenth century. This is followed by an analysis of the historical roots of both the pluralist and the unitarian nature of Italian *sindacalismo*, with an examination of the 'White' (*sindacalismo Cattolico* – Catholic) and the 'Red' (*sindacalismo Rosso* – Socialist) wings of Italian unionism. The chapter will then detail the pluralistic experience of unionism during the period of social unrest in the 1960s, followed by an analysis of union trends since the 1980s. Historical forces and socio-economic and political conditions which explain the duality between pluralism and unitarism in the history of Italian trade unionism will be the focus of attention.

2. The Historical Background of *Sindacalismo*

It is not possible to explain the nature and the evolution of Italian trade unionism without examining the conditions which accompanied their origins as well as the socio-economic and political context in which they have developed. Italy is a unique case among Western European industrialised economies. More than twenty years under the fascist state impacted the trade unions at the time of their development. Although there is little evidence that Italian trade unions represented the organised interests of the working class in the immediate aftermath of World War II, the history of social struggle and union mobilisation during that period appears very rich (Couffignal 1979). It is therefore relevant to examine the history of *sindacalismo* in order to point out how certain specific conditions typical of the nineteenth-century Italian socio-economic and political context help explain the emergence of unionism and its subsequent resurgence and development after 1945. In particular, one can distinguish three different structural factors which had an influence on the development of the Italian postwar *sindacalismo*.

The first factor is the comparatively late emergence of the industrial revolution in Italy. This reflects a specificity of Italian capitalism, often represented by a high number of family-owned small–medium firms in comparison with big industrial companies found elsewhere. Diverse factors explain the late industrial development of the Italian economy. Among these is geography; the Alps represented a structural impediment to trade. In addition, lack of energy resources, the high demographic increase in the birth rate in comparison with national GDP growth, and the consequent high migration rate especially to the US also explain the tardy development of the Italian economy. The complex political structure of the country, which in the mid nineteenth century was composed of numerous small, independent states, also contributed to slow industrial growth. As Lenti (1973: 10) argued: 'in Italy the geographical conditions allowed the survival of the different self-independent states on one hand. On the other hand, however, they constrained the emergence of a homogeneous economic and industrial system within a newly unified nation state'. It was only at the beginning of the twentieth century that political unity, created by the industrial *bourgeois* in the North of Italy, provided the stimulus for the economic development of the country. But this economic development did not cover homogeneously the entire Italian peninsula. The area which benefited most was the North, and in particular, the Piemonte and the Lombardia regions. The socio-economic divergence between the North and South of Italy began in this period, with all the social and cultural consequences which it represented.

A second factor explaining the character and the nature of the Italian postwar unionism is the importance of the agricultural sector, mainly concentrated in the South. Rapid industrialisation in the North led to the maintenance of a highly concentrated and underdeveloped 'pre-capitalist' agricultural area in the South. Italian *sindacalismo* originated in the traditional system of the 'cooperative' and the cultural associations in the South. Indeed, the mobilising nature of the Italian *sindacalismo* comes from the agricultural sector of the South. There has always been a problem of reconciling the 'agricultural' and the 'proletarian' soul in the history of Italian trade unionism. More specifically, there have always been different motives at the heart of workers' struggles in industry and agriculture. Whereas in industry workers' struggle is aimed at defending jobs, in agriculture workers struggle mainly to find a job. As Abendroth (1967) argued, the political divergence between the workers' movement in the North and the peasants' social movement in the South came to an end in 1926. After World War I this resulted in a 'political alliance between the two workers' movements as the only way to fight against the bourgeois of the State' (Gramsci 1920).

Finally, another historical influence on postwar *sindacalismo* is the absence of a collective history of the Italian working class as a 'mass' social movement. This absence is the result of heterogeneity in the working class and the combined effect of late industrialisation on one hand, and the regional economic disparities between the North and South on the other. In contrast to the French experience, in which facts and people of both the post- and the prewar period remained alive in the memories and actions of the newly organised working class, the Italian trade union movement was unable to integrate the diverse historical moments and to create a collective working class culture. Thus the culture behind the organising strategies of the trade unions as mobilising social forces, rather than the collective culture of the working class as such, remained as historical memory of the Italian labour movement (Agosti et al. 1970).

The combination of late industrialisation, marked economic regional disparity, the origins of the Italian unionism in the agricultural sector, the weak culture of the working class, and the period of the fascist dictatorship contributed to define the basis from which Italian postwar trade unionism developed. On the other hand, it can be also argued that Italian *sindacalismo* has been greatly affected by earlier historical events. The birth of industry – at the end of the nineteenth century – coincided with the political unity of the country. At that time there was no experience of trade union organisation in Italy. The first trade union organisation was created in 1893 and coincided with the establishment of a territorial structure for the organisation of trade unions, such as the Labour Chambers (*Camere del Lavoro*). It is important to note that the constitution of the Labour

Chambers appeared one year after the birth of the Socialist political party. This shows the predominance of political parties over the autonomy of Italian trade unions. Union and political actions are strongly integrated in a project which sees trade union organisations as searching for solutions to working class social problems primarily through social dialogue with public institutions rather than through negotiation with the private employers. At the same time, the constitution of the *Rerum Novarum*[1] at the beginning of the twentieth century encouraged the persistence of diverse ideologies and thereby helped to shape the pluralistic nature of the trade union movement. As the next section will illustrate, the *Rerum Novarum* represents the basis of the different ideological orientations which characterised Italian trade unionism since its origins.

3. The Roots of 'Pluralism' in Italian Trade Unionism: 'Red' and 'White' Unions

Two different experiences distinguished Italian unionism at its inception: the 'White' and the 'Red'. Both developed inside the evolving *Rerum Novarum* at the beginning of the twentieth century. Both developed gradually and gave rise to a period of intense ideological pluralism which shaped the union movement until the beginnings of the fascist corporatist period in 1922–6 (Zaninelli 2007). Why was the Italian prewar period characterised by the emergence of 'White' (Catholic) and 'Red' (Socialist) ideological (or political) pluralism? One reason is the long and well-known conflict between the Church and the state in the prewar period, which led to a strong division between the Catholic component and the interests of the state. Secondly, the desire to implement a system of social protection led in the first instance to the development of new Catholic-oriented forms of

1 *Rerum Novarum* is an association which aims to use trade unionism primarily as an instrument for political action.

social assistance and charity for the weakest groups in society. Subsequently, these measures assumed an antagonistic, Socialist-oriented character. This trend was accompanied by the development of new means for the protection of workers' rights, such as collective bargaining and strike action. Thirdly, as the result of the first stage of industrialisation – from the end of the nineteenth century until World War I – there was a split regarding the protection of workers' interests. More specifically, there were differences in the typology of union engagement with social protection depending on whether the workers were attached to the industrial, the agricultural or the textile sector, and whether workers were landowners. Workers in the industry tended to be Socialist and left-oriented and, therefore, part of 'Red' unionism, with a higher propensity for struggle and social conflict. Other workers were part of the 'White' wing of unionism, less prone to conflict, and more interested in a conciliation of interests.

Although they had divergent ideological roots, both 'White' (Catholic) and 'Red' (Socialist) unionism shared several commonalities. For example, the territorial and professional trade union organisational structure, which reflects the current structure of union organisation in Italy, was similar. Moreover, although 'Red' unionism was conflict prone and 'White' unionism was more geared toward achieving compromise through a peaceful resolution of diverse interests, the instruments for trade union action, such as collective bargaining and the strike, were the same. Some industrial relations and sociological literature posits an historical and ideological link between 'White' unionism and the Italian trade union confederations CISL (*Confederazione Italiana Lavoratori*) and UIL (*Unione Italiana Lavoratori*), which have, respectively, Catholic-Christian and Liberal affiliations. Likewise, a link is indicated between CGIL (*Confederazione Generale Italiana del Lavoro*) and the 'Red' wing of the Italian *sindacalismo* (Craveri 1977). Yet, if pluralism is conceptualised as expressing not only different ideological but also diverse cultural and socio-economic positions, the continuity between certain trade unions organisations and some ideological (political) orientations has limits. Craveri's account does not take into consideration the significant transformations that occurred in the diverse trade unions organisations across historical periods. As Cova (2007) observes, CISL was created in the midst of two formative events: the fascist dictatorship, which helped to destroy the 'voice' of the emergent trade union movement, and World War II. Therefore, in the postwar period the experience of CISL – as well as of Italian unionism overall – is regarded as weak because of its historical isolation from developments in other Western economies. The result has been a loss of memory on the part of traditional trade union organisations which arose in the prewar period. More generally, to highlight the isolation and the lack of development of Italian trade unionism during the fascist period, Zaninelli (2007: 29) argues that 'in 1945 Italian unionism as a cultural and social force was out of touch with other trade union movements in most of the developed industrial economies'. In 1945, Italian *sindacalismo* was culturally outmoded and isolated and, therefore, it was not considered a political and social actor capable of participating in the political and socio-economic life of the country. A wave of revitalisation was therefore needed.

4. The Unitarian Experience in Postwar Unionism

In the postwar period the goal of the politically divided Italian working class was to establish unity within the trade union movement. Three factors explain this choice. Firstly, the memory of the fascist period, which had used ideological and political divisions within trade unions as a tool to dismantle the right of free association of workers. As Horowitz (1972: 300) argues, 'because of the lack of trade union unity after World War I it was difficult to counter fascism'. Secondly, in the post-World War II period creating unity in the divided union movement was seen as the only means to re-establish democracy in the national institutional context. In other words, trade union unity was required if the working class was to be the dominant political force in society. Thirdly, the defeat of fascism has to be explained not only as the result of the military opposition by the *Alleati* troops but also as the result of strike activity in the industrial triangle of Turin–Milan–Genova in 1943–4 (ESI 1949). Both the widespread character of the strikes in the North, and the close relationship between economic and political struggle, contributed to the process of Liberation from fascist domination in 1944. It is not a coincidence that the negotiation for trade union unity (the so-called 'Pact of Rome') took place at the very time Italy declared itself a country free from fascism.

In the Pact of Rome in June 1944, representatives of the former Communist, Socialist and Catholic unions agreed to establish a single organisation, the *Confederazione Generale Italiana del lavoro* (Cgil). As Hyman (2000) argues, Cgil was in essence a political creation, an expression of the shared commitment of the three main political tendencies to a consensual process of postwar reconstruction. This unity had its parallel in the participation of Socialist and Communist ministers in De Gasperi's first Christian Democratic (DC)-led government. Thus Cgil expresses the institutionalisation of pluralism in postwar Italian trade unionism. This occurred in a particular period characterised by the need to create unity as the way to contribute to the economic revitalisation of the country. This intent is clearly stated in the stated objectives of Cgi: 'trade unions should examine all important initiatives in order to proceed with postwar socio-economic reconstruction.' Although the Pact of Rome was progressive in regards to its economic and political goals and meanings, it also had shortcomings. No specifics were offered on the nature of, and the best means to protect, working class's interests. In addition, the Pact of Rome proved an ineffective instrument in resolving the unions' organisational problems. The institutionalised nature of union pluralism under the Pact explains this shortcoming. Finally, although the Pact established trade union autonomy from political party control, this autonomy did not exclude, under certain circumstances, the pursuit of unity of action with the political parties. As a result it can be argued that Cgil suffered from imprecision in the way it upheld union autonomy and its stance on trade union pluralism. Cgil may well have been the expression of trade union unity in postwar Italy, but at the same time it was also the 'voice' of ideological or political union pluralism. It expresses trade union autonomy from political parties but it also indicates the capacity of the unions to intervene in the political sphere with (or without) the political parties. And because of its contradictory nature, Cgil soon encountered difficulties. These difficulties also reflected Cgil's relatively low degree of political consciousness and the lack of experience and training of Cgil members.

The period of unity in Italian postwar trade unionism was short-lived. The strains of the Cold War were reinforced by domestic political divisions. These were linked to the dominant parliamentary position of the newly-established DC party under De Gasperi, and the powerful opposition status of the Communist (PCI) party (after its brief period as member of the governing coalition). Within a few years, Cgil was confronted by two breakaways. The splits weakened labour both politically and industrially, allowing major as well as smaller employers to victimise union activists and assert virtually unilateral authority in the workplace. The splitting of Cgil was the counterpart of a political project, beginning in the late 1940s, characterised by the Christian Democrats' political ambition to mesh closely with the American foreign policy. At that time the De Gasperi government made clear that the US would have provided economic assistance to Italy, but only if the PCI was marginalised (Romero 1992). Hyman (2000) argues that systematic intervention by the Americans encouraged divisions in Italian trade unionism. The influence of the Catholic Church and, in particular, of the Vatican was also relevant in the splintering process. More specifically, the role played by Acli (*Associazioni Cristiana e dei Lavoratori Italiani*) was crucial in the creation of the Catholic faction of the movement. The mission of the Acli was to represent the interests of the Italian workers by creating a broad Catholic and therefore non-Communist confederation.

The pretext for the splits occurred in July 1948, soon after the DC's electoral victory and the attempted assassination of communist leader Palmiro Togliatti. The latter event prompted a wave of strikes and protests, which the communists, supported by socialists and radicals, sought to control (Harowitz 1963). In October 1948 the Catholic fraction of Cgil created a 'free' Cgil or Lcgil (*Libera Confederazione Generale Italiana del Lavoro*), which had been preceded by Acli's public call for an 'autonomous and democratic Italian trade union movement' (Grandilone 1959). The hostility of Cgil to both the Marshall Plan and the evolution of the global unionism led the Republican and Social-democratic factions to breakaway from Cgil and create the Fil (*Federazione Italiana del Lavoro*) in 1949. A year and a half later, Fil and Lcgil merged with the support of Acli and created the trade union confederation CISL (*Confederazione Italiana dei sindacati lavoratori*). One month later the anti-clerical section of the republicans and the socialists in Cgil established UIL (*Unione Italiana del Lavoro*). In the same period another confederation, CISNAL (*Confederazione Italiana Sindacati Nazionali Lavoratori*), was created by some nostalgic sympathisers of the monarchy and Mussolini (Romero 1989). In opposition to the highly centralised CGIL, CISL emphasised the relative autonomy of its sectoral organisations. This indicated to some degree the 'economic' rather than the 'political' orientation of CISL. CGIL remained easily the largest confederation, dominated by the communists but with a significant left-socialist minority (Hyman 2000).

Splintering in the postwar Italian union movement illustrates the impact of political contingences in the evolution of trade union structures. Although the ideological variable was dominant in 1943–50, it alone cannot explain the dynamics of trade union development in this period. Structural factors in the Italian economy as well as the evolution of the working class movement are also important features. Trade unions organisations, which emerged in the immediate postwar period, aimed at creating a structural unity between the workers in agriculture and the traditional industrial proletariat. The 1944 creation of Cgil was the concrete expression of this desire. Yet the competing union traditions, cultures and structures undermined such unity in practice. It can also be argued that the political nature of Italian unionism emerged as an inheritance of fascism. Accordingly, militant trade union members were 'political' actors. In addition, political parties have traditionally served as the incubators for trade unions. Therefore, although historical conditions in 1944 permitted the emergence of trade union unity, political conflicts and changes in the national and international socio-economic context subverted the unitarian experience and fanned the flames of internal union division. However, as the following section illustrates, union unity re-emerged in 1960–70.

5. Unity of Action and Social Unrest: The Period of 'Hot Autumn'

In the second half of the twenty century, Italian trade union practices were profoundly impacted by socio-economic and political developments. It is important to note first that by 1950 the process of trade union division was completed with the creation of the three main union confederations. Each confederation was characterised by a different ideology and political party affiliation. CGIL, with the largest membership, joined the PCI and embraced an ideology of militant class struggle. CISL was dominated by the Christian democrats. However, it would be wrong to consider CISL a Catholic trade union. CISL has always insisted on its religious neutrality. Nevertheless, in line with the Catholic social doctrine, CISL supported the advancement of workers' interests by strengthening their organised integration in society. Finally, UIL distinguished itself from CISL and CGIL by its insistence on the need to intervene actively in all problems related to economic and social policy (Bedani 1995).

Ideological division of the Italian trade unions movement was itself a factor of internal union redefinition. Franzosi (1995) argues that the re-invention of Italian trade unionism in the second half of the twenty century was also in many respects a result the escalation of industrial militancy in the same period. More specifically, the widespread social unrest in 1969 – the so-called 'hot autumn' (*autunno caldo*) – stemmed from deep discontent by a new urban workforce, primarily those coming from the South of Italy and, therefore, unaccustomed to the cost of a city life or the intensification of work in the factories. Thus social conflict during the 'hot-autumn' was essentially the expression of the mobilisation of the 'rank-and-file' structures into unions' organisational machinery. In this sense it represented the unity of union action (the social conflict) against the pressure of Italian capitalism. The 'rank-and-file' committees, which provided some coordination during the struggles, were institutionalised as trade union-based factory councils, displacing the old system of the

Commissioni Interne. This contributed to accelerate the process of union democratisation at Italian workplaces.

The big industries were the protagonists during this period of social conflict. Worker response over matters of wages, health and safety, pace of work and shifts at work generated this discord. For some observers, the ideological and political splits among the main trade unions confederations as well as the weak workplace union structure facilitated the achievement of unity through common social action in 1968–70 (Cella 1971). By recalling the Marxian concept of 'trade union conscience' (*coscienza sindacale*) in this period, unity of action was the mechanism used by trade unions to revitalise their internal organisation while at the same time seeking to neutralise the power of capitalism. Thus it can be argued that the unity of interests which clearly emerged since 1968–9 was the condition for the working class as a whole to advance itself socially and increase its power in society. However, for the sake of precision we must also look at the period from 1960 to 1965, when the foundation of trade union unity was laid. For it was in these years the collective interests of workers were expressed in the fight for the renewal of bargaining agreements in the metal sector. Stimulated by this fight, CGIL, CISL and UIL began a dialogue with each other after 1965.

There are two principal reasons that explain the unitarian approach followed by the Italian trade unions in this period. First, the important socialisation role adopted by trade unions in 1960–5 began to produce its first results. A new spirit of collectivism emerged at the workplace, which reinforced a sense of common social identification among workers. Second, in 1965 the centre-left collapsed as a political and economical force. In line with what Engels had observed in Britain in 1881, the decline of the purely political workers' organisation in Italy in 1965 was accompanied by a resurgence of trade unions as organisations representing the interests of a new socially constituted working class.[2] Thus a shifting political context, in which both the union confederations and the 'rank-and-file' operate, made unity possible in the trade union movement. Unity stemmed from the

2 Accornero (1967) has provided a clear historical analysis of this phenomenon.

desire of political parties to re-create a unitarian experience, which should be not simply the result of political agreement among the three main union confederations, as it was during the Pact of Rome in 1944. Unity was to represent something more deeply rooted, an expression of similar economic and social interests. Unity was to express workers' autonomy against any form of dependency, whether political parties or capital.

In 1968–9 the drive toward unitarism came to fruition. At the base of this upsurge there was an acknowledgment by the Italian working class that unity was necessary to regain the power of autonomy while struggling for the improvement of working conditions under Fordism. As indicated, the metalworking sector became the centre for the reconstitution of the trade union unity. The three main union confederations for the first time organised jointly at the workplace in order to prepare for collective negotiations for the improvement of working conditions. As a result in 1970 and 1971 a unitarian union structure was established. It was accompanied by the creation of a union centre for research and development, a monthly newspaper (*Unita' Operaia*), and a union training centre. In addition, the trade unions promoted a unitarian campaign which increased the membership to more than 90,000. The momentum for a Unitarian union structure was characterised by three important historical events: the joint trade union congresses in 1969; the joint meetings (so-called Firenze I, Firenze II, Firenze III) organised by the three general trade unions confederations CGIL, CISL and UIL in 1970; and the creation of a joint Unitary Federation (*Federazione Unitaria*) CGIL-CISL-UIL in 1972 (Forbice 1973).

Despite the genuine attempt to create a unity driven by the collective interests of the working class, there still remained the problem of how to guarantee the effective and concrete autonomy of the Italian trade union movement against the political parties. In the history of the Italian trade unionism, gaining autonomy from the political parties is a crucial issue. The conditions under which the Italian *sindacalismo* resurged after liberation from fascist domination have shown how difficult it has been for unions to act independently from politics. In the public debate following the 'hot-autumn', the role of the political party, as well as trade unions in the political system, was re-opened and widely discussed. For some unionists close to CGIL at that time, creating trade union unity did not imply the marginalisation of the political parties; they sought to strengthen union organisation as a collective body while reinforcing its role in the struggle against capital. As Baglioni states, the aim was to constitute trade unions 'as a political force as the response of the autonomous working class. This is because the representation of the social conditions of the working class cannot be delegated to official political parties' (Baglioni 1975: 138). In this respect, we can consider the unitarian experience of trade unions in the 'hot-autumn' period as not 'a-political' but rather as a mean to promote a mass political struggle.

In 1972–3 two important internal events challenged labour unity once again. First, the different approaches taken by the three main trade union confederations in response to the request by the main Italian employer organisation *Confindustria* to find a solution to the economic and social crisis. Second, the creation of the Unitary Federation CGIL-CISL-UIL in 1972 coincided with the election of Giovanni Leone as President of the Republic. He was elected with the support of the votes of the traditional fascist party, so-called *Movimento Sociale Italiano* (MSI), which precipitated elections to create a new government coalition. During these elections the trade unions emerged as important political forces, which rekindled their internal ideological differences. However, as the next section will illustrate, the pluralistic nature of the Italian trade union movement re-emerged with some new and distinctive characters which, sometimes, did not exclude moments of unity.

6. Contemporary Trends in the Italian Trade Union Movement

During the early 1970s, Italy's socio-economic stability was seriously under threat. The consequences of the 'hot autumn' had led to rapidly growing labour costs, a dramatic rise in industrial conflict and the open contestation of traditional forms of work organisation in large firms. At the same time,

Italy's competitiveness and foreign trade deteriorated. Moreover, because of its extremely high dependence on imported raw materials, especially oil, and rapidly growing labour costs, Italy experienced in the 1970s and early 1980s one of the highest price-level increases among the OECD nations. Confronted with the unbearable costs on the Italian economy, the leaders of three major trade unions confederations began to develop a new strategy aimed at enhancing their joint participation in national economic policy in exchange for wage moderation and self-restraint in industrial conflict. This strategic shift, know as 'Eur-line' was characterised by 'political exchange' between unions, employers and the government (Pizzorno 1978). It rested on important institutional innovations introduced in the 1970s, including comprehensive labour law reform (the *Statuto dei Lavoratori* or Workers' Statute); the introduction of an unemployment benefit fund (*Cassa Integrazione Guadagni*); the introduction and the subsequent major redefinition of the wage indexation mechanisms (*scala mobile*).[3] Both the Workers' Statute, the 1975 reform of the *scala mobile* and the unemployment benefit fund constituted the building blocks on which Italy's system of economic 'social concertation'[4] had been erected. It was created on the basis of a strong union unity of workers' interests.

The first attempt at 'social concertation' in Italy took place in 1977–9 when the union confederations, although politically often at odds, began to bargain jointly and directly with the government. In particular, the three main trade unions negotiated wage moderation in exchange for substantial changes in the government's tax, energy and agricultural policies; a reform on state finances; and a legislative package involving industrial restructuring and reconversion that included, among other things, youth employment

3 The 1975 reform of the *scala mobile* was 100 per cent indexation of industrial workers' wages. This reform was accompanied by another important agreement over the *Cassa Integrazione Guadagni,* which extended the duration of state-funded partial unemployment benefits and guaranteed 80 per cent wages in the event of lay-offs.

4 Social concertation describes the nature of the compromise in Italy's industrial relations. It implies government, employer organisations and trade unions sharing responsibilities in regulating economic and social policies while concluding tripartite agreements.

guarantees, vocational training initiatives and pension reform. In 1979, as part of this strategic shift towards 'social concertation', the three union confederations also jointly embarked on organisational reform which promoted new union structures at both regional and territorial levels, besides the existing national, sectoral and local union structures. The confederations hoped that this more centralised structure would provide them with the organisational control and resources necessary to pursue their new strategy based on participation in national policy making.

The second attempt at concertation, took place in 1983 in the form of a tripartite agreement aimed at reducing the cost of labour, particularly through a revision of the *scala mobile*. Unlike the first attempt, this initiative was made without unity in union ranks. The Communist component of the CGIL rejected this proposal while promoting in 1984 an electoral referendum aimed at abrogating the government decree. The referendum resulted in support for the government's position. Thus after just twelve years following the birth of the Unitary Federation CGIL-CISL-UIL, trade union unity was defeated once again. This reduced the likelihood of creating the equivalent structures for neo-corporatist bargaining in Italy, but it also dashed many of the dreams of social reforms associated with the 'hot autumn'. What caused the defeat of the project of union unitarism, under the programme of 'social concertation' during the 1980s? Locke and Baccaro (1996) argue that the demise of an Italian variant of neo-corporatism during the 1980s provoked the re-emergence of old political and ideological divisions among CGIL, CISL and UIL. On the other hand, Regalia and Regini (1998) point out that the failure of the social reforms of the *Cassa Integrazione Guadagni* in the 1980s as well as the *scala mobile* accord in 1975 had the undesired effect of eroding support among workers and, therefore, of reopening ideological fault lines within the CGIL-CISL-UIL Unitary Federation. As a result union membership declined gradually and employers were able to exploit episodes of worker protest and displays of intolerance by militants. The so-called 'march of the forty thousand' (*La Marcia dei Quarantamila*) Fiat middle managers and white-collar workers against the unions – immediately interpreted by its leaders and its observers as signalling the 'defeat' of the unions (Baldissera 1988) – is perhaps the best known episode in this climate of difficulty and internal union dissatisfaction, which accompanied the dismantling of union unitarism in the 1980s.

At the beginning of the 1990s, the strength of confederal trade unionism in Italy had diminished further. Union difficulties were compounded by inter-union rivalry following the break-up of the Unitary Federation. This represented, among other things, an impediment to attempts to reform workplace representation. Subsequently, however, a number of changes, notably the reform of the workplace representation system, revitalised the relationship with the rank-and-file which had been broken in mid 1980s, and also improved relationships between unions. These developments dramatically improved the prospects for confederal trade unionism. In a climate of restored union public visibility and renewed popularity, the debate on union reunification was revitalised. This was accompanied by the resumption of united action and by CGIL's decision at the beginning of 1990s to dissolve its internal party factions. As a result in the first half of 1990s outright reunification of the confederal unions became a real prospect. The most significant event of this re-emergence of union unity was the resurgence of 'social concertation' in 1992–3, which was characterised by a consistent programme of social reforms on incomes policies and collective bargaining. The revival of concertation was a crucial feature in the development of Italy's industrial relations. It is often seen a giant leap towards the institutionalisation of Italy's industrial relations and, therefore, it is seen to contribute to overcome the voluntaristic and mainly informal mechanisms that have traditionally characterised industrial relations (Alachevic and Burroni 2001; Regini 1995). More specifically, voluntarism and low institutionalisation in the Italian context principally meant that collective bargaining developed without a formalised framework until the early 1990s, which gave clear definition to procedures, rules of behaviour, wage levels and a host of other issues. In particular, the 1993 tripartite agreement on income policy, labour policy and the structure of collective bargaining was a first, important step toward further regulation of collective bargaining and of social negotiation. For the first time respective competences were attributed to the national-sector and company or local bargaining levels. This led to the establishment of rules and procedures for the conduct of collective bargaining. In so doing, the 1993 tripartite agreement reinforced the decentralisation of collective bargaining while linking the increase in wages to the company's level of productivity. In addition, a renewed system of workplace representations based on the Unitary Representative Units (*Rappresentanza Sindacale Unitaria* or RSU) was established, social negotiation practices were clarified, and new relations between centre and periphery reinforced through the development of a territorial level for social negotiation. The 1993 tripartite agreement emerged as the Italian response to the climate of increasing competitiveness in external product markets as well as the new political and institutional Maastricht forces which imposed the necessity to join the Euro-zone.

As indicated, one of the most important innovations introduced by the 1993 Tripartite agreement was in the area of collective bargaining. Although the balance between centralised and decentralised bargaining was to be maintained through the introduction of 'minimum standards' at central level, the setting of those standards was dependent on power relations. Disagreements emerged between *Confindustria* and within the union confederations over the merits of decentralised collective bargaining. The former was usually in favour of excluding the small and medium enterprises from decentralised collective bargaining. CGIL sought to maintain centralised national collective bargaining, while CISL and UIL approved the decentralised structure of collective negotiation as the expression of their approach to 'participative' industrial relations. With the passing of the economic and political emergencies, which had made possible the development of 'social concertation' in the early 1990s, a climate of disagreement among the three confederations suddenly re-emerged. This climate helped to slow down the implementation of the decentralised bargaining agenda while partially undermining the content of the 1993 agreement. It also jeopardised the unity of the unions and contributed to weakening their influence while accentuating their ideological differences. Thus it may be argued that when 'social concertation' was formally put under discussion in the 'White Paper' on the reforms of the labour market presented by the Berlusconi government in October 2001, the influence of the Italian unions had already been weakened.[5] On the other hand, as has been argued elsewhere (Pulignano 2007), under the D'Alema centre-left coalition in 1996, and therefore well before Berlusconi came to power, the existence of a 'bipolar' system (a parliamentary majority and the existence of an opposition) had already exacerbated the political divisions between the three union confederations. The core of the disagreement was which role the trade unions were to play under the new government. At that time the CGIL held that the trade unions could dialogue and conclude agreements only with politically friendly governments. Conversely, CISL and UIL viewed trade unions as autonomous actors, and considered the willingness of the trade union to dialogue as being not dependent on the political attitude of the government. Thus when the Berlusconi government started its political attack on the trade unions in 2000, the ideological divergence among the Italian union confederations was already sharp. Unions had already elaborated different interpretations concerning the costs and the benefits of diverse situations and, therefore, had already weakened their position in the political and social arena.

Ichino (2006) has suggested that union pluralism in Italy has been the main cause of the fragmentation of representation. This position is also supported by trade unions leaders, who see the trade unions themselves under the centre-left coalition led by Romano Prodi since April 2006 carry on having fragmented positions due to their pluralistic view. Two main examples are here reported in order to illustrate this process. First, the positions of trade unions towards the Biagi Law: CGIL follows the political position of the Prodi left-right government in accordance to which that law must be cancelled and rewritten; conversely, CISL and UIL believe that the law must be re-discussed by the social parties beforehand. Second, the trade unions' political disagreement over the structure of decentralised collective bargaining is one of the major impediments to the development of the third (company) level of decentralisation of collective bargaining

5 The programme of reforms introduced by Berlusconi in 2001 included three important initiatives in the vital areas of labour market institutions, the pension system and taxation.

(Negrelli and Pulignano 2008). In this regard, following the idea of the 'participative' nature of the employment relations, CISL and UIL support the idea of a third (company) level of decentralisation; CGIL opposes it because of its 'antagonist' ideology concerning labour relations.

7. Concluding Remarks: Towards an Historical Interpretive Framework for Italian Unionism

My thoughts on the dualism between pluralism (or division) and unity in the history of the Italian trade union movement has been inspired by the analysis of the labour historian Mario Romani. The results of his studies have been recently collected by Mario Napoli (2007). To explain the experience of pluralism and unitarism in postwar Italian trade unionism, Romani (1988) reflected on two vital elements: social protection and worker consensus. More specifically, the achievement of a consensus among workers through the enlargement of the scope for social protection is the principal reason for the creation of worker associations and, therefore, of the Italian trade union movement. In this context, Romani explains the duality pluralism-unity while using two analytical concepts, union autonomy and union democracy. These concepts are important in order to explain what happened in Italy in the three main historical phases we have examined: 1922–6; 1944–8; and post-1950. In all three periods trade unions have been relatively weak autonomous and democratic forces in society. In each period the achievement of unity of action represented the attempt by the three principal trade union confederations CGIL, CISL and UIL to cope with the changes in the institutions (including the law and political coalitions), the market and the society. In other words, absorbed by the pragmatic aims of the 'political exchange' on one hand, and guided by the need to quickly respond to the occurring changes in the market and in the society on the other, Italian unions had to be united. Nevertheless, this did not always occur in a climate of ideological consensus. In some cases unions were reluctant to jointly adhere to important agreements for social reforms because of their different political affiliations. In this context, we can explain the failure of historically relevant Unitarian experiences of the Italian trade unions, such as, for example, the fall of the Unitary Federation CGIL-CISL-UIL in 1984.

Trade unions' diverse ideologies remain strongly rooted in Italian *sindacalismo.* One novelty of union pluralism is that the latter is not only entrenched in the different unions' culture and ideologies but it is also part of the diverse union techniques and methodologies, their behaviour, their way to shift from action to associative moments with the employees. To what extent can the new pluralism constrain the development of unity in the future of Italian trade unionism? Generally speaking, recognition of the pluralism in the strategies and tactics as well as of the different spheres of decision making is the point of departure for any trade union confederation. This implies that the presence of the associative dimension and general workers' interests on one hand, and unionism and democracy on the other hand, should encourage the creation of union unity regardless of ideological diversity. Ideological diversity will always be a hallmark of the Italian trade union movement. Yet the capacity of trade unions to act in unity in the future will likely depend on their ability to concretely enhance their own autonomy while contributing to the creation of a common project for social and economic change. This depends on the critical capacity of trade unions to set themselves as autonomous forces in society. As Carera (2003) argues, because trade unions represent the collective interests of the workforce, they need to establish themselves as 'free' and 'autonomous' forces in society. In this context, political action cannot be marginalised. It becomes the unions' tool to protect the collective interests of the working class.

Suggested Reading

Abendroth, W. (1967) *Historie du movement ouvrier en Europe*, Paris: Maspero.

Accornero, A. (1967) *Dalla rissa al dialogo*, Rome: ESI.

—— (1976) (ed.) *Problemi del movimento sindacale in Italia 1943–1973*, Milano: Feltrinelli.

Agosti, A., Andreasi, A. and Bravo, G.M. (1970) *Il movimento sindacale in Italia. Rassegna di studi*, Turin: Einaudi.

Alacevich, F. and Burroni, L. (2001) 'Collective Bargaining, Social Pacts and Employment Policies in Italy: Towards a New Model of Industrial Relations?', in Alaluf, M. and Prieto, C. (eds) *Collective Bargaining and the Social Construction of Employment*, Brussels: ETUI.

Baglioni, G. (1975) *Gli aspetti propulsivi di un processo unitario di massa, Quaderni di Rassegna Sindacale*, 9(29): 128–45.

Baldissera, A. (1988) *La svolta dei quarantamila. Dai quadri Fiat ai Cobas*, Milan: Edizioni Comunita.

Carera, A. (2003) (ed) *La cognizione della CISL. Testimonianze per una storia della Federazione pensionati in Lombardia*, Rome: Edizioni lavoro.

Cella, G.P. (1971) *Il Sindacato in Italia nel decennio 1960–1970*, Trento: Instituto superiore di science sociali dell'Universita' di Trento.

Couffignal, G. (1979) *I Sindacati in Italia*, Rome: Editori Riuniti.

Cova, A. (2007) 'Il Sindacalismo dalle origini alla nascita della CFdl' in Napoli, M. (ed.) *Alle radici del Sindacalismo Italiano*, Milan: Diritto e Ricerche.

Craveri, P. (1977) *Sindacato e istituzioni nel dopoguerra*, Bologna: il Mulino.

Forbice, A. (1973) *La federazione CGIL, CISL, UIL fra storia e cronaca. Inchiesta nel movimento sindacale*, Verona: Bertani Editore.

Franzosi, R. (1995) *The Puzzle of Strikes: Class and State Strategies in Postwar Italy*, Cambridge: Cambridge University Press.

Grandilone, M. (1959) *Storia del Sindacalismo – Italia*, Milan: Giuffrè.

Gramsci, A. (1920) *Alcuni Temi della questione meridionale*, Roma, Editori Riuniti.
Harowitz, D.L. (1963) *Storia del movimento sindadcale in Italia*, Milan: Giuffrè.
Hyman, R. (2000) *Understanding European Trade Unionism: Between Market Class and Society*, London: Sage.
Ichino, P. (2006) *A che cosa serve il sindacato?*, Milan: Mondadori.
Lenti, L. (1973) *Grandeur et servitudes de l'économie Italienne*, Paris: Calmann-Lévy.
Locke, R. and Baccaro, L. (1996) 'Learning from Past Mistakes? Recent Reforms in Italian Industrial Relations', *Industrial Relations Journal* 27(4): 289–303.
Napoli, M. (2007) (ed.) *Alle radici del Sindacalismo Italiano*, Milan: Diritto e Ricerche.
Negrelli, S. and Pulignano, V. (2008) 'Change in Contemporary Italy's Social Concertation', *Industrial Relations Journal* 39(2): 63–77.
Pizzorno, A. (1978) 'Political Exchange and Collective Identity in Industrial Conflict', in Crouch, C. and Pizzorno, A. (eds) *The Resurgence of Class Conflict in Western Europe Since 1968*, London: MacMillan.
Pulignano, V. (2007) 'Understanding the Changing Influence of Trade Unions in Contemporary Italy' in Phelan, C. (ed.) *Trade Union Revitalisation: Trends and Prospects in 34 Countries*, Oxford and Bern: Peter Lang.
Regini, M. (1995) *Uncertain Boundaries: The Social and Political Construction of European Economies*, Cambridge: Cambridge University Press.
Romero, F. (1989) *Gli Stati Uniti e il sindacalismo europeo 1944–1951*, Rome: Editrice Lavoro.
Zaninelli, S. (2007) 'Dal Sindacalismo Bianco alla nascita della CISL e della UIL', in Napoli, M. (ed.) *Alle radici del Sindacalismo Italiano*, Milan: Diritto e Ricerche.

Trade Unions and the Politics of Renewal in Spain in Historical Context: Making and Enacting Regulation and Representation

MIGUEL MARTÍNEZ LUCIO AND KERSTIN HAMANN

1. Introduction

Placing issues of union change and renewal in a historical context is increasingly important but challenging. Firstly, some scholars assume a 'golden age' of labour organisations that resides from the mid- to late twentieth century (see Hyman 1995) and then discuss issues of change and adaptation in relation to such broad concepts as globalisation and privatisations, for example. However, the development, crisis and transformation of the labour movement is often more complex. The origins of trade union identity in specific national contexts are varied – trade unions emerged and formed in variable circumstances. The impact on their strategic preferences and the focus of their activities are in part path-dependent. Furthermore, not only does history relate to origins, choices and constraints; it is also the subject of active political intervention as the memory and purpose of the past is contested by different groups and individuals within, between and beyond trade unions. The case of Spain is no exception. For almost half of the twentieth century (1939–75) the country was a dictatorship under the right-wing General Francisco Franco. The sheer scale of the murderous liquidation of the trade union movement in the late 1930s and 1940s marks a moment of history that configures many of the origins of the post-Franco labour movement. However, this configuration is also influenced by the more subtle aspects of state regulation of the employment relations and the development of some sort of Fordist model of production. In addition, the 1960s witnessed the emergence of a new independent labour movement with a strong social character that played a pivotal role in the constitution of Spanish democracy. The political dimension of Spanish industrial relations is a key factor in the origins of the new industrial relations system. Yet at the same time it is the unions' choices, developments and calculations that have been shaped by this past from the late 1980s onwards in a context of extensive industrial restructuring and change that marks a new set of departures and issues within Spanish industrial relations. In effect, history is both context and contest. It is a point of origin and contested departures.

This chapter locates the development of Spanish trade unions in such a historical context. We first outline the civil war and early Francoist years in an attempt to underscore the coercive nature of state action and its impact on the labour movement. We then discuss some of the ways in which industrial relations became organised during the 1940s to the 1960s within an authoritarian context. We assess the manner in which a new independent trade union movement began to form in the final decade or so of the dictatorship and explain how political differences based on different historical trajectories marked the development of this movement in the 1970s. We locate the discussions of political differences – primarily between the socialist UGT and the then communist-oriented CCOO – in terms of how trade unions coped with the extensive economic crisis and restructuring of the 1980s. The failure of centralised mechanisms of control and neo-corporatist ventures gave way to a new set of developments in the 1990s as trade unions began to enter into a range of debates on how best to service and support a 'new workforce'. The question of social and political identity became refracted onto a discussion of the purpose and future roles of trade unions as a link between civil society and the state. We conclude by arguing that the present-day trade union movement is stretched between the different interests and segments of class and social constituents. We evaluate the legacy of history in terms of how the identity of Spanish unions has been contested, how unions have tackled the question of regulating employment and society across time, and how their resources and activism have been shaped.

2. Authoritarianism and Struggle in the Postwar Period

Whilst the year 1945 marks not just the end of Fascism in Europe but also the end of World War II, for Spain it is less significant. The end of the Spanish civil war in 1939 had installed a right-wing dictatorship under General Francisco Franco that lasted until his death in 1975. The civil war had been a bitter struggle between pro-democracy Republicans and the right-wing coalition led by the armed forces. The trade union movement – be it the socialist *Unión General de Trabajadores* (the UGT) or the *Confederación Nacional de Trabajadores* (CNT) with its anarcho-syndicalist politics – were liquidated. Many in these movements and in the communist movement were executed or exiled or were forced to lead clandestine lives (Sartorius and Alfaya 1999; Preston 1993). In effect, the dictatorship imposed a full stop in the history of Spanish industrial relations and trade unionism. The decision by the victorious allies not to invade Spain in 1945 and to leave Franco in power meant that Spain would reside under the shadow of the 1930s until well into the 1970s. For some, this legacy is still present because no one has ever been tried for the crimes of the Francoist regime, although the minority government of the PSOE Prime Minister Zapatero, elected in 2004 and re-elected four years later, began to address some of the issues through the Law of Historical Memory, but the initiatives were in the main symbolic.

The role of the secret police and the use of concentration camps did not diminish for well over a decade after 1939 (Lafuente 1999). However, it has been noted that some UGT activists remained, organising to the best of their ability within very difficult circumstances in various parts of Spain (Maravall 1978). The main trade union confederations established themselves in exile and set up committees and organisational structures, although they were mostly tokenistic and concerned with lobbying foreign governments. Many left and liberal activists in and around the older labour movement participated in the trade unions of such countries as France, Britain and especially Mexico, where exile communities were established. In some cases these communities became the source of trade union leadership in the post-Franco period, as in the case of UGT construction sector.

Despite this forced internal and external dispersal of trade unionists, the state could not allow a vacuum in its industrial relations system. Coercion, no matter how extensive, could be but one part of a politics of industrial relations and the regulation of employment in favour of employers and capital more generally. The first decade of the dictatorship developed a range of 'reforms', in great part led by *Falangists*, the fascist wing of the Francoist 'alliance'. These reforms began to put in place what amounted to a shadow system of industrial relations. In terms of representation, the *Organización Sindical Española* (OSE) was developed. This 'vertical union' brought worker and employer representatives into the national level of this state body down to the regional and sectoral level (Ellwood 1976). The idea was based on a state corporatist approach (Schmitter 1975), which used a nationalist and anti-class discourse to ensure a manufactured dialogue between labour and capital. A large part of the labour ministry's remit was in the hands of this organisation, although the representatives on such bodies were normally henchmen of the dictatorship. Secondly, a system of 'representation' was developed within the workplace and in companies. This system of representation was neither independent nor free of state influence, and it functioned on behalf of employer interests. Thirdly, and more importantly in terms of its enduring influence, the state passed what are termed labour ordinances, a set of detailed regulations of employment categories and classifications. They configure the position and jobs of individuals and whilst employers perhaps did not always take them seriously, the ordinances assisted in organising employment relations and in establishing the need for regularity and certainty that was state-directed and for the most part favoured employers. The fourth dimension was cultural and symbolic. That is, various educational institutions addressed skill and cultural-related issues in the framework of a quasi-fascist discourse that paid homage to labour as a part of the Spanish national identity. The *Universidad Laboral* in Gijón is a classic example of the way in which the iconography and structures of sixteenth-century Spain influenced the architecture of labour-related buildings. The culture of the right was fused with the culture of the organised labour movement around concepts of nation (what Laclau and Mouffe 1984 would call a 'point of articulation'). This therefore meant that labour was represented visually through sculpture and a dedicated architecture as a vital but politically passive and silent part of the Spanish Francoist project, which in turn assisted in undermining the independent voice of labour.

This industrial relations strategy was complemented by an industrial and economic strategy that was in great part statist in its approach to supporting capital. Whilst the extent to which Spain was Fordist in the 1940s and 1950s has been questioned (Barbiano 1995), with some arguing that it was more organised around strong supervision and control and less on co-ordinated and structured production systems, the state played a major role in assisting the development of Taylorised production processes and developing a mass production system. For example, the development of joint ventures between the SEAT car company and FIAT of Italy in the 1950s (Miguelez Lobo 1976), the development of a vast state holding company of industrial and other entities in the form of the *Instituto Nacional de Industria* (INI), and the direct intervention in workplace re-organisation by various state bodies meant that a system of mass production was developed, albeit without a clear link with mass consumption in the 1940s and 1950s. This began to change in the 1960s, however. Increasingly large and integrated industrial and working-class districts began to emerge on the outskirts of Madrid, Barcelona and other cities. Heavy industry – such as ship building, steel, or mining – had a strong state input. In effect the state organised large parts of the economy in relation with capital or on its own. It could be argued that this was never a pure model of Fordism given the role of direct intervention and the heavy reliance on authoritarian politics. However, one can distinguish the intensive reorganisation of the working class and a steady move from an uneven industrial and an expansive agricultural background to a more industrialised and organised, yet closed, system of capitalism.

These developments formed the background for the resurgence of independent organised labour. One could argue that the years from 1939 to 1958 were ones which in some respects mimicked the experience of organised capitalism (Lash and Urry 1987) and Fordist state approaches of the postwar period in other West European countries. The difference with most of Western Europe was that social rights were underdeveloped and political rights were limited in a context of coercive state strategies. There was a highly precarious and informal dimension to jobs and employment generally in such sectors as agriculture (Barbiano Mora 2003). Yet by the mid- to late 1950s a series of events occurred that shaped the origins of the new Spanish labour movement.

First, the coercive aspects of the state began to dissipate partly because the liquidation of the Spanish left exhausted itself and the regime had completed a great part of its objectives. Second, with the visit of US President Eisenhower in the 1950s and the internal tensions within the Francoist alliance with the ongoing marginalisation of the *Falangist* (fascist) wing, it became evident that opening Spain to international capital and Europe would be a priority (Preston 1993). Third, the more hierarchical and dictatorial model of decision making and state intervention had by the 1950s not improved Spain's economy compared to 1936 (Ellwood 1976). The Francoist alliance was not successful in delivering economic gains and it increasingly lagged behind developments in Western Europe. Fourth, within the Francoist alliance the military wing was incapable of providing intellectual leadership and a basis for renewal, leaving the door open for groups that emerged from the Opus Dei and the technocratic wings of the state. These began to reform the Spanish economy by partially opening it to foreign trade (Tamames 1997), modernising aspects of state intervention, tolerating some degree of openness in elections for positions in the works committees of firms and allowing quasi-collective bargaining to take place in the OSE system. This facilitated, albeit minimally, some of the voice mechanisms of the industrial relations system.

The late 1950s witnessed spontaneous strikes and assembly meetings led by 'commissions' of workers in various industrial areas, especially in the north of Spain, such as Asturias, where political memories of the 1930s and the general strikes there continued to influence worker perceptions. These were organised around specific issues and grievances, and they were led by alliances of communists, independent trade unionists and labour-oriented Catholic radicals (Ruiz 1988). Over time these actors began to develop a system of representation and independent structures throughout various parts of Spain. They brought together assembly-led movements that emerged in relation to specific issues; soon, however, they began to create a national network that would eventually form the Workers' Commissions (*Comisiones Obreras* – CCOO). The commissions began to constitute the spine of the independent labour movement and were increasingly influenced by the Spanish Communist Party and various other left organisations. They developed a socio-political identity and linked workplace and community struggles through an alliance with urban movements and neighbourhood associations (Martínez Lucio 1987). This would configure a social and political identity 'assembly-ist' in nature, linking economic and social struggle. Castells (1981 and 1983) pointed to the emergence of innovative and mobilisation-based urban movements in Spain as a major feature of the new landscape of urban politics. Hamann (1998) points to the role of the assembly as a key feature of trade union processes in Spain, becoming more central to their identity and not just their activities (especially in the CCOO and other leftist unions).

Furthermore, in the 1960s the CCOO developed a strategy of infiltrating the OSE and especially the embryonic works councils by presenting independent candidates in elections. In 1968 over one thousand workplace delegates were expelled from their elected posts when the government began to realise the extent of infiltration. In contrast, the CNT was unable to find a space for its reinvention within Spain and the UGT did only marginally better. Part of the reason was the decision not to engage in a strategy of infiltration but another reason was the inability to connect with the struggles and tactics of the assembly-driven new labour movement, thus providing the communists with a space for influencing the trade union movement that they had not previously enjoyed. A whole new generation of trade union leaders emerged from the workplace that would increasingly drive the new movement. Bargaining processes became more complex with worker demands being relayed directly or indirectly to the employers and state officials. A system of *de facto* negotiation crept into sectors such as car manufacturing and the construction industry. Hence, political action and social struggles were tied to industrial relations as activities. This period contributed several characteristics to the new Spanish labour movement:

the role of mobilisation, the position of protest, the link to social movements and struggles, and politicised labour relations. Industrial conflict became more overt and occurred on a range of issues and across various points of the negotiating process. This legacy would be vital to the mobilising character of Spanish organised labour but it would also provide a challenge to organisation building later on.

3. Rebuilding Industrial Relations and Trade Union Identity after the Dictatorship

Although Franco's death in 1975 was anticipated because of his declining health since the 1960s, the assassination of Carrero Blanco, his right-hand man, in 1974, and the increasingly open nature of the regime meant that his succession would not be uncontested. After Franco's death and the subsequent coronation of the King of Spain, a new political elite took control within the regime under Prime Minister Adolfo Suárez. This elite formed the basis of a new, unstable and short-lived centre-right alliance that acknowledged the need for political transition and pacts with the opposition parties (especially the Socialists and the Communists). The transition witnessed considerable political mobilisation and especially large-scale industrial conflict led primarily by the CCOO. It is likely that Spanish political elites saw the prospect of a united labour movement led by the Communist Party as a significant turn of events for the established socio-economic system. The re-establishment of the socialist UGT for a short period of time was regarded as creating more moderate options within the Spanish labour movement. The strategies varied – CCOO saw a necessary link between negotiation and mobilisation; the UGT did not. The former also considered a link with social movements necessary; the latter did not, preferring instead a programme of state-led welfare development. The CCOO was to some extent more democratic in terms of internal discussion and grass-roots interventions, whilst the UGT was more centralist and built upon a weaker network of workplace activists. These differences in class discourses (Martínez Lucio 1988) configured a political schism over the meaning of wage and social struggles. This was to provide a model of union affiliation similar to that of France and Italy with its politically identified trade unions. Perez Díaz (1980) argued that this moderate dimension to trade unionism was underpinned by a vast majority of Spanish workers who – it was found in a range of surveys – did not always share the more militant views of unions such as the CCOO. The reality was that the UGT found a social basis for its trade unionism, although how much this was due to moderate views or the critiques of communists has not been the subject of extensive study.

Another stumbling block to trade union organising – although it could be argued that such a schism allowed more institutionalist strategies to emerge – was the brake put on mobilisation as a consequence of the explicit and implicit political pacts that were established to stabilise democracy around specific economic and political agendas (such as an acceptance of a monarchy in exchange for a liberal democratic process). More importantly, the late 1970s and early 1980s found trade union leaders managing mobilisation and conflict in order to stabilise the political and economic climate and context. This is a matter of great conjecture but what can be said is that trade unions at this stage found themselves increasingly subservient to political interests and contingencies (see Ferner 1988 for a discussion of political contingency more generally). With the failed 1981 military coup the management of industrial relations and other issues, such as the regional issue, became of paramount importance to Spain. Yet this management established a legacy that evidenced massive trade union membership decline (reflected in affiliation rates, see Table 1) after the rapid increases of the mid-1970s.

Table 1. Union affiliation rates in Spain, 1977–2003

Year	Affiliation Rates (%)	Year	Affiliation Rates (%)
1977	18.5	1991	19.3
1978	28.5	1992	21.5
1979	24.7	1993	22.9
1980	13.8	1994	22.7
1981	13.1	1995	16.3
1982	13.2	1996	16.1
1983	13.9	1997	15.7
1984	13.9	1998	16.4
1985	14.2	1999	16.2
1986	13.6	2000	16.1
1987	14.7	2001	16.1
1988	15.1	2002	16.2
1990	16.8	2003	16.3

Sources: Jordana (1996: 215); Visser (2006: 45).

Thus Spanish unions developed to a large extent simultaneously with the new democratic system after the end of the Franco dictatorship in 1975. Clearly, unions did not develop from scratch at that time, but rather built upon foundations reaching back to the pre-authoritarian period as well as experiences during the dictatorship. These foundations differed for what became the two dominant unions in democratic Spain. The UGT relied in many ways more on its pre-authoritarian history, including its close and fraternal relationship with the Socialist Party while the CCOO built on its experiences during the dictatorship (see Hamann 2009). These trajectories were important when unions and the industrial relations system more generally were redefined during the transition to democracy and during the early years of the new Spanish democracy. Given their ideological differences, their different histories and identities, it is not surprising that unions were highly competitive during the transition and beyond. This competition was reflected in and reinforced by the industrial relations institutions that were incrementally constructed at this time. The process of union legalisation favoured a pluralist union system over a unitary one by pitting union confederations against each other. The initial fragmentation – over 400 national and approximately 2,400 subnational unions registered when unions were legalised (Zufiaur 1985: 206–7) – was partially overcome through the rules guiding union elections at the level of the workplace, but it indicated pervasive ideological and organisational splits that manifested themselves in a pluralist rather than unitary union system. By the time the democratic industrial relations framework was finally adopted, unions found themselves in a position in which they competed against each other for the same workers. Once unions were legalised, the nature of the future labour relations system became a subject of immediate concern. The preferences of the major union confederations diverged on at least three distinct, yet related, dimensions: the type of union movement (unitary or pluralist), the system of union representation in the workplace, and the rules for union elections in firms (see Hamann 2008 for a detailed discussion of these issues).

First, the debate over 'unity' versus 'plurality' in the union movement divided the two major unions. CCOO preferred a unitary movement, whereas the UGT supported the establishment of a pluralist system based on associational unionism. In contrast, building upon the role of the Workers' Commissions during the dictatorship, CCOO presented an example of a class union, envisioned a union movement that included all workers, and downplayed the role of union organisation. Instead, CCOO was conceptualised as a socio-political movement or 'a new type of union' (*sindicato de nuevo tipo*). The idea of a unitary union movement all but died in 1977, and the union elections in the spring of 1978 sharpened the competition between the two major unions.

Second, the issue of a unitary or pluralist system had implications for the type of workplace representation unions preferred. The discussion lasted three years (from the legalisation of the unions in April 1977 until the adoption of the Workers' Statute in March 1980), interrupted by the 1978 union elections, during which the unions shifted their position from fundamental opposition to basic agreement (see Marín Arce 1997: 78). CCOO advocated assemblies open to all workers, members or not, as the cornerstone of workplace representation. In contrast, the UGT favoured the introduction of union sections in the firm, in which union organisations would fight for the interests of their members.

Finally, a two-tier system was adopted. Works committees representing all workers should exist parallel to union sections. However, the resulting emphasis on the works committees, which had bargaining power at the workplace level and were legitimised through elections by all workers, and the decree-law regulating the first union elections with open lists for enterprises between six and 250 workers – the vast majority of enterprises in Spain – were much closer to CCOO's preferences than the UGT's vision.

Union sections only obtained full legal recognition in the 1985 Organic Law of Union Freedom; before then, their existence was based on several pacts and agreements between the unions and employer organisations, such as the July 1979 ABI (Basic Interconfederal Agreement) and the 1980s AMI (Interconfederal Framework Agreement), both between the UGT and the employers' organisation CEOE. Members of the works committees are elected by all workers in the firm[1] in elections to be held every two years (every four years after 1982), and comprise members of different unions as well as non-affiliated and independent candidates. Their most important tasks include the negotiation of collective contracts with employers that are extended to cover non-unionised workers, the organisation of strikes, and the convocation of meetings with workers. The role of the union sections lies primarily in organising candidate lists for elections to the works committees, providing legal and other services to union members in the firm, and maintaining contact with the national sector federation and confederation as well as recruiting new members. Union sections also have some limited collective bargaining rights.

1 Workers must have been employed for at least one month before they are eligible to vote. Union membership is not linked to the right to vote.

Third, given the significance of the works committees, the rules guiding the 'union elections' is crucial. In addition to the obvious purpose – the composition of the works committees – the elections also determine the 'most representative' unions (those with 10 per cent of the delegates nationally or 15 per cent at the level of the Autonomous Communities), which have the right to represent workers in collective bargaining on levels higher than the firm. Union elections are thus of significance far beyond the workplace.

The first union elections were of considerable political salience. This is in part because the principal indicator of union strength is the results of the workplace elections rather than union membership, especially since collective bargaining agreements are extended to non-unionised workers and workplaces without union representation. Together, these rules define a union system that has been labelled alternatively 'institutional unionism' (see Miguélez 1999: 199), 'voters' trade unionism' (see Martínez Lucio 1998: 199), or 'electoral unionism' (see Martínez Lucio 1992: 501). The importance of workplace union elections for defining relative union strength had implications for union strategies. Organising and recruitment were de-emphasised while worker mobilisation at union election time became paramount.

These first elections established the union system more clearly. The CCOO emerged as the clear winner with more than 55 per cent of the delegates – a result that was hardly surprising given the CCOO prominence during the later part of the dictatorship. Yet the results also firmly established the UGT as the strong second major union confederation, which *de facto* established a pluralist union movement. The highly fragmented union movement that had come into existence shortly after the legalisation of unions thus quickly developed into one dominated by the UGT and CCOO, to which some regional and sector-specific unions were added.

4. Spanish Social Democracy in the 1980s and 1990s: Building Regulation in a Context of De-Regulation

The Challenge of Restructuring and the Capacity of Labour

Economic restructuring in Spain took place primarily during the 1980s, once democracy had been established. When the PSOE took office in 1982, it was faced with major economic challenges, and motivated to restructure the economy by the prospect of joining the European Union (then the European Community). Most citizens expected González' government to redefine Spanish politics and to fulfil his campaign promise of *cambio* (change), referring to economic and social modernisation. The political context was finally stabilised, even to the point where a major shift in the party system with the virtual disappearance of the UCD and the dominance of the Socialist Party did not pose a threat to the stability of democracy. This stabilisation of democratic politics, however, did not translate into an immediate stabilisation of industrial relations politics; instead, the actors, issues, and arenas of the industrial relations system remained in flux throughout the PSOE's time in office. This instability was in part a response to the concurrent changes in the national, European and global economy, but was also driven by the unions' historical legacies and the PSOE's policy choices. At the same time, the basic rules and institutions of the labour relations system remained largely unaltered, even though employment regulations underwent significant modifications (Hamann 2009).

The PSOE government pursued a policy course that was marked by the government's rhetorical emphasis on 'modernisation', referring to implementing economic adjustment in order to prepare Spain for entry into the European Community. This policy course, which included macroeconomic adjustment and industrial restructuring, came as a surprise to unions, which had expected more expansionary policies. The PSOE's economic policies contributed to the problems of organised labour during the 1980s and 1990s, thus partly explaining the growing distance between the unions and the PSOE (see Gillespie 1990), and they provide the framework to understand the strategies unions developed in response that led to their renewal towards the end of the PSOE period. Despite the loss of the close linkages to leftist parties, Spanish unions remained inherently political actors. The burning issues of the Socialist era – economic adjustment and peaking unemployment rates – called for government involvement in labour market policies. Consequently, union action continued to focus to a considerable extent on the political process in an attempt to influence the government's macro-economic, social and labour market policies.

Thus the challenge for Spanish industrial relations and trade union strategies was, and still is, that they have to construct organised and modern systems of industrial relations and employment regulation in two very different and competing contexts. The first is the legacy of Francoist regulation, which frames many of the more bureaucratic features of the employment relations and, as in the cases of the labour ordinances (which have been steadily reformed), created ambivalent defensive aspects to trade union strategies in the face of greater de-regulation and flexibility in the labour market. Secondly, this ambivalence with the past has been exacerbated by the need to find more co-ordinated approaches by the state and labour for regulating the economy and the labour market in a context of greater globalisation, competition and change at a time of fragmenting labour markets and greater numerical flexibility, which has been very high in Spain.

The Limitations of Neo-Corporatist Agendas

In many ways, the defining feature of industrial relations in the 1980s and also since the mid-1990s has been the existence of a number of social pacts, addressing a variety of issues ranging from employment creation to the structure of collective bargaining. Yet, bi- or tripartite national bargaining through pacts (also sometimes referred to as neo-corporatist bargaining in the literature) has never been institutionalised and has never been systematically applied across a consistent set of issues or policies. Thus union involvement in policy making has remained contingent on the government's willingness to negotiate with unions and employers, and has been inconsistent over time (Martínez Lucio 1992, 1998; Hamann 2001). Furthermore, the unions were not always satisfied with the results and implementation of the social pacts. In fact, the pacts of the early to mid-1980s led the unions to question the PSOE government's commitment to the pacts. In addition, crucial parts of the government's economic, social, and labour market policy agenda were not negotiated with the unions but instead legislated, often against the vociferous opposition of the unions. The relationship between the unions and the government deteriorated in response, exemplified in the national general strike called by the two major unions against the government's social and employment policies in December 1988 and followed by several other general strikes over the next few years.

There are two views regarding the tradition of social pacts. The first tends to see it as a strategic process that aims to legitimate government decisions, and placate organised labour on a range of issues, which, however, does not lead to deep institutional relations over longer term issues in economic and social policy (Martínez Lucio 1998, 2000; Hamann 2001, 2009). That is not to imply that complex informal process and modes of information sharing are not possible within such bodies as the Social and Economic Council (*Consejo Económico y Social*). Hence, a series of ongoing dialogues on a range of issues has existed; yet they are increasingly on the supply-side dimensions of the economy and less on the demand side (Martínez Lucio 2002). For some, market colonisation and strains on the political exchanges in Spain have been extensive (Molina and Royo 2007). Still others (Guillén et al. 2008) suggest that the sheer amount of agreements both nationally and regionally cannot be regarded as minimal or symbolic – they count at least 23 major national bipartite or tripartite agreements. As Encarnación (2003: 8) argues: '... Spain is deservedly regarded as the paradigmatic model of a pacted transition ... every kind of pact has been attempted in Spain: from secretive gentlemen's agreements to grand social and economic accords enjoying tremendous public fanfare.' In addition, the impact of co-ordinated national bargaining and political exchanges has affected wage increases across time, suggesting an ongoing national dialogue even if the forums are not always transparent and concrete.[2]

5. Renewing Trade Unions in a New Economic and Social Context[3]

The context of Spanish trade unions is one of having to forge industrial relations customs and systems in a context of a dual transition (Martínez Lucio 1998). The challenge after the dictatorship in the 1970s has been to 'make' and 'negotiate' an industrial relations system and methods of bargaining and dialogue with the state and employers (the artefacts of modern Keynesian welfare structures) at a time when industrial structures, social regulation, and organised capitalist systems have given rise to disorganised and post-industrial change (see Lash and Urry 1986 for a discussion of the concepts, and Molina and Rhodes 2007 on the changing nature of capitalism in Spain). The two majority unions, the CCOO and UGT, have therefore steered policies of renewal in a context where they have had not just to defend but to develop forms of labour relations and regulation simultaneously. Many additional contextual factors are due to the time-space compression of political and economic developments in democratic Spain as with migration waves, feminisation of the labour market, emergence of changing educational outcomes, and social and familial change. The relevant point for this chapter is that Spanish trade unions face a context of change at all levels and a project of 'regularising regulation' that in effect provides them with a curious set of challenges. Judging the outcomes and

2 We are grateful to María González Menéndez (Universidad de Oviedo) for the information regarding this impact.

3 The next few sections and the following discussion are based on an article written by Miguel Martínez Lucio (2008).

choices of industrial relations is therefore a difficult exercise: hence this chapter's focus on the processes rather than outcomes.

Whilst the system of industrial relations is regulated and formally quite extensive, the focus of trade union strategy has been the extension of the form and content of collective bargaining. Bargaining coverage is substantial – reaching around 80 per cent of workers – in Spain and most workers have their basic terms and conditions of employment covered by collective agreements. However, the UGT and CCOO have, to varying degrees and regardless of differences at specific moments, formulated approaches concerning the extension of the content of collective bargaining as well as its effectiveness. Collective bargaining in Spain does not always cover a wide range of issues effectively, especially with respect to its implementation in small and medium-sized firms. Since the 1980s it has steadily been co-ordinated through sector-level agreements that increasingly provide a framework. This approach has been supported by a range of policies and campaigns around health and safety, working time, employment stability, and others, which have highlighted the need to secure a more systematic and coherent system of joint regulation between employers and unions. In addition, the support services for bargaining, and the research function and expertise underpinning them, have been a focus for trade union development and organisational consideration. In terms of the European dimension there has been a greater investment in co-ordinating European Works Councils as modes of worker representation in larger transnational firms. This is visible in the European Trade Union Congress's TRACE project and the CCOO's impact in the project.

This strategy towards collective bargaining and joint regulation has generally dovetailed with a strategy of 'regularising', effectively operationalising and extending aspects of state regulation. The need for better health and safety regulation and inspectorates, for greater control of employment contracting, for a systematic approach to learning and training for working people, and the development of a social state generally have been a basis for campaigning since the 1970s and the focus of a range of mobilisations. The UGT considers this part of its social democratic focus and support of the welfare state development. This has been the case with the CCOO as well, but it has been more firmly lodged in its identity of being a mobilising and 'socio-political' union. Whilst, steadily, this latter concept has been re-crafted to be less about its links with civil society and more about its support for a social state, the demands for social regulation have been extensive. It can be perceived that over time trade union leaders and activists at various levels realise that the effectiveness of state intervention is questionable, and over time a 'strategy' emerged that witnessed trade unions directly intervening in the development and implementation of these forms of activities itself. The input into health and safety structures, the role of trade unions in employment contracting through various bodies, and the development of information and services show the trade union movement taking on a series of public responsibilities. These are never as extensive as the case of social security in Belgium or the historical case of housing in Germany. In some cases forays into social housing led to serious issues of accountability and mismanagement in part due to the novelty of this engagement for unions, as was the case with the UGT in 1990s.

However, a new logic of engagement emerges emphasising training and learning. Training and development have been the focus of dedicated institutional strategies and concerted reform during the last decade. The social costs of extensive industrial restructuring during the 1980s and 1990s, high levels of unemployment, severe problems of labour market access for younger and female workforce (and a new immigrant workforce), and the continuing legacies of underinvestment in basic educational skills all combined in the 1990s to give an impetus to a strategy for lifelong learning and training in general. By the early 1990s a range of pacts between trade unions, employers and government engaged with the reform of training and established objectives for the adoption of lifelong learning: Both unions and employers in 1992 showed that both sides of the employment relation were committed to reform, drawing the government into a tripartite agreement later that combined state resources with a new levy on employers, half of which is spent on lifelong learning (Sánchez Reinón 2001). The joint management of training and the pivotal role of sector level collective agreements in articulating training needs and strategy is now quite common, with negotiation over accreditation since 1996 (EIRO 1998; Homs 1999; Martínez Lucio et al. 2007; Sánchez Reinón 2001). This strategy was supported by greater trade union intervention in the process of skill and job re-classification. One of the concerns that emerged in the 1990s was that whilst the number of both unemployed and employed being trained was increasing (Consejo Económico y Social 1998), the social partners were inconsistent in applying, administering and supporting lifelong learning. It seemed that unions were engaged mainly for the recruitment possibilities (Rigby 2002). However, trade unions clearly see learning strategies – be they in community centres, the workplaces of larger companies or as a service to smaller companies – as a way of linking into new needs and demands within the workforce and tying regulation back into the fabric of the labour market (Rigby 2002). At the national level, this corresponds to a new institutional role that they had historically been denied. The political and national exchanges around skill appear to be more stable than on such issues as health and safety and employment contract regulation.

In such cases of strategic renewal it is hard to isolate a moment of reflection and deliberate decision making as these strategies are the outcome of a range of historical concerns, calculations and reflections. Yet they seem to reflect a shift in the way the 'socio-political' is redefined and the way the main unions link the state, civil society and labour market. Various concerns appear to underpin this shift: the need for a broader conception of servicing, an awareness of the limited reach of state intervention in the labour market beyond particular areas such as dismissals and legislation, the awareness of a decline in communist and left politics and the marketisation of social democratic positions since the 1980s, and the manner in which trade unions appear isolated and having to follow more independent positions in political if not state terms. In the late 1990s and early 2000s the unions faced the need to work in a political context shaped by the conservative *Partido Popular* government. Hence, a strategy of renewal emerged with a strong leaning towards the state and questions of 'social' service delivery. This is very much propelled by a view that the modernisation of state administration requires a strong trade union input that is visible even in some of the public sector activities of the public administration sections of the two main unions. This dovetails with a professionalisation of trade unionism in terms of its various internal departments and approaches (Hamann and Martínez Lucio 2002). At the regional level – the level of the *autonomías*

– one begins to see the union structures reflect this as well through local pacts, local engagement with learning and related activities.

6. Rethinking Representation

This re-orientation is paralleled by an extension of new forms of communication. The trade unions link this new logic of support to the way they approach general and particular communication. In terms of branding and new forms of communication the role of the Internet has been important despite some discontinuities (Martínez Lucio 2003). Levels of innovation in this area have been extensive. However, a new system of communication has emerged that did not systematically incorporate information related to trade union branches, works council activity, or broader discussions around assemblies. The manner in which unions connect with the workforce in terms of alternative communication appears different from the Internet presence. For example, the role of the assembly and the workplace were disconnected from the new iconography and information systems of the unions, which were primarily service driven. In fact, any discussion regarding the role of the Internet must realise that whilst the assembly and workplace activism has historically been important to the CCOO in particular, the extent of workplace-level trade union activism (see Ortiz 1999) is variable. Hence, this disconnection between the new form of communication and the workplace may therefore emerge due to both national strategy and the unevenness of the union within the workplace, thus limiting demand for such information sources.

Another core feature of the trade union strategy to communication is tied to trade union elections. The role of the trade union election is central to the system of representation as it determines levels of workplace representatives, works council members, and levels of representation at the level of the state's representative bodies on various matters. The elections face few difficulties in most of the larger workplaces (however, we discuss some challenges below). It is in the small and medium-sized firms that trade unions establish teams of organisers who visit the firms with the aim of getting elections held and representatives elected. How effective these representatives are once they are elected is another matter given the paternalistic culture of many employers. Yet these teams form the basis of linking with this disorganised sector, and of creating what would be similar to the Anglo-Saxon 'organising' model. The work of many of such teams tends to reference the learning and support services outlined above, not just for workers but the employer too. In some cases, the teams continue to visit and support the representatives and workforce of this workplace which, referencing relevant collective agreements signed at the provincial or sectoral level, cover their basic terms and conditions. Yet such workplaces are nevertheless exposed and isolated within the labour relations system.

Hence, for both major unions, communication and organising strategies are linked to the issues raised above in terms of the renewal of regulation. What appears to be less prevalent (although research in this area is somewhat less apparent) is the role of community engagement and presence. The grassroots and social presence of trade unions appears to be a declining feature of their activity. For the UGT this is relevant because of the historical and mystical role of the *Casa del Pueblo* (People's House); for the CCOO because of its very conception of being 'socio-political' and of having grown from neighbourhood and workplace struggles. This remains a feature of the trade unions due to the presence of local union offices and centres, although they are less in number than at the time of rapid growth during the years of democratic transition in the late 1970s. Some initiatives were framed around immigrant communities but how they connect to these dimensions is a topic of discussion. Trade unions are beginning to address such groups through various organisational structures and services; whether these activities are an extension of their bureaucracy and become internalised, as with the case of women and gender issues, demands further clarification.

These activities by the major unions have left significant parts of civil society and the precarious economy excluded and thus created grounds for smaller unions to organise. The roles of the CGT and CNT, amongst others, which organise on a minority basis in key sectors, have attempted to play a direct role on community, migrant and vulnerability issues. Yet they are caught by their lack of resources and access to state resources and networks. Others, such as USO, continue to try to establish a link between these open spaces and the more formal activities of the trade union movement. But they are dependent on invitations into formal arenas of discussion due to their poorer results in trade union elections and diminished resources. This is not to say that political mobilisation around specific campaigns and issues – normally related to the labour market and welfare – have not continued to be a hallmark of Spanish industrial relations. The role of strategic general strikes of a short duration but with a high media impact has been a feature of trade unions' strategy, majority and minority.

Trade union revitalisation appears to be occurring across various dimensions (Hamann and Martínez Lucio 2007). It is difficult to establish what the actual outcomes of these strategies are in terms of membership and impact, but the multiple roles being adopted focus on sustaining and developing particular services and regulatory processes across a variety of practices. Yet challenges remain and they emerge at various levels: the nature of the new labour market, the increasing non-accessibility of new groups of workers and of service sectors, the weakness of workplace representation, and the organisational issue of changing internal union governance.

The fragmented nature of society and labour market boundaries mean that trade unions have been caught representing one particular dimension of workers and in the process may exacerbate dualisms and differences. The challenge of the labour market in Spain with its diverse contractual and increasingly individualised systems has been the concern of many observers (see Alonso 2007: 181–214). Traditional nuclei of workers in stable and larger workplaces continue to form the basis of the union leadership and activism (Jódar et al. 2004). This is also apparent in the gender imbalance of union membership even if the influx of women in the labour market has been substantial (Blanco 2004). Changes are visible in the transitional nature of the workforce, necessitating the differentiation between those locked into a peripheral labour market context and those in transition (Jódar et al. 2004), but trade unions still appear to be struggling to capture a new and extensive set of activists within the 'new workforce'.

This issue of boundaries also involves the sectoral dimension. Royle and Ortíz (2006), in a detailed study of the retailing sector (large-scale hypermarkets, established department stores and employers), observed some reticence towards trade unions. The idea that industrial relations in Spain are regulated because of the presence of trade union elections in most workplaces and the extensively juridical character of the law is challenged by the authors' findings. The increasingly transnational character of employers also raises challenges: Contradictory outcomes are present in sectors such as banking and finance as they deploy more sophisticated human resource management techniques, a subject which remains relatively understudied.

In addition, drawing from comparative industrial relations perspectives, the workplace in Spain tends to have weaker workplace representatives when compared to organised sectors in the United Kingdom (Ortiz 1999; Blyton and Martínez Lucio 1995). Such organised workplace roles in the United Kingdom are concentrated within specific sectors with traditions of trade union organisation, but in the 'core' industrial relations sectors in Spain local workplace representation is less prevalent and depends on the structure of works councils. This apparently minor point is actually highly relevant. It means that management communication, new forms of participation and new forms of flexible working are not responded to in a consistent manner by trade unions throughout the firm (for a detailed case study see Ortiz 1999).

The ability to maintain internal political plurality and an open approach to factions and debates pose a particular dilemma for Spanish unions even though this is rarely a topic of academic study. The UGT has never really been as predisposed to such internal debate as the CCOO and whilst within the CCOO the space for intervention is formally broader, the 'majority' leadership faction and position is based around a modernising coalition that is increasingly less concerned with the cult of factions (the issue of declining democratic spaces is discussed in Rigby et al. 1999). This factor is significant for a discussion of the question of how debates and positions can evolve around new employment issues. In Spain one could argue that the political choice is between and not within unions, which guides the logic of democratic trade union elections and trade union history.

Yet with a strong monopoly of trade union representation based on two unions whose conviviality has been significant during the past decade, the question is how meaningful debates actually emerge. Given the weakness of workplace activism, and the increasingly symbolic status of community structures, the spaces for consistent and meaningful internal debate may require some further attention in academic and trade union terms.

It has been argued that there is a potential tension between the *modernising* drive and the *socio-political* inheritance of the trade unions (Hamann and Martínez Lucio 2007). Yet it may be that the potential links between these two and the debate about organisational purpose and visions of society may provide trade union renewal in Spain with a particular identity that is less technocratic and procedural than, for example, the Anglo-Saxon experience. These tensions and contradictions are not new; if anything, they are accentuated in Spain due to the challenging context of Spanish unions and not solely matters of strategic intentions. The tendency of labour relations scholars to isolate the institutional dimension in favour of the political context is ill advised given examples such as the Spanish case. It could be argued that unions are engaged in creating flexible structures and tactics that can be deployed in these difficult contexts of changing workforce demographics, economics, and politics. In this respect one could – with great caution – (ab)use Gramsci's term and describe what is being discussed as an 'institutional' war of position (Gramsci 1971). This occurs in terms of a deployment of campaigns, temporary structures and services across a range of new workers, local communities and workplace environments. Yet this particular approach carries its own contradictions and issues as well, such as reliance on state resources, which is most visible in terms of public funding in the area of learning, for example.

7. Conclusion: The Dilemmas Facing the Spanish Labour Movement

Trade union renewal should be understood in relation to its context and in relation to a developing sensitive understanding of what it is unions 'are' and 'do'. Three issues need to be understood: (1) the national regulatory context, (2) the complex position of trade unions in any specific conjuncture and the structural tensions brought by the employment relation, and (3) the way strategic choices are made.

First, the literature on Spanish industrial relations has clearly established the problem of contradictory developments and contexts. The emergence of complex and highly dualist labour markets with competing interests and constituencies has provided trade unions with a challenge to the renewal of representation. However, the national economic and regulatory context has not helped, given the challenge of modernising regulation and social forms of state action in an increasingly globalised, de-regulated context. Trade unions are stretched between accommodating to economic change and monitoring it. They are caught having to extract from capital but also having to make capital work effectively; this also applies to its relation to the state function. Some competing political projects have not been congruous in recent years. Trade unions appear to be a synthesis of roles and functions in the wake of the gaps left by regulatory development in a market context. They may end up as the 'caretakers' of the regulatory processes, a term once used by Stuart Hall (1988) to discuss social democracy historically but that seems more relevant now.[4]

Secondly, this leads to greater complexity of the position of trade unions. The need to find links between regulation and civil society – to be at the intersection where the trade union can 'socialise' regulation and organised employment on the one hand, and assist the impact of regulation socially – brings forth a range of challenges. Trade unions have

4 This approach requires a view of regulation as being contested with functions that can be provided by various actors (MacKenzie and Martínez Lucio 2005).

always been caught in contradictory positions in capitalist society and have had to sustain 'a delicate balance between grievance and satisfaction, between activism and quiescence' (Hyman 1971: 37). Wright Mills (1948: 8–9) argued that trade unionists were 'managers of discontent' making 'regular what might otherwise be disruptive, both within the industrial routine and within the union which [they seek] to establish and maintain [operating as] an agent in the institutional channelling of animosity'. In the 1970s and 1980s Panitch (1980) discussed how political involvement in neo-corporatist forms of decision-making that traded cuts in direct wages for increases in social wages formalised this tension. The tensions of trade union intervention are part of their function but what now emerges is that trade unions are caught at different points of the employment relation as they reach out to different types of workers (who previously may have been simply ignored or asked to be secondary to a core workforce that was normally gendered and racialised, i.e. male and white). They are also caught between the state and civil society in terms of the delivery of different social forms of regulation and social services, on the one hand, and articulating interests in civil society on the other. New forms of trade union action, and the resources required for new and multiple roles, create a tension not just based on making unions relevant but of responding to the stresses of developing multiple roles. Questions of form need discussion and not just strategy and action: The current problem is not one of decline but of multiple roles and possibilities within an organisational framework that needs to be more flexible, inclusive and resourced (see Martínez Lucio 2006 for a discussion on the way the crisis of organised labour may have been misconceived). Trade unions are now managers of discontent on a broader basis and across a variety of roles in a context where the social is secondary to the market.

The third factor refers to political choice. What makes unions respond in the way they do and have done? Choices evolve and are made during critical moments – these calculations are vital to the study of trade unionism forcing us to take a more historical approach and a more sensitive realisation of how the future is understood in terms of threats and opportunities. Without considering this we end up studying and evaluating the actions and decisions without the framework of meaning that was generating it and may perpetuate it even after it may be deemed to have failed. Hyman (2007) points to the need to understand union modernisation more carefully in terms of issues such as strategic capacity, the role of resources and resourcefulness, the nature of leadership and democracy, and the impact of structures and legacies. Trade unions learn like any other organisation and habits are created that need to be dissected and maybe even challenged. Yet for all this, Hyman (2007) argues that renewal and change need a continuing interest in participation, social networks, the formulation of leaders, activists and intellectuals as well as visions based on justice and distribution. The socio-political aspect is a required ingredient if unions are to avoid modernising in purely managerial terms.

We might need to evaluate at least two narratives. The first narrative states that trade unions have in effect sold themselves to a role that is limited, supply-side in orientation, based on the reproduction of labour and mainly service-delivery driven. Within this picture, trade unions are seen to use their radical legacies as questions of 'branding' in order to sell their new roles. We have, therefore, witnessed the ultimate incorporation of labour into the state. Yet the second narrative would argue that the state is fragmenting and that trade unions are some of the few organisations in modern societies to effectively, democratically and socially provide the supports and visions required in an age of continuous change, especially in the light of highly fragmented social movements. This is a legacy of earlier trade union struggles where trade unions had to cope with unsupportive and uneven state structures and employers. The crisis of social democracy and the failure of other left currents have also left trade unions abandoned and without favours from capital and the state in the way it once was – this is especially the case in the Anglo-Saxon contexts. In Spain, unions have received few systematic favours since the beginning. The labour movement has to make regulation 'work', and to provide support in a system where it also presents a critique of the modus operandi. Trade unions are left with the legacy of the choices that underpinned the nature of the Spanish political transition and the difficulty of coping with memories and political legacies. If we are to understand trade union change reference to these factors is vital for an appropriate discussion. Choice and context are symbiotically related.

Suggested Reading

Alonso, L. (2007) *La crisis de la ciudadanía laboral*, Barcelona: Anthropos.

Amsden, J. (1972) *Collective Bargaining and Class Conflict in Spain*, London: Weidenfeld and Nicolson.

Barbiano Mora, J. (2003) 'Mercado laboral y condiciones de trabajo durante el Franquismo: Algunas caracteristicas, algunos efectos' in Ortiz Heras, M. (ed.) *Memoria e historia del Franquismo*, Cuenca: Almud Universidad de Castilla La Mancha.

Barbiano, J. (1995) *Emigrantes, cronómetros y huelgas*, Madrid: Siglo XXI.

Blanco, J. (2004) 'El sindicalismo español frente a las nuevas estrategias empresariales de trabajo y empleo', *Cuadernos de Relaciones Laborales* 22(2): 93–115.

Blyton, P. and Martínez Lucio, M. (1995) 'Industrial Relations and the Management of Flexibility: A Comparison of Britain and Spain', *International Journal of Human Resource Management*, 6(2): 271–92.

Castells, M. (1981) *Crisis urbana y cambio social*, Madrid-Mexico: Siglo XXI.

——(1983) *The City and the Grassroots. A Cross-Cultural Theory of Urban Social Movements*. Berkeley: University of California Press.

Consejo Económico y Social (1998) *Memoria Annual*, Madrid: Consejo Económico y Social.

Encarnación, O. (2003) 'The Legacy of Transitions: Pact-Making and Democratic Consolidation in Spain', Center for Advanced in the Social Sciences Estudio/Working Paper 2003/193, Juan March Institute Madrid.

EIRO (1998) Comparative Supplement, 'Collective Bargaining on Training' at www.eurofound.europa.eu/eiro/1998/04/word/es9801220s.doc

Ellwood, S. (1976) 'La clase obrera bajo el regimen de Franco', in Preston, P. (ed.) *España en crisis: La evolución y decadencia del regimen de Franco*, Madrid: FCE.
Ferner, A. (1987) 'Public Enterprise and the Politics of 'Commercialism': Changing Industrial Relations in the British and Spanish Railways', *Work, Employment, Society* 1:179–203.
Fishman, R. (1990) *Working-Class Organization and the Return to Democracy in Spain*. Ithaca: Cornell University Press.
Foweraker, J. (1989) *Making Democracy in Spain: Grassroots Struggle in the South, 1955–1975*, Cambridge: Cambridge University Press.
Gillespie, R. (1990) 'The Break-up of the "Socialist Family": Party-Union Relations in Spain, 1982–89', *West European Studies* 13(1): 47–62.
Gramsci, A. (1971) *Selection from the Prison Notebooks*, London: Lawrence and Wishart.
Guillén Rodriguez, A., Gutiérrez Palacios, R., González Begega, S. (2008) 'Pactos sociales en España', *Cuadernos de Información Económica* 203(marzo–abril): 173–81.
Hall, S. (1988) *The Hard Road to Renewal*, London: Verso.
Hamann, K. (1993) 'Afiliación, movilización y aliados políticos: Las incognitas del poder sindical español, 1970–1988', *Cuadernos de Relaciones Laborales* 3: 107–25.
—— (1998) 'Spanish Unions: Institutional Legacy and Responsiveness to Economic and Industrial Change', *Industrial and Labor Relations Review* 51(3): 424–44.
——(2001) 'The Resurgence of National-level Bargaining: Union Strategies in Spain', *Industrial Relations Journal* 32(2):154–72.
——(2008) *The Politics of Industrial Relations in Spain*, unpublished typescript, University of Central Florida, Orlando.
——(Forthcoming 2009) 'The Institutionalization of Unions and Industrial Relations in Spain' in Field, B. and Hamann, K. (eds) *Democracy and Institutional Development: Spain in Comparative Theoretical Perspective*, Basingstoke: Palgrave Macmillan.
——and Martínez Lucio, M. (2003) 'Strategies of Labor Union Revitalization in Spain', *European Journal of Industrial Relations* 9(1): 61–78.

——and Martínez Lucio, M. (2007) 'Trade Union Revitalisation in Spain', in Phelan, C. (ed.) *Trade Union Revitalisation: Trends and Prospects in 34 Countries*, Oxford and Bern: Peter Lang.

Homs, O. (1999) 'La Formacíon de los trabajadores: ¿A mas formacíon mayor cualificacíon?' in Miguelez, F. and Prieto, C. (eds) *Las Relaciones Laborales en España*, Madrid: Siglo veintiuno.

Hyman, R. (1971) *Marxism and the Sociology of Trade Unionism*, London: Pluto Press.

——(2007) 'How Can Trade Unions Act Strategically?', presented at *Industrial Relations in Europe Conference (IREC)*, Centre of Industrial Relations and Negotiations (CIRN), Athens, 26–8 July.

Jódar, P., Ortiz, L., Marti, J., Martin, A. and Alós, R. (2004) 'Los perfiles de la afiliacíon sindical', *Cuadernos de Relaciones Laborales* 22(2): 35–61.

Jordana, J. (1996) 'Reconsidering Union Membership in Spain, 1977–1994: Halting Decline in a Context of Democratic Consolidation', *Industrial Relations Journal* 27(3):211–24.

Laclau, E. and Mouffe, C. (1984) *Hegemony and Socialist Politics,* London: Verso.

Lafuente, I. (1999) *Tiempos de Hambre,* Madrid: Temas de Hoy.

Lash, S. and Urry, J. (1987) *The End of Organised Capitalism*, London: Polity.

MacKenzie, R. and Martínez Lucio, M. (2005) 'The Realities of Regulatory Change: Beyond the Fetish of Deregulation', *Sociology*, 39(3): 499–517.

Maravall, J.M. (1978) *Dictadura y disentimiento político*, Madrid: Alfaguara.

Marín Arce, J.M.. (1997) *Los sindicatos y la reconversión industrial durante la transición*, Madrid: Consejo Económico y Social.

Martínez Lucio, M. (1987) 'El sindicalismo madrileño en un contexto de cambio', *ALFOZ*: 44–50.

——(1992) 'Spain: Constructing Institutions and Actors in a Context of Change' in Ferner, A. and Hyman, R. (eds) *Industrial Relations in the New Europe*, Oxford: Blackwell.

——(1998) 'Spain: Regulating Employment and Social Fragmentation' in Ferner, A. and Hyman, R. (eds) *Changing Industrial Relations in Europe*, 2nd ed., Oxford: Blackwell.

——(2002) 'Strategic Corporatism for a "Flexible Age"? State, Capital and Labour in Spain during the 1990s' in Compston, H. and Berger, S. (eds) *Policy Concertation and Social Partnership in Western Europe*, New York: Bergen.

——(2003) 'New Communication Systems and Trade Union Politics: A Case Study of Spanish Trade Unions and the Role of the Internet', *Industrial Relations Journal* 34(4): 334–47.

——(2006) 'Trade Unionism and the Realities of Change: Reframing the Language of Change' in Alonso, L.E. and Martinez Lucio, M. (eds) *Employment Relations in a Changing Society: Reassessing the Post-Fordist Paradigm*, Basingstoke: Palgrave Macmillan.

——(2008) '¿Todavía 'Organizandores del Descontento'? Los Retos de las Estrategias de Renovación Sindical en España', *Aixus* (18 June): 119–30.

——Skule, S., Trappmann, V. and Kruse, W. (2008) 'Regulating New Skills and New Work: A Comparison of German, Norwegian and Spanish Policies on Transferable Skills', *European Journal of Industrial Relations* 13(3): 323–40.

Miguélez, F. and Prieto, C. (eds) (1991) *Las relaciones laborales en España*, Madrid: Siglo XXI.

Molina, O. and Rhodes, M. (2007) 'The Political Economy of Adjustment in Mixed Market Economies: A Study of Spain and Italy' in Hancké, B., Rhodes. M. and Thatcher, M. (eds) *Beyond Varieties of Capitalism: Conflict, Contradictions and Complementarities in the European Economy*, Oxford: Oxford University Press.

Ortiz, L. (1999) *Convergencia o Permanencia de los Sistemas de Relaciones Laborales*, Madrid: Instituto Juan March de Estudios e Investigaciones.

Panitch, L. (1981) 'Trade unions and the Capitalist State', *New Left Review* 125: 21–45.

Perez Díaz, V. (1980) *Clase Obrera, Partido y Sindicatos*, Madrid: Fundación INI.

Preston, P. (1993) *Franco*, London: Harper Collins.

Rigby, M., Smith R., and Lawlor, T.E. (eds) (1999) *European Trade Unions: Change and Response*, London: Routledge.

Rigby, M. (2002) 'Spanish Trade Unions and the Provision of Continuous Training: Partnerships at a Distance', *Employee Relations* 24(5) 500–15.

Royle, T. and Ortiz, L. (2006) 'International Framework Agreements in the Global Retail Supermarket Sector: An Effective Mechanism for Trade Union Revitalisation and Worker Representation?' paper presented to IREC, Ljubljana, 31 August–2 September.

Ruiz, D. (1988) *Historia de Comisiones Obreras (1958–1988)*, Madrid: Siglo XXI.

Schmitter, P. (1974) 'Still the Century of Corporatism?', *Review of Politics* 36(1): 85–131.

Sánchez Reinón, M. (2001) 'Third National Agreement on Continuing Training Implemented', http://www.eurofound.europa.eu/eiro/2001/09/word/es0109202fes.doc

Sartorius, N. and Alfaya, J. (1999) *La Memoria Insumisa*, Madrid: Espasa.

Tamames, R., Rueda, A. and Valverde Fuertes, J. (1997) *Estructura económica de España*, 23rd ed., Madrid: Alianza Banco Urquijo.

Visser, J. (2006) 'Union Membership Statistics in 24 Countries', *Monthly Labor Review* (January): 38–49.

Wright Mills, C. (1948) *The New Men of Power: America's Labor Leaders*, New York: Harcourt Brace.

Zaragoza, A. (ed.) (1988) *Pactos sociales, sindicatos y patronal en España*, Madrid: Siglo XXI.

Zufiaur, J.M. (1985) 'El sindicalismo español en la transición y la crisis', *Papeles de Economía Española* 22: 202–34.

The Swedish Model of Industrial Relations: Self-Regulation and Combined Centralisation-Decentralisation

ANDERS KJELLBERG

1. Introduction

Several aspects of Swedish industrial relations differ greatly from those in most other countries, particularly in comparison with non-Nordic countries. At the same time considerable historical continuity can be discerned. Contemporary Swedish industrial relations in many respects have their roots in the late nineteenth and early twentieth centuries. Both the historical continuity and the persistent international diversities indicate a high degree of institutionalisation of national industrial relations.

To begin a characterisation of Swedish industrial relations some useful dimensions might be noted:

- collective agreements – legislation
- cooperation – confrontation
- self-regulation – state regulation
- centralisation – decentralisation

These dimensions are closely related (see Table 1 below). Collective agreements are a key instrument for self-regulation on the part of trade unions and employers' associations. It presupposes that the labour market parties recognise each other and consequently cooperate in a basic sense. A high coverage of collective agreements without the support of state extension mechanisms in turn requires a high level of centralisation on both sides, making possible the existence of national industry agreements.

As we will see, the very high union density rate in Sweden (73 per cent in 2007) has been promoted by a combination of both centralisation and decentralisation. Consequently, not only do different dimensions of industrial relations interact, but also the opposite poles within each dimension. In Sweden the threat of state regulation in some periods played a prominent role in the growth of self-regulation. In other periods confrontation between the labour market parties combined with a relatively passive state fostered cooperation and self-regulation. In the early 1900s several important compromises were concluded after conflict or threats of conflict. In contrast to the US, legislation and other forms of state intervention in Sweden functioned neither as an obstacle to, nor as a fulcrum for the breakthrough of trade unionism, with one notable exception: the rapid expansion of private sector white-collar unionism in the 1930s benefited from legislation in 1936 that came in response to strong demands from this category of unions.

Since the late 1930s Swedish industrial relations have been dominated by collective agreements, cooperation, self-regulation and a combination of centralisation and decentralisation. A break of sorts occurred in the 1970s with the introduction of a series of labour laws and in the 1980s with a struggle over wage-earner funds. In the 1990s employers sought to completely decentralise wage formation. Yet at the end of this decade the unions and employers' associations within manufacturing industry signed an agreement on wage formation and cooperation (the 1997 Industry Agreement) reminiscent of the 1938 basic agreement between the peak organisations. Once again the Swedish model of self-regulation and combined centralisation-decentralisation demonstrated its vitality on the eve of the twenty-first century.

The increased activity of state mediators since the 1990s, including the creation of a more powerful mediation institute in 2001, suggests a new mix of self-regulation and state regulation. European Union institutions, in particular the EC court (in the important Vaxholm/Laval case) have deprived the Swedish labour market parties of some of their autonomy. The Swedish centre-right government that took office in 2006 has rejected employer demands on restricted conflict rights, but the EC court did not hesitate to intervene in the Swedish labour market regarding such issues. Nevertheless, in 2007 the private sector labour market parties started talks on a new basic agreement to replace the 1938 agreement, yet another sign of the considerable tenacity of the Swedish model of self-regulation. In 2008 these talks were transformed into regular negotiations, but still in November this year no agreement was concluded.

2. The 1938 Basic Agreement: Victory for Self-Regulation

In the first four decades of the twentieth century Sweden was marked by a high rate of labour conflicts. Some disputes directly involved the peak organisations LO (Swedish Federation of Trade Unions) and SAF (Swedish Employers' Confederation), including the momentous 1909 strike and lockout which ended in a severe defeat for the union movement. The spirit of cooperation surrounding the basic agreement between LO and SAF, the 1938 'Saltsjöbaden Agreement', stood in sharp contrast to the 1909 mood of confrontation and intransigence. As the social democratic policy for recovery during the deep depression of the 1930s was threatened by labour conflict, not least in the building sector, the state pressured the labour market parties to find a solution. Under the threat of state intervention LO and SAF opted for industrial relations regulated by themselves, i.e. self-regulation. On the initiative of the employers, government representatives were excluded from negotiations that began in 1936 (Johansson 1989: 135ff). Although the social democratic government indirectly played a role in the Saltsjöbaden Agreement, it was neither tripartite, nor did tripartite deliberations precede it. The agreement established a set of rules, procedures and bipartite bodies to regulate relations between the labour market parties. The aims were to construct a smoothly collective bargaining system and make state regulation superfluous.

Considering the strong links between the social democratic party and the blue-collar confederation LO, it is noteworthy that the basic agreement reflected the interests of employers, particularly as the social democratic reign would endure for 44 years in succession (1932–76, 1982–91, and 1994–2006). Preventing state interference in industrial relations was a top priority within LO. Since the social democratic government remained dependent on support from other parties, anti-union legislation, for example on restricted conflict rules, was always a possibility (Johansson 1989: 142). And of course social democratic defeats might occur in future elections. LO received several significant employer concessions in exchange, above all advance notice in case of redundancies. From 1938 onwards SAF *de facto* also abstained from any further attempts at using strike-breakers in conflicts with LO unions (Therborn 1983–4: 583; Lundh 2002: 180f). In 1931 five workers were killed by military forces when they demonstrated against the use of strike-breakers in a small community in Ådalen in northern Sweden. The strike-breakers were introduced by SAF to carry out stevedoring work in connection with a strike at a pulp mill owned by a non-member of the organisation (Flink 1978: 63, 141f, 149).

Above all, the Saltsjöbaden agreement promoted union growth. At the end of the 1930s less than every second LO member was employed by SAF firms. A high density in the LO-SAF area was considered a prerequisite to guarantee industrial peace and to promote peaceful industrial relations (Söderpalm 1980: 34, 117f). Thus LO and SAF agreed that it was desirable to increase density and coverage on both sides. SAF agreed to increase its coverage among employers, particularly in manufacturing industry (*Saltsjöbadsavtalet 50 år*: 117; Söderpalm 1980: 34). Between 1940 and 1980 SAF doubled its coverage within manufacturing from 40 per cent to about 80 per cent of blue-collar workers (Kuuse 1986: 152). During the decades after World War II the SAF associations recruited large numbers of small firms in order to prevent wage competition in the predominantly tight labour market. Increased coverage of national collective agreements thus fulfilled an important role in the cartel strategy of employers. Almost all blue-collar unions were already affiliated to LO, but a large share of small and medium-sized enterprises remained outside employers' associations. Between 1939 and 1948 the number of enterprises affiliated to SAF associations almost doubled, to be doubled again within the next twenty years.

The spirit of cooperation following the 1938 agreement removed the fear of joining unions in SAF-affiliated companies. The recruitment of union members was facilitated as SAF firms could not refuse recognising unions or signing collective agreements. In 2006 about 76 per cent of all private sector workers (including white-collar workers) were employed by enterprises affiliated to the SAF successor SN (Confederation of Swedish Enterprise) or to other employers' associations.[1] That meant a somewhat higher rate of organisation among employers than among unions: in 2006 private-sector union density was 71 per cent and in 2007 just 68 per cent. As much as 87 per cent of all private-sector workers were covered by collective agreements in 2007. Including the public sector the share was 92 per cent. It should be noted that no state mechanisms exist in Sweden to extend collective agreements to firms not affiliated to employers' organisations. Instead extension requires negotiations between non-affiliated companies and local union branches. Indeed, in 1934 LO rejected a proposal from the social democratic government to extend collective agreements by law to non-affiliated companies (Söderpalm 1980: 22).

1 The density of employers' organisations in Sweden is far too low in the EU and Eurofound statistics. According to *Industrial relations in EU Member States 2000–2004* (p. 13) and *Industrial Relations in Europe 2004* (Jelle Visser) SN contains only 55 per cent of Swedish wage and salary earners in the private sector (Table 1.5). The correct share for SN in December 2006 was 64 per cent. Including about 20 other private sector employers' associations, most of them small, the share was 76 per cent (excluding business organisations within and outside SN, only employers' associations included). The calculation resulting in the 55 per cent density, besides missing all private sector employers' organisations outside SN, apparently also has missed transforming full-time equivalents (SN statistics) into individuals (Labour force statistics).

3. Centralised Employers' Associations

Although the 1938 Saltsjöbaden Agreement is an important milestone in the history of Swedish industrial relations, there is considerable continuity dating back to around 1900. Within a period of less than ten years, the most important peak organisations of employers and unions were founded and path-breaking compromises between them concluded.

The Swedish Employers' Confederation SAF came into being only four years after the LO's creation in 1898. The 1902 political strike was the immediate cause of the employers' joining together in SAF. The Engineering Employers' Association (VF) in that same year reorganised into an effective and centralised nationwide organisation. The appearance of powerful employers' organisations just after the turn of the century suggests that employers at that time viewed the labour movement as menacing, especially given the close connection between the social democratic party and the union movement. Swedish strike statistics shed light on the employers' vulnerability. Out of 490 work stoppages with a known result during the period 1895–1902, the workers achieved clear victory in 243 cases, the employers in 63, while 184 conflicts were settled by mutual concession (*Arbetsstatistik E:I*: 333). Not even large enterprises were able to cope with the unions in the long run. They possessed neither the size nor resources of giant US companies, nor was the state prepared to assist them in repressing the unions (Kjellberg 1983: 211ff). Scandinavian employers had to rely almost exclusively upon their own collective strength, expressed in employers' confederations equipped with far-reaching powers. Both SAF and VF from the start were dominated by big enterprises. VF, which did not join SAF until 1917, together with the Metalworkers' Union, continued to play a key role in Swedish industrial relations due to the prominence of the highly export-oriented engineering industry in the Swedish economy.

In the years following 1902 several large lockouts (1903, 1905, 1909), or threats thereof (1906, 1908) occurred. Such trials of strength often ended in compromises revealing the failure of the employers to defeat the unions. In both the Engineering Agreement of 1905 (between VF and the

Metalworkers' Union) and the December Compromise of 1906 (between SAF and LO) basic trade unions rights were recognised, in the latter case in exchange for accepting employer prerogatives. The Engineering Agreement, which among other things contained rules on minimum wages and piecework, can be described as the decisive turning-point in the relationship between the union movement and large-scale industrial employers.

Almost from the start, VF and SAF advocated nationwide collective agreements within each industry. The purpose was to attain uniformity so as to avoid the possibility of spear-heading tactics by the unions (Schiller 1967: 58ff.). Until the pivotal 1909 conflict, industry-wide national agreements were concluded with fifteen to seventeen trade groups. The ambition of SAF to regulate the system of industrial relations, however, far exceeded nationwide agreements *within* various industries. During the 1909 strike-lockout SAF even tried to force LO to sign a basic agreement that included a negotiation procedure for the entire SAF-LO area (Schiller 1967: 70ff.). A written proposal was outlined by the Executive Director of the SAF with the 1905 Engineering Agreement as a prototype. The 1909 conflict lasted two months. Involving 285,000 workers, of whom almost 30 per cent were non-union, it was from an international perspective quite unique. In the wake of the conflict LO in 1909 and 1910 lost every second member. In the absence of a relative balance of power between the labour market parties during the conflict it was not followed by a compromise or any agreement at all.

The centralising of employers' organisations had centralising effects on the unions. The LO, originally intended as a purely defensive confederation, dramatically increased its interventionist role, far in excess of the authority originally conferred to it. LO was conceived as a body with very limited tasks, one that lacked its own financial resources. Unlike the Danish and Norwegian union confederations, the Swedish LO did not give economic assistance in case of strikes. But the employers' frequent use of lockouts or threats thereof forced LO to take a more active stance. The outcome of the 1909 conflict produced a temporary setback, however, leaving both LO and SAF in a rather passive role. The SAF-affiliates, however, continued the employer policy of negotiating national agreements even with relatively weak unions like the Textile Workers' Union.

With a downturn in the business cycle, and the major defeat in 1909, union density, having reached a high point in 1907 (38 per cent of non-agricultural blue-collar workers), was more than halved within four years and did not recover entirely until 1920 (Kjellberg 1983: 50). Recovery resulted almost exclusively from efforts by the national unions and their locals (Hadenius 1976: 32). In the early 1920s SAF once again used lockouts on a massive scale. Due to high unemployment LO avoided responding likewise and considerable wage reductions followed. But times soon changed. In 1925 the unions successfully combated a large SAF-lockout. Despite an unfavourable business cycle, the workers achieved a status quo agreement, ending the employers' hegemonic position in the labour market. In contrast to most countries Swedish union density of non-agricultural blue-collar workers expanded considerably in the 1920s, from 38 per cent in 1920 to 55 per cent in 1930, despite severe membership losses during the deep recession at the beginning of the decade (Kjellberg 1983: 50, 220).

From an international perspective, Sweden's labour conflicts until the mid-1920s were distinct in both size and duration (Shorter and Tilly 1974). The first major decrease in the annual number of workers involved in strikes or lockouts occurred in the mid-1920s. At the same time the coverage of collective agreements was extended. By 1930 80 per cent of all industrial workers in Sweden were covered by collective agreements, compared to two-thirds in Denmark and about 40 per cent in Norway (Ericksen 1932: 676).

4. Self-Regulation of the Part of Unions: The 1941 Centralisation of LO

During the 1930s, the LO's growing control over affiliated unions was manifested during several labour market conflicts, and in the centralising consequences of the 1938 agreement. A radical change in 1941 shifted authority to make decisions from the affiliated unions to LO. Similar centralising changes took place within the affiliated unions, depriving members of voting rights regarding collective agreements. Only advisory membership referenda were allowed. The increased powers of the union leadership would pave the way for the introduction of centralised bargaining in the 1950s. The centralisation of LO in 1941 may be described as self-regulation *on the part of unions themselves* (*unilateral* self-regulation) and as a supplement to the *bipartite* self-regulation implemented by the Saltsjöbaden Agreement (Table 1).

One aim of centralisation was to curb the influence of communists, who wielded power in LO unions organising seamen, paper workers and building workers, all of which were involved in militant wage struggles and labour market conflicts during the depression years of the 1930s. The key role of the building trades in the recovery programme led the social democratic government to exert pressure on LO, which in turn forced the unions involved to call off a large building strike in 1933–4. A government commission (1935) recommended that LO centralise and that the labour market parties define rules of conduct safeguarding industrial peace. Only if the parties failed to introduce such rules would the state become involved. The employers also desired reform of the union movement's rules of decision-making (Höglund 1978: 55ff). The 1936 LO congress appointed a committee to present a proposal regarding centralisation at the 1941 congress; SAF therefore did not pursue this issue in the 1936–8 Saltsjöbaden negotiations. Yet centralisation in 1941 was very much a natural consequence of the 1938 agreement.

The 1941 LO report, *The Union Movement and Industry*, made no mention of the principal motive for centralisation presented at the 1936 LO congress – paving the way for a solidaristic wage policy (Hadenius 1976: 49ff, 57ff). Nevertheless, the strongest support for centralisation came from low-wage unions, while the Metalworkers' Union, which in 1936 had championed centralisation, now criticised the imminent weakening of national unions affiliated to LO. As late as the 1950s, solidaristic wage policy played a subsidiary role and would only appear later as a prime motive for centralisation. In 1941 the chief motive for centralisation was avoiding state interference in collective bargaining (Hadenius 1976: 60ff,

65). Without increased powers for the LO, the Saltsjöbaden Agreement would be an insufficient guarantee.

Centralisation in Sweden was quite different from the corresponding processes in Denmark and Norway. Although collective agreements distinguish all Nordic countries, Sweden is in a class by itself with respect to self-regulated wage formation and conflict resolution (Elvander 2002b). The Danish state has played a prominent coordinating role since the 1930s by the authority of state mediators to link ballots of draft settlements. In Norway a similar procedure was introduced by the union movement itself, included in the 1935 basic agreement. The more fragmented union structure in Denmark and Norway made centralisation by coordinated ballots more or less necessary. The Danish and Norwegian states intervene far more actively in collective bargaining than in Sweden, although the exact form of state intervention varies.

Table 1. The Swedish model of self-regulation (bipartite and unilateral) and combined centralisation and decentralisation

	Centralisation	Decentralisation
Self-Regulation	A. On the part of unions *and* employers' associations* Engineering Agreement 1905 and December Compromise LO-SAF 1906 Saltsjöbaden Agreement LO-SAF 1938 Basic Agreement in Government Sector 1966 Centralised bargaining LO-SAF and PTK-SAF Industrial Agreement on wage formation 1997 Central agreements LO-SN and PTK-SN on other issues than wages Negotiations in 2008 LO-PTK-SN on a new basic agreement to replace the 1938 agreement	A. On the part of unions *and* employers' associations* Frequent local negotiations on piece-work Workplace agreements The 1983 Engineering Agreement concluded without preceding participation in the LO-SAF negotiations Decentralisation of collective bargaining since the 1990s: (1) centralised bargaining on wages abolished from 1990 (2) industry agreements kept, but substantive contents successively less detailed and increasingly left to local negotiations Increased space for individualised wage setting

Self-Regulation	B. On the part of unions *or* employers' associations** Centralised employers' associations (VF and SAF) Transition to industrial unionism in the 1920s Centralisation of LO 1941 Solidaristic wage policy (LO) Public sector bargaining cartels (white-collar workers) PTK (bargaining cartel for private sector white-collar workers) 1973 Bargaining Council for unions in engineering industry 1992 Unions within Manufacturing 1996 Intensified internal coordination within LO and SAF/SN	B. On the part of unions *or* employers' associations** Workplace union organisations ('Union clubs') since the 1890s Employers' associations expanded their regional organisation (VF from the 1970s) SAF decision in 1990 to abdicate from collective bargaining
State Regulation	Laws on labour court and collective agreements 1928 Law on right of association and negotiation 1936 (white-collar workers) Stabilisation agreements 1990–93 (Rehnberg) Increased *de facto* role of state mediators since 1993 National Mediation Office 2001 Role of the Bank of Sweden in fighting inflation	Laws on co-determination (MBL), board representation, employment protection (LAS), trade union representatives strengthen union workplace organisations (1970s) EU regulation on European Works Councils implemented by Swedish law EC court verdict in the Vaxholm/Laval case: decentralisation in the sense of increased autonomy of the individual foreign employer to decide wages, but centralisation by the intervention of the EC court into national wage formation and conflict rules.

* Bipartite self-regulation
** Unilateral self-regulation

5. The Role of the Swedish State in Industrial Relations

Until the 1970s the Swedish state can best be described as non-interventionist in industrial relations. The most important legislation before the 1930s were the 1928 laws on collective agreements and on labour court, creating a labour court and making labour conflicts during contract periods illegal. The passing of the 1928 laws, under a liberal government (1926–8), prompted a massive one-day protest strike, but within a few years the union movement accepted the new legislation. Disputes over the interpretation of collective agreements were submitted to the newly established labour court. SAF agreed wholeheartedly that unions should play a role in curbing illegal strikes (Andersson 1990: 138f). Twenty years earlier SAF had objected to similar proposals because sympathy lockouts during contract periods would also become illegal (Göransson 1988: 224f). But the 1928 laws satisfied SAF's requests on the legality of sympathy conflicts and on the avoidance of compulsory arbitration in collective bargaining. In 1928 the employers by and large wanted to preserve the traditional autonomy of industrial relations, including a certain liberty of action during contract periods. Swedish employers benefited from one of the most extensive lockout rights in Europe.

The labour court itself, formally representing a tripartite mode of regulation, in practice functions as a bipartite body as 'party representation is considerable and the "neutral" members cannot perform their duties properly unless they enjoy the confidence of the labour market parties' (Fahlbeck 2002: 94f).

Compared to the liberals, the conservative party had a more passive attitude towards labour legislation (Andersson 1990: 49). The new conservative government (1928–30) tested an alternative line of action when it called together a 'Conference on Industrial Peace' later in 1928, inspired by the Mondist movement. While the 'Delegation on Industrial Peace', appointed by a social democratic government in 1926, brought legislation to the fore, the conservative initiative emphasised voluntary action on the part of the labour market parties (de Geer 1976: 130ff).

Until 1921, when universal suffrage was introduced, the liberals blocked conservative proposals on labour legislation. The liberal leader Karl Staaff considered it wrong to legislate on such issues as long as the workers did not have full voting rights (Nycander 2002a). The social democrats supported the liberal governments of 1905–6 and 1911–14, and participated as a coalition partner in the liberal-led government 1917–21. The alliance between liberals and social democrats rested on the common struggle for universal suffrage. As a lawyer, Staaff in the 1890s defended the right of workers to dissociate themselves from strike-breakers. Liberals and social democrats together protested against the 1901 anti-union law aimed at protecting strike-breakers. Apart from this law no anti-union legislation was introduced in Sweden. In contrast to USA and several continental European countries, the Swedish state on the whole did not act repressively towards the union movement. The 1931 Ådalen events, mentioned above, formed an exception.

6. The 1938 Basic Agreement: Paving the Way for Centralised Bargaining

As a result of the Saltsjöbaden Agreement two bipartite bodies were established. The Labour Market Council dealt with conflicts considered dangerous to society, while the Labour Market Committee was a body for information and negotiation on matters of general interest. The activities of the latter resulted in a series of 'cooperation agreements' between LO and SAF: on worker safety stewards and labour-management safety committees (1942), vocational training (1944), works councils (1946), and time and motion studies (1948).

The 1938 Saltsjöbaden Agreement and the 1941 centralisation of LO paved the way not only for the cooperation agreements, but also for the long period of centralised bargaining between LO and SAF beginning in the 1950s. The ideological and political stance of LO also pointed in that direction: the positive attitude to economic stability and growth, the preparedness to accept 'social responsibility', and the aspirations for a 'solidaristic' wage policy. Centralised bargaining was also encouraged by the close relationship between the LO and the social democratic government, as well as the preference for self-regulation over state regulation (a preference common with SAF).

Despite all these favourable circumstances the road to centralised bargaining was not free of difficulties. LO had conflicts with membership demands for wage increases when wage restraint was maintained during World War II (Sweden was not a participant), and a significant communist-inspired metalworkers' strike occurred in 1945. In a situation of dammed up wage demands and economic boom the 1946–7 bargaining rounds resulted in large wage increases including substantial wage drift. In 1948–50, faced with the possibility of government wage regulation, the LO chose the least objectionable alternative: a voluntary wage-freeze. Such a policy exposed unions to obvious risks; long-term wage restraint would alienate members from their own unions. The proposed solution to the dilemma of combining membership demands and 'social responsibility' was outlined in a report to the 1951 LO congress. Solidaristic wage policy was assigned the double role of expressing solidarity between workers and promoting economic stabilisation (Meidner 1974: 14f). According to what later became known as the Rehn-Meidner model (after the LO economists Gösta Rehn and Rudolf Meidner), the *government* was responsible for preventing inflation through a restrictive economic policy. If the unions were given the primary responsibility in the fight against inflation, they would risk losing members. The unions did have an important stabilising role, but it was not principally one of wage restraint.

The 1951 report recommended a reinforced co-ordinating role for LO in collective bargaining, but the affiliated unions were not yet prepared for such responsibility. The first centralised bargaining round (1951–52) came about after government pressure on LO. At first LO advocated loosely co-ordinated negotiations. The model of a uniform, strictly centralised bargaining round had to be forced through by SAF (de Geer 1986: 116ff). When centralised bargaining was resumed in 1955–6, SAF was the initiator, but centralised collective bargaining was not established on a more permanent basis until the next bargaining round (1956–7). SAF then had to force LO to the negotiation table (de Geer 1986: 139ff).

The introduction of centralised bargaining should be seen in the light of inflation and labour shortage, matters of grave concern to employers and the government. It was therefore no surprise that the initiative in 1951–2 was taken by SAF together with the government. SAF would play a key role in the establishment of the system. Centralisation was an instrument to solve internal *employer* problems, such as the lack of discipline and co-ordination between SAF-affiliates and between firms. SAF was eager to resolve the negative effects of 'scissoring' caused by employers' associations that concluded agreements at separate points of time (de Geer 1986: 325, 327). Employers were also motivated by a desire to overcome the problem of mobilising support to lockouts involving a limited number of employers. In particular it was difficult getting employers who already had concluded agreements to join sympathy lockouts. Another important motive was to prevent state intervention into industrial relations, revealing once again the preference for self-regulation as opposed to state regulation. In 1951–2 the social democratic finance minister expressed a clear threat of government regulations if excessive wage increases were granted. The principal SAF motive for centralised collective bargaining, however, was to secure industrial peace for at least one year (de Geer 1986: 327, 328ff).

Why did SAF not enforce centralised negotiations during the bargaining rounds following upon the 1952 centralised agreement? During these years of recession considerable divergences between industries with respect to the business cycle removed the basis for co-ordinated action. Not until the end of 1955, when a more uniform and auspicious economic situation appeared, and substantial demands for wage increases were expected, did SAF, after positive signals from LO, strive for centralised bargaining once again (de Geer 1986: 326). That was the beginning of a long period (1955–83) of centralised collective bargaining.

7. Solidaristic Wage Policy

Not until the end of the 1950s did unions consider centralised bargaining as a necessary instrument for implementing a solidaristic wage policy. Not surprisingly, no substantial levelling out of wages took place until the 1960s (Meidner 1974: 37, 52 ff). In a 1961 LO report industrial restructuring was recommended to attain more equal wages. The solidaristic wage policy in itself, however, would have an impact on the industrial structure by making some low-wage firms unprofitable. To facilitate structural change, an active labour market policy played a key role. Paradoxically, it was owing to the employers that the traditional union demand for solidaristic wage policy was eventually realised on a large scale. LO's lack of internal unity and discipline could only be overcome by external forces. As a result, the living conditions of the Swedish working class from the 1960s rapidly became more homogeneous.

With the solidaristic wage policy LO found a formula facilitating the simultaneous fulfilment of solidarity and 'social responsibility'. As a consequence, neither state regulation of wages, nor regular income policy was put on the agenda in the 1960s. Expanding export industries could, without government intervention, benefit from wage restraint at the same time as 'structural rationalisation' was speeded up. Special attention was attached to low-wage industries like textiles, garments and service trades. By the added bargaining power provided to unions in these sectors, the decline of employment accelerated in stagnating industries like garments due to worsened terms of trade versus low-wage countries. To secure 'full employment' and transfer workers to expanding areas the active labour policy fulfilled an important role. The Labour Market Board held a strategic position as a promoter of geographical and occupational labour mobility. State regulation (active labour market policy) thus supplemented self-regulation (solidaristic wage policy). From a union perspective it was of vital importance that the government did not intervene directly in collective bargaining. If so, unions would risk appearing as superfluous. The solidaristic wage policy thus offered an opportunity to live up to the objective of the 1951 LO report, that is 'preserving a system under which wage formation take place by collective agreements between free organisations and without state involvement in the form of compulsory arbitration or laws regulating wages' (LO 1951: 145f).

Solidaristic wage policy meant that high-wage groups in engineering and other export industries received relatively small increases in their industry agreements, but they were at least partly compensated by local wage drift, stimulated by the frequent use of piece-work in these strongly expanding industries. *All* categories of workers could thus benefit from the rapid economic growth in Sweden during these decades, in particular groups which in many countries to a large degree remained unorganised. In addition, solidaristic wage policy functioned as cement strengthening the unity of workers, which certainly increased the propensity to join unions.

8. Centralised Self-Regulation under Pressure

The Swedish model of self-regulation under the auspices of the confederations LO and SAF could be labelled 'centralised self-regulation' (Kjellberg 1992: 94; Kjellberg 1998: 79). With roots in the early twentieth century the model step by step was consolidated in 1938 (the basic agreement LO-SAF), 1941 (LO centralisation) and the mid-1950s (establishment of centralised bargaining LO-SAF). In the 1970s the new white-collar bargaining cartel PTK entered as a third actor at the central level. The heyday of the classical model, dominated by the LO-SAF axis, occurred in the 1950s and 1960s. In the 1980s the employers gradually changed bargaining strategy to become strong proponents of decentralised bargaining. By the time of the 1997 Industrial Agreement, however, centralising forces regained the initiative.

Another departure from the traditional Swedish model of industrial relations occurred with the series of labour laws on co-determination introduced in the 1970s. In general, a number of interacting circumstances caused this break with self-regulation, among them the anti-authoritarian political-ideological climate of the time, the aspirations of political parties to benefit from the growing demands for the democratisation of society, the accelerated structural rationalisation of industry followed by frequent layoffs and employers unprepared to comply with growing demands on co-determination. Some of the new laws came about on the initiative of political parties, while others primarily originated from unions.

9. Labour Legislation in the 1970s

Union legislative initiatives did not come from top union leaders but rather from a radicalisation from below. A prominent example is the process preceding the 1976 Law on Co-determination. It should be observed that this law, like most labour legislation enacted in the 1970s, was designed to be followed up by agreements at different levels. The law, however, also requires employers to negotiate major changes in operations, working conditions and terms of employment affecting union members (Kjellberg 1998: 106f). The 1946 LO-SAF agreement on works councils provided a forum for information and advice, but no obligation on information and nothing about negotiations. In contrast to German works councils, workers were exclusively represented by unionists. Shortly after the revision of the agreement in 1966, the Metal president expressed his hope that the employers now should apply the formula 'Consultation before decision' (Kjellberg 1981: 68ff). The Metalworkers' magazine in 1967 reported several flagrant violations of this principle in connection with large-scale layoffs in the engineering industry. In the next year the Stockholm branch sought to convince the 1969 Metal congress to work for legislation on co-determination. Under pressure from delegates, the Metal president switched from a very moderate position to declaring his full support for legislation. Just a week later LO appointed a committee, led by the vice president of the Metalworkers Union, to determine the best line of action: agreement, legislation or a combination of the two. In its report to the 1971 LO congress the committee declared legislation unavoidable, but that any law should be followed up by agreements in order to achieve a desirable adjustment to varying conditions in different industries and firms. Supplementary agreements were also necessary to prevent employers from considering 'industrial democracy' a burden. For the first time the employer prerogative was being questioned in a LO report. The LO leadership considered legislation as necessary due to the unreasonable attitude of employers. On the initiative of the LO president (who was a social democratic member of parliament) a government committee was appointed, which in 1975 presented the report 'Democracy at the Workplace'.

Although the impetus for the 1976 Law on Co-determination came from the union movement, a multitude of circumstances impinged on the process. The student and youth movement, and the intensified public debate on unsatisfactory conditions and unequal power relations in working life certainly appeared as a challenge to the union movement. The great wild-cat strike at the state-owned mining company LKAB in 1969–70, followed by a wave of wild-cat strikes in the engineering industry, demonstrated the growing tensions in the Swedish model of the 1950s and 1960s. Due to the solidaristic wage policy, miners' wage increases lagged behind and did not compensate for the increased intensity of work. One of the principal demands of the striking workers was to be treated as 'human beings', not as 'machines'. This signified an implicit critique of the positive attitude of the union movement towards technological change and rationalisations. A 1966 LO report expressed in cautious terms a growing awareness about 'adjustment problems' among workers exposed to change. The economic and technological development in combination with a radicalised ideological-political climate caused rising demands for influence. As the employers were not prepared to comply with these demands, legislation on co-determination became the dominant union strategy. In 1976 parliament passed the Law on Co-determination, which came into effect from 1977. Due to the hostile attitude of private sector employers, an agreement on co-determination between SAF and LO-PTK was not signed until 1982 (Kjellberg 1998: 106ff).

The fear of 'sitting at two chairs' was the traditional union argument against co-determination in firms. In addition, the preference for self-regulation and flexible solutions initially made the top union leadership sceptical towards legislation on these issues. The liberal party, eager to win back white-collar workers lost to social democrats in the struggle over occupational pensions in the late 1950s, proposed representation for employees on company boards (Nycander 2002b: 222f, 237ff). The conservative party made similar initiatives and the social democratic government prepared legislation on union representation on company boards. Such political pressures forced LO to act. In 1972 LO invited SAF to negotiate on board representation, but due to resistance from leading companies in SAF no agreement was reached (Schiller 1988: 67ff). In practice, the employers preferred the anticipated legislation. By that route SAF could prevent the deep split among its members from growing worse. One possible reason for LO to negotiate was the risk that the liberal party, in case legislation was adopted, would take the credit. In any event, the result was the 1973 Law on Board Representation, the first in a series of labour laws during that decade. Employment protection was another area is which political forces succeeded in pushing through labour legislation. Despite the appointment in 1969 of a government commission on employment protection, it was not until 1973 that LO turned to legislation on this issue. Nycander characterises the social democratic party as the driving force for the 1974 Law on Employment Protection (Nycander 2002b: 259ff, 272ff).

10. Centralisation and Decentralisation

Although the extensive labour legislation introduced in the 1970s implied a departure from the classical Swedish model of self-regulation, it also contained important elements of continuity. Most laws were framework laws to be implemented by agreements. The laws on employment protection and co-determination, however, also required the employers to negotiate in case of redundancies and important changes. The aim of the Law on Trade Union Representatives (1974) was to make certain that, to the extent possible, negotiations took place at workplace level. The law strengthened unions at the workplace by establishing the right to union activities on paid working-time provided such activities were related to the workplace. Union officers at local branches were guaranteed access to workplaces, an important right for small workplaces without union representatives.

The labour legislation of the 1970s thus extended the powers and tasks of unions at the workplace and increased the resources of union workplace organisations. Due to such new laws and the juridification of industrial relations, a large-scale government-supported education of union representatives was launched. In the wake of the 1982 SAF-LO/PTK Co-determination Agreement, a multitude of local forms of co-determination appeared: negotiations, project groups and bipartite bodies. Compared to the far-reaching aspirations of the 1970s to shift power towards unions, workplace industrial relations were now characterised by cooperation and employer initiatives. Headed by the Metalworkers' Union, the union movement tried to regain the initiative through the concept of 'Good Work' (1985), later 'Developing Work'. In a labour market still characterised by 'full employment' and high labour turnover, several large firms had an interest in creating attractive workplaces and, by increased pay differentiation, to encourage workers to climb a skills 'ladder' (Kjellberg 1998: 109ff). The depression in the early 1990s shifted the focus of workplace unions to employment protection, while employers accelerated the introduction of lean production methods and flexible working arrangements. The employer demands for abolishing the Law on Employment Protection, in the first instance protecting elderly workers, may be explained by the intensified efforts to increase productivity.

The collective bargaining system was untouched by the labour laws of the 1970s. Long before unions at workplaces received extended negotiation rights on co-determination, workplace unions played a prominent role in collective bargaining. Until the mid-1950s wage negotiations took place in a two-tier system: industry agreements followed by workplace negotiations under the auspices of workplace 'union clubs'. Under the era of centralised bargaining the LO-SAF level (from the 1970s also the PTK-SAF level) was added. The result was a three-tier system. Including the local union branch, negotiating at workplaces without union representatives, another level was necessary, although the negotiations always were concentrated to three levels.

The combined centralisation and decentralisation of Swedish trade unions and industrial relations goes far toward explaining high union density. *Centralisation* is required for central compromises guaranteeing union rights and reducing fears about joining unions at the individual workplace. It also increases the share of workplaces represented by unions provided a high coverage of employers' associations. Another illustration of interaction between central and local levels to the advantage of unions is that bargaining power at national level facilitates local negotiations, particularly at workplaces with weak union representation. Centralisation is also a prerequisite for solidaristic wage policy and for avoiding extensive state regulation of industrial relations. Finally, strong confederations and national unions facilitate international union cooperation.

Decentralisation refers to the extensive coverage of union workplace organisations vertically integrated into national unions. The workplace 'clubs' bring unions close to rank-and-file members and offer unique chances for reciprocal communication between unions and members. They also constitute an arena for formulating demands and delivering goods where the workers are. Union workplace organisations promote membership recruitment not only from a *social* aspect (face-to-face contacts) but also from a *utility* aspect (results of union activities directly at the workplace) and by reducing fears about joining unions. A Swedish survey demonstrates that the existence of a union workplace organisation is extremely important for creating positive attitudes about union membership (Kjellberg 2001). The decision to *join* a union is highly influenced by the workers' immediate social environment at the workplace (colleagues and union representatives), while the major reasons for *maintaining* one's membership are related to the ability of the union to achieve satisfactory results and provide protection in unanticipated situations. In both cases, the workplace union has a key role in attracting the support of workers. When asked about which part of the union they identify as 'the union', most members have the workplace union in mind. This union level plays a strategic role for successfully dealing with issues like 'developing jobs', work environment, achieving co-determination in companies, and transforming European Works Councils into effective bodies of influence. Last but not least, negotiations by workplace unions adapt national agreements to the individual workplace, a role of increasing importance since the 1990s and the decentralisation of collective bargaining. A growing part of the concrete contents of national collective agreements are left to the local level.

On the other hand, both *one-sided* centralisation and *one-sided* decentralisation may be highly problematic for unions. Power relations are often strongly biased to the employers' advantage in such cases. After World War II Dutch unions had to abstain from their workplace presence in order to be accepted as cooperation partners at central level. Similarly, one-sided decentralisation results in fragmentary union coverage, as in the US, Japan and Britain. Generally speaking, industrial relations systems with a strong decentralised *or* centralised bias militate against a high union density, while a *combination* of centralisation and decentralisation offers more sanguine prospects for unions.

11. Separate Blue-Collar and White-Collar Unions

In addition to the blue-collar confederation LO, Sweden has two white-collar confederations: TCO (Swedish Confederation of Professional Employees), founded in 1944, and SACO (Swedish Confederation of Professional Associations), founded in 1947. Sweden contains the most class-segmented union movement in the world by the existence of separate national unions and union confederations for blue-collar workers (LO), university-educated professionals (SACO) and other white-collar workers (TCO). This pattern persists despite increasingly diluted borders between SACO and TCO unions due to the heightened educational level of TCO groups like teachers.

According to the theory of workers' collective behaviour elaborated by the Norwegian sociologist Sverre Lysgaard, a common identity and feeling of solidarity may arise among workers at the same workplace or in the same work group (the principle of *nearness*) and among those with a similar occupation or profession (the principle of *similarity*; Lysgaard 1985). Both sources of solidarity are reflected in the Swedish union structure. Besides the extensive network of union workplace organisations there are a number of occupational and professional unions, in particular among white-collar workers. The largest SACO affiliate, the Union of Graduate Engineers, combines different sources of solidarity by being a professional union containing several workplace 'clubs'. All SACO affiliates are professional unions. Many TCO unions and some LO unions are occupational unions, organising teachers, police officers, electricians, painters and so forth. Most LO unions, like *IF Metall*, are vertical unions although restricted to blue-collar workers.

The separation of blue-collar workers, university graduates and other white-collar workers into different unions and confederations create rather homogenous recruitment areas for Swedish unions, most pronounced among LO and SACO unions, while vertical TCO unions like the large *Unionen* have a very heterogeneous membership. In countries where blue-collar and white-collar workers are organised by the same unions, many of the latter abstain from membership due to difficulties identifying themselves with blue-collar dominated unions. The political orientation of blue-collar unions might also repel many white-collar workers. The strong links between Swedish LO and the social democratic party still constitute a severe barrier for mergers between white-collar and blue-collar unions. In short, both social and political reasons make the existence of separate, politically independent white-collar unions and confederations instrumental for the high union density in Sweden.

12. The Rise of White-Collar and Female Unionism

The increasing share of white-collar workers within labour force, combined with their high and rising density, is reflected in considerable shifts between union confederations. LO's membership share declined from 79 to 49 per cent from 1945 to 2007. Until 1975, TCO's share increased from 14 to 32 per cent (33 per cent in 2007). Over the last three decades SACO's share has quadrupled (14 per cent in 2007).

Of the fifteen largest unions in 2008, no less than nine were white-collar unions: five TCO unions, three SACO unions and one independent union (Table 2). In 1950 all but one of the top-fifteen unions were blue-collar LO unions. Eight of the fifteen largest unions in 2008 had a clear majority of women but only two unions in 1950 had a female majority. The women-dominated Municipal Workers' Union (LO) in 1977 passed *Metall* as the largest Swedish union. In 1950 most members of the Municipal Workers' Union were men, but in 2008 women comprised eight out of ten members (Tables 2 and 3). The teachers' unions in TCO and SACO have also undergone a feminisation process. The merger in 2006 between *Metall* and another LO union (in turn formed by mergers of unions numbered 6, 9 and 14 in Table 3) did not prevent the white-collar union *Unionen*, formed in 2008 by a merger between two vertical TCO unions, from becoming the second largest Swedish union and the largest private sector union.

Table 2. The 15 largest national unions in Sweden, 1 January 2008

(1)	(2)	(3)	(4)	(5)	(6)	(7)	(8)	(9)	(10)
1	Municipal (LO)	529,100	81	G/M	BC	V	LO	1910	
2	*Unionen*	412,400	45	M	WC	V	TCO	2008	FI, PTK
3	*IF Metall*	316,000	21	M	BC	V	LO	2006	FI
4	Teachers (TCO)	177,000	83	G/M	WC	O/P	TCO	1991	OFR, PTK
5	Commercial (LO)	129,000	66	M	BC/WC	V	LO	1906	
6	Municipal (TCO)	127,400	73	G	WC	V	TCO	1936	OFR
7	Communication	94,600	28	M/G	BC/WC	V	LO	1970	
8	Graduate Engineers	93,500	22	M/G	WC	P	SACO	1954/ 2007	FI, PTK
9	Nurses	91,700	92	G/M	WC	O/P	TCO	1965	OFR, PTK
10	Building	86,200	1	M	BC	V	LO	1949	
11	Government employees	70,200	66	G	WC	V	TCO	1938	OFR
12	Supervisors	70,200	20	M/G	WC	O	Independ	1928	OFR, PTK
13	Transport	58,400	16	M	BC	V	LO	1897	
14	Teachers (SACO)	56,900	67	G/M	WC	P	SACO	1912	OFR, PTK
15	Lawyers/ economists	52,000	55	G/M	WC	P	SACO	1940	PTK

(1) Rank by size.
(2) Category of workers organised by the union.
(3) Number of active union members. Unemployed, persons on labour market programs and SACO members on leave included. Pensioners, self-employed and students excluded.
(4) Share of women.
(5) Most members in government sector (G), in market sector (M).
(6) Blue-collar union (BC), white-collar union (WC).
(7) Vertical (industrial) union (V), Occupational union (O), professional union (P).
(8) Affiliated to confederation. Independ. = Independent.
(9) Year of foundation.
(10) Affiliated to FI (*Facken inom industrin* = Unions in Manufacturing), OFR (*Offentliganställdas förhandlingsråd* = Public Employees' Negotiation Council), PTK = Council for Negotiation and Cooperation, formerly the bargaining cartel 'Federation of Salaried Employees in Industry and Services'.

Table 3. The 15 largest national unions in Sweden, 31 December 1950

(1)	(2)	(3)	(4)	(5)	(6)	(7)	(8)	(9)
1	*Metall*	211,800	7	M	BC	V	LO	1888
2	Building	111,100	1	M	BC	V	LO	1949
3	Municipal (LO)	85,900	42	G/M	BC	V	LO	1910
4	Railways	69,100	5	G	BC/WC	V	LO	1899
5	Commercial (LO)	66,600	43	M	BC/WC	V	LO	1906
6	Factory	60,100	20	M	BC	V	LO	1891
7	Manufacturing industry, SIF	59,700	25	M	WC	V	TCO	1920
8	Wood	56,300	2	M	BC	V	LO	1924
9	Textile	47,400	51	M	BC	V	LO	1898
10	Agricultural	42,900	7	M	BC	V	LO	1918
11	Transport	39,700	9	M	BC	V	LO	1897
12	Paper	37,900	6	M	BC	V	LO	1920
13	Food	37,900	27	M	BC	V	LO	1922
14	Garment	35,400	81	M	BC	V	LO	1889
15	Forest	30,800	0	M	BC	V	LO	1918

13. The LO-SAF Axis Challenged

Centralised bargaining in the 1950s and 1960s was facilitated by the near monopoly of the LO-SAF axis in the classical Swedish model. With the rapid expansion of public sector and white-collar unions in the 1970s this situation was broken. The private sector TCO and SACO unions in 1973 formed the white-collar cartel PTK to bargain with SAF. Two TCO public sector bargaining cartels were formed in 1967 and 1976 respectively. By becoming the largest Swedish union in 1977 the Municipal Workers' Union challenged the position of the Metalworkers' Union within LO.

As a result, the LO-SAF negotiations covered a shrinking share of workers. With militant white-collar unions and cartels demanding substantial wage increases, LO was forced to revise its own demands. Solidaristic wage policy, based upon the privileged position of the LO-SAF axis, lost its role as an alternative income policy. Instead the government tried to restrict wage increases by income policy, but with limited success.

Despite oil shocks and declining economic growth, total wage costs rose 700 per cent between 1970 and 1992, but due to inflation and repeated devaluations real wages increased only 10 to 20 per cent. As centralised bargaining no longer promoted labour peace and 'socially responsible' wage increases, dissatisfaction grew among employers from the mid-1970s. The segmentation of the industrial relations arena made wage negotiations much more complicated. Swedish unions were divided into blocs of relatively equal strength – LO (private sector blue-collar workers), PTK (private sector white-collar workers) and a third bloc of LO and TCO public sector unions. SAF itself had become more heterogeneous by the inclusion of employers' associations in private services resulting in growing internal tensions.

Despite the 1980 lockout of 750,000 workers the new militant leadership of SAF failed to transform the great conflict into 'an investment for the future'. In the next year a SAF-PTK conflict at four big engineering companies risked spreading to an additional large number of white-collar workers. These events contributed to the employers' reconsidering a shift in strategy, from centralised to decentralised bargaining. The erosion of wage differentials combined with 'full employment' caused high labour turnover in export industries and undermined local wage formation as a tool for promoting productivity, flexibility and quality (Kjellberg 1998). Together with the Metalworkers' Union, the Association of Engineering Employers (VF) in 1983 left the central negotiations of LO-SAF. *Metall* was prepared to take this step as the solidaristic wage policy of LO had widened the gap between skilled workers and lower-level white-collar workers, causing *Metall* losing members to the TCO white-collar union in manufacturing industry (SIF).

14. A New Mix of Self-Regulation and State Regulation and of Centralisation and Decentralisation

In 1990 SAF decided to dismantle its bargaining unit, but it soon resumed a prominent role in the collective bargaining system. Since 1995 SAF (and its successor SN) has strengthened its role as co-ordinator of the affiliated employers' associations. The conflict between the different goals of the organisation became conspicuous in the 1990s. The aspirations for a completely decentralised and individualised wage formation stood in sharp contrast to SAF's *de facto* growing cartel function in collective bargaining.

Faced with a wage-price spiral and economic crisis, SAF considered several alternatives to cope with the situation. After SAF's rejection of centralised bargaining, the social democratic government (in office since 1982) in 1990 proposed a two-year general pay freeze and strike ban, but after protests from the Municipal Workers' Union and many local unionists the government resigned. It soon was replaced by a new social democratic government (1990–1) which succeeded by using more consensual methods, but now the state was assigned a key role in wage formation. A government commission persuaded the peak organisations to accept the tripartite 1991 'stabilisation agreement', followed by a similar agreement in 1992 (Kjellberg 1998). Due to this super-centralisation to overcome bargaining segmentation, and with unemployment of a scale not known since the 1930s, the wage-spiral was effectively curbed for the moment. The policy of 'full employment' now lost its privileged position to the advantage of 'the fight against inflation' as top priority for Swedish governments.

The stabilisation agreements comprised a moment of extreme state regulation and centralisation. After that a new mix of self-regulation and state regulation began to evolve. Long before the newly strengthened mediation institute was set up in 2001 the role of state mediators increased by informal means. In the 1993 bargaining round they assumed a *de facto* coordinating function. Two years later the sharply diverging economic performance between industries and sectors prevented a replication of the previous round and made the 1995 round the most conflictual for many years. In general the agreements exceeded the expected European average rate of wage growth. From a stabilisation perspective the 1995 round failed, although the result certainly would have been worse without the efforts of the mediators.

Based on the experience of the 1995 bargaining round SAF intensified its demands on legislation restricting conflict rights and upgraded its role as coordinator between affiliated employers' associations. The government encouraged the labour market parties to find forms of negotiations and wage formation compatible with the European norm. As in the 1930s the alternative was considerably increased state regulation. If state mediators gained the powers LO hoped, they would also be able to coordinate collective bargaining across the whole labour market. This idea did not attract the unions within manufacturing industry. They were aware that something had to be done but preferred self-regulation. With most of their members in firms heavily dependent on exports the unions in manufacturing had a clear interest in gearing down wage increases to save those jobs that had not been lost in the depression at the beginning of the decade. In both 1993 and 1995 the employers headed by the Association of Engineering Employers (VF) demanded completely decentralised bargaining to restore Swedish competitiveness and to obtain a more individualised and flexible wage-setting. National agreements should contain nothing but a peace clause. To counter such demands the LO union *Metall*, together with the white collar TCO union SIF and the SACO-affiliated Association of Graduate Engineers (CF), formed a common organisation, the Bargaining Council in the autumn of 1992. As a result the system of national collective agreements was maintained, although a gradual decentralisation of the contents of the agreements took place. In 1993 the employers, however, scored an important success by the, still valid, agreements with the former TCO union of supervisors concentrating all wage formation at the workplace level. Among LO unions, fears grew that other white-collar unions would take the same path.

To forestall both completely decentralised wage formation and increased state regulation – and to prevent wage inflation – the presidents of SIF, CF and six LO unions in manufacturing industry wrote an article, 'Moderate wage increases – our responsibility' (June 1996), inviting the employers in manufacturing to deliberate on industrial development, training and wage formation. As a result, the organisation 'Unions in Manufacturing' was formed. The following year these unions and twelve employers' association in manufacturing concluded the Agreement on Industrial Development and Wage Formation, usually known as the Industry Agreement. It has clear parallels to the 1938 basic agreement with respect to origin (threat of state regulation), contents (negotiation procedure, conflict resolution) and the spirit of cooperation. By the 1997 Industry Agreement a certain re-centralisation took place. The 1938 Saltsjöbaden Agreement paved the way for centralised LO-SAF bargaining, but the 1997 agreement set the LO-SAF axis aside. Instead it expressed a cross-collar alliance reflecting the growing importance of white-collar unions. The preference of the Swedish state for self-regulation by the labour market parties was demonstrated by the exemption of manufacturing industry and sectors with similar agreements from the powers of the new 2001 mediation institute. In any event, the Mediation Office has important tasks in wage formation, in particular as building and large parts of the trade and transport sectors still have no cooperation agreements (Kjellberg 2007: 277f).

A limitation of the Industry Agreement is that it only covers the manufacturing sector, which employs a shrinking share of workers while employment in private services expands. Until the 2007 bargaining round the Industry Agreement was considered a success and a key component in a model of wage formation combining growing real wages and low nominal wage increases to the advantage of Swedish competitiveness. In addition to the coordination within Unions in Manufacturing, the internal coordination in both LO and SN play important roles in the Swedish model of wage formation. Furthermore, the Mediation Office in different ways seeks 'to promote an efficient wage formation process' (Kjellberg 2007). Coordination is facilitated since most agreements last for three years and expire at about the same time. Such large bargaining rounds occurred in 1998, 2001, 2004 and 2007 (the next is in 2010).

In 2007, ten years after its birth, the Industry Agreement for the first time was tested in a tight labour market. The 2007 bargaining round resulted in higher wage increases than during the previous ten years. It was reminiscent of the 1995 round when centrifugal forces resulted in a breakdown of the internal coordination within the Swedish Employers' Confederation, SAF (the predecessor of SN). In 1995 the SAF federation containing the booming pulp and paper industry conceded wage increases above what others considered acceptable.

Through its strong internal coordination the LO acquired a dominating influence in the 2007 bargaining round. The LO had a twofold aim: agreements in manufacturing industry should set the norm but low-wage unions should have the right to demand more and to receive support from the other LO unions. When the Commercial Employees' Union (LO) in 2007 threatened to strike, the Swedish Trade Federation (affiliated to SN) concluded an agreement strongly criticised by the SN leadership for being too costly. After the 1995 debacle, the pulp and paper employers were forced to discipline themselves, not least by the SAF associations behind the Industry Agreement. The failed SN coordination in 2007 was different as it challenged the export-oriented manufacturing industry as a norm-setter in wage formation.

15. Manufacturing Industry Challenged by Private Services

A rift between manufacturing and private services has lately appeared across unions and employers associations. In 2007 the Commercial Employees' Union and eight other LO unions within private services and home market trades started to cooperate more closely. On the initiative of the Swedish Trade Federation and another SN-affiliate, a network ('The Service Sector in Cooperation') directed against the dominant position of manufacturing industry in collective bargaining, was formed by five SN-federations and seven unions, all of them in private services. One of the participants is *Unionen*, formed in 2008 when a TCO union in manufacturing industry (SIF) merged with a TCO union in private services (HTF). Consequently *Unionen* stands with one foot in each camp. It remains to see whether it will serve as a bridge between different groups or will itself be rent by conflicts. The president of Union (the former SIF president) declared early in 2008 that the LO unions in manufacturing – and consequently indirectly LO itself by its coordination – have too large an influence on the demands put forward by Unions in Manufacturing (Kjellberg 2008). She also called into question the leading role of manufacturing industry in collective bargaining and also stressed that IT, transport and other trades in private services are exposed to international competition. The employers in private services agree, but their reasons may be quite the opposite of unions. Several employers want to get rid of the manufacturing norm not to increase wages *more* – as unions desire – but *less*.

By the SIF-HTF merger into *Unionen* the private service sector has attained strong representation in Unions in Manufacturing. The hitherto leading union in this group, *IF Metall*, in 2008 criticised LO's priority of low-paid women. Most of these are employed in private services and public sector in contrast to the male-dominated *IF Metall* (Table 2). It is true that women-dominated Commercial Employees' Union (LO) succeeded relatively well in the 2007 round, but it should be observed that the *IF Metall* members have much better prospects than commercial employees to compensate rising inflation by local negotiations and wage drift. Probably not by chance, the Commercial Employees' Union demanded substantial wage increases in a business cycle favourable to wage drift and a prospering trade sector. Despite the tight labour market many unions in 2007 paid great attention to increased minimum wages and individual guarantees. By that the decentralisation of the concrete contents of national agreements since the early 1990s was partly reversed. Unions now considered it important to heighten minimum wages in the absence of Swedish legislation in this respect and considering the EC court verdict in the Vaxholm/Laval case restricting the right to strike for the introduction of Swedish collective agreements in firms from other countries temporarily employing foreign workers in Sweden. Unions also had to respond to a growing discontent among rank-and-file members with the unsatisfactory results of local wage-setting. In 2008 the nurses union (TCO-affiliated) struck for for almost six weeks for this very reason. A third union argument for increased minimum wages was to neutralize the feared down-ward pressure on wages due to reduced benefit levels in the unemployment insurance.

In 2008 the Association of Swedish Engineering Industries, the largest SN-affiliate, proposed that Swedish minimum wages should be determined by the state. The main argument is to prevent unions from using minimum wages in collective agreements as an instrument to set the norm for foreign workers posted in Sweden. If so, minimum wages would be pressed upwards considerably as the wages actually paid to Swedish workers generally are far above the minimum level, which in the first place is aimed for young workers without much skills or experience. Despite that, Swedish minimum wages (by collective agreements) are higher than in other European countries (mostly by legislation). It is argued that increased minimum wages would cause a strong inflationary pressure.

16. A New Basic Agreement?

In recent years the Confederation of Swedish Enterprise (SN) has intensified its demands for legislation restricting conflict rights (a ban on sympathy conflicts and more). The employers regard unions as too powerful, at least in the short run. In a country heavily dominated by large transnationals such as Sweden, however, firms in the long run have superior power due to their capacity to move production abroad. Another employer demand is to abolish the Law on Employment Protection introduced in the 1970s. To the disappointment of SN the centre-right government in office since 2006 has refused to comply with any of these demands and declared that it prefers self-regulation to state regulation in industrial relations. From an employer perspective state regulation therefore seems to be closed as an option. This forms an important part of the explanation why SN in September 2007 invited LO and the white-collar PTK to negotiate a new basic agreement, replacing the 1938 Saltsjöbaden Agreement.

The prospects for success seem much better than in 1998 when deliberations between LO, TCO and SACO on an 'Alliance for Growth' collapsed (Kjellberg 2000: 559ff). The failed internal SN coordination in 2007 and the search for a model of wage formation that functions well in periods of tight labour markets and declining productivity (previously Swedish productivity had increased rapidly) make up a common basis for negotiations. Already in the summer of 2007 the LO president announced her willingness to meet the employers to find common solutions. While the employers seek re-regulated conflict rights and more flexible employment relations, LO and PTK demand improved adjustment possibilities for workers losing their jobs. In addition, the unions would like a much more positive employer attitude to Swedish collective agreements for foreign workers temporarily posted in Sweden. Supporting the Latvian company Laval financially in its complaints to Swedish unions, it was no surprise that SN welcomed the verdict of the EC court.

In contrast to the SN demands on new and changed legislation, LO's expressed interest in bi-partite talks in the summer of 2007 might be interpreted as a move to forestall legislation by the right-led government, or more correctly: in case a new right-led government would take office after the 2010 elections. The strategy of SN might be that LO is more prepared to make concessions under such a government than under a social democratic, as was the case during the collapsed talks in 1998 (social democrats were in office 1994–2006). Were the 2008 negotiations to fail, SN could then appeal to the government for the necessity of legislation. On the other hand, the employers would risk that a future social democratic government would change the legislation, i.e. the classical argument for self-regulation.

17. Union Density Decline

From an international perspective, union density in Sweden, Denmark and Finland is very high, about 70 per cent. In contrast to another Nordic country, Norway (with less than 55 per cent union density), unions in these countries have an important role in the administration of unemployment insurance. In Sweden union-run funds have a long history. That of the

Metalworkers' Union was founded in 1897 and was transformed into a state-supported fund in 1942. Fear of negative effects of state regulation delayed the decision to join the Swedish Ghent system, introduced in 1935 and reformed in 1941. As late as 1940 only about 20 per cent of LO members belonged to a *state-supported* unemployment fund (Edebalk 1996: 129). The widespread existence of union unemployment and conflict funds is an important component when explaining why Swedish union density increased so much in the 1920s, a decade of high unemployment and numerous labour conflicts.

On the other hand, the significance of union unemployment funds should not be exaggerated. Particularly in Sweden, a substantial and growing proportion of workers are affiliated to such funds without being union members (Kjellberg 2006). During the 1980s this phenomenon expanded among Swedish private sector white-collar workers. In the 1990s it spread to blue-collar workers and to public sector employees. In 2007 more than every seventh member of a union-led unemployment fund was not a union member.

To explain the high union density other characteristics of Nordic industrial relations also have to be taken into consideration, such as the combined centralisation and decentralisation and the high degree of self-regulation of industrial relations. The division into LO (blue-collar), TCO (white-collar) and SACO (university graduates) in Sweden has promoted the very high union density, on average about the same for blue-collar and white-collar workers: 74 and 73 per cent in 2007 (in private sector 70 and 65 per cent respectively).

Union density declined after the mid-1980s, only to rise again in the early 1990s when a very tight labour market turned into mass unemployment. The sharp shift to depression was followed by both rising union density and by an accelerated share of non-union members in unemployment funds. Besides the administration of such funds, Swedish unions in depressed times have another important function for membership recruitment. According to the Law on Employment Protection unions are assigned the task of negotiating in case of redundancies.

Since the mid-1990s Swedish union density has declined, particularly among young workers (Table 4). A contributory factor is that every second worker aged between 16 and 24 today has a temporary job compared to every third worker fifteen years ago. Changed attitudes are also part of the picture.

Table 4. Union density by age in Sweden 1990–2007 (%)

Age	1990	1993	2000	2006	2007	1990–2007	1993–2007	2006–2007
16–24	62	69	52	46	40	−22	−29	−6
25–9	78	81	74	68	64	−14	−17	−4
Sum 16–29	69	76	64	58	53	−16	−23	−5
30–44	85	86	82	77	74	−11	−12	−3
45–64	88	89	88	85	82	−6	−7	−3
Sum 16–64	81	85	81	77	73	−8	−12	−4

Note. Employed workers' yearly averages. Full-time students working part-time excluded. Labour force surveys.

Looking at the average density a substantial part of its decline before 2007 – in all about 0 to 1 percentage points per year – was caused by the shrinking employment share in manufacturing industry and the public sector. In the span of one single year, 2007, union density declined almost four percentage points (from 77 to 73 per cent), which is quite unique in modern Swedish history (we have to go back to 1909 to find a larger decline) and extreme also by international standards. The size of the decline cannot be explained by anything other than the profound changes in the unemployment insurance introduced by the centre-right government in 2007. Unemployment funds were ordered to finance a larger part of benefits, and they therefore had to raise their fees considerably. In 2006 fund members paid 90–100 SEK per month (10 SEK is valued at one euro). From January 2007 most fees rose to about 340–70 SEK a month. Due to the abolition of tax reduction, the net increase was even higher. Large numbers of members experienced a six fold net increase, often from about 60 SEK (100 SEK with 40 per cent tax reduction) to about 360 SEK (with no tax reduction). The considerably increased fund fees have caused massive membership losses in both unions and funds. The union-led funds lost almost twice as many members (10 per cent of members) as the unions (6 per cent). Blue-collar funds and unions in private services have been particularly hard hit. In general their members pay the highest fund fees while the wages are among the lowest in the labour market. Conversely, the members of the 'academic' SACO unions, many of which are at the top of the wage scale, have to pay considerably less. A new phenomena is the rapidly growing share of union members standing outside unemployment funds, some because they cannot afford paying high fees, while others believe the risk of becoming unemployed is sufficiently remote.

The precise rise in the fund fee depends on the rate of unemployment among its members. The goal is to force unions to moderate their wage claims. During the period 1989–2006 the funds redistributed membership fees in a solidaristic way. Together with the high degree of state subsidies, this meant that virtually no connection existed between fees and rate of unemployment among the members of a fund (Holmlund and Lundborg 1999: 403). The government changed this in 2007 by abolishing the redistribution system and considerably increasing fund fees, particularly in industries hit by high unemployment. The Swedish economists Bertil Holmlund and Per Lundborg argue that unemployment-related fund fees would fit well as a 'policy that raises the marginal cost of wage increases' which would be 'unambiguously good for employment' (Holmlund and Lundborg 1999: 413). The idea is that by pressing unions to lower their wage demands more jobs would be created. A more direct effect of decreased government support to unemployment funds can also be discerned. In a Ghent system the degree of state subsidies to the insurance is denoted as 'one of the crucial factors' influencing union density. Decreased subsidies would have a negative impact on union membership and consequently result in more moderate wage increases by influencing the power of balance between the labour market parties. Conversely, heavily subsidised Ghent systems 'always raises the unionisation rate' and weakens wage moderation (or increases wage pressure) (Holmlund and Lundborg 1999: 412).

To sum up, a less state subsidised system and higher fund fees would (1) deter trade unions from high wage claims, and (2) *de facto* weaken unions not applying such behaviour as they will lose members as a result of increased fund fees. The implicit assumption is that union fees in a Ghent system have to increase about as much as fund fees. Usually fund fees are included in union dues, but from 2007 some unions have separated them. In a 2005 bill submitted by the party dominating the government ('the Moderates') the logic is formulated as: 'Less generous conditions in the insurance will in addition make it more costly for a trade union to pursue wage claims which might cause unemployment among its members' (*Politik för arbete och välfärd*: 44). By introducing such mechanisms the state thus want to confront unions with the choice between moderate wage claims or losing members. Hitherto massive membership losses have occurred, while other effects of this variant of state regulated wage formation are harder to discern. Even the government's own 'Fiscal Policy Council', headed by professor Lars Calmfors, in 2008 characterised the changed financing of the unemployment insurance as a failure as it provides little incentive for restraint in wage formation and as many unemployed will be left without coverage in the next economic slowdown. A possible future effect of the reform, not mentioned by the council, concerns the development of union density. Under previous periods of high unemployment Swedish union density in general has increased. With fund fees linked to the rate of unemployment, the next recession might have an opposite effect or at least curb union growth.

18. The Swedish Model at the Crossroads

As is evident from this chapter, the Swedish model of industrial relations is facing severe challenges, but there are also prospects for revitalisation. The accelerated decline of union density might in the long run undermine the legitimacy of the Swedish model in which collective agreements play a prominent role. Despite the absence of extension mechanisms the coverage of collective contracts is very high. If the steep fall in unionisation is not halted, it might be impossible to maintain either the high collective agreement coverage or the Swedish model of labour market regulation. Already before 2007 the share of workers covered by collective agreements declined: from 94 per cent in 2005 to 92 per cent in 2007. Among private sector workers the share fell from 90 to 87 per cent.

Other challenges facing unions is the outcome of the Vaxholm/ Laval case. The restricted conflict rights regarding collective agreements for foreign workers posted in Sweden might help undermine the coverage of collective agreements. Not by chance, the Confederation of Swedish Employers (SN) welcomed the verdict of the EC court. SN increasingly has been demanding a ban on sympathy conflicts and other restrictions on conflict rights.

On the other hand, both unions and employers have a common interest in a wage formation process that functions smoothly both in tight labour markets and recessions. The 1997 Industry Agreement demonstrated the vitality of the Swedish model of self-regulation. The possibility that the 2008 negotiations for a new basic agreement will be successful cannot be precluded.

Note. This chapter was written with financial support from the Swedish Council for Working Life and Social Research (project: Union Density in Global Perspective).

Abbreviations

LO	*Landsorganisationen* (Swedish Confederation of Trade Unions)
Metall	*Svenska Metallindustriarbetareförbundet* (Swedish Metalworkers' Union)
PTK	*Privattjänstemannakartellen* (Federation of Salaried Employees in Industry and Services), later: *Förhandlings- och samverkansrådet* (Council for Negotiation and Cooperation)

SACO *Sveriges Akademikers Centralorganisation* (Swedish Confederation of Professional Associations)
SAF *Svenska Arbetsgivareföreningen* (Swedish Employers' Confederation)
SIF *Svenska Industritjänstemannaförbundet* (Swedish Union of Clerical and Technical Employees in Industry)
SN *Svenskt Näringsliv* (Confederation of Swedish Enterprise)
TCO *Tjänstemännens Centralorganisation* (Swedish Confederation of Professional Employees)
VF *Sveriges Verkstadsförening* (Swedish Engineering Employers' Association)

Suggested Reading

Andersson, S. (1990) *Mellan Åkarp och Saltsjöbaden*, Stockholm: Almqvist and Wiksell International.

Arbetsstatistik E:I, Stockholm 1909.

De Geer, H. (1976) 'Arbetsfreden i Sigtuna', *Scandia* vol. 2.

—— (1986) *SAF i förhandlingar*, Stockholm: SAF.

Edebalk, P. (1996) *Välfärdsstaten träder fram*, Lund: Arkiv.

Elvander, N. (2002a) 'The New Swedish Regime for Collective Bargaining and Conflict Resolution: A Comparative Perspective', *European Journal of Industrial Relations* 8: 197–216.

—— (2002b) 'The Labour Market Regimes in the Nordic Countries: A Comparative Analysis', *Scandinavian Political Studies* 25: 117–37.

Ericksen, E. (1932) 'Scandinavian Employers and Collective Labour Agreements', *International Labour Review* 26(5): 676–91.

Fahlbeck, R. (2002) 'Industrial Relations and Collective Labour Law: Characteristics, Principles and Basic Features', in Wahlgren, P. (ed) *Stability and Change in Nordic Labour Law*, Stockholm: Almqvist and Wiksell International.

Flink, I. (1978) *Strejkbryteriet och arbetets frihet*, Stockholm: Almqvist and Wiksell International.
Göransson, H. (1988) *Kollektivavtalet som fredspliktsinstrument*, Stockholm: Juristförlaget.
Hadenius, A. (1976) *Facklig organisationsutveckling*, Uppsala: Statsvetenskapliga föreningen.
Holmlund, B. and Lundborg, P. (1999) 'Wage Bargaining, Union Membership and the Organisation of Unemployment Insurance', *Labour Economics* 6: 397–415.
Höglund, S. (1978) *Storföretagen, Svenska Arbetsgivareföreningen och beslutsordningen i arbetarnas fackliga organisationer*, Umeå: Department of Sociology.
Johansson A. L. (1989) *Tillväxt och klass-samarbete*, Stockholm: Tiden.
Kjellberg, A. (1981) 'Från industriell demokrati till medbestämmande', *Arkiv* no. 21–2.
——(1983) *Facklig organisering i tolv länder*, Lund: Arkiv.
——(1992) 'Sweden: Can the Model Survive?' in Ferner, A. and Hyman, R. (eds) *Industrial Relations in the New Europe*, Oxford: Blackwell.
——(1998) 'Sweden: Restoring the Model?' in Ferner, A. and Hyman, R. (eds) *Changing Industrial Relations in Europe*, 2nd Ed., Oxford: Blackwell.
——(2000) 'The Multitude of Challenges Facing Swedish Trade Unions', in Waddington, J. and Hoffmann, R. (eds) *Trade Unions in Europe*, Brussels: ETUI.
——(2001) *Fackliga organisationer och medlemmar i dagens Sverige*, Lund: Arkiv.
——(2006) 'The Swedish Unemployment Insurance – Will the Ghent System Survive?' *Transfer* 12:1.
——(2007) 'The Swedish Trade Union System in Transition: High but Falling Union Density', in Phelan, C. (ed.) *Trade Union Revitalisation: Trends and Prospects in 34 Countries*, Oxford: Peter Lang.
——(2008) 'Ett nytt fackligt landskap bland tjänstemännen', *TAM-Revy* no. 1.
Kuuse, J. (1986) *Strukturomvandlingen och arbetsmarknadens organisering*, Stockholm: SAF.

LO (1951) *Fackföreningsrörelsen och den fulla sysselsättningen*, Stockholm.
Lundh, C. (2002) *Spelets regler*, Stockholm: SNS.
Lysgaard, S. (1985) *Arbeiderkollektivet*, Oslo: Universitetsforlaget.
Nycander, S. (2002a) 'När liberalerna kämpade för facket', *Arena* no. 5:38–41.
——(2002b) *Makten över arbetsmarknaden*, Stockholm: SNS.
Meidner, R. (1974) *Samordning och solidarisk lönepolitik*, Stockholm: Prisma.
Politik för arbete och välfärd (2005–6) Bill to Riksdagen (m010).
Saltsjöbadsavtalet 50 år (1989) Stockholm: Arbetslivscentrum.
Schiller, B. (1967) *Storstrejken 1909*, Göteborg: Akademiförlaget.
——(1988) *Det förödande 70-talet*, Stockholm: Allmänna Förlaget.
Shorter, E. and Tilly, C. (1974) *Strikes in France 1830–1968*, Cambridge: Cambridge University Press.
Söderpalm, S.A. (1980) *Arbetsgivarna och Saltsjöbadspolitiken*, Stockholm: SAF.
Therborn, G. (1983–4): 'The Coming of Swedish Social Democracy', Milano: 'Annali' della Fondazione Giangiacomo Feltrinelli.
Thörnqvist, C. (1999) 'The Decentralization of Industrial Relations: The Swedish Case in Comparative Perspective', *European Journal of Industrial Relations* 5: 71–87.

Trade Unionism in Britain since 1945

KEITH LAYBOURN

1. Introduction

British trade unionism grew rapidly during World War II, its membership increasing from 6,053,000 in 1938 to 7,803,000 by 1945. Subsequently it expanded to a 1979 peak of over thirteen million members (12,128,708 affiliated, TUC *Report* 1971: 1), more than half the workforce. The Labour Party, which formed the immediate postwar Labour governments under Clem Attlee, ostensibly represented trade union interests even if the relationship was a 'contentious alliance' (Minkin 1991). As a result, jointly with employers and the governments, trade unionism helped shape policies in British society (Middlemass 1980). Yet, since the late 1970s trade union membership has declined by almost half despite an increasing workforce, as Labour governments have attempted to contain strikes and wages, as Margaret Thatcher, the Conservative Prime Minister, challenged trade union power, and as the emergence of a global economy has meant a shift from industrial production to service industries. As a result trade union membership now hovers around seven or eight million (the TUC claiming around 6.5 million members since 2004) and unions represent less than 30 per cent of the total workforce in public services and only about 20 per cent of those in the private sector. This has been the counter revolution of our time. In addition the Labour Party, defeated in four general elections between 1979 and 1992, was forced to re-assess its relationship with the trade unions, hoping to maintain the connection whilst reducing trade union influence in an attempt to democratise the party and distance itself from trade union militancy that blighted its fortunes in the 1970s and 1980s. Thus the majority of workers in Britain in 2008 are no longer represented by trade unions and collective bargaining as they were before the 1980s, and trade unions no longer exert the political influence they once held. In modern industrial relations it is the government, the EEC, community campaigns and even the Citizen's Advice Bureau who between them are as likely as trade unions to represent the workers and defend them in the workplace (Abbott 2004).

The implications of these fundamental changes are dramatic because they mean that collective bargaining with trade unions impinges on management much less than it once did and because there is an obvious gap in industrial representation for workers. If trade union influence declines then it is clear that other bodies will become increasingly important in a workplace which is rapidly changing and littered with New Labour partnership agreements between workers and employers as well as individual rather than collective arrangements. There is no guarantee, then, that workers will be as effectively and collectively represented as they were in the 1950s and 1960s. It is always possible that trade unions might recover some of their former influence but if they do so then it will be in a very different political and industrial climate than that which prevailed between 1945 and the late 1970s. The changes of the 1980s have challenged the TUC and trade unions to respond, to become far more attuned to the new American-style management system, to be significantly less confrontational, more legalistic and increasingly inclined to offer their members a wider range of services. Nevertheless, the trade unions and the Labour Party still hold to the belief that they are bonded by the traditional roots of the past. Indeed, in 2005 Tony Dubbin and Ian McCartney of the Joint Chairs of National Trade Union and Labour Party Liaison (TULO) Organisation – a product of the Trade Union For Labour (TUFL) organisation and campaign that emerged after Labour's general election defeat in 1987, to pump funds into the Party and provide up to £5,000 for each parliamentary by-election – emphasised that the 'financial and organisational support of the trade unions was central to the historic accomplishment' of a third consecutive

Labour government.[1] Yet the strong links between Labour and the trade unions are not what they once were as the Labour Party has adjusted in the 1990s to a more democratic voting system that reduced the power of the trade union block vote in the local constituency parties, at conference and in leadership contests.

2. An Outline of Industrial Relations and Trade Unionism, 1945–79

After World War II British trade unions enjoyed better relations with the British state than they ever enjoyed during the interwar years with the coal lockout and the General Strike of 1926, which directly affected about three million trade unionists. In contrast, trade unions leaders and particularly Ernest Bevin, the wartime Minister of Labour, had been an integral part of the political and industrial arrangement in Britain that had won the war. In 1945 trade unions saw their governments, the Clem Attlee Labour governments of 1945 to 1951, run the nation. Despite problems trade unions showed enormous restraint in the pursuit of wage increases until at least the devaluation of the pound by more than 30 per cent in 1949. Strike levels had been low up to that point but tensions grew thereafter. Even then, in 1949 and 1950, the number of industrial disputes fell dramatically. Whilst there had been 2205 disputes involving 531,000 workers in 1946, with days lost numbering 2,835,000, there were only 1,339 strikes involving 302,000 workers and 1,389,000 days lost in 1950. It was not until the 1990s that the number of days lost through strike action was ever that low again (Wrigley 1997: 24).

1 *General Election 2005. The TULO Strategy Delivered* in the TULO Box, unlisted. The Labour History Study and Archive Centre, 103 Princes Street, Manchester. There is a large number of unlisted boxes on this material and that of the Trade Union For Labour (TUFL) in the archive.

The Conservative Party also adopted a more tolerant attitude to the trade union movement. R.A. Butler chaired the Party's Industrial Committee in 1947 and produced *The Industrial Charter* which offered a 'Worker's Charter' setting out good practice for employers in their relations with workers. This re-emerged in the 1950 general election when the Conservatives undertook to enforce their commitments once in power. Following the Conservative Party's general election success of 1951, Winston Churchill, the new Prime Minister, decided that he would adopt a tolerant attitude towards trade unionism by appointing William Monckton, a moderate political figure, as Minister of Labour. Churchill himself established good relations with Vincent Tewson, then General Secretary of the Trades Union Congress, and the Conservative government attached trade union representatives to even more consultative committees than even Attlee has done (Campbell et al. 1999a; Wrigley 1997).

The political consensus that sought to maintain good relations between government and the trade unions continued under the Conservative premiership of Sir Anthony Eden (1955–7) and Harold Macmillan (1957–63). They were 'One Nation Tories' who wished to maintain the alliance between the government, employers and trade unionists. However, there were already signs emerging that this commitment to good relations, and the consequent pledge to full employment, was under threat from a rising concern to control inflation. Indeed, in June 1958 the Inns of Court Conservative Unionist Society published a study entitled *A Giant's Strength* which emphasised the need for measures to control wage rises, some of which emerged in the 1960s and others of which emerged in the ill-fated Industrial Relations Act of 1971 (Wrigley 1997).

There were other signs that the postwar consensus on full employment, social reform and free collective bargaining was beginning to be challenged. On 6 January 1958 Peter Thorneycroft, the Chancellor of the Exchequer, Enoch Powell, Financial Secretary to the Treasury, and Nigel Birch, Economic Secretary to the Treasury, all resigned from Macmillan's Cabinet which had refused to keep down government expenditure. Such an action would of course have challenged the consensus with trade unions by raising unemployment, reducing social expenditure and curbing wage rises. The views of the Thorneycroft rebels were, ultimately, to become dominant when Thatcher became Conservative leader in 1975 and then prime minister between 1979 and 1990, but in the 1950s they could not be tolerated by Macmillan whose ruthlessness in politics earned him the accolade 'Mac the Knife'.

Between 1961 and 1979, trade unions in Great Britain were greatly affected by the prices and incomes policies administered by both Conservative and Labour governments. This period started with Selwyn Lloyd's July 1961 'pause' in rises in wages and salaries. As Chancellor of the Exchequer, Lloyd reported to the House of Commons on the final report on the Council on Prices, Productivity and Incomes, which asserted that Britain was increasing incomes whilst productivity was lagging. The pause was to be the basis of a new long-term policy: 'That policy is that increases in incomes must follow and not precede or outstrip increases in national productivity.'[2] This pay pause was applied for nine months to the public sector alone. There had been similar pay blocks in the past although they had always been applied to small groups of workers. However, in the wake of this pay pause, the government set up a tripartite forum composed of government, employers and the trade union. It was known as the National Economic Development Council, or 'Neddy'. Its purpose was to advise government in its efforts to adopt long-term planning. 'Neddy' met for the first time on 7 March 1962 to discuss ways 'to increase the rate of sound growth'.[3] The government also announced the formation of the National Incomes Commission in 1962, known as 'Nicky', to offer impartial advice on profits and productivity (Laybourn 1992; Wrigley 1997).

George Woodcock, General Secretary of the TUC between 1960 and 1969, hoped that 'Neddy' would be a forum for the discussion of economic issues but was unwilling to allow it to challenge free collective bargaining. Nevertheless, successive governments generally made their own individual arrangements for controlling wages. The public sector was subject to a wage ceiling of between 2 and 2.5 per cent in 1962 and, later, Harold

2 *Parliamentary Debates*, Commons, 5th Series, 645, cc.222–3, 25 July 1961.

3 National Economic Development Council (1963), *Growth of the United Kingdom Economy 1961–1966*, London, HMSO, viii.

Wilson's Labour governments set a voluntary wages and prices agreement between 1964 and 1966 before imposing a statutory policy from 1966 to 1970. Under the voluntary agreement a pay norm of 3.5 per cent was set in April 1965 and special cases were put to the short-lived National Board of Prices and Incomes.

In July 1966 a sterling crisis led to a six-month pay freeze and a statutory prices and incomes policy. After that there was a period where only a small number of exceptional cases were allowed increases on grounds of productivity. The policy was relaxed in August 1968 and abandoned in January 1970 (Laybourn 1992).

Edward Heath's Conservative government of 1970–4 intended not to use an incomes policy but hoped to control public pay rises through the 1971 Industrial Relations Act. Heath's government also attempted to apply a year on year reduction in pay rises of one per cent and use the National Industrial Relations Act, set up by the 1971 Act, to enforce agreements it arranged with the threat of fines of between £5,000 and £100,000. This policy was shattered by the coal mining dispute of 1972, giving rise to power shortages and leading to the three-day week and the 1972 dockers' strike. Subsequently Heath's policy became far more complex (Laybourn 1992: 190–8). Between November 1972 and April 1973 Stage One was a freeze on pay, prices, profits and dividends. Stage 2 from April until November 1973 allowed wage increases from £1 per week (a flat rate sum to help the lower paid) plus 4 per cent up to a maximum of £250. Stage Three from November 1973 allowed increases of up to 7 per cent of the total pay for a group of employees, for each person £2.25 per week or 7 per cent up to a maximum of £350 per annum. On top of this there was a 1 per cent margin allowed for productivity rises, sick pay schemes and holiday entitlement and threshold agreements which gave increases of 40 pence per week for each percentage point that the Retail Price Index rose above 7 per cent. This scheme was wrecked by a further miners' strike in 1973 and 1974 which led to Heath's general election defeat in 1974. What consensus seemed to exist in national policy-making was beginning to break down (Campbell et al. 1991b).

The new Labour government led by Harold Wilson (1974–6) and James Callaghan (1976–9) was also faced with curbing wage inflation. The

Wilson administration removed the hostile 1971 Act and introduced some social reform but found that the economic crisis, which led it to apply to the International Monetary Fund for a loan in 1976, undermined its ability to follow through with increased social expenditure for the poorer members of society. As a result the 'social contract' it operated with the trade unions, ostensibly curbing trade union wage demands in return for government social expenditure, soon proved worthless. Phase One, operating between July 1975 and July 1976, limited pay to £6 per week maximum with no increase for those earning more than £8,500 per year. Phase Two from July 1976 to July 1977 allowed for increases of 5 per cent with a £2.50 per week minimum increase and a £4 per week maximum. For 1977–8 the Callaghan government allowed up to a 10 per cent increase plus a self-financing productivity agreement and, for 1978–9, a maximum increase of 5 per cent. Denis Healey, Labour's Chancellor of the Exchequer, later admitted that he had set the figure too low and that this was responsible for the 'Winter of Discontent' of 1978–9.[4] This had begun with the Ford workers' strike of 24 August 1978 and climaxed with the one-day local authority workers' strike of 1,250,000 workers on 22 January 1979, although the more protracted grave diggers' strike in Liverpool produced the contentious and embarrassing newspaper headline that the dead might have to be 'Buried at Sea' (Campbell et al. 1999b; Laybourn 1992: 198–203).

The pattern of industrial relations in Britain had been one of voluntary collective bargaining until the 1960s and 1970s when governments intermittently attempted to impose controls and curb inflation with calamitous results. However, the law was already beginning to undermine the legal power of trade unions.

4 D. Healey (1989) *The Time of My Life*, London: Penguin, 398, 462.

3. The Law

Historically, the Trade Disputes Act of 1906, which had reversed the Taff Vale Judgement of 1901 and restored trade union immunity from prosecution in industrial disputes, had been replaced by the Trades Disputes Act of 1927 which took away the right of trade unions to take sympathetic strike action. However, unions still retained legal immunity for normal strike arrangements and in 1946 the right of sympathetic strike action was also restored. In 1964 all this was altered dramatically when the *Rookes v Barnard* case removed much of the immunity trade unions had enjoyed when calling strikes. This was followed by the House of Lords judgement in *Stratford v Lindley* which again challenged the right of sympathetic strike action.

These legal actions were supported by the Conservative and Unionist Party, then in government, which produced a pamphlet called *The Giant's Strength.* It criticised closed shops, restrictive practices, secondary strike action and demarcation disputes. The Labour Party responded by declaring that it would restore trade union immunity once in government, which it did with the 1965 Trades Dispute Act, and it examined the activities of trade unions and employers' associations through a royal commission chaired by Lord Donovan. The Donovan Report, published in 1968, suggested that industrial relations should continue to be dealt with by voluntary, not legal, means whilst aiming to reduce unofficial disputes by strengthening the power of the trade unions over local shop stewards.

Neither the Labour government nor the subsequent Conservative governments were happy with these suggestions. Harold Wilson had Barbara Castle, who was at the Department of Employment and Productivity, examined the Donovan recommendations and she produced a White Paper, *In Place of Strife* (1969), which sought to interfere with voluntary collective bargaining although it offered protection to workers against unfair dismissal. It was quickly rejected by the Trades Union Congress, now led by Victor Feather, an old Bradford friend of Castle. Its main recommendation was that strike ballots should be called before major disputes and that there should be conciliation pauses before minor disputes. The proposals were stopped by pressure imposed by trade unions on the Labour MPs and through the efforts of Robert Mellish who got the White Paper dropped at a Cabinet meeting on 17 June 1969 (Campbell et al. 1999b).

Although out of office the Conservative Party took *The Giant's Strength* and incorporated its main ideas into its pamphlet *Fair Deal at Work* (1968) which favoured a comprehensive legal structure whereby collective bargaining would be enforced by law, a sixty-day conciliation pause would be introduced, and compulsory ballots would have to be held in order to call strikes. It was this pamphlet which led to the Heath government's Industrial Relations Act of 1971, with its requirement of compulsory ballots for major strikes, voluntary registrations for trade unions and the possibility of individual trade unionists being imprisoned if they broke the law. It was an act that was rejected by both employers and trade unionists because they feared that it would lead to a worsening of industrial relations and, in any event, the miners' strike of 1972 and the release of the 'Pentonville Five' nullified its influence. The latter case had occurred in July 1972 when the National Industrial Relations Court (NIRC) ordered dockers to stop 'blacking' vehicles used by the Midland Cold Storage Company at Stratford in East London. Following a complex set of negotiations and NIRC decisions the dockers refused the order and five of them were arrested and jailed, an action that resulted in a national strike of 170,000 dockers which forced the government to release them within two days: 'No sooner were the dockers in Pentonville than the Official Solicitor appeared like a fairy godmother to "spring" then from jail and in the process to deal the Act a mortal blow' (Barber 1976: 2).

The Labour government withdrew the 1971 Act in 1974 and replaced it with the Trade Union and Labour Relations Act of 1974 and the Employment Act of 1975 which positively encouraged voluntary industrial relations within the context of the 'social contract'. The Labour government also sought to implement the Donovan Report. However, it did nothing about increasing worker participation in determining firms' industrial policy and it ignored the findings of a Committee of Inquiry under Lord Bullock set up to expand industrial democracy. In a climate of failure over the social contract Labour had returned the law on industrial relations to the pre-1971 situation where trade unions had legal immunity for strike action.

4. The Challenge of the Thatcher and Major Government, 1979–97

From the mid-1960s trade unionism has been on the defensive but it was to face even more pressure and a sharp reversal of fortunes during the Thatcher and Major governments of 1979 to 1997. Thatcher's new Conservative administration kept its distance from the trade unions and reduced the importance of the National Economic Development Council, 'Neddy', its monthly meetings being reduced to quarterly ones in 1984 before being eliminated after the 1992 general election. A raft of legislation on trade unions and employment law was introduced to reduce trade union power at a time when the Thatcher administration abandoned the idea of full employment and a comprehensive state welfare (Laybourn 1991).

A battery of Conservative economic and industrial strategies pounded the trade unions. The lack of commitment to full employment – which saw unemployment rise to well over three million, well above the 1.25 million it had inherited from Labour in 1979 – saw trade unions lose muscle in the labour market (TUC *Report* 1981:1). Furthermore, in 1988 young people (16 to 21) were removed from the protection of wages councils, which had emerged after the Trades Board Act of 1909, and these councils were themselves ended in 1993.

The Conservative Party's general election manifesto of 1979 declared the intention to weaken the closed shop arrangement (which required that everyone in a firm be a member of the ensconced union to gain a job), to confine picketing to those involved in a dispute, and to provide money for unions to hold secret ballots for union elections. But these were to be implemented in a step by step approach which Jim Prior, Secretary of State for Employment, admitted was geared to 'put the onus on the trade unions'.[5] This perhaps explain why Prior's Bill of 1980, which allowed union strike ballots to be paid out of public funds, was generally seen to be an innocuous measure (Wrigley 1997).

The Thatcherite challenge to existing industrial relations was slow to develop. Indeed, there was no immediate action to deal with the secondary picketing associated with the steel strike of January to April 1980. However, the 1980 Act divided the unions between those who supported the TUC embargo on using public money to finance strike ballots and those who did not. Yet the pace of action against the unions quickened under Norman Tebbit who replaced Prior and introduced the Employment Act of 1982 and the Trade Union Act of 1984, both of which broached the thorny question of the closed shop.

According to Tebbit the 1982 Act was 'my greatest achievement in government' and 'one of the principal pillars on which the Thatcher economic reforms have been built' (Tebbit 1991: 233–4). It banned the pre-entry closed shop but above all removed the trade union immunity from civil action for damages arising from strikes. The TUC held a special conference at Wembley in April 1982 to mount campaigns against the 1980 and 1982 employment acts and to oppose the use of public funds to finance strike ballots. In the wake of this, and the 1982 Act, the Conservative government published a Green Paper in January 1983, a consultative document entitled *Democracy in Trade Unions*, which became the basis of the 1984 Trade Union Act. This Act gave legal immunity to trade unions if they held a secret ballot before a strike, demanded ballots every five years for the principal voting members of trade union executive committees, and required ballots to be held every ten years in order to establish or continue with political funds.

Such legislation tended to be counter-productive and galvanise trade union opposition. Indeed, despite the 1984 Act most of the ballots supported strike action and 52 of the 53 unions that held ballots on political funds voted in favour of them; a further 20 unions also held ballots and agreed to establish political funds for the first time (Taylor 1993: 300).

5 J. Prior (1987) *A Balance of Power*, London, 158.

It was in this context of anti-trade union legislation that many union strike battles, including the coal miner's strike of 1984–5, were lost. The fight against pit closures had begun 9 March 1984 at pits in Yorkshire and Scotland where notification of pit closures had been made. It occurred without the holding of a national strike ballot, involved the National Union of Mineworkers (NUM) sending out 'flying' pickets from Yorkshire to Scotland and Kent, and led to mass picketing and violence, most notably at Ollerton in Nottinghamshire, and later at the Orgreave coke plant. The law was used against the NUM, most notably on 14 March 1984 when a High Court injunction was granted to stop the flying pickets, though the National Coal Board chose not to use it. Later court actions led to the sequestration of union funds. The full power of the law was used against the miners and they were finally forced to return to work on 3 March 1985. It was clear that the Conservative government was winning the battle with trade unions.

Just before the 1987 general election the Conservative government issued a Green Paper, *Trade Unions and Their Members* (1987) which referred to the miners' strike of 1984–5 and the right of trade union members not to be intimidated by threats from union leaders. Then Thatcher, following her third successive general election victory in 1987, pressed forward with new trade union legislation, and most particularly the 1988 Employment Act which, whilst it was clothed in terms of the rights of individual members, was in fact designed to inhibit the right to take industrial action. The Employment Acts of 1989 and 1990 followed up this attack, the latter effectively outlawing trade union closed shops and secondary strike action.

John Major replaced Thatcher as Prime Minister in 1990 and, after his 1992 general election victory, introduced a range of other measures which impacted industrial relations, including the 1993 Trade Union Reform and Employment Rights Act. Another Green Paper, *Industrial Action and Trade Unions*, published in November 1996, also advocated a new batch of proposals which would have seen the immunity of trade unions removed and courts deciding whether or not a strike was disproportionate in its impact upon the community. However, just as employers found the 1971 Industrial Relations Act to be an impediment in dealing with trade unions, the Confederation of British Industry and other employer organisations, often representing large firms, found that the proposals a danger in conducting organised voluntary industrial relations. They still preferred to deal with trade unions who could deliver agreements rather than with many individuals or small groups of workers. Despite the new legislation the Tory strategy, as was the case of the Labour strategy, remained committed to voluntary collective bargaining.

5. Thatcher's Reasons for Curbing Trade Union Power and the Decline of Trade Union Representation

The Thatcher revolution had been brought about by the driving desire to curb the trade union power that had humbled Heath's government in the early 1970s. Apart from the general ideological commitment to the right-wing policies of Frederich von Hayek and Milton Friedman the hostility to trade unionism was also partly fashioned by the writings of the Bow Group and also by Sir Keith Joseph's pamphlet *Solving the Union Problem as the Key to Britain's Recovery*. These endorsed the view that trade union power and strikes, along with the burden of the welfare state, had caused Britain's comparative economic decline after 1945. Britain's strike record has often been noted and historians have written about the 'British disease'. However, strike activity is by no means exclusive to the British and in fact there was little that was exceptional about strike rates in Britain. Indeed, Thatcher's attack on the unions was based on a false premise. The Donovan Commission (1965–8) examined the statistics of the International Labour Organisation and concluded that Britain was by no means the most strike-prone nation in the world. It stated that 'While this country has a comparatively large number of stoppages, they are of fairly short duration and do not usually involve very large numbers of people.' The principal concern was that the majority of strikes were unofficial, not supported by the trade unions. 'Over these three years (1964–66) each unofficial strike involved an average of 300 workers and lasted a little over 2 and one half days. By contrast each official strike involved an average approximately 1370 workers, lasted nearly three times as long, and caused the loss of over twelve times as many working days' (Donovan 1968: paragraphs 365, 368, 96–7).

The *Ministry of Labour Gazette,* the *Department of Employment Gazette*, and the *International Labour Office Year Book,* further established that Britain was in the intermediate level of strike action in the 1950s and 1960s, falling to the lower levels of strike action from the 1970s onwards (Wrigley 1997: 24–5). It is true that the number of strikes in Britain and the number of days lost more than doubled in the 1970s but in many other countries, such as Australia, Canada, Italy and the US, the per capita incidence of strikes was higher. The fact is that Britain was not a particularly strike-prone economy and that strikes represented only a small proportion of the days of work lost by industry. Indeed, Richard Hyman has estimated that in 1970, a high point of strike activity in Britain, only ten million working days were lost due to strike activity, while 20 million days were lost through industrial accidents and 300 million days were lost because one million people were unemployed (Hyman 1992: 33–4). Strikes contributed to the problems of British industry but constituted only a small part to Britain's loss of productivity. Notwithstanding this evidence, the Thatcher onslaught was based upon the impression, cultivated by the 'Winter of Discontent', that trade union strike action was bringing Britain to its knees.

The impact of the Thatcher attack was dramatic; the 13,289,000 trade unionists of 1979 declined to 8,089,000 in 1995. The figures are now even lower, with the TUC currently claiming about 6,500,000 members. Trade union density for men (trade unions as a proportion of the male workforce) fell considerably from 63.1 per cent in 1979 to 34.6 per cent on 1995 – although that for women did rise from 34.5 per cent to 39.5 per cent in the same years (Wrigley 1997: 24). The anti-trade union legislation of the Conservative government has clearly been responsible for much of this decline by undermining the notion that workers had to be represented by a trade unionism. Yet other factors were also at work.

First, the old staple industries – such as cotton, coal mining and engineering – which often had 80 per cent or more of the workforce in a trade union – have declined since World War II and even more rapidly since the 1980s. This is also true of some of the light and new industries of the 1930s, such as the car industry, where new machinery and control by foreign companies have combined to weaken trade union organisation by reducing the power of the labour force. Secondly, this decline of the old large blue-collar industries has led to the fragmentation and disaggregation of the working class. In a more complex industrial society the unity of the blue-collar workers is obviously far less formidable than it once was (Hyman 1992: 150–68). Thirdly, the composition of the working class has therefore changed. White-collar occupations have been expanding since 1960, and by 1979 about 40 per cent of the workforce was white collar, and about 44 per cent were members of trade unions. In other words, only a minority of white-collar workers deemed it necessary to join a trade union compared with the declining older staple industries where the percentage of organised workers in the twentieth century had traditionally been much higher. In addition, a weakened trade union movement operating in a fluid labour market where individualism has become more important than collectivism has led to a move from multi-employer to plant-level bargaining (Hyman 1992: 150–68).

6. The Trades Union Congress Response to the Challenge

Faced with the Thatcher challenge to trade unionism Len (Lionel) Murray, TUC General Secretary (1973–84), said that 'The TUC will find its way to influence – just like a stream when blocked finds a new channel.' His successor Norman Willis (1984–93) was similarly optimistic, stating that 'It will be said of us that we did our best, and if we do it together it will be said we did our best and it was good enough' (Taylor 2000: 234). As time went on it became clear that this confidence was misplaced although the TUC has certainly made serious attempts to respond to the challenge of declining union influence.

Murray presided over attempts to make the 1970s 'social contract' succeed but he soon became convinced that the Labour government and the TUC should bargain with each other rather than relying on a cosy relationship. Such bargaining was evident in the late 1970s, particularly as trade unions became frustrated over pay; during the 'Winter of Discontent' of 1978–9 Murray was reluctant to accept the government's pay norm of 5 per cent imposed upon his members. Yet both the government and the TUC feared a political backlash and issued a joint statement insisting upon their future intent to improve their mutual understanding of each other's position in the hope that such conflict could be avoided (TUC *Report* 1979: 1–2). The statement was issued too late to stem the tide of reaction against both trade unionism and the Labour government; in March 1979 a parliamentary vote of no confidence in the Labour government led to a general election in May 1979 in which Thatcher triumphed.

At first the TUC did not fear the Thatcher government: 'We simply did not believe what she said she would do and we didn't believe that most Conservatives did either.'[6] Murray later admitted that the TUC had completely misjudged the moment in not recognising that Thatcher represented a mood-swing against trade unionism in Britain which had been strengthened by the 'Winter of Discontent'. The TUC thus failed to react adequately to the actions of the Thatcher government until it formed a fund to defend unions against the 1982 Act and held a one-day conference at Wembley in the spring of 1982 to indicate its non-co-operation with government legislation. After the Labour defeat in the general election of 1983, however, Murray introduced a 'New Realism' into his speech at the TUC Conference in 1983. He stressed the need for the TUC and its affiliates to recapture the lost ground and to listen more carefully to the needs of its members (TUC *Report* 1983: 464).

This 'New Realism' became evident shortly afterwards when the TUC refused to give backing to the National Graphical Association in its dispute with the *Stockport Messenger*. Subsequently, the coal mining strike of 1984–5 saw the TUC giving general support to the National Union of

6 *The Observer*, 2 September 1984.

Mineworkers but it is clear that Arthur Scargill, the miners' leader, was in any case reluctant to make the association closer for fear of losing control of the dispute to the TUC.

When Norman Willis replaced Murray as General Secretary in September 1984, the TUC membership was declining rapidly in the new hostile environment. Willis failed to exert much influence in the year-long miners' dispute and was present when the tripartite arrangement of the NEDC, 'Neddy', was finally laid to rest by the Major government in the autumn of 1992. Tebbitt had wanted its demise rather earlier and recalled in his memoirs that 'Somehow that old corporatist tripartite forum escaped the axe, much to my personal irritation as I detested wasting a morning in an agony of boredom when I had better things to do' (Tebbit 1991: 164). Despite criticisms of his weak leadership, Willis began a Special Review process for trade union policies in 1987, following up with more initiatives at the TUC Conference in 1988. Under Willis the TUC certainly lost prestige, confidence and some direction but it was striving to confront the new industrial challenges and it did retain some influence on the Advisory, Conciliation and Arbitration Service, the Health and Safety Commission, the Equal Opportunities Commission and the Commission for Racial Equality.

Indeed one should not underestimate the extent to which Willis presided over change. Representatives from the NEC of the Labour Party, the TUC and the Parliamentary Labour Party (including Tony Blair), set up a People at Work Review Group at the end of 1987. They decided to establish a workers' charter of rights as part of a programme which included the improvement of industrial relations through partnership between employers and employees. In the 1988 Draft Report partnership agreements were considered to be a 'vital component of economic efficiency'.[7] Also, the 1989 Labour Party Conference accepted 'A Charter of Rights for Employees' through its policy statement *Meet the Challenge Make the Change: A New Agenda for Britain*; which agreed to the introduction

7 Box LP/RD People at Work, PD 1526A/ May 1988, Draft Report, 5/4 at the Labour History Study and Archive Centre.

of a national minimum wage once Labour was in office and outlined the partnership agreements in industry that it wanted to establish. The TUC and the Labour Party examined a variety of partnership agreements in the late 1980s, and they have found favour at most TUC Congress meetings since 1996.

These developments occurred when the Labour Party, as part of its process of democratisation, set up a Review Group on the Link between Trade Unions and the Labour Party in 1991. It received numerous letters from constituency Labour parties (CLPs) wishing to retain the existing links with trade unions but facing a declining affiliation membership and fee income.[8] The Review Group soon grasped the true magnitude of the declining contribution of the trade unions. In 1949 there had been 80 unions with 4,946,000 members affiliated to the Labour Party as against 41,000 members from Socialist societies and 723,000 from CLPs. In 1979 there were 59 unions with 6,511,000 members affiliated to the TUC (about half the trade union membership), compared to about 54,000 affiliated members of socialist societies and 675,000 CLP members. But 1979 was the peak. By 1991 CLP affiliation was down to 261,000, Socialist society affiliation down to 54,000 and trade union membership affiliation down to 3,900,000. By 1996 trade union affiliation numbers were little more than 3,000,000. Because of declining CLP membership the influence of trade union membership on the Labour Party increased but the decline of trade union members led to a decline in the trade union contribution to the General Fund Income of the Labour: it was 88 per cent in 1978, 76 per cent in 1982 and 55 per cent in 1991.[9]

The Review Group, which included Tony Blair, published its final report in June 1992 and concluded that trade unions were varyingly under-represented and over-represented in different parts of the party structure

8 TU-LP Link Review Box, LPGS, not fully referenced, Labour History Labour History Study and Archive Centre.

9 Ibid., RG15, August 1992 JWL/RL rozry13, Draft Report on Trade Union Affiliation and the TUC, tables A, B and C. This was drawn up by Lewis Minkin, informed the Review Body, but does not seem to have been fully prepared until just after the Review Body reported to the party.

and that this had to be adjusted in order to reduce the power of the trade union block vote in leadership elections and at conferences. At the same time the Labour Party had to adjust as it became less dependent upon the trade unions.

The Low Pay Unit (LPU), an independent body organised by Chris Pond and partly funded by the London Borough Grants Committee, was a factor in this move to a more emollient TUC and trade union policy. It noted the government's *New Economic Survey, 1990* observation that 'nearly half the British workforce earned less than the LPU low pay threshold – showing the ever-widening divide between those at the bottom and those at the top of the earnings league.'[10] *The New Review,* and its sister journal *News Brief,* published by the LPU's Wages' Rights Office, campaigned strongly against low pay and in favour of a national minimum wage; opposition to the idea of a national minimum wage was led by *Conservative Pay News,* largely published by Michael Howard for the Conservative Party. Out of this debate it became clear that the trade unions were failing their members.

Willis was replaced as General Secretary of the TUC by John Monks (1993–2003), who was much more of an arch moderniser like Tony Blair. Monks announced his 'Campaign for Change' on 1 March 1994 (TUC *Report* 1994: 11). This included the commitment to re-arrange the membership of the General Council and the committees connected with the annual Women's Conference and the annual Black Workers' Conference. The underlying idea was to make the TUC more representative of the membership. At the 1996 TUC Congress Monks launched his 'New Unionism', in response to New Labour, stating that 'For seventeen years trade unions have been painted as part of Britain's problems. Our challenge is to prove that we are part of the solution,' adding that 'Trade unionism is at the crossroads' and 'Unless public policy changes and above all else unless we change we shall be forced down the road marked Retreat' (TUC *Report* 1996: 60; McIlroy 1995; McIlroy 1998). Monks supported the new partnership agreements advocated by New Labour, seeing partnership as a way of

10 *The New Review*, no. 7, December 1990/January 1991, p. 11.

promoting job security. Indeed, he reported to Tony Blair on 7 September 1999, repeating what he had written in the foreword to the TUC's document on partnership in April 1999: 'I endorse the clear message of the TUC that Britain works best when unions and employers work together (TUC 'Partners in Progress' April 1999).

Most trade unions, sometimes reluctantly, accepted the need for partnership agreements. What has helped the TUC to sell this new approach, however, has been the publication of the White Paper *Fairness at Work* in May 1998 by the Labour government which provided a raft of social reforms, including the statutory minimum wage and the £4 billion Welfare to Work programme. In April 1999 the Labour government introduced the £3.60 per hour national minimum recommended by the Low Pay Commission, even though this was far below what the trade unions wanted. This upset the TUC and the trade unions though not as much as the Labour government's insistence in the Employment Relations Act of July 1999 on the need for 40 per cent unionism in an agreed bargaining unit before unions could secure the recognition that would allow them to bargain for their members. This latter action annoyed Monks who berated the Labour government's reluctance to recognise trade unions and expressed criticisms at the June 1998 TUC's Fairness at Work Conference (Taylor 2000: 266). He complained that:

> We are cast in the role of stooge – to be used as a contrast to New Labour – not modern, not new or fashionable, old, in decline, in hock to sectarian politics which resonate with only a tiny proportion of the British people [...] There is little public acknowledgement of change in trade unions or of the positive partnership role of unions in raising standards of performance as well as terms and conditions of work.

In his lecture to the Manchester Statistical Society in February 1999, he emphasised the need to raise standards to gain security for the workers: 'everyone wants a sense of respect'. And in March 2000 a confident Monks stressed that 'We are in the best position for decades to start to grow once again. But it won't happen if we go on as we are' (Taylor 2000: 266–7).

7. British Trade Unionism: Crisis, Continuity and its Future in the Workplace

By the mid-1990s British trade unionism had lost its primacy in the workplace (Gallie et al. 1996). Collective bargaining had declined dramatically: 'by the end of the 1990s the official Labour Force Survey showed that only 44 per cent of employees were in a workplace where unions were recognised and only 36 per cent had their pay and conditions determined by collective bargaining' (Hyman 2001: 105).

The loss of trade union capacity to bargain voluntarily for the nation's workforce was the result of Thatcherite legislation, which made it difficult for trade unions to defend the rights of their members, the structural changes in the workforce, and the rising unemployment that occurred during the 1980s. There may be nothing inevitable about this decline and it may be reversible (Hyman 1992). However, whilst the TUC was looking towards reform and change, the responses of individual trade unions to the challenge were uneven and seem to have been more effective in public than in private industries (Fairbrother 2000: 336–7). It would also appear that New Labour's social partnership schemes are far from delivering the industrial and social benefits that were suggested.

There have been glimmers of hope though. A recent survey suggests that employers are still inclined towards trade union representation in the workplace, albeit less so than they were (Gallie et al. 1996). Employers in establishments of 25 to 500 employees have generally not changed their opinion on trade unions and approximately 40 to 50 per cent of them encouraged their own employees to join a trade union. Ominously, however, private industry employers in smaller establishments do not encourage trade unionism: a mere 17 per cent in firms with fewer than 25 employees encouraged trade union membership, compared to 47 per cent in firms employing between 200 and 499.

Trade unions have had to respond to this situation. The decline in trade union membership, the diversification of the labour market and employer resistance has forced them to be flexible in their recruiting activities, offering a variety of services including reductions on consumer goods, holidays and the like. What has emerged increasingly is the need to recruit workers with people of similar personal interests and age. In other words, young workers are increasingly being recruited and represented by young workers. There is a similar tendency for minority groups, such as minority ethnic women, to be recruited and represented by their own age and ethnic groups (Healy et al. 2004: 105).

Black and ethnic groups represented about 10 per cent of the British population in 2001 but were underrepresented in trade unions. By the early 1990s some efforts were being made to address this and by 2004 the black and ethnic numbers in trade unions had increased (Healy et al. 2004). Some unions, though not all, were making serious attempts to get both ethnic groups and women into trade union organisation. Case studies, based on interviews with 55 black women and ten union officers in the CWU (Communication Workers' Union), NATFHE (National Association of Teachers in Further and Higher Education) UNISON, and USDAW (Union of Shop, Distributive and Allied Workers) (Healy et al. 2004) have revealed some variable progress.

All four unions are affiliated to the TUC and send representatives to both the TUC Women's and Black Workers' Conference, yet women and black workers are not represented proportionally in any of the unions. CWU is a male-dominated union of 300,000 members of whom 21 per cent are female and 7 per cent black. Only 6 per cent of the Executive were women (Healy et al. 2004: 109). This was despite the fact that the TUC in 1980 had launched *The Black Workers' Charter*, and the Black Workers' Conference in 1993 had asked the TUC to assess the progress of black workers in the trade union movement. NATFHE with 65,000 members had 47 per cent female membership, 4 per cent black membership and 25 per cent women membership of the executive. UNISON, with 1,300,000 members had 72 per cent female membership, 10 per cent black membership, 58 per cent of women at conferences and 62 per cent on the executive. USDAW with 300,000 members, 60 per cent female and 5 per cent black, had 44 per cent female representation at conferences and 52 per cent of its executive was women. Recent research emphasises that many women still work in male-dominated environments, do not always get involved in union work and are not properly represented in the union structure (Healy et al. 2004).

It is clear that there are problems and contrasting cultures within the unions which have made it difficult for both women and ethnic groups to be effectively represented. The CWU attracts members from the Post Office, British Telephone, cable television, engineers, computer operators and other telephone companies and is male orientated with all that implies. Nevertheless, following the racist murder of Stephen Lawrence the CWU commissioned an inquiry, a transparently critical one as it turned out, into the state of race equality in the union (Healy et al. 2004: 110–11).

NATFHE has also gone down this route. Its National Executive Committee (before it merged with the university teachers union in 2006–7) had a national executive committee which included two black representatives, one lesbian or gay representative, and one from the disabled minority. Also at least 25 per cent of the NEC had to be female (Healy et al. 2004: 110). Following the formation of the Stephen Lawrence Task Group NATFHE appointed an officer to co-ordinate this group and became involved in the initiation of the Commission for Black Staff in Further Education with the Further Education Funding Council.

UNISON was formed in 1993 and is the largest trade union in the United Kingdom. It has 70 seats on its NEC. Election procedures ensure that at least 60 per cent of the NEC is composed of women, including 14 reserved seats for low-paid women. UNISON has 2000 local branches which deal with issues for women and black members, which are fed through to the Black Members or Women's National Conference. In mid-2001 there were two black women on the NEC (Healy et al. 2004: 111).

USDAW has had equality officers since 1985 and a National Race Relations Committee since 1991. It appointed a Women and Equalities Officer in 1999 with responsibility for black, gay, lesbian and disabled members' interests. However, there is still an uneven distribution of equality structures in USDAW.

Changes in trade union thinking, action and recruitment result from the need to widen their potential net, but trade unions must also accept that they are no longer in control of the workplaces and that they are increasingly dealing with globalised employers able to shift production from one country to another (Fairbrother 2000). Trade unionism will no doubt remain vital in many workplaces but it will be weaker in many and disappear altogether in others, and in many workplaces it will have to reconstitute itself in different forms.

Since 1979, then, trade unions have had to change tack. The pre-1939 class conflict model of trade unionism was replaced between 1945 and the 1970s by a model which involved the trade unions in national planning with government and employers at the national level. Despite the general equanimity of national discussions industrial relations at the company level often remained hostile and class based. Since the 1970s industrial relations have again changed dramatically; the composition trade union membership has changed, and there has been increasing emphasis on social partnership between unions and employers promising a shared stake in the success of the enterprise. The TUC in 1998 declared that 'Employers are now beginning to appreciate that as partners trade unions can add value to their business and business performance'.[11] However, recent surveys suggest that labour-management partnerships are a mixed bag; there are opportunities for some progress in the services industries but they have undermined workers' interests in the aircraft industry.

In the aircraft industry partnership in high-performance work systems involve greater organisational flexibility, working in self-managed teams and, so it is argued, jobs are designed to make them intrinsically more interesting for the individual (Danford et al. 2004: 167). Yet, despite innovations which focus upon the employees

> ... there is little evidence of two-way communications of employee influence over decision-making that affected their working lives. Instead, in what some interviewees described as a climate of fear, we found consistent managerial opposition to meaningful employee participation and more than this, a pattern of exclusion from discussions and decisions that implicate job security and employee futures (Danford et al. 2004: 185).

11 This as a statement made by Bill Connor of the shopworkers' union USDAW; Connor later became chair of the TUC Social Partnership Task Group.

In other words, the promised 'social cohesion' was largely rhetorical. Whilst employees delivered their part of the bargain, the employers did not. The implication is that in this age of globalisation it is militant trade unionism, not partnership that is required in order that employers and employees share the rewards of industry fairly. Some evidence suggests that the partnerships may be useful where they are 'shallow partnerships', often in the service industries, but even here the benefits are often intangible and may serve more to revitalise unions (Oxenbridge and Brown 2004: 187–206).

Further evidence also suggests that trade unions are not making significant advances in new expanding employment sectors despite trade union membership campaigns and the social partnership arrangements. Evidence of union growth in new areas is not encouraging. One study suggests that trade unionism among software workers in the information technology industry is declining rather than expanding, with membership density falling from 16 per cent to 12 per cent. Indeed, examining five anonymous small to medium-sized firms in Scotland one survey makes it is clear that only Beta, the largest with 275 employees, had union representatives (Hyman et al. 2004: 39, 44). The level of unionisation is higher amongst the more than half a million call-centre workers in Britain, although the varied nature of the industry means that there is immense variation and that unions have great difficulty organising these workers (Bain et al. 2004: 62–81).

Given that the majority of British workers are not now represented by trade unions, worker representation is no longer dominated by voluntary collective bargaining, reorganised trade unionism, or partnership agreements. Instead it is more likely that workers receive, and will continue to receive, some protection of their rights from other sources. In 1994 the European Court of Justice ruled that European Union information and consultation measures should apply to all employers whether or not they had trade union members. Employee representatives have now to be elected on particular issues, laws on the length of the working day and week have to be abided by, and, since 2007, employees have had the right to work beyond the age of 65 – although the British government modified this too at the behest of the employer not the employee. There have been European Union laws concerning redundancy since the mid-1970s, and ones concerning health and safety were passed in 1977 and 1997 (Hall and Terry 2004: 207–8).

In this new, increasingly non-unionised Britain the workforce is also being represented and organised by bodies other than trade unions. Agencies have proliferated since the 1980s. Agency workers often think that they would not be represented by trade unions – 'I am not aware of a trade union that deals with temping work' (Druker and Stanworth 2004: 231). The Citizens Advice Bureau handled only about 140,000 enquiries on wages and conditions in 1974–5 but over 600,000 in 2001–2, by then about 10 per cent of its workload (Abbott 2004: 245).

Local community campaigns have also battled for concessions on behalf of unrepresented workers. One successful example has been the East London Living Campaign (Wills 2004: 264–76). The problem in East London was that many individuals were hired by private contractors to provide essential services – such as cleaning, catering, portering, security and related activities – at around the national minimum wage of £3.70 per hour in 2001. They had no sick pay, no pension rights, no London allowance, nor many of the rights normally associated with employment. In June 2002 about 300 of these low-paid workers employed by ISS Mediclean to provide domestic, portering, catering, car parking, security and switchboard work at Whipp Cross Hospital in East London joined a picket line outside the hospital demanding a living wage. They had joined the East London Communities Organisation (TELCO), formed in 1995, to take in part in a campaign and membership of the local UNISON branch increased from 61 to about 350 amongst contract workers. They wanted and eventually won parity in terms and conditions with NHS staff. Similar action took place at the Homerton and other hospitals in the East End, and settlements were secured quickly. In other words, here was an example of trade union action combining with community action to improve the lot of low-paid workers. It was the first modern British example of a successful local campaign to win a living wage for workers in an attempt to reverse the trend towards widening income differential of the previous twenty years. In 2003 TELCO consisted of about 40 schools, mosques, community centres and trade union branches which represented about 50,000 people.

8. Conclusion

British trade unions enjoyed their greatest success between 1945 and the mid-1970s. Along with employers, they were called into discussions with government, they represented more than half the British workforce, and they effectively managed voluntary collective bargaining arrangements. Since the 1980s their influence has declined rapidly. They now represent little more than a quarter of the British workforce, their influence on voluntary collective bargaining is greatly reduced and other forms of worker representation have had to emerge to fill the gap. Trade unions have, of course, changed with the times but this has meant that they have offered a variety of social services to their workforce – well beyond the old collective bargaining arrangements – to retain and increase membership and, because of legislation, have less industrial muscle than in the 1970s. In effect, their position is no stronger than it was in the inter-war years and they are increasingly faced by new challenges, not least the weakening relationship with the Labour Party. Notwithstanding these, and other, dangers trade unions still have an established place in the British pattern of industrial bargaining arrangements and have evolved. However, the idea of worker representation based almost solely upon trade unions is now very much a thing of the past. Indeed, it is difficult to believe that the 'New Realism', in the words of John Monks, means that the trade unions and the TUC 'are in the best position to start to grow once again'. The TUC and trade union initiatives have not been enough to reverse the recent decline of British trade unionism.

Suggested Reading

Abbott, B. (2004) 'Worker Representation through the Citizen's Advice Bureaux' in Healy, G. Heery, E., Taylor, P. and Brown, W. (eds) *The Future of Worker Representation*, Basingstoke: Palgrave Macmillan.
Bain, P., Taylor, P., Gilbert, K. and Gall, G. (2004) 'Failing to Organise – or Organising to Fail? Challenge, Opportunity and Limitations of Union Policy in Four Call Centres' in Healy, G., Heery, E., Taylor, P. and Brown, W. (eds) *The Future of Worker Representation*, Basingstoke: Palgrave Macmillan.
Barber, R. (1977) *Trade Unions and the Tories*, London, Bow Group.
Campbell, A., Fishman, N. and McIlroy, J. (eds) (1999a) *British Trade Unions and Industrial Politics: The Post-War Compromise, 1945–64*, Aldershot: Ashgate.
—— (eds) (1999b) *British Trade Unions and Industrial Politics: The High Tide of Trade Unionism 1964–79*, Aldershot: Ashgate.
Danford, A., Richardson, M., Stewart, P., Tailby, S. and Upchurch, M. (2004) 'Partnership, Mutuality, High Performance workplace: A Case Study of Union Strategy and Worker Experience in the Aircraft Industry' Centres' in Healy, G., Heery, E., Taylor, P. and Brown, W. (eds) *The Future of Worker Representation*, Basingstoke: Palgrave Macmillan.
Donovan Commission (1968) [Royal Commission on Trade Unions and Employers]; Associations 1965–1968, *Report*, London, HMSO.
Druker, J. and Stanworth, C. (2004) 'Agency Voices: The Role of Labour Market Intermediaries in Worker Representation', in Healy, G., Heery, E., Taylor, P. and Brown, W. (eds) *The Future of Worker Representation*, Basingstoke: Palgrave Macmillan.
Fairbrother, P. (2000) *Trade Unions at the Crossroads*, London: Mansell.
Gallie, D., Penn, R. and Rose, M. (1996) *Trade Unionism in Recession*, Oxford: Oxford University Press.
Healy, G., Bradley H. and Mukerjee, N. (2004) 'Inspiring Activists: The Experience of Minority Ethnic Women in Trade Unions' in Healy,

G., Heery, E., Taylor, P. and Brown, W. (eds) *The Future of Worker Representation*, Basingstoke: Palgrave Macmillan.
Hall, M. and Terry, M. 'The Emerging System of Statutory Worker Representations' in Healy, G., Heery, E., Taylor, P. and Brown, W. (eds) *The Future of Worker Representation*, Basingstoke: Palgrave Macmillan.
Hyman, J., Lockyer, C., Marks, A. and Scholarios, D. (2004) 'Needing a New Program: Why is Union Membership so low among Software Workers?' in Healy, G., Heery, E., Taylor, P. and Brown, W. (eds) *The Future of Worker Representation*, Basingstoke: Palgrave Macmillan.
Hyman, R. (1992) 'Trade Unions with the Disaggregation of the Working Class' in Tegino, M. (ed.) *The Future of Labour Movement*, London, Sage.
—— (2001) *Understanding European Trade Unionism: Between Market, Class and Society*, London: Sage.
Laybourn, K. (1992) *A History of British Trade Unionism c. 1770–1990*, Stroud: Alan Sutton.
McIlroy, J. (1995) *Trade Unions in Britain Today*, Manchester: Manchester University Press, 2nd Ed.
—— (1998) 'The Enduring Alliance? Trade Unions and the Making of New Labour 1994–1997', *British Journal of Industrial Relations* 36(4): 537–64.
Middlemass, R.K. (1979) *Politics in Industrial Society: The Experience of the British System since 1914*, London: Andre Deutsch.
Minkin, L. (1991) *Contentious Alliance: Trade Unions and the Labour Party*, Edinburgh: Edinburgh University Press.
Oxenbridge, S. and Brown, W. (2004) 'A Poisoned Chalice? Trade Union Representation in Partnership and Co-operative Employer-Union Relationships' in Healy, G., Heery, E., Taylor, P. and Brown, W. (eds) *The Future of Worker Representation*, Basingstoke: Palgrave Macmillan.
Taylor, R. (2000) *The TUC: From the General Strike to New Unionism*, Basingstoke: Palgrave Macmillan.
Tebbit, N. (1991) *Upwardly Mobile*, London: Futura.

TUC, *Report*, London: TUC, various dates and pages given and various reports.

Wills, J. (2004) 'Organising the Low Paid: East London's Living Wage Campaign as a Vehicle for Change', in Healy, G., Heery, E., Taylor, P. and Brown, W. (eds) *The Future of Worker Representation*, Basingstoke: Palgrave Macmillan.

Wrigley, C. (1997) *British Trade Unions and Government 1945–1995*, Manchester: Manchester University Press.

Eastern Europe

The History of Trade Unions in Hungary, 1945–2002

LÁSZLÓ NEUMANN

1. Background

In the fifty years prior to World War I Hungary underwent major economic growth, industrialisation and modernisation. A significant share of industrial workers was of ethnic German origin and trade union development followed the German model, transmitted by Austrian trade unions. In 1890 the Hungarian Social Democratic Party (MSZDP) was created, which reorganised the union movement and established the Trade Union Council, the national umbrella organisation of the craft unions. Union membership grew quickly: in 1906 there were 130,000 registered members, growing to 215,222 by 1917 (Lux 2002).[1] In addition to their traditional roles (collective wage bargaining, organising strikes, participation in grievance procedures), local trade unions also functioned as component organisations of the MSZDP (Sipos 1991).

The evolution of trade unions and the MSZDP was broken not so much by World War I but by the rightist white terror following the 1919 Hungarian Soviet Republic. The counter-revolutionary forces and governments persecuted both the MSZDP and its trade unions. By the end of 1919 membership of social democratic trade unions dwindled to 212,408 while Christian socialist trade unions, enjoying the support of the regime, had a membership of approximately 120,000 (Lux 2002). In 1924 conditions

1 Figures refer to the territory of Greater Hungary, in existence until the end of World War I.

for the MSZDP and trade unionism were set by the Bethlen-Peyer pact. In this agreement the government legalised the party, trade unions, and workers' welfare and cultural institutions, but social democrats were required to support the government's fundamental domestic and foreign policies and were prohibited from forming alliances with liberal and democratic parties. Furthermore, railway, postal and public employee unions remained banned and the organisation of agricultural workers was outlawed. In 1935, following the Italian model, the fascist Gömbös administration sought to replace trade unions with corporations but managed only the introduction of statutory regulation on working time, minimum wages and paid holidays. By 1938 35 per cent of the 300,000 'factory workers' (workers at establishments employing more than twenty) were unionised, with the highest concentrations in printing and heavy industry (Rézler 1940). In the war years, however, union memberships fell to a record low level; according to police estimates, in early 1942 there were not much more than 70,000 organised workers. Trade unions were finally outlawed in October 1944, when the fascist Arrow Cross Party came to power.

2. The Road to the Communist Takeover (1945–8)

After the war, the MSZDP's decision to cooperate with the Hungarian Communist Party (MKP) had a major impact on union evolution. The MKP had been a small, illegal group during the war, but it became a significant political power in Hungary when its emigrant leaders returned with the Soviet occupying forces. In 1948 the cooperation of the two 'labour parties' evolved into formal merger, which in fact meant the Communists' annexation of their 'ally' and the elimination of parliamentary democracy, thereby completing the Communist takeover.

With the Soviet army's advance, trade unions were established in liberated areas, and they represented a significant force in the Hungarian National Independence Front, the umbrella organisation of the five parties of the new democratic regime. Their nineteen representatives were among the 230 members of the Provisional National Assembly set up on Soviet prompting on 22 December 1944. The National Centre of Hungarian Trade Unions was created on 7 February 1945 in liberated Budapest. The Communists usually demanded the secretary-general's position in trade unions and central organisations, which gave them real power, and they allowed the social democrats to have the presidency. Furthermore, the Communists held a majority in the central leadership of several craft unions, such as the miners, construction workers, drivers, meat industry workers, public employees, postal workers, doctors and iron workers.

Disagreement between the Communist and social democratic leaders of the National Centre over the issue of the principle of organisation sharpened in early 1945. The Communists advocated workplace and sectoral level organisation while social democrats insisted on craft unionism. The National Centre eventually reached a compromise permitting both. Trade unions were created in previously unorganised occupations as well, such as public employees, engineers, doctors and teachers. With the masses joining, membership grew rapidly and reached 850,831 by December 1945.

Upon liberation, self-governing bodies known as 'works committees' were created spontaneously as workers took it upon themselves to manage the seriously damaged plants. They assumed responsibility for cleaning away debris and restarting production. According to a government decree of June 1945, a works committee was to be elected in all plants with over twenty employees. From the autumn of 1948, works committees were transformed into trade union committees, with new objectives and responsibilities in line with the new political order.

In the area of wage policy the trade unions' first achievements were the 'stabilisation' of collective agreements which specified in-kind remuneration for workers in addition to cash payments. Given the hyperinflation at that time, the daily 'one-dish meal' meant a considerable improvement in workers' living standards, as was textile workers' entitlement to a certain length of textile, which could be used as hard currency on the black market. In 1945 and 1946, collective agreements regulated wages, hours, terms and conditions of work in a total of 323 occupations in 178 industries. The National Wage Setting Committee was created on 7 May 1945 to coordinate and review collective bargaining and local wage determination. From 1947 the National Centre concluded three national collective framework agreements covering manufacturing industries, small-scale industry and commerce (Tóth 1997). By that time, however, the National Wage Setting Committee was dominated by the Communists, and in October 1947 the committee introduced a new national wage regulation system for manufacturing. Production norms were raised, resulting in wildcat strikes (Kozák 2007).

In 1946 the National Centre was active in the Communist campaigns to rebuild destroyed railways and bridges ('the bridge battle') and to restart coal mines ('the coal battle'). Trade unions also supported monetary reform to curb hyperinflation and stabilise the economy. Work competitions were held to rebuild the destroyed country as quickly as possible. Trade unions also supported the Communist Party on broader social issues and direct political actions; they endorsed land reform, the purge of the state administration, and nationalisation. In March 1948 Hungarian-owned factories employing over 100 workers were nationalised in a coup-like move by the Communists that bypassed both the parliament and the government. In a symbolic act, the designated worker-directors responsible for nationalisation assembled in the banquet hall of the Ironworkers' Trade Union.

In early 1948 the MKP sought to merge the two parties. In February the crypto-Communists in the SZDP ousted the so called 'rightist' anti-merger leaders from the party and initiated a purge of non-Communist members. The two parties merged on 12 June 1948 under the name of Hungarian Workers' Party (MDP) with an essentially Communist political programme. Simultaneously, social democrats were removed from trade union leaderships, starting at the February 1948 Presidium meeting of the Trade Union Council. After the party merger, 95 per cent of trade union leaders, all members of the National Centre, and all secretaries of industry federations were MDP members (Lux 2002).

3. The Stalinist Dictatorship (1949–56)

In March 1948 István Kossa, the Communist president of the National Centre, urged a complete reorganisation of the trade union movement. Reorganisation on the Soviet model essentially entailed organisation along industrial rather than craft lines, and the implementation of the principle of 'one workplace – one trade union'. The seventeenth Trade Union Congress in October 1948 endorsed this plan and created the National Council of Trade Unions (SZOT) as the peak organisation in the industrial and workplace trade union hierarchy. After industry directorates (i.e. supervising authorities of nationalised industrial production) were created in the summer of 1948, trade unions were reorganised so that each sectoral trade union became the partner of a single economic authority. By December 1950 the fifty craft unions had been replaced by nineteen national sectoral unions. In the course of reorganisation the Communists fired several trade union officials and replaced them with their own appointments. At the same time, senior trade union officials were given positions in the top organs of the Communist Party. This was the case of Sándor Gáspár, who, with the exception of a short interval, headed SZOT from 1952 until 1988. The structure of SZOT was as centralised as that of the Communist Party. The government then merged the various social security systems and put the new organisation under SZOT control.

With the Communist takeover, trade union functions fundamentally changed. The 4 June 1948 resolution of the Political Committee of the MKP stated that 'the greatest shortcoming of union activity is that the trade union has played the *transmission belt* role only to a small extent' (i.e. the role of implementing the party's goals at the workplace and mobilising workers to work towards these goals) (Lux 2002). In February 1949 the plenary session of SZOT adopted new statutes for workplace trade union committees. According to the statutes, one of the most important tasks of the committees was to organise work competitions and meet production plans set by various state organs. The trade unions' remit was reduced to the supervision and enforcement of legal provisions regulating employment and the collective agreement, and the provision of social, cultural and educational services to members. Trade union committees were forbidden to confront company management either in collective interest representation or in individual grievance procedures as the settlement of industrial conflicts belonged to bodies outside the trade union.

In late 1948 and early 1949, trade unions lost their political independence and were henceforth directed by the top leadership of the MDP. As one of the top leaders of the MDP put it in 1952, 'trade union activists are party functionaries and have to do party work in the trade union'. Some trade union leaders resented the harsh regulations and tried to retain the role of interest representation despite the new hostile environment. This approach, however, invited fierce anti-trade union attacks by the party leadership, except during the period of political thaw in 1953.

Production was increased primarily through work competitions. At the celebratory work shift organised in honour of Stalin's seventieth birthday, and later in the Stakhanov work competitions, individual performances amounting to increases of several thousand per cent were reported. While participation in the work competitions was essentially compulsory, the achievements of champion workers had little impact on overall production rates. For that purpose, norm setting was introduced. As a first step, the Political Committee of the MDP accused trade unions of 'syndicalism' and of not fighting hard enough to implement the Party's economic policy. Next, the government issued a decree on central norm setting and increased the compulsory performance level by about 17 per cent. As a consequence of the norm setting in 1952 workers' earnings fell by 6 to 12 per cent. Organising work competitions, however, became increasingly difficult because of workers' resistance; high performances served as excuses for increasing norms, which then further reduced earnings.

Criminal law was another tool to increase performance through, for instance, expanding the definition of sabotage, which was punishable by five years imprisonment. Despite such harsh measures, work discipline was a constant problem. In 1950 and 1951 absenteeism soared, especially during agricultural peak seasons. Leaving the workplace without proper excuse was also a crime; in 1952 and 1953 15,000 such cases were tried by courts. The statutory forty-eight hour work week was rarely observed, and overtime performed as part of work competitions was often unpaid. Seven-day work weeks were a common practice in mining and construction (Institute).

From the early 1950s, trade unions no longer concerned themselves with workers' earnings and the terms and conditions of employment. Their role in the social and cultural lives of their members changed too. With the creation of workplace trade unions, earlier neighbourhood groups disintegrated and trade unions ceased to be organisers of the social life of workers, thereby losing their traditional role as a movement (Lux 2000). Members became alienated from trade unions which failed to serve their members at the workplace or in the community. The role of union members amounted to little more than paying membership fees and demonstrating their subordination and passivity towards the leadership.

The Communist takeover signified numerous other societal changes for trade unions as well. Freshly promoted and reliable Party members replaced experienced social democrats as shopfloor supervisors. Three-quarters of shopfloor supervisors in heavy industry were replaced between 1945 and the summer of 1951 (Varga 1984). At the same time, with forced industrialisation from 1948 onward, the urban labour force grew rapidly; between 1949 and 1956 330,000 industrial jobs were created. The majority of new recruits had peasant backgrounds, and the large-scale employment of women in industry began at the same time too. With this mass influx of new labour, those aware of pre-1948 union traditions became a minority. Attitudes toward work also began to change considerably; commitment to one's profession became less important and the hierarchy within the working class less respected (Institute).

4. The Revolution and Reprisals (1956–62)

An escalation of social tensions in the early 1950s formed the background of the 1956 revolution. In addition to political goals, workers had a long list of grievances – high norms, long working hours, low wages, intolerable working conditions, and the lack of effective interest protection. In the summer of 1956, skilled workers in several factories expressed discontent, and their revolt was supported by the workplace trade union committees (Pittaway 2007). The general dissatisfaction of workers was voiced at the September 1956 session of SZOT. The president of the council, Sándor Gáspár, declared that unions must henceforth concern themselves with wages. He proposed that older organised workers and trade union leaders' with knowledge of wage matters be involved in trade union work. Gáspár called upon the central committees of the various unions to act quickly whenever wage disputes arose and devise possible solutions. (It is now conceded by Polish Communist leaders that 'wage tensions' touched off the Poznan demonstrations of 28 June.)

The day following the outbreak of revolution on 23 October, Workers' Councils were created to represent workers' political goals. They received strong impetus on 26 October, when, in the hope of retaining some control over the events, both the party and the trade union hierarchy endorsed them. Together with the representatives of the University Revolutionary Students' Committee and of the Writers' Union, SZOT signed a communiqué upholding the revolutionary demands. The first item on the list of demands reflected the revolutionary atmosphere: 'All power should belong to the new democratic national government so that it can ensure the country's independence and the development of socialist democracy'. This alliance played a crucial role in the events on 28 October that led to the withdrawal of Soviet troops. On 31 October the Presidium of SZOT resigned and the Provisional Executive Committee of the National Federation of Free Hungarian Trade Unions was created, with the formerly imprisoned social democrat Miklós Vas-Witteg as president. The new Committee declared that trade unions were independent from the Party and government, and announced that the trade union federation was quitting the (Communist) World Federation of Trade Unions. The Committee also declared that the primary task of trade unions was the protection of the interests of workers. On 1 November the Presidium of SZOT called for sectoral trade union leaders to resign and to create 'free trade unions' with provisional executive committees.

Meanwhile Workers' Councils took over the direct management of plants and also assumed a role in local political leadership. In several cases armed plant guards were organised to protect factories. SZOT declared that Workers' Councils were 'the most direct manifestation of the fact that workers are the responsible masters of the plants', but in fact Workers Councils' primary role in the revolution was national level policy making rather than self-governance or representing workers' interests. The remarkable chain of events had been set in motion by a wave of nationwide strikes lead by the Workers' Councils. Strikes were to be suspended in support of the new Imre Nagy government, but this plan was abandoned when the Soviets invaded on 4 November. The Workers' Councils led the resistance. They called for a national strike to force the Soviets to reinstall the Imre Nagy government. In addition to workplace Workers' Councils, several regional councils were set up, the most important of which was the Greater Budapest Central Workers' Council. Workers' Councils also became the principal revolutionary institutions in large rural industrial cities (Győr, Pécs, Debrecen and Miskolc). During the week following 4 November, they took control of public administration, issued newspapers in several cities and helped supply shops with needed goods. Their power was based on the fact that, possessing the strongest available weapon (the strike), they were in the best position to negotiate with the Soviets (Institute).

The establishment of the Greater Budapest Central Workers' Council (KMT), and its close cooperation with various revolutionary intellectual groups, posed a threat to the collaborating Kádár government, which feared that a dual power system was being created. This government had no choice but to negotiate with the KMT delegates, understanding that restarting work in factories was a prerequisite to stabilising the government's power. The KMT ordered workers to return to work on 16 November but the government reneged on its promise to create a National Workers' Council. Amidst protests and demonstrations, an increasing number of Workers' Council leaders were arrested. On 9 December regional workers' councils were banned and the leaders of KMT were arrested too. In December the KMT was still planning a national strike, but in several rural cities the government declared its intent by opening fire on street demonstrators. Workers' councils lost their influence, and in the spring of 1957 they were banned by government decree.

Trade union leaders supporting Kádár issued a declaration on 11 November in which they assured the government of their support and urged workers to return to work: 'Only work can put goods in the shops, bread on the table, warmth in homes and transportation in the whole country. Only work can bring forth order, peace and calmness' (Lux 2002). By late November, however, trade unions had lost influence in workplaces, and former stewards were often not allowed to enter at all. In the factories democratic trade union elections were held under the supervision of Workers' Councils. Press and textile industry workers set up their own respective unions. In such a situation, the national union leadership saw no alternative to cooperation with the KMT. In a communiqué they announced that they would act independently of the party and the government and recognise the working class' right to strike (Institute).

Upon the collapse of the Revolution, Workers' Councils were gradually liquidated. Nearly two-thirds of the victims of reprisals in the wake of the Revolution were working class. In the emigration wave of 1956 and 1957, a large number of skilled workers left the country. After the Revolution the government saw pacification of the working class as its primary task; in early 1957 wages were raised significantly, and shops carried a greater supply of goods. After 1956 the unemployment benefit was temporarily introduced because the Revolution generated a minor wave of unemployment. At the same time, the trade union leadership, with the social democrats removed, quickly forgot about its reform ideas. At the March 1957 meeting of chief stewards, for example, speakers criticised the union leadership and insisted on independence from the Party and the right to strike. With the escalating retaliation after the revolution, however, their proposals fell on deaf ears.

5. Consolidation and Reform (1963–85)

In 1961 the slogan 'Anyone who is not against us is with us' opened a new era. Political thaw brought about greater freedom in the private lives of citizens. The consolidation of the Kádár regime was based on the de-politicisation of society. In the late 1950s the country's leadership began reflecting the new spirit by giving workers higher wages and a better life, for instance by mitigating the housing shortage. Until the 1980s, living standards increased steadily though only moderately. By the late 1960s the majority of the population had bought fully into the consumer culture that had developed over the previous decade. Many workers in the western industrial city of Győr were, according to a 1968 sociological study, 'already busily satisfying their demands for additional consumer durables: they had their TV sets, washing machines, motor-cycles, and were now spending money improving their apartments, buying refrigerators or even cars' (Pittaway 2006; Héthy and Makó 1972: 144). People accepted the regime largely in exchange for higher living standards achieved also through improved wages and the expansion and extension of welfare provisions. It was during the Kádár era that all employees (including members of agricultural cooperatives) became entitled to old-age pensions and that a generous system of child-raising supports was introduced.

From the 1960s onwards a relatively wide range of income earning possibilities became available. The so-called 'second economy' appeared first in agriculture; after forced collectivisation in 1960–61, cooperative members were now allowed to sell what they produced in their household plots. This new phenomenon fundamentally changed workers' options, not only because a large part of the working class were in reality commuters from villages but also because the second economy of industrial production gradually became tolerated too. Legal and illegal 'second jobs' mushroomed, and by the 1980s these sometimes became small private businesses. From as early as the 1960s, the regime also tolerated the informal wage struggles of workers in strong bargaining positions. The above mentioned study in Győr, and later other sociological studies found that workers who occupied a key position in the production structure fought for higher wages by restraining their performance and performing well-paid overtime instead of their regular work. In the somewhat exaggerating words of István Kemény, 'The factory, then, is in fact governed by two powers, the management and the spontaneously formed elite, both of which seem to carry equal weight' (Kemény 1986: 187). As formal wage setting at the company level belonged to the competence of the 'plant quadrangle' (management, the Party, the Communist youth organisation and the trade union), the informal bargaining position of elite workers challenged the authority of the company management. Other groups of workers managed to raise wages by changing companies. Other workers had both a job in a state run company providing a modest yet stable wage and extra income earned in the second economy (Kertesi and Sziráczki 1985). On the whole, from the 1960s, the segmentation of the working class increased. At the bottom of the hierarchy were those marginalised workers for whom only low paying impermanent jobs were available. Informal collective action was not an option for them as company managers could exploit in-house rivalry among such workers.

In the 1960s and 1970s, party control over trade unions was maintained as over 80 per cent of the SZOT apparatus were party members. At the local level, trade union officials identified themselves with the company management and trade union cadres often advanced their careers by becoming managers themselves. Trade union officials most often tolerated informal wage bargaining. Throughout the Communist era, workers remained alienated from trade unions, which were never regarded as credible defenders of their interests. A popular joke at the time held that 'one of the world's most superfluous things is a trade union'.[2]

By the mid-1960s, industrial growth based on new labour recruits from agriculture was exhausted. The need to run the economy more efficiently forced the Party leadership to introduce reforms. The 'new economic

2 This joke is also quoted by Kemény (1986). A more vulgar version asks: 'What are the three most useless things in the world? Answer: The pope's prick, a nun's tit, and a trade union.'

mechanism' was introduced in 1968, which increased company autonomy against central leadership and gave company managers financial rewards for increasing productivity. Restrictions on changing workplaces were lifted in an effort to make the labour market more efficient. The Gáspár-led SZOT, however, fuelled by Party hardliners, played a major role in the ultimate failure of the reforms. SZOT first launched a media campaign against the 'migrant birds' – workers changing workplaces too frequently – then attacked managers' high incomes pretending it was voicing the workers' dissatisfaction. The anti-reform attack by the trade union centre culminated at the 22nd SZOT Congress in 1971 at which speakers blasted the 'negative' consequences of reform, demanded an end to high incomes for managers, and called for increased taxes on small private businesses (Soós 1984). Ultimately reform measures were revoked. The freedom of changing workplaces was gradually restricted and incomes were regulated in a way that ensured that wages in the large industrial enterprises were higher than in other sectors. In the spirit of restoration, in 1976 an overall revision of norms was ordered, which, however, never took place because of the resistance of the workers. Companies were unable to meet plans because workers refused to work overtime (Kemény 1984). The Gáspár-led SZOT leadership launched an unsuccessful anti-reform campaign as late as in 1983 when private entrepreneurship was legalised. As a consequence of this failure, administration of the social security system was taken away from SZOT and placed under government supervision in 1984.

The reforms had promised a shift towards real interest representation by trade unions. Rezső Nyers, the guiding spirit behind the new economic mechanism, wrote in March 1968 that it was 'desirable that trade unions represent the interests of their members and of employees in a way that makes them a special partner of management and of the state' (Lux 2002). This idea was put in practice by an amendment of the Labour Code in 1967, which gave unions the right to file complaints (demurrer) in search of in-house solutions for grievances and also made it possible for companies to conclude collective agreements at enterprise level. While the institution of demurrer essentially gave trade unions the right of veto in cases of unlawful employer measures, trade unions hardly ever used it in practice, partly because of central instructions. The Party leadership fretted about trade unions' veto right so SZOT instructed company unions that they should use it only as 'a last resort' (Lux 2002). Nonetheless, collective agreements became essentially obligatory, although their content was mostly limited to drafting the local rules of implementing the law in terms of company objectives. Evidence that local unions were being strengthened against the centre could be seen in the fact that as of 1968 locals retained fifty per cent of membership fees rather than the previous thirty-five per cent.

Stewards' committees – an institution that had existed before World War II – were introduced in 1975 as a means of more direct representation for various groups of employees.[3] Yet throughout the 1970s, even union competences were formally expanded, attendance at membership meetings fell significantly. Still, union density in the period was relatively stable as a result of trade unions' undertaking community functions such as social security, holidays, work safety, and provision of facilities for cultural and sports activities. It should be noted, however, that these trade union functions were more limited than in the Soviet Union. For instance, health care always remained a state service.

6. The Growth of Trade Union Pluralism (1987–90)

By the mid-1980s the two pillars of consolidation began to crumble: increasing living standards and full employment proved unsustainable in the face of the country's large debt burden that had been mounting since the oil shocks. Trade union leaders felt increasing pressure from members for more effective representation. In 1987 part of the SZOT leadership cautiously started to criticise the Party's economic and income policy. In 1988 they

3 Prewar 'chief-stewards' committees' comprised blue collar employees and often foremen, as opposed to the 'professional' trade union apparatus and leadership, which was comprised largely of intellectuals. In wage bargaining militant stewards and moderate union leaders were often in conflict.

made an alternative proposal concerning the introduction of VAT and a personal income tax system. An unemployment benefit was also introduced on SZOT proposal. At that time, negotiations between the government and SZOT, mostly on income and social policy issues, were regularly covered by the media. Obviously, the government wanted to share the responsibility for the unpopular measures. As an extension of the bilateral negotiations, in December 1988 the tripartite National Interest Reconciliation Council (OÉT) was created, in which SZOT was the sole organisation representing employees; the employers' side was represented by organisations of companies and cooperatives, but the private sector were not invited. Despite the existence of OÉT, in 1989 it was the SZOT president (Sándor Gáspár resigned as president in 1988 and Sándor Nagy was elected) with whom the prime minister agreed on real wages and the budget.

In 1988 eight local strikes were reported and twenty more in the following year. In some occupations (for instance, mining) workers protested against government decisions on wages and benefits. Most strikes took place at national state-run companies, where workers demanded independence, a lawful option by that time, and workers at local sites were driven by the illusion of self-governance. These incidents made it urgent to implement a strike law, even though under the Communist regime strikes were outlawed. Reformists in SZOT pushed for a strike law and the newly established independent trade unions were determined to have a say in it.

The independent trade unions were movements of intellectual elites (researchers, teachers and artists). The Democratic Trade Union of Scientific Workers (TDDSZ), the first independent trade union, was set up on 16 May 1988 largely by intellectuals, some of whom were also founders of the Alliance of Free Democrats (SZDSZ), the second biggest party in the first free elections. SZDSZ was the successor of the democratic opposition which worked more or less illegally in the 1980s, the members of which, following the model of the Polish Solidarnosč, decided to set up a free trade union before the formation of oppositional parties was legalised. As opposed to Solidarnosč, however, Hungarian independent trade unions, having only a few thousand members in 1988 and 1989, never became a mass movement. At first SZOT did not take seriously the challenge of independent trade unions, and they did little to prevent them except to launch a defamatory campaign against the leadership in the media.

In December 1988, the four independent trade unions of intellectuals (scientists, special education teachers, filmmakers and teachers) established the Democratic League of Independent Trade Unions (LIGA), the first alternative confederation. LIGA was closely connected to the newly formed pro-democracy parties and its programme included the fundamental grass-roots reform of the trade union movement. The fist action of LIGA was its involvement in the strike law debate. The right to strike was an important political issue for the democratic opposition too, and it was one of the twelve demands of mass demonstrations that took place on 15 March 1989. By that time opposition parties were organised and that summer Round Table negotiations were held between the Hungarian Socialist Workers' Party (MSZMP), which was still in power, and the opposition on the best means to achieve the transition to democracy, including free elections and a new constitution. LIGA took part in these negotiations. Obviously, LIGA was primarily concerned with the idea of a radical political change and the traditional demands of workers were of secondary importance.

At the same time, MSZMP sought to involve new players in negotiations in order to strengthen its position, and 'social organisations', among them SZOT. In September the SZOT leadership declared its independence from the Party, and President Sándor Nagy resigned from the Party's Central Committee. At that time SZOT wanted to assume the role of a mass left wing party to replace the disintegrating MSZMP, and it pushed for legislation to allow trade unions to put up candidates in parliamentary elections. Nevertheless, SZOT, with is crumbling and discredited structure and passive membership, was unable to influence events, and having lost all of its political clout, withdrew from the Round Table negotiations.

At the Round Table negotiations, agreement was reached only on ceding political power, and although economic transition was on the agenda, the various sides could not reach a compromise on the issues of privatisation and macroeconomic policy. Meanwhile, the incumbent parliament passed economic laws that allowed state enterprises to transform into private businesses and for managers to privatise assets for themselves. The public uproar over the so-called 'spontaneous privatisation' and other local employee grievances led to the formation of new unions of blue-collar workers under the auspices of LIGA. The same sort of grievances resulted in the spontaneous erection of Workers' Councils in summer 1989, mostly in the industrial plants in Transdanubia (Herend, Pét and elsewhere). Those founding the blue-collar unions recognised that over the past forty years the name 'trade union' had become discredited and hence called their organisations Workers' Councils in reference to the self-governing bodies in the 1956 revolution. Local Workers' Councils, however, were first given legal and then political support by the Hungarian Democratic Forum (MDF), one of the most important of the oppositional forces, which became the governing party in the first free elections. In addition to the grassroots Workers' Councils, the legendary leaders of the 1956 Workers' Councils championing socialist ideals joined the movement. Additionally, a group of leftist intellectuals urged the introduction of workers' self-management. This movement soon found partners among intellectuals who promoted employee share ownership programmes as the best means of privatisation (Szalai 1994). In a September 1989 decision the Supreme Court recognised Workers' Councils as trade unions. First the Information Office of Workers' Councils, a national umbrella organisation, was set up; then in February 1990 the National Federation of Workers' Councils (MOSZ), which later became a trade union confederation, was created amidst bitter ideological and power struggles between the various factions. Several other independent trade unions were created, coming together as the Solidarity Workers' Alliance.

The restructuring of SZOT began after its December 1988 national conference. Sectoral trade unions were transformed into federations, and many local trade unions became independent. Central direction was abolished, the interest representation objectives of trade unions were reinstituted, and union internal democracy was established. By early March 1990, SZOT ceased to exist and was re-established as the National Association of Hungarian Trade Unions (MSZOSZ). Not all sectoral unions joined the new confederation, however. Several organisations did not accept the MSZOSZ statutes or assumed a politically neutral position by keeping an equal distance from both the MSZOSZ and the independent trade unions. Under the coordination of the Trade Union of Chemical Workers, unions not joining MSZOSZ formed their own confederations. Some of them founded the Alliance of Autonomous Trade Unions (ASZSZ). As rivals to TDDSZ, the less radical Trade Union of Scientific Workers (TUDOSZ) and the Confederation of Unions of Professionals (ÉSZT) were also created. Finally, public employees and civil servants set up the Trade Unions' Cooperation Forum (SZEF) as an organisation separate from the Autonomous Alliance. On the other hand, many trade unions remained independent, and even those affiliated to confederations enjoyed a high degree of autonomy in terms of their representation policies. This was a period dominated by a decentralised trade union structure, and partly due to the unions' organisational features, the evolving system of collective bargaining also became decentralised, with most bargaining taking place at the company level (Neumann 2007).

On 25 May 1990 six union federations – MSZOSZ, LIGA, Solidarity, ÉSZT, the Autonomous Alliance and MOSZ – established the Trade Union Round Table, which later was joined by SZEF as well. The primary function of the Round Table was to determine who should constitute the employees' side in the future social dialogue. Later the redistribution of trade union assets became the major issue on the agenda. On 1 August, the tripartite Interest Reconciliation Council (ÉT) was established as the successor of OÉT and included representatives of the seven trade union federations and private employers' associations. ÉT became a major political actor on 28 October, when the country was paralysed by the 'taxi-drivers' blockade' organised in protest against the petrol price hike. ÉT reached an agreement with the representatives of drivers at a meeting aired live on television. In his night-time interview Prime Minister József Antall acknowledged that ÉT was a significant organisation, even though it was not involved in the upcoming budget discussions.

During the political shift, trade union membership did not shrink drastically. In 1997 SZOT had a membership of 4.4 million and the new confederations and independent trade unions boasted nearly 4 million members at the end of 1990. While the independent trade unions were politically very significant, their membership remained small. As opposed to Poland, the independent trade unions were not a mass movement playing a major role influencing events. On the contrary, in 1988 and 1989 it was political change that brought about the renewal of the trade union movement.

7. Trade Union Infighting and the Transitional Recession (1990–4)

Discussions at the Trade Union Round Table from autumn 1990 revealed wide differences of political opinion among the trade union confederations. With respect to privatisation, for instance, MSZOSZ opposed state revenue-driven privatisation and championed the protection of the 'nation's assets'. Solidarity and MOSZ demanded that employees be sold shares at a preferential rate as part of privatisation. At the same time, the Autonomous Alliance regarded the creation of the social safety net as the most important task, and LIGA suggested that a special fund should be set up from privatisation revenues to alleviate expected social and employment problems. By 1991 the conflict between the old and new trade unions deepened; they could not agree on how to determine the national weight of the various confederations or how to divide inherited trade union assets. LIGA and the Workers' Councils proposed to hold trade union elections to resolve the impasse, while MSZOSZ and the Autonomous Alliance held that representation should be based on the results of the works council elections, and small trade union federations insisted that representation should be based of self-reported membership size. Eventually, LIGA and the Workers' Councils withdrew from negotiations on 7 February, and the Round Table was dissolved. It should be noted that the redistribution of assets was not an urgent problem; the two new trade union confederations were at that time generously supported by AFL-CIO, although the Workers' Councils received less than LIGA.

LIGA and the Workers' Councils turned to MDF and SZDSZ, the strongest parties at the time, to solve the problems of trade union legitimacy and the redistribution of assets. Meanwhile, conflicts within trade unions escalated when MSZOSZ tried to transfer trade union assets into a joint venture before legislation giving it permission (the contract was annulled in court). The first freely elected parliament passed two bills in July 1991 to settle the dispute and to promote 'equal opportunity' for the new trade unions. The first legal provision prescribed that authorisation of the check-off system had to be renewed, i.e. each trade union member was free to decide whether to remain in the union or not. The other law required that assets be handed over to an asset management organisation (VIKSZ), and then distributed among trade unions according to election results. In relation with the latter law, the Hungarian Socialist Party (MSZP) accused the parties voting for the bill of violating the constitution, and MSZOSZ, which possessed the assets, refused to report what it actually held. For a year the government and the 'old' and 'new' confederations fought over the means to redistribute the assets. Eventually, in November 1992, the seven confederations reached an agreement on what share each of the confederations would receive from the inherited SZOT assets. Debates on the distribution of the rest of the sectoral assets and on the national representation of confederations were postponed until the setting up of two new institutions, the works councils and social security self-governments, the latter including elected representatives of employees. The trade union confederations – except for Solidarity, which foundered – gained legitimacy when they were recognised by international organisations (ETUC, TUAC, ILO) and became members.

The law prescribing the redistribution of assets was upheld by the Constitutional Court, but two other court decisions in 1990 were less benign. One deprived local trade unions of the right to obtain information on individual wages from employers. The other revoked unions' automatic right to collectively represent employees, i.e. in case of conflicts they could represent employees at court only on the individual authorisation of each of the concerned employees. These two decisions were based on liberal economic notions of protecting the individual's freedom against trade unions. These decisions laid the foundations of the 1992 Labour Code, which cancelled several trade union rights inherited from the Communist era. And thus the two decisions dramatically influenced the workplace role of trade unions. The Labour Code excluded them from individual wage determination therefore wage bargaining is only a framework (for instance, it can cover about the annual average wage increase), and limited trade unions' role in collective representation in industrial conflicts. As a consequence 'job control' unionism and heavy participation in grievance procedures remained stifled even after the collapse of Communism.

The first freely elected government also pursued an ambivalent trade union policy. First, wanting to break away from the past, it championed the idea of strengthening new trade unions and of stripping the nomenclature of its trade union assets. Second, it sensed that it is MSZOSZ and the rest of the successor organisations that have a mass base. Prime Minister József Antall could do nothing but negotiate with the MSZOSZ chief because only he could talk to the miners called to strike by himself (Kozák 2007). Third, the government had to find a way out of the economic crisis, and the only realistic solution seemed to be the privatisation of state enterprises and a radical restructuring of industries through inward foreign direct investment. Although in its elections campaign MDF promised gradual transformation, it was expected not able to escape taking radical steps. And to do so it had to break the economic and political influence of old trade union lobbyists but, agreeing with his fellow conservative politicians in the West, Antall did not consider that strengthening the new trade unions was desirable, either. Also, there were extreme right groups in MDF demanding the temporary banning of trade unions, measuring their representativeness annually and nationalising their assets. Under these conditions it counted as success for the president of the Workers' Councils, an MDF MP too, who lead the lobbying for employee share ownership programmes that he managed to have a bill passed in 1992 that introduced a scheme similar to the American ESOP.

After long political bargaining and legal wrangling social security self-government elections were held on 21 May 1993. The 39 per cent turnout was higher than expected, giving 45 per cent of the votes to MSZOSZ, 13 per cent to LIGA, 13 per cent to Workers' Councils and 8 per cent to KESZOSZ (a Christian trade union established on government prodding), 8 per cent to SZEF and 6 per cent to the Autonomous Alliance. In the pension insurance self-government elections, held on the same day, MSZOSZ candidates received 50 per cent of votes. Solidarity did not even meet the criteria to put up candidates. While LIGA and the Workers' Councils did better than their actual workplace weight, MSZOSZ hegemony was undisputable. Moreover, at the first works council elections held in late May 1993 the vast majority of votes were cast for MSZOSZ and the Autonomous Alliance.

During the term of the first freely elected government a deep economic crisis hit the country with unemployment reaching a record high 13 per cent in 1993. The government tried to mitigate social tensions by generous unemployment benefit at the very beginning, and then tolerated (and mostly funded) various forms of early retirement schemes. Eventually, closure of state enterprises and mass redundancies were carried out without major industrial actions. In state enterprises and cooperatives about one million jobs were lost, causing a similar drop in trade union membership. New jobs were created in non-unionised small enterprises and green field foreign investments. At the same time changes did not impact the public sector, where trade unions kept the majority of their membership. Nevertheless, the objective of legislation in this sector was to create a 'Beamte-type' employment and therefore the space for collective bargaining became limited. In the private sector trade unions were continuously losing ground as a result of dwindling membership, changes in the labour law and the managements' increasingly militant anti-trade union behaviour. At the same time, however, trade unions became important players at the national level, such as in national interest reconciliation fora, labour market institutions and social security self-governments.

Warning strikes and strike calls of MSZOSZ were politically very important industrial actions from 1991 to 1993. In June 1993 trade unions of public employees organised demonstrations mobilising several tens of thousands and announced a strike alert. Social policy demands of MSZOSZ and SZEF met with the claims of the discontented losers of the economic transition. The landslide victory of the SZOT successor organisations in the 1993 social security and works council elections also heralded a leftwing political turn, and trade unions became one of the strongest economic policy bases of the reorganised left. (Thoma 2000) This not only legitimised MSZOSZ but its alliance with MSZP formed in March 1992 also helped MSZP to win the 1994 general elections and dozens of trade union leaders won seats in the parliament, including MSZOSZ president Sándor Nagy, who thus won the legitimacy war, too.

By that time the political lines of the other confederations changed somewhat compared to what it had been at the time of the change of the regime. In contrast to MSZOSZ and SZEF, the rest of the SZOT successors remained neutral in party politics – especially the Autonomous Alliance emphasised its distance from all of the parties. With the first free elections LIGA lost its political role it had played in the National Round Table negotiations and many of its founders left their trade union career for a political one. The shrinking 'liberal' trade union ceased to be important for SZDSZ, too. On the right side of the political scene, MOSZ first approached MDF and later FIDESZ when it became the leading power of the right. Around 1993 MOSZ announced that it was a Christian socialist organisation and was admitted in WFL while the rest of the confederations joined ICFTU.

8. Trade Unions under Subsequent Governments (1994–2007)

As promised in their election campaign, the MSZP-SZDSZ coalition winning the 1994 elections started negotiations with employers and trade unions to conclude a social pact. Negotiations lasting nearly eight months proved to be unsuccessful as trade unions refused to waive the right of strike in exchange for vague economic promises by the government. Hardly a month after the failure of the negotiations, the government announced its austerity measures called the Bokros package (after finance minister Lajos Bokros) in a coup-like move, without consulting ÉT. These measures included the substantial reduction of real wages and of pensions as well as social policy reforms (for instance, various universal benefits became means tested provisions, envisaged tuition fee in higher education). First trade unions in ÉT unanimously protested against both the content and the way of the introduction of the package, then SZEF and MSZOSZ made several amendment proposals, all rejected by the government. Trade union leaders, who were MPs of the governing party argued for the necessity of the 'economic adjustment' programme and eventually voted for the bills implementing the package. Pressed mostly by dissatisfied sectoral union leaders, Sándor Nagy eventually resigned as MSZOSZ president but was promised important government position by the prime minister. In László Thoma's argument: 'For trade unions the Bokros package was Waterloo... They knew that supporting the programme might erode their political capital, but they also knew that implementing the programme is a fundamental national interest ...' Trade unions were the ultimate political losers of the Bokros package for they were blamed for the drastic drop in living standards and the government was given the credit for the economic stabilisation the programme brought about.

The Bokros package caused real wages drop by 14 per cent and only public sector trade unions were able to achieve some compensation. In September 1995 the Teachers' Union organised a demonstration mobilising 80,000 to 100,000 people but later refrained from actions and only held press conferences to protest. Meanwhile the MSZOSZ president tried to get some concessions, mostly in back-stage negotiations (Thoma 2000). Eventually, in 1996 SZEF managed to conclude a three-year agreement with the government to increase public employee salaries at a higher rate. By the end of the term of the government in 1998 SZEF became the most important trade union confederation due to its successful negotiations and large membership as restructuring and the consequent unemployment hit the big companies while in the public sector, though earnings dropped, employment security remained high. Similarly, trade unions in public utility companies, especially in transportation and energy industries, remained strong. An exceptional solution in the privatisation of the electricity industry in 1997 was that a significant share of privatisation revenues was transferred to an employment promotion foundation managed by trade unions and the sectoral collective agreement was extended prior to selling the enterprises. The Autonomous Trade Union Confederation, representing primarily employees of public utility companies, significantly strengthened by the mid-1990s.

In 1995 trade unions and the government clashed over the amendment of the Labour Code. The draft bill submitted by the government promised greater flexibility for employers by allowing collective agreements to deviate from the law to the detriment of employees, and trade union officials were given the option of cash compensation for unutilised time-off. In 1995 the government could not reach a compromise with the social partners in ÉT but in 1997, when the law was amended the next time, it forced trade unions to agree. Between the two amendments, however, significant changes took place in the national social dialogue system. Instead of the earlier co-decision mechanisms of ÉT, the government wanted to reduce trade unions' role to mere consultation. In this the government was helped by a Constitutional Court decision revoking the competence of the county level social dialogue fora to distribute employment policy resources. As a solution in compliance with constitutional requirements, a rule was introduced that only those organisations could participate in the decision-making which belong to national level organisations participated at the ÉT. This, however, made the legitimacy of ÉT members an urgent problem. In the course of 'reforming' ÉT this was an excuse to set up representativeness criteria, which otherwise was urged by MSZOSZ and SZEF, too. These larger confederations wanted to squeeze the smaller ones out, the Workers' Councils and LIGA in particular. Allied with the governing party, they seemed to want to take revenge for the 'anti-trade union' legislation of the previous government. The current government was willing to help them, though for a high price. Allegedly, the deal was that the trade unions were to support the reform of the pension insurance system; indeed, helped by MSZOSZ the government introduced private pension funds in 1996. While the large confederations could not altogether push LIGA and the Workers' Councils out, they were made to accept provisional voting rules that significantly reduced their role on the trade unions' side in ÉT. The 1998 works council elections were meant to finally settle the issue of representativeness and then only trade unions receiving nationally 10 per cent of votes were to participate in ÉT. This would have meant that the two confederations created at the time of the change of the regime would have undoubtedly lost their places in ÉT. Because of the change of governments in 1998, however, this regulation was never introduced.

Intertwining between union leaders and the governing party largely discredited the trade union movement. Diminishing assets of health insurance funds, corruption scandals in connection with the privatisation of trade union holiday homes and close ties of trade unions to economic and political elites were much discussed in the media. Trade unions were deep in a legitimacy crisis once again. Between 1994 and 1998 both the representativeness and membership of trade unions drastically fell, unionisation was estimated to have dropped to 25 per cent.

One of the main causes of MSZP's losing the elections in 1998 was corruption permeating privatisation and trade unions. The first thing FIDESZ, the biggest party in the new right-wing coalition, did was to abolish the scandal-ridden social security self-governments. The right-wing government saw trade unions as parts of a strong economic and political network of the left and sought to politically annihilate them. As FIDESZ ideologue Gyula Tellér put it:

> Employees after 1990 the MSZP leadership was reassured that the forces propelling the change of the regime had been unable to destroy several of the embedded structures of socialist society and MSZP can rely on these remaining 'coagulated structures' as formal tools of exercising power in order to sooner or later regain and ultimately stabilise their own power. [...] One of these structures are trade union bureaucracies, which are relentlessly tapping any current government for money but are weak and submissive in the face of the owners and managers of private companies. Another of these structures is ÉT, the macro level interest reconciliation system set up in the last minutes of the socialist era. In ÉT trade unions were integrated in the social security self-governments and in certain large companies and banks – in which they had interests – and in the personal network of socialist affiliates, who actually directed and run the unions.[4]

In this spirit, the FIDESZ-led government was never even bothering to hide its intention to concentrate powers. To this end it also reorganised the institutions of national social dialogue: the competence of the National Labour Council, set up as a successor of ÉT, was restricted to consultation on labour issues, and the Economic Council, including powerful economic

4 Tellér Gyula: Az MSZP mint bukott vállalkozás. Magyar Nemzet (4 April 2002).

players outside employers' associations as well as civil organisations, was set up with an essentially representation function (Héthy 2002). In 1999–2000 the FIDESZ administration doubled the minimum wage – an increase trade unions would never even have dared to demand – but revoked the social partners' co-decision right in determining the minimum wage. Although with this move FIDESZ could discredit trade unions, it also confronted employers' organisations because this increase of the minimum wage undermined the viability of small and medium sized enterprises and the competitiveness of low-wage industries. Parallel with increasing the minimum wage, eligibility criteria for the unemployment benefit were made stricter to compel the unemployed to seek jobs. Another wage policy measure was that in 2001 the government raised civil servants' salaries, but at the same time failed to raise the lower salaries of public service employees. The government did not have any policy concerning workers in the traditional sense; its social policy mainly served to strengthen the better-off middle class, and pensions were hardly raised.

During the term of the right wing government, trade unions did not achieve any considerable success with strikes either. As earlier, strikes were staged at state owned sectors. In the 1999–2000 railway strikes and in the protest demonstrations organised by health care workers in 2000 the government adamantly refused to give concessions. The heavy-handed management of the railway strike deterred trade unions from organising more strikes. While in the 1990s annually 21.5 working days were lost through industrial action per 1,000 workers, in 2001 as few as 3.5 were lost.

The government and trade unions also clashed over the amendment of the Labour Code, partly introduced to carry out EU accession legal harmonisation. The debate of the draft legislation started in 1999 but because of the conflicts the bill was passed by the parliament only in 2001. Changes in the regulation of working time exclusively served employers' interests to make working time more flexible and reduce labour costs by allowing more possibilities of deviation for collective agreements and also individual work contracts from the law to the detriment of workers. The labour law reform was opposed by five trade union confederations. With the exception of the pro-government MOSZ, trade union confederations staged a joint demonstration mobilising 50,000 people but the government did not step back on the important issues. The anti-trade union policy of the government forced the so far hostile confederations to cooperate, and even to start negotiations on mergers. At the same time, as a consequence of the amendment, not only working conditions changed but also wage supplements connected to flexible work. The wage conflicts, however, were not of national significance for usually they took place in the decentralised company collective bargaining or even in individual wage bargaining. In this sense, the government largely succeeded in depoliticising wage issues in the private sector.

While ETUC supported the Hungarian trade unions' struggle, the EU did not object the Labour Code amendment as it was formally in compliance with the EU directives. At the same time, the government of Hungary, a candidate country, was severely criticised by the EU for stifling the national level social dialogue. Strengthening sectoral social dialogue institution started under the FIDESZ government with EU PHARE funding. Earmarked state funding for social partners began at the same time, with trade unions and employers usually getting the same amount.

Meanwhile union density kept shrinking: according to HCSO Labour Force Survey, it was 19 per cent in 2001 and only 17 per cent in 2004. By membership size and mobilising capacity, transportation and public sector (health care and education) trade unions were the strongest – exactly the sectors which remained in state ownership, except for utilities. Although reforming these areas had been long inevitable, the subsequent governments kept postponing it out of fear of antagonising employees, local governments and the consumers/service users. In other words, this was a time bomb handed over from government to government until 2006.

The 2002 general elections were won by the left again, and MSZP and SZDSZ formed the government. With the swing of the political pendulum, trade union policy made a 180-degree turn too. The social dialogue institutions were spectacularly restored – in a symbolic act, the national tripartite forum was given back its original name OÉT of 1998. Labour legislation remedied the greatest trade union grievances. Furthermore, as promised in its election campaign, the government significantly raised pensions and public employee salaries, and also increased funding for social partners. It was a clearly euphoric time for trade unions. With this government policy MSZP's primary goal was not any longer to meet the demands of its considerably weakened political allies but to improve the living standards of its constituency. By 2002 the two large parties (MSZP and FIDESZ) were engaged in a bitter power struggle in which fighting for votes was the most important concern. In its election campaign, MSZP was busy to outbid the right wing's populist political promises with similarly ungrounded leftist promises, and tried to keep them after coming to power. With the very active support of trade unions demanding 'European wages', this policy put the country right on the road to the next budget crisis in 2006. History, to a certain degree, seems to repeat itself: the crisis will be overcome by an austerity package and the reform of the welfare state in which trade unions will not have a say; and this will strengthen one of the confederations (this time LIGA headed by István Gaskó), which in alliance with the opposition parties will put the government under pressure.[5]

Suggested Reading

Héthy, L. and Makó, C. (1972) *Munkásmagatartások és a gazdasági szervezet*, Budapest: Akadémiai.

Héthy, L. (2002) *Social Dialogue and the Expanding World: The Decade of Tripartism in Hungary and in Central and Eastern Europe 1988–99*, Brussels: European Trade Union Institute.

Institute for the History of the 1956: *Hungary 1944–53* at http://www.rev.hu/history_of_45/index.htm

5 The events after 2002 are covered by Neumann (2007) and the EIRO reports and annual reviews on Hungary. http://www.eiro.eurofound.eu.int/2008/country/hungary.html

Kemény, I. (1986) 'Trade Unions and Workers' Interest in Hungary', in Pravda, A. and Ruble, B.A. (eds): *Trade Unions in Communist States*, London: Allen and Unwin.

Kertesi, G. and Sziráczki, G. (1985) 'Worker Behaviour and Labour Market.', in Galasi, P. and Sziráczki, G. (eds) *Labour Market and Second Economy in Hungary*, Frankfurt: Campus.

Kozák, L. (2007) *A független magyar szakszervezetek története és harcai*, Budapest: LIGA.

Lux, J. (2002) *A szakegyletektől a Szaktanácsig*, Budapest: mimeo.

Neumann, L. (2007) 'The State of Trade Unionism in Hungary' in Phelan, C. (ed.) *Trade Union Revitalisation: Trends and Prospects in 34 Countries*, Oxford and Bern: Peter Lang.

Pittaway, M. (2006) 'A Home Front in the Cold War: Hungary, 1948–1989', *History in Focus* 10, at http://www.history.ac.uk/ihr/Focus/cold/articles/pittaway.html

——(2007) 'A magyar forradalom új megközelítésben: az ipari munkásság, a szocializmus széthullása és rekonstrukciója, 1953–1958' in Gyáni, G. and Rainer, J.M. (eds) *Ezerkilencszázötvenhat az újabb történeti irodalomban*, Budapest: 1956-os Intézet.

Rézler, G. (1940) *Magyar gyári munkásság*, Budapest.

Sipos, P. (1991) *Die Sozialdemokratische Partei Ungarns und die Gewerkschaften 1890–1944*, Budapest: Akadémiai.

Soós, K.A. (1984) 'Béralku és 'sérelmi politika' (Adalékok a mechanizmus-reform 1969. évi első megtorpanásának magyarázatához)', *Medvetánc* 2–3.

Szalai, E. (1994) *A civil társadalomtól a politikai társadalom felé*, Budapest: T-Twins.

Thoma, L. (2002) 'A baloldal dilemmája: a szakszervezet' *Mozgó Világ* 1.

Tóth, F. (1997) *Bevezetés a munkaügyi kapcsolatokba (Jegyzet)*, Gödöllő: Gödöllői Agrártudományi Egyetem.

—— (1998) *Konszenzuskereső évek*, Budapest: Autonóm Szakszervezeti Szövetség.

Varga, L. (1984) *Pató Pálok vagy sztahanovisták?*, Budapest: Magvető.

Trade Unionism in Poland since 1945

DAVID OST AND MICHAL WENZEL

1. Introduction

Our chapter outlines key developments in the history of Polish trade unionism from the end of World War II to today. In the case of Poland, of course, the end of World War II did not lead to the revival of prewar unions or industrial relations, but to an entirely new social system with new actors and new rules. Then, in 1989, the social system changed once again, though this time the key trade unions of the 1980s remained the dominant ones afterward, with some new, smaller unions emerging over time. We begin with a discussion of the postwar period, turn to the conflicts that wracked the world of labour during the communist period, and then look at the rise of Solidarity and the great transformation in Polish unionism that began in 1989 and continues today.

One of the factors that makes the study of Polish labour so important, and so complex, is that unlike in any other country in modern times, even other former communist countries, it is labour protest that has consistently driven political changes. The crucial turning points in Poland since 1945 have all been driven by strikes, demonstrations, and organisations of workers. The definitive break with Stalinism occurred in 1956, after massive strikes in Poznan. The Gomulka period came to an end in 1970, after strikes and protests on the Baltic Coast. Gierek's regime suffered its first major crisis in 1976, when its plan to raise prices was met with militant labour opposition in Radom and Ursus. The beginning of the end of the communist system can be dated to 1980, when workers formed Solidarity, and the system's final denouement was provoked by a wave of labour unrest in various industrial cities in 1988, which drove the ruling Communist Party to the bargaining table, and to give up a power a year later.

Yet while *workers* played a role in all the key events of the postwar period, it was not necessarily trade unions that did so. Until 1980, Polish trade unions were run by the ruling Party, which tried to contain discontent and, when that failed, to squash it. Labour opposition thus expressed itself for a long time chiefly in non-institutional form, before organising under the Solidarity umbrella in 1980.

2. Trade Unions before Solidarity (1944–80)

Although the fundamental constraints on trade union activity remained constant throughout the state socialist years, there was real variation in the specifics. Our overview of Polish trade unionism will therefore be chronological, with references to key historical events of political-economic history. We will discuss the official roles of unions as well as their actual functioning. While scholarly analysis and empirical studies about the initial postwar period are scarce, due mainly to political restrictions on research at the time, several research projects from the 1970s and 1980s provide reliable data and information.

Basic Features

'Official' trade unions under state socialism must be considered in the context of the political and economic system under which they operated. The very concept of 'organised labour' acquired a different meaning in postwar Poland than in western capitalist economies, hinging on the distinction that Polish unions were essentially state institutions. Even in theory they were not supposed to be independent. Instead, they were legitimately subject to interference both by the ruling Communist Party and by enterprise management. In practice, unions performed a role of 'transmission belts' from the Communist Party to the masses, much as Lenin (1965) argued they should. Unions helped in recruiting potential party leaders and activists from the ranks of workers, and implementing party policies in the workplace.

Poland embraced a statist model of industrial relations, different both from the pluralist and corporatist models distinguished by Schmitter (1981). Work relations were regulated by the state, and unions had no real autonomy. The principle of political control operated from the very beginning. The first president of the postwar Central Commission of Trade Unions, Adam Dolinski, was a leading Communist Party activist, as were two other of the remaining four national union leaders. From 1948 until 1980, all top trade union officials were Party members, as were most factory union leaders. The merger of political and labour activities occurred on all levels: at the top, the national union president was a member of the Communist Party politburo, and thus obliged to enforce its resolutions. In enterprises, the factory's Party organisation exercised chief control and, together with the firm's director and union representative, it co-managed the enterprise. The aim of the unions was to help enterprises meet the economic plan and to keep the workforce moderately satisfied. This second function became more important after the early years of state socialism, and thus gave the unions a degree of leeway to occasionally defend workers against management. For the most part, however, maintaining employee satisfaction meant administering the vast social welfare functions of the socialist enterprise. Trade unions ran vacation homes and summer camps, provided loans for needy workers, and, in some cases, helped employees get apartments. Unions were organised along the so-called production principle, according to which each enterprise had only one trade union. This meant that unions often grouped workers of many different professions. The trade union in the coal mine, for example, represented both the underground miner and the on-duty nurses. Unions in the communist era were thus *industrial unions*, rather than professional or craft unions.

Postwar Organisation (1944–55)

Officially sanctioned trade unions emerged after World War II region-by-region, as the Soviet army took control of Polish territory. Thus the first trade union councils were formed in eastern Poland, in Bialystkok and Lublin, in August 1944 (Rusiecki 1974: 29). Soon after, unions were also organised on the voivodship and the county (*powiat*) level into regional councils. At the top, on the national level, stood the umbrella organisation Central Commission of Trade Unions, renamed in 1949 as the Central Council of Trade Unions (CRZZ).

The primary cells of trade unions in enterprises were called 'workplace councils' (*rady zakladowe*). These started out as genuine institutions of workplace democracy, created by small groups of workers in the wake of the Nazi defeat in order to keep the firms running and defend them against sabotage by retreating German troops. In order to contain any anti-regime pressure that might issue forth from these councils, the new Communist government quickly embraced them, issuing a decree in February 1945 that mandated the election, by secret ballot, of such councils in all public or private factories of twenty workers or more (Kenney 1997). Formally, the workplace councils were charged with representing the professional interests of employees vis-à-vis the employer. They were responsible for monitoring and controlling working conditions, quality of production, and cultural and welfare facilities. They were to make formal agreements with management over workplace regulations, co-operate with management in hiring and firing, and mediate conflicts between employee and management. Management had a responsibility to consult workplace councils before enacting measures to raise productivity, increase discipline, or make safety, technical, and organisational improvements (Czech and Dermin 1983). In practice, however, given the increasing level of control of unions by Party officials, this formal recognition of workers' councils meant their *de facto* disempowerment.

The economy was progressively taken over by the state in these early postwar years, and trade unions actively helped implement this. According to the Party, the role of trade unions was to 'defend the working class from exploitation by the private sector and from pathologies in the state apparatus', and to 'reinforce the people's government, supporting it on the economic and political fields' (Czech and Dermin 1983: 206). In practice, this meant making life difficult for private entrepreneurs (such as by organising the so-called 'citizen control of prices'), and helping ensure production in state enterprises (such as by sponsoring labour competitions, or organised contests between workers to see who could achieve the highest output targets, or organising campaigns aimed at reducing absenteeism).

The Communist Party, officially called the Polish United Workers Party (PZPR), took complete control of the political system in 1949. The next years, until Stalin's death in 1953, were marked politically by the suppression of all opposition and the imposition of a brutal authoritarianism, and economically by the beginning of the '6-Year Plan' for the rapid industrialisation of the country. Trade unions were seen as instrumental agents for mobilising the workforce and fighting off alleged 'enemies' aimed at sabotaging the effort. 'The relics of reformism and syndicalism, which we see in all those who underestimate the importance of production targets … or [propose] the theory of "independent trade unions", must be thwarted with all vigilance', thundered the programmatic declaration of the national trade union congress of 1949 (Kwartalnik 1978: 40). As one prominent observer put it, 'dictatorial solutions, having been used in the political sphere … were now being applied in economic policy too'. The Party began 'applying all means, including violence, to assure that production targets are fulfilled' (Gilejko 1972: 61).

Reform, Backlash and Stabilisation (1956–70)

The industrialisation of 1949–55 required tremendous sacrifice from workers, for despite the huge increases in production, the standard of living did not rise correspondingly. Brutal methods of enforcing production plans, combined with continuing poverty, led to growing workers' frustration. In 1956 that frustration exploded. This was made possible first of all by the political change in the Soviet Union. In February 1956, in a secret speech delivered to the Twentieth Congress of the Communist Party, Nikita Khrushchev condemned the 'mistakes and deviations' of the Stalinist past.

In denouncing Stalin, Khrushchev was also denouncing the communist leaders of Eastern Europe put in place by Stalin. As it happened, the Polish Stalinist leader, Boleslaw Bierut, died in Moscow shortly after the famous secret speech. When he was replaced by Edward Ochab, the political climate grew milder.

From de Tocqueville we know that revolutions start not when times are bad, but when they are getting better. In June 1956 a pay dispute erupted in the huge Cegielski metal manufacturing plant in Poznan. Officials first agreed to concessions, such as the payment of bonuses for overtime caused by increased output targets, but later withdrew from the agreement. The news about the aborted agreement triggered widespread street protests, and then riots. Authorities called in the army, which suppressed the demonstrations with live fire. The exact number of casualties is unclear to this day, but most estimates point to about 60 to 80 people dead, with over 500 wounded. Throughout this conflict, the official trade unions and striking workers stood on opposing sides. In the initial negotiations, the CRZZ and the Ministry of Machine Industry were on one side, with plant workers' representatives on the other. Former CRZZ president Kazimierz Witaszewski was now head of the political office in the army, and took an extreme hard-line position in the dispute.

Political reform came to Poland in October 1956, in large part as a result of the fallout from the Poznan events. Wladyslaw Gomulka, a communist leader who had been imprisoned during the Stalinist years, was released and made head of the Communist Party. The new leadership was greeted with a great deal of hope; people anticipated liberalisation, greater freedom, and a certain degree of independence from the Soviet Union. Some expectations were met: the new leadership allowed the publication of critical and independent publications, reversed the collectivisation of agriculture, and allowed some independent Catholic deputies into parliament. Within a few years, however, most of these political gains were reversed.

Similar developments occurred in industrial relations. In November 1956, a new CRZZ leadership denounced what the unions had done in the previous years, calling this a time when unions 'ceased to be a genuine representative and defender of the interests of working people', and 'pushed unions into becoming mobilisers of production, while neglecting the needs of the working class' (quoted in *Przeglad Zwiazkowy* 1956: 4–5). As a gesture of reform, and also to mollify the labour unrest that had been percolating since Poznan, the new Gomulka leadership now established workers' councils (*rady robotnicze* – not to be confused with 'workplace councils', *rady zakładowe*, or the official trade union cells). As open acknowledgement that the trade unions had become widely discredited in the workplace, workers' councils were intended to be institutions for the participation of workers in firm decision-making processes. Formally, they were to be consulted on a wide range of matters: economic plans, enterprise development, allocation of profits, output norms and pay rates. Within a few years, however, this experiment ended. As it happened, it was the official unions, despite the change of leadership, which forced the demise of the council movement. In part, this was because some of the official responsibilities of the councils overlapped with that of the trade unions, such as consulting over pay rates and revenue allocation. Mostly, however, unions simply opposed the competition, and felt threatened by the support the council movement had received. The Party also began fearing the workers' councils, having seen workers take them more seriously than the Party apparently hoped. And so, in 1958, when the political mobilisation of 1956 had definitively passed, Gomulka, speaking at the Fourth Congress of the CRZZ, proposed the creation of so-called 'conferences of worker self-management', which would bring together workers' councils, workplace councils and the enterprise party cell. With the passing of the law in December 1958, workers' councils effectively disappeared (Góralski 1982: 49). In the following decade, known as the 'little stabilisation' (1958–68), trade unions chiefly focused on their role as provider of welfare benefits (such as organising cultural events, arranging holidays in union-owned or enterprise-owned resorts, and procuring scarce consumer goods), and political and economic mobiliser of the workforce. Methods of enforcing production plans became less coercive, but unions still saw such activity as part of their function. At its Fifth Congress in 1964, the PZPR listed some of the tasks of trade unions: 'constantly increasing production through increasing labour productivity and improving enterprise cost-efficiency, supporting workers in rationalisation initiatives, spreading the idea of work competitiveness, and increasing the professional qualifications of employees' (Kondrat and Pulikowski 1984: 61).

Political stability came to an end in 1968, when the country was wracked by student protests and a wave of intellectual dissent. The Party responded by turning to its nationalist wing, and initiating an anti-intellectual and anti-Semitic purge, and it used the trade unions to send its message. Enterprises would close down for hours at a time, and bus employees to take part in 'spontaneous' demonstrations in which 'the working class' carried banners denouncing students and 'Zionists'. But if Party officials thought workers were now safely on their side, they soon found out how wrong they were. In December 1970 strikes erupted in cities all along the Polish coast: Gdansk, Gdynia, Szczecin and Elblag. The direct cause of the protests was price hikes for meat; the indirect cause was the long-lasting stagnation in living standards, and a sense that no change was imminent. The protests were particularly strong in the shipyards, whose largely skilled workforce faced especially acute cutbacks (Laba 1991). Strikes turned to street protests, culminating in the burning down of Communist Party headquarters in Szczecin and mass demonstrations in Gdansk. As in 1956, the Party reacted with force. The army and police opened fire on protesting workers, killing at least 39 and wounding over 1,000. Three thousand people were arrested (Goodwyn 1991; Eisler 2000). The decision to use force was taken by the PZPR Politburo. One of its members was Ignacy Loga-Sowinski, the president of CRZZ.

In retrospect, it can be said that this is where Solidarity began. This was the first time in postwar Polish history that a workers' opposition movement persevered, despite severe repression. In December 1970 Gomulka was replaced by Edward Gierek, party leader from Katowice, but rather than stifling labour activism, the leadership change only served to intensify it. Renewed strikes in January 1971 forced Gierek to travel to the Baltic Coast and concede to a list of demands presented by the strike committee. In Szczecin, the committee, led by Edmund Baluka, formed itself as the independent 'Workers Commission', which was allowed to exist outside the official trade union structure in order to monitor fulfilment of the demands negotiated with Gierek. One of those demands was for free elections of shipyard union officials (Baluka and Barker 1977). Ironically, it was the satisfaction of this radical demand that led to the upstart workers' defeat. For when Baluka and others won the contested elections and entered the official union structure, they lost their independent base of committed activists, and in the subsequent months were crushed from within, with Baluka himself ultimately driven into exile.

This experience paved the way for Solidarity because it taught workers that they could not defend themselves *within* the official unions, but only by forming an alternative to them. It was the political organisation KOR, or Workers' Defence Committee, that first proposed the organisation of parallel civic institutions as a strategy for opposing the communist system. KOR was formed in 1976 by intellectuals such as Jacek Kuron, Adam Michnik and Antoni Macierewicz, in order to defend workers persecuted for organising strikes earlier in the year. Two years later, in large part thanks to KOR's success in renewing ties between workers and intellectuals, Gdansk opposition activists Andrzej Gwiazda and Krzysztof Wyszkowski formed the 'Free Trade Unions of the Coast', and soon recruited a Gdansk 1970 strike veteran named Lech Walesa.

Growth and Crisis (1970–80)

In addition to the rise of oppositional trade union activism, the 1970s witnessed change in the party management of the economy. In contrast to previous leadership, the Gierek regime took substantial measures to improve living standards. Consumption rose fast, especially in the first half of the decade. With new access to global capital as a consequence of détente, the state also embarked on an energetic modernisation of industry, though inadequate organisation of the economy and the late 1970s global recession resulted in a fast-growing budget deficit a crippling international debt.

The official unions also began to change as well. They remained, as before, a way for the party to control the workforce, recruit promising future cadre, and organise distribution of welfare provisions and entitlements. But mobilisation methods now changed; there was less coercion and more positive incentives. Unions organised more sports and cultural events, and the number of employees vacationing in union-run resorts rose quickly. For a short time in the early 1970s, due in large part to the 1970–1 strike wave, unions even started to more forcefully defend workers' basic economic interests. Unionists felt a need to redefine their activity. 'Let the Party be a party, the government a government, and let trade unions be trade unions', went a motto popular for a time.

By the latter part of the decade, however, the tide of change had ebbed (Widera and Gardawski 1984). Party leaders still tried to improve the economic conditions of workers, as the low commitment Gomulka had shown in this area was seen as the chief reason for his demise, but the more participatory and inclusive experiments in industrial relations were brought to a halt. If anything, the official trade unions became even more closely tied to political leaders. Centralisation also tightened. The CRZZ assumed greater control over the regional (voivodship) trade union councils, and it pressured factory union cells to sever horizontal ties to other unions in the same sector in favour of more vertical subordination to the national union leadership.

The year 1976 witnessed a brief strike wave, triggered by the same proximate cause as the 1970 strikes: a sharp rise in the price of meat. News of the price hikes pushed workers in most industrial plants in the city of Radom to go on strike and, after the plants were locked out, onto the streets. The protests were apparently spontaneous. The demonstrations were harshly pacified by the police, and massive arrests followed. The CRZZ did not support the workers; at a plenary meeting in December 1976 the CRZZ president declared that 'the working class and millions of people turn away from the organisers [of the Radom strikes] with disgust' (Kondrat and Pulikowski 1984: 85), thereby making clear that the unions were going to treat strike activists the same way.

The CRZZ's own rules, it might be noted, did allow for the possibility of a strike. At its Fourth Congress in 1958, it declared that in the case of persistent violation of employee rights, as a last resort, after a complex mediating procedure had been exhausted, a union had a right to stage a short warning strike lasting several minutes. Although that rule remained valid until the end of the CRZZ's existence in 1980, there is not a single record of it ever being invoked. Every strike between 1958 and 1980 took place despite the opposition of the official trade unions (Góralski 1984: 50).

Unions according to Workers

What did workers think of their unions? It is one thing to say that unions, until 1980, were subordinate to Party authorities and worked closely with management. But trade unions are worth what members get out of them. Were members able to use these unions for their own benefit? Did unions themselves try to compensate for their lack of autonomy by performing well in other areas? How did workers see trade unions – as ally, enemy, something irrelevant?

We can get some answers to these questions from a large survey of trade unionists conducted in 1979, a year before the postwar model ceased to operate. Extensive research was conducted in industrial enterprises in Warsaw and Katowice. The results of that research provide unique insight into workers' attitudes in the 1970s (Gilejko 1980; Widera and Gardawski 1984).

The aim of the survey was to measure the fit between what workers expected of their unions and what they actually got from their unions. As for expectations, first place went to the provision of welfare services. Trade union members expected unions to do such things as organise holidays, summer camps, sporting events and funerals. Second, they expected unions to improve working conditions. Lower-ranked expectations were pay and housing problems. Issues related to the defence of employee interests, however, were only rarely mentioned. As for union accomplishments, or what members actually got from unions, the list of items is dominated by the distribution of various welfare entitlements, chiefly those concerned with organising vacation and free time. Some respondents noted improved working conditions, and better-supplied workplace factory cafeterias. Workers did not notice much effect of trade unions regarding pay increases or housing issues (Gilejko 1980: 63, 205).

Overall, the survey indicates that workers had a restrictive view of the role of trade unions, largely accepting the official model. Workers tended to see themselves as clients of unions, not as active participants in shaping them (Gilejko 1980: 51). However, unions underperformed in the role of benefactor: only about half of the members believed they got some benefits from them.

As for attitudes to professional unionists, workers tended to see them as people who occupied prestigious positions which gave them access to power and a lighter work load. Consequently, they did not believe these professional activists were qualified to speak on behalf of the rank and file. The professional union activists themselves, meanwhile, who tended to be older, with seniority, and often members of the party, acknowledged that their union activity brought them certain benefits. But they believed they defended general societal interests, not their own (Gilejko 1980: 59, 207).

Despite their misgivings, workers did not want to part with their unions. Most believed that if the unions disappeared, their conditions would decline. Yet we can see cleavages here that would be important for the future. For example, women were more worried than men about a hypothetical absence of unions. The older were more worried than the younger. The lesser skilled were more worried than the highly skilled. In other words, young and skilled male workers were least attached and least appreciative of the official trade unions. This is the group that would soon go on to form the backbone of Solidarity. Overall, workers generally accepted trade unions in 1979, but their acceptance was shallow. As events only a year later would show, they accepted the prevailing union model only because they saw no alternative.

3. Trade Unions during Late Communism (1980–9)

Solidarity

The end of the postwar model of trade unionism came in August 1980. The strike wave started once again in the shipbuilding plants on the Baltic Coast, and soon swept to other big industrial centres (Laba 1991). And once again the direct cause of the strikes was food price increases. This time, however, workers had learned the lessons of 1971, and so their first demand, the one they treated as non-negotiable, was not for the rescinding of the price hikes but for legalisation of trade unions independent of the ruling party. Unable to break the strike, and limited in its opportunities because of the severity of the economic crisis, the authorities accepted the demand, signing the historic Gdansk Agreement on 31 August 1980.

Party authorities at first hoped to limit the formation of independent unions to Gdansk. But workers from all over the country began forming their own strike committees to demand independent unions, and flocked to Gdansk to learn how to do it. On 11 September a strike settlement in Katowice explicitly extended the Gdansk Accord to the whole country. A week later, independent union activists meeting in Gdansk decided to seek registration of a single national union called 'Solidarity'.

The official unions found themselves in a hopeless crisis. Cognisant of the stakes, CRZZ had originally taken a hard-line position against the recognition of Solidarity. At a CRZZ meeting of 19 August union president and Politburo member Jan Szydlak vowed that 'we shall not give up power and shall not share it'. But Szydlak was soon deposed and removed from the Politburo, and in October 1980 the CRZZ dissolved itself. A new central body called the Associative Commission of Sectoral Trade Unions was formed in its place, though it never attained great significance.

From August 1980 until the imposition of martial law in December 1981, Solidarity was the biggest and most important trade union in Poland, with a total membership of about 7 or 8 million members (Wenzel 2008). What did it do as a trade union? It let loose a popular, participatory union experiment, creating one of the most democratic organisations in the history of trade unionism. There were two reasons for this openness to participation from below: first, the ideology and political commitments of the union's founders and leaders, many of whom were influenced by New Left self-management ideas popular in the 1970s (Ost 1990), and second, the constant threat from the Communist Party-state, which never fully adapted itself – and never *could* fully adapt itself – to the existence of an independent organisation. If the first factor made activists sympathetic to a broad, participatory union, the second factor virtually required it, since the best way to thwart repression was to have too many activists to be repressed. Thus, anyone who wanted to get involved could do so, and being involved often meant simply coming to meetings and sympathising with the cause. This was because Solidarity was not just a trade union but a vehicle for a national, democratic uprising (see Touraine 1983). Union meetings were frequent and widely attended, and they concerned not just workplace affairs but also politics and history. Every factory had a factory newsletter, and Solidarity took these over too. Solidarity offices in 1980–1 had the look and feel of centres of political radicalism, with activists engaged in the kind of direct democratic participation common to revolutionary moments. Journalists at the time compared it, not without reason, to the enthusiastic collective action present at the Paris Commune, to Spanish anarchist strongholds during the Civil War, or even to the early Russian soviets. This was direct democracy at its finest.

This is not to say that Solidarity did not help improve working conditions. It did, largely because of the presence of these strong, self-confident workers' organisations in each firm. Local Solidarity unions became vigilant in monitoring safety and social conditions. This was a big boon, for example, in mining, which had a particularly bad safety record in the 1970s, due to perilous round-the-clock work shifts aimed at extracting maximum amounts of Poland's sole export commodity with a stable, hard-currency outlet. Mining deaths and accidents dropped considerably with the appearance of Solidarity.

In December 1981, the ruling PZPR declared martial law, suspending all trade union activity. (Formally it was the army that declared martial law, but the army leader and party leader was the same Wojciech Jaruzelski, and the party quickly resumed all governing power.) Most Solidarity leaders were arrested, and strikes were quickly suppressed. It was only in 1983 that Poland officially allowed trade union activity again, but even then it allowed only small enterprise unions, no national organisations, and it did not allow the re-legalisation of Solidarity. In 1984 it did allow the formation of a national trade union coordinating committee for the small, largely pro-government trade unions that had formed – this became the National Council of Trade Unions, known by its Polish initials as OPZZ – but it still did not allow for the revival of Solidarity.

Solidarity did continue to exist during this time, but chiefly as an underground political organisation. Underground union cells also existed in many factories, but even these did not do much trade union work *per se*. In part, this was because the political leadership of underground Solidarity wanted to de-emphasise labour activity. Solidarity during martial law became largely a political body with political ambitions, and trade union activity was seen not only as something secondary to political activity, but even as something that could harm that political activity by allowing untrained workers to become leaders and thus alienating potential supporters (Ost 2005).

On the other hand, even if it had wanted to pursue trade unionism, there is not much that could have been done, given the nature of the system. Just as Solidarity could not be a 'classic' trade union in 1980–1, it could not be so afterwards. This was due to the economic system, not the political one. It is worthwhile exploring this point, not just to explain what Solidarity did and did not do in the 1980s, but to explain the particular dilemmas and problems in the 1990s, after the collapse of the communist system.

The economic system posed the greatest barriers to trade unionism. Some unions can fight their way to prominence under a capitalist dictatorship, as in Spain during the late Franco years or South Africa in the late apartheid years. But Solidarity could not behave like the famous *Comisiones Obreras*, or Workers' Commissions, that existed illegally in Spain in the 1960s and 1970s. The *Comisiones* were active in firms that needed some consent from the workforce, since these were privately owned firms that hired mostly skilled male labourers producing goods that the firms hoped to sell on the world market, in a context where the owners and an increasingly technocratic state bureaucracy hoped to join the European Union. The *Comisiones* could act as an underground trade union negotiating pay rates and working conditions because the other side was made up of private owners who had an economic incentive to have a satisfied workforce, or at least not a completely hostile workforce, and a political incentive to show that they nominally respected the autonomy of the workforce. The Congress of South African Trade Unions, or COSATU, had a similar ability to pressure employers because those too needed skilled labour that only blacks had (lesser-skilled whites having been given their mostly supervisory positions due to race alone), and because they needed to sell their wares on a world market whose customers had become increasingly hostile to apartheid.

In Poland, as in other state socialist countries, although it was going through a period of substantial economic reform of its own, firms were still state-owned, employing – or rather over-employing – large numbers of men and women of different skills, producing goods and services that were not intended to be competitive on the world market, and the sale of which would not redound to the individual benefit of anyone. Not only was there no economic incentive for enterprise mangers to negotiate with trade unions, but the workforce was too diverse for a trade union that could represent all their economic interests. Capitalist firms seeking to succeed on the world market, and existing where previous political struggles have made democracy a guiding principle, have incentives to negotiate with unions in ways that state-owned firms which exist more to provide employment to people than to produce competitive products, and existing in a context of assured single-party rule, simply do not. In the state socialist context, moreover, pacts with independent trade unions do not even make much sense, since economic plans are being made from above. The problem for trade unions under state socialism stems not from Lenin's mandate that unions serve as 'transmission belts' implementing party policies, but from that system's very concept of an economy, where state ownership, top-down planning, and full employment take precedence over everything else.

Official Trade Unions in the 1980s

Following martial law, the PZPR set about the task of rebuilding an official union movement. In 1983 it allowed only the revival of factory unions; in 1984 it allowed those unions to group together under the umbrella organisation of the National Council of Trade Unions (*Ogólnopolska Porozumienie Związków Zawodowych*, or OPZZ). OPZZ described itself as an authentic, apolitical union movement, in contrast to Solidarity. Solidarity members and activists treated these unions as a political project of the party, and treated those who joined as offering a kind of support to the regime.

Membership in OPZZ was not compulsory, and workers faced no sanctions for not joining. That in itself indicates the extent to which OPZZ really was a different kind of trade union than had existed in the communist system in the past. The official line of the party at this time was that the rise of Solidarity was a legitimate expression of justifiable working class discontent, but that Solidarity had become 'politicised' and taken over by 'counter-revolutionary' forces. OPZZ was presented as the kind of union workers 'really' needed, and it even had the formal right to strike. Indeed, some Solidarity activists initially wanted to test the limits of the new trade union law by joining an OPZZ union and trying to turn it into a more militant union like Solidarity. Solidarity leaders discouraged such a move, however, and so OPZZ arose as a kind of official, pro-party trade union federation, though with considerable more autonomy than official unions had had in the past.

In terms of what OPZZ unions actually did at the workplace, they essentially continued the model of official trade unions of the 1970s. They were concerned primarily with employee welfare services (cultural and sports events, holidays, summer camps, emergency financial aid, housing issues), defended employees in case of conflict with management, concerned themselves with health and safety issues, and also joined with management to improve work efficiency. The workplace OPZZ leader was often incorporated into enterprise management.

Aside from committed Solidarity activists, workers generally had a positive opinion of OPZZ unions. Membership went up to about 3 million by 1989. But they were also seen as having only a very limited scope for independent action, as being too dependent on management. OPZZ unions seem to have been hampered by an institutionalised incapacity to achieve structural change either in the enterprise or at the national level. A significant barrier to their growth was their political involvement on the side of the party at a time of intense domestic and cultural conflict (CBOS 1985, 1986, 1988a).

OPZZ also had competition from employee councils *(rady pracownicze)*, which were reintroduced in 1981, at the height Solidarity's power, as a form of employee participation. Because of martial law, these councils had only limited influence on the functioning of the enterprise, and they were often dominated by middle management (although underground Solidarity activists began to get involved with them by the late 1980s). They competed with OPZZ in social welfare work, and empirical research (CBOS 1988b) shows there was typically a degree of hostility between the two.

4. Systematic Transformation and Beyond (1989–2008)

What happened after the fall of the communist system in 1989? It is here where Solidarity lost its bearings. Just when it was able to be a trade union again – with firms becoming marketised and privatised, and those of its cadre who were interested chiefly in politics or professional advancement able finally to go off freely into government or business – it did not quite know how to be one. Of course, things were not going to be easy. There were not yet private owners with whom to negotiate agreements, but state-owned firms with uncertain economic prospects, which no union wanted to drive into bankruptcy. As a result, Solidarity had severe difficulties restoring its membership base to the 1980–1 levels. It resisted the government in some areas, such as wage controls and privatisation policy. On the latter, for example, where the government wanted to weaken employee councils and sell off firms to whomever it chose, Solidarity insisted on the rights of the workforce to monitor the sale of firm assets. This signalled the start of a pattern for Solidarity in the next decade: it acted as a defender of workers' rights as owners, but not as a defender of workers as workers.

Contradictions between the role of Solidarity as a civic-political movement and the trade union appeared (Wenzel 1998). Ironically, some Solidarity leaders may not have wanted to build strong unions. Lech Walesa articulated this principle at the very outset of the transition, in September 1989, telling his supporters, 'We will not catch up to Europe if we build a strong trade union'. At the time, of course, Walesa was both a union leader and preparing to be a presidential candidate, and so took a broader perspective. He declared, for example, a union 'umbrella' over economic reform, meaning that Solidarity would generally vouch for the new policies and do its best to help them succeed.

In enterprises, Solidarity cells tended to work closely with the new management. The union worked with employee councils to elect new managers, frequently from Solidarity ranks, and then cooperated with the new leaders to push the firm towards market reforms and privatisation. In a 1994 survey of unionists from 95 manufacturing firms throughout the country, over half the Solidarity respondents, when asked why they were involved in the union, said they did so in order to *promote* market reform and *speed* the privatisation process, while less than one-fifth mentioned fighting the effects of shock therapy (Ost and Weinstein 1999). Interestingly, most of them also tended to believe that firms did not need much employee representation in the long run. That is, they believed that *state-owned* firms required extensive employee input, but chiefly in order to guarantee against abuse by state bureaucrats. Private firms, however, unionists believed did *not* require much input, since the owners themselves would make sure things went right.

It is no surprise, then, that union membership began to decline. This resulted from a number of factors: drastic downsizing of the old manufacturing base, the new political situation (belonging to Solidarity no longer served as a sign of political protest), rapid growth of the informal sector and of tiny private firms, and the unwillingness of Solidarity to strongly defend its members due to the union leadership's own belief in the need for radical reform. In 1991 Solidarity had 3 to 3.5 million members. By 1996 that dropped to 1.2 million, and by 1999 to about 900,000.

Of course, Solidarity was not the only union now, besides OPZZ. In fact, 1989 brought about an enormous growth in the number of trade unions, if not in the number of trade union members. The new trade union law of 1990 allowed multiple unions to exist in a firm, permitting a founding committee of as few as ten employees to establish a union. The law, in fact, promoted the multiplication of unions, since union officials enjoyed such benefits as protection from dismissal and an enterprise-financed office and salary. Big firms in particular saw a steep rise in the number of unions, which spurred a competition for members, on which the legal privileges depended. By 2006, about half of the unionised workforce was employed in firms where more than one union existed (CBOS 2006). Although the call for 'trade union pluralism' was central to Solidarity in 1980, this principle has become dysfunctional today as a model for the articulation of interests, since industrial conflict negotiations must be conducted sometimes with miniscule unions. In May 2008 the Tripartite Commission put forward a proposal to change the trade union law so as to require negotiations only with unions that represent a significant percentage of the workforce in an enterprise. Both Solidarity and OPZZ supported the proposal. In 2002 the Tripartite Commission itself changed its rules so as not to be forced to invite tiny unions to its meetings. This resulted in the formation of a third large national union organisation, a confederation known as Forum of Trade Unions (FZZ). (OPZZ is also a confederation, while Solidarity is a unitary union.) These three remain the dominant trade unions in Poland today, with Solidarity and OPZZ stronger than Forum.

It was around the end of the last century that unionism started to change (see Gardawski 2003). A number of factors contributed to this. Perhaps most important is that time had passed, a new generation was emerging, and ideas about the benefits of market economies that seemed convincing in 1989 no longer appeared so certain. Solidarity was in bad shape by 2000. It was burdened with responsibility for an unpopular government. In 1997 the Solidarity Electoral Action coalition, made up of over thirty small self-defined right-wing parties, and led by Solidarity's president Marian Krzaklewski, had come to power and introduced a number of painful systemic reforms. The economy started to fall into recession. Unemployment, which had hit a post-1989 low of 10.4 per cent in 1998, started to rise dramatically, to 15.1 per cent in 2000 and 19.8 per cent in 2002, the highest among the eastern European countries slated to join the European Union. What made this recession different from the previous one is that this one could not be blamed on the old communist system. Many rank-and-file unionists started blaming it on Solidarity. Ten years earlier, many in Solidarity were happy to be associated with tough reforms, but no longer. Being associated with a governing party was taking its toll, and Solidarity responded by cutting back its ties with politics and by becoming more committed to defending their members than to defending economic reform or to promoting the fortunes of right-wing political parties.

Solidarity had been active in politics throughout the 1990s. In the 1991 elections it fielded a group of candidates and won parliamentary representation. In 1996 it founded Solidarity Electoral Action and helped bring it into power. But the increasing unpopularity of that government alerted leaders to the perils of political activism, and so in May 2001 Solidarity formally severed its ties to Solidarity Electoral Action. A year later it voted Marian Krzaklewski out of office, electing a new leader, Janusz Sniadek, who is much less committed to politics than Krzaklewski ever was. It is not totally clear that this separation from politics will last indefinitely. In 2005 Solidarity did not formally endorse any party, but the Law and Justice led by the Kaczynski brothers, which won the elections, did put Solidarity candidates on its electoral lists. OPZZ, meanwhile, has also seen its long-standing organisational and personal ties to the Democratic Left Alliance weaken over time, although some OPZZ leaders still serve as SLD deputies. The dominant party at the time of this writing, Civic Platform, does not have ties with any unions.

When unions put less stock into making gains through political connections, they put more into doing so by workplace organising, and that is also something that has been expanding since around 2000. In the 1990s, unions did almost no organising work in the new private sector. By the beginning of the twenty-first century, they have developed more sophisticated organising techniques and have become increasingly effective in sectors where unions were previously absent. Solidarity started putting more energy into a Union Development Office, and both Solidarity and OPZZ started organising drives in the private sector, particularly in retail (hyper-markets).

Part of the reason good old-fashioned union work has become more in vogue in Poland has to do with the changing times. In 1989 unionism was associated in many people's minds – especially Solidarity supporters – with the struggle against communism, not protection against capitalism. By 2000 many older workers began to think that they really needed unions in the new society after all, while a new generation emerged that had work experience *only* in a market economy. The perspective of activists changed too. In 1989 many Solidarity activists had a number of opportunities open to them: they could exit to better-paying and higher-status jobs in management, government, private business, or civil society. In 2000 those options were largely gone. Union officials themselves needed the union more than before. Finally, the firms had also changed. The massive workforce reductions of the 1990s were in the past. Firms were leaner than before, with less unskilled workers and less women. As manufacturing work became based more in skilled male labour, skilled male labourers got more involved in unionism. One of the reasons this group had not been very active in unionism in the early post-communist period is that it did not want to protect the jobs of the lesser-skilled labourers, working chiefly because of the social employment policies of the old regime. Skilled workers wanted these unskilled labourers out. By the turn of the century, they *were* out, and unionism now took on a different meaning. All of this meant that factory unions are now led by different kinds of people than in the past: fewer political activists, and more focused on workplace issues.

5. Density Rates

Before we present data on union density rates in the postwar period, a word of caution. There are at least three reasons why it is misleading to compare union density from 1944 to 1980, during the 1980s, and after 1989. First, unions in the three periods were essentially different types of organisations bearing the same name. In the first postwar years, membership was connected with state efforts to transform the economy. In the 1970s, union membership was automatic and largely compulsory. In the 1980s, membership had as much to do with making a political statement as with enterprise-level activity. It was only after 1989 that unions became truly voluntary and largely, though not entirely, shed their political functions. Second, statistics for the years prior to 1980 are not reliable. This was noted even by agencies that produced them; sometimes reservations were officially published. Third, measurement methodology differed. For the years 1944–80, we have the official numbers given by CRZZ, based on statistics given by member unions. There is a high probability of inflated numbers. For the years 1980–2008, data from public opinion surveys are available. Therefore, reliable comparisons can be made for the last 28 years.

According to CRZZ statistics, union density rose from 59 per cent in 1945 to 72 per cent in 1955 and 81 per cent in 1960. Density passed 90 per cent at the start of the 1970s, and in 1978 rose to a high of 97 per cent of all employees, for a total of 13.4 people in trade unions (*Zwiazki Zawodowe w liczbach* 1979).

For the years 1980–2008, we use national public opinion research, provided by the Public Opinion Research Centre, CBOS. In 1983 it began asking questions about union membership, in representative nationwide surveys of the entire adult population, using retroactive declarations to assess 1980–1 membership. According to these sources, 65 per cent of employees belonged to a trade union in 1981, the majority to Solidarity. The drop in density from 1978 to 1981 can be accounted for by the fact that membership ceased being automatic and compulsory. From 1984 to 1988, only OPZZ unions were legal. However, Solidarity acted clandestinely, and many people still considered themselves to be members. According to public opinion declarations, 35 to 40 per cent of employees belonged to unions during these years.

Since 1989, union density has fallen systematically, from 28 per cent in 1991 to 17 per cent in 2008. Solidarity is the strongest (5 per cent of all employees), followed by OPZZ (4 per cent), and Forum (2 per cent). The remaining 6 per cent belong to unions unaffiliated with any national-level organisation (Wenzel 2008).

In Poland, as in other developed countries, the manufacturing sector has declined and the service sector has grown. Since unions were strong in manufacturing, the loss of these jobs has meant a net loss for unions. This has been a tendency throughout the EU and in all OECD countries (Ebbinghaus 2002). The Polish trends in this regard are thus typical. Density rates are low in comparison to most western EU states, although not as low as in France (where unions, nevertheless, have a great deal of clout), while the impact and scope of collective bargaining is much lower in Poland than in the west.

Today, unions are at their densest in the public sector. In the private sector, unions are more prevalent in privat*ised* industries than in the new private sector. In this new private sector they are very weak, due to such factors as the high number of jobs in micro-enterprises, the inability or unwillingness of established unions to organise there, management obstruction, and the low social capital of much of this workforce. Some highly educated white-collar occupations, such as doctors, nurses, teachers, and civil servants, are especially well-organised, mostly in unions belonging to OPZZ or to nationally unaffiliated unions. Solidarity today is mostly a blue-collar union.

6. Conclusion

We have written about positive changes in the Polish trade union movement since 2000, with the emergence of a more committed group of activists. Is this trend likely to continue? Will unions grow stronger in the future? As far as unionism in manufacturing is concerned, there are good arguments for both possible answers to the question. Supporting the 'yes' answer, that unions will grow stronger, we have already pointed to some factors: the survival needs of union officials, the transformation of the post-communist firm (the removal of surplus workers that makes the remainder more amenable to unions), and the rise of a new generation. There are also two international factors promoting continued union development: incorporation into the European Union, and emerging international labour solidarity. Even if the EU is going through a neo-liberal turn, as many have argued (van der Pijl 2006), its laws and institutions still recognise unions as a constitutive part of the European political economy, and as necessary 'social partners' in governance. Polish unions have received resources and legitimacy, and they have gained important international labour contacts from the EU, and this is likely to continue. As for international labour solidarity, this includes aid from trade unions in old EU countries as well as from elsewhere. The

American AFL-CIO and Change to Win union federations have devoted resources to teach organising techniques (the Service Employees International Union advised in the building of Solidarity's Union Development Office), and west European trade unions have become increasingly interested in working with Polish and other east European unions because west European corporations have been heavily investing there. Precisely because capital mobility encourages a 'race to the bottom', unions are becoming more internationally oriented as a form of self-defence, and this can only help relatively weak eastern European unions.

On the other hand, there are still formidable obstacles to the re-emergence of a strong union movement in Polish manufacturing. The giant state-owned firms of the past have cut their workforce drastically, if they have stayed in business at all, and have increased hiring of temporary workers and 'independent contractors' (the latter often the same employees as before, pressured to give up their formal employment). Numerous small firms and micro-firms entered the market. The result is that many employees simply do not have the chance to unionise, and unions have become concentrated in elite sectors of the manufacturing world, and in the public service sector. Ideologically, the media remains largely critical of trade unions, particularly in the manufacturing sectors, and intellectual support for unionism – always important in creating a general climate favourable to working class collective action – has declined dramatically over the years. Organisationally, the large number of small firms run by managers largely hostile to unions makes organising very difficult. All in all, the legacies not of communism but of post-communism, with its backlash against the idea of strong trade unionism, present formidable problems for the future (see Ost 2006).

Things look differently in the non-manufacturing sectors. Today, both structural economic change and different levels of workforce mobilisation have changed the structure of Polish trade union membership a great deal. In 2008 the typical union member is no longer a factory worker. Unionisation is highest among white-collar employees, especially those who are relatively well-educated and working for the state. The most highly unionised sectors today are in health care, education, and civil service. Some of these groups have shown savvy organising capacities of late. In 2007 nurses staged a remarkable 10-week protest action, including a tent city set up opposite the Prime Minister's office in Warsaw, to demand higher wages and better working conditions. Though they did not win their demands, they enjoyed strong support from local citizens, and demonstrated a resolve that suggests growing strength in the future.

Of course, the continued institutional division of the Polish labour movement, chiefly along the lines of past political affiliations, remains a problem. While tensions and hostility between Solidarity and OPZZ are not as great as in the early 1990s, to say nothing of the mid-1980s, they still do take their toll. At the factory level, the two unions usually do manage to cooperate harmoniously, but the continuing differences at the national level prevent a unified approach to issues like improving labour legislation or organising the unorganised. There is hope that this will change in the future, for reasons such as the emergence of a new generation, to whom the old battles seem arcane, and in order to enable greater functional cooperation with both the European Union and European trade unions. Perhaps the greatest development in recent years is that the wariness towards trade unions that was sometimes apparent within the ranks of unionists themselves (Ost 2005), due to the legacy of Solidarity as an anti-communist movement, seems to be a thing of the past.

In the future, then, unions are likely to remain strong in public sector services, and to be increasingly divided in the manufacturing sectors between those who have clout (skilled labourers in larger firms, with the potential for cross-border labour alliances) and those who do not (lesser skilled workers in small firms, producing non-branded items). As for the latter, the old paradox holds: that those who need union protection the most, get it the least.

Suggested Reading

Baluka, E. and Barker, E. (1977) 'Workers Struggles in Poland', *International Socialism* 94 (January), available online at http://www.marxists.org/history/etol/newspape/isj/1977/no094/baluka.htm

CBOS (1985) *Samorząd pracowniczy w przedsiębiorstwach przemysłowych*, research report available at: www.cbos.pl

—— (1986) *Ocena działalności związków zawodowych przez pracowników gospodarki uspołecznionej*, research report available at: www.cbos.pl

—— (1988a) *Opinia społeczna o działalności związków zawodowych w latach 1983–1988*, research report available at: www.cbos.pl

—— (1988b) *Rola rady pracowniczej w uspołecznieniu zarządzania* przedsiębiorstwem, research report available at: www.cbos.pl

—— (2006) *Układy zbiorowe pracy, łamanie praw pracowniczych i 'szara strefa' w zatrudnieniu*. research report available at: www.cbos.pl

Czech, S. and Dermin, R. (1983) *Ruch zawodowy na Śląsku Opolskim w latach 1945–1980*, Opole: Instytut Śląski.

Ebbinghaus, B. (2002) 'Trade Unions' Changing Role: Membership Erosion, Organisational Reform and Social Partnership in Europe', *Industrial Relations Journal* 33 (5).

Eisler, J. (ed.) (2000) *Grudzień 1970 w dokumentach MSW*, Warsaw: IPN.

Gardawski, J. (2003) *Konfliktowy pluralizm związków zawodowych*, Warsaw: Fundacja im. Friedricha Eberta.

Gilejko, L. et al. (1980) *Realizacja podstawowych funkcji zwiazków zawodowych, ich ocean w srodowisku pracowniczym i postulowany model dzialania*, Warsaw: SGPiS-IGS.

Gilejko, L. (1972) *Związki zawodowe w procesie przemian społecznych w PRL* Warsaw: Inst. Wyd. CRZZ.

Goodwyn, L. (1991) *Breaking the Barrier: The Rise of Solidarity in Poland*, New York: Oxford University Press.

Góralski, W. (1982) *Spór o związki zawodowe, Vol. 2*, Warsaw: IWZZ.

Kenney, P. (1997) *Rebuilding Poland: Workers and Communists 1945–1950*, Ithaca: Cornell University Press.

Kondrat, R. and Pulikowski, W. (1984) *Związki zawodowe – doświadczenia i perspektywy*, Warsaw: Książka i Wiedza.

Kwartalnik Historii Ruchu Związkowego (1978), No. 4.

Laba, R. (1991) *The Roots of Solidarity*, Princeton: Princeton University Press.

Lenin, V. I. (1965) 'The Role and Functions of the Trade Unions under the New Economic Policy', in *Collected Works*, Vol.33, second edition (Moscow: Progress Publishers, 1965), at http://www.marxists.org/archive/lenin/works/1921/dec/30b.htm

Ost, D. (1990) *Solidarity and the Politics of Anti-Politics*, Philadelphia: Temple University Press.

——(2005) *The Defeat of Solidarity: Anger and Politics in Postcommunist Europe*, Ithaca: Cornell University Press.

——(2006) 'After Postcommunism: Legacies and the Future of Unions in Eastern Europe', in Phelan, C. (ed.) *The Future of Organised Labour*, Oxford: Peter Lang.

Ost, D. and Weinstein, M. (1999) 'Unionists against Unions: Towards Hierarchical Management in Post-Communist Poland', *East European Politics and Societies* 13 (1).

Przeglad Zwiazkowy (1956), No. 12.

Rusiecki, J. (1974) *Od A do Z o związkach zawodowych i organizacjach społecznych w Polsce*, Warsaw: Książka i Wiedza.

Schmitter, P. (1981) 'Interest Intermediation and Regime Governability in Contemporary Western Europe and North America' in Berger, S. (ed.), *Organising Interests in Western Europe*, Cambridge: Cambridge University Press.

Touraine, A. (1983) *Solidarity*, Cambridge: Cambridge University Press.

Van der Pijl, K. (2006) 'A Lockean Europe?', *New Left Review* 37: January/February.

Wenzel, M. (1998) 'Solidarity and Akcja Wyborcza Solidarność: An Attempt at Reviving the Legend', *Communist and Post-Communist Studies*, 31(2): 139–56.

——(2008) 'Dynamika przynależności do związków zawodowych w latach 1980–2008', in Gardawski, J. (ed.) *Polacy pracujący i ich instytucje*, Warsaw: PWN (forthcoming).

Widera, W. and Gardawski, J. (1984) *Spoleczno-organizacyjne uwarunkowania artykulacji interesow robotniczych przez przedsierpniowe zwiazki zawodowe. Raport koncowy z badan*, Warsaw: SGPiS.

Związki Zawodowe w liczbach (1977, 1979) Warsaw: IW CRZZ.

Ukrainian Trade Unions since 1945

PAUL KUBICEK

1. Introduction

Under Soviet rule, Ukrainian trade unions, like other organisations in Ukraine, were doubly repressed, subjected to the ideological dictates of the Communist Party and rule by Moscow. In the late 1980s, thanks in large measure to the reforms of Soviet leader Mikhail Gorbachev, Ukrainian workers were able to organise and push for political reforms and national independence. Most workers, however, did not abandon their communist-era unions, which became one of the most conservative organisations in post-Soviet Ukraine and worked against the development of independent or 'alternative' unions. All Ukrainian unions, however, struggled with post-Soviet economic reforms, as economic collapse created pain for their members and privatisation and globalisation have brought in new owners that are frequently ill-disposed toward unions. Never particularly strong, trade unions in post-Soviet Ukraine are rather weak today, and most have experienced steep declines in membership. Some unions were actively involved in Ukraine's democratic 'Orange Revolution' but their place in Ukrainian society remains uncertain.

2. Trade Unions in Soviet Ukraine

Different views exist relating to the role of trade unions in the Soviet Union. Many observers emphasised the fact that Soviet trade unions were not 'unions' in the usual Western sense of the term (Conquest 1967; Ruble 1981). They were not independent organisations whose chief function was to protect and advance the interests of workers. Rather, trade unions, like all organisations in the Soviet Union, were linked to the Communist Party and they were utilised to support the goals of the regime: plan fulfilment, worker productivity, and social controls. The plenum of the Soviet All-Union Central Committee of Trade Unions announced in 1946 that its chief goal should be 'the organisation of the multi-million masses of workers, engineers, technicians and employees for the struggle to fulfil and over-fulfil the 1946–1950 Plan' (Conquest 1967: 156). Insofar as they became mouthpieces of the Party, Soviet trade unions were at times referred to, in Lenin's terms, as 'transmission belts' from the Party to the people and 'schools of communism'. Soviet ideology even maintained that there could be no basis for fundamental disputes between workers and the administration of a given enterprise, as the elimination of private property and collective ownership had ended the basis for exploitation of labour. Unions were organised on both territorial (e.g. distinct Russian, Ukrainian, Kazakh organisations) and branch (industry-specific) principles, and membership was based on the production principle, meaning that all workers in an economic sector (e.g. manual workers, supervisors, bookkeepers, secretaries) became members of the same union. All unions, however, were subject to rules of democratic centralism, ensuring that directives from above, ordered by the Party, would be carried out. Simon Clarke and his collaborators conclude, 'Although the Soviet Union was nominally a workers' state, Soviet workers were systematically denied any institutional channels through which they could express and articulate their own interests, grievances and aspirations' (Clarke et al. 1995: 2).

Some scholars, while not disputing the notion that unions were appendages of the Party-state, note that Soviet trade unions performed a 'dual functioning' role that included efforts to represent and defend workers. According to this line of argument, whereas trade unions were generally expected to follow orders 'from above', they were also charged with protecting workers from abuses of power by individual managers, including unjust dismissals and creation of unsafe working conditions. Changes in Soviet labour law in the 1950s gave wider powers to local trade unions, which were empowered to conclude collective agreements with individual enterprises on work conditions. Many aspects of labour policy, including wage scales, continued to be set at the national level. Nonetheless, as the Soviet Union became less overtly repressive in the 1960s and 1970s, some writers suggested that unions began to play a role in national policymaking through corporatist institutions and development of 'institutional pluralism' in which unions bargained with other actors over state policy (Hough 1979). Ultimately, unions helped maintain the 'Soviet social contract', according to which workers received job security, rising wages, and a host of benefits in return for their political passivity (Cook 1993). Workers were thus incorporated into the system, albeit in such a manner that they forfeited the right to engage in independent political or economic activity.

These debates over the unions' 'dual role' overlook a fundamental element of trade unions and industrial relations in the Soviet Union: unions' work as an arm of management within the enterprise. The unions were given responsibility for doling out a variety of social benefits (e.g. housing, day care, social insurance, sports facilities, 'houses of culture', vacation lodging, subsidised goods) nominally under the control of the state or the individual enterprise. They thus functioned as a sort of social welfare agency, perhaps gaining some legitimacy from the workers but at the same time re-enforcing a paternalistic mode of economic relations. Their control over various benefits helped ensure that workers would stay in line and follow union (in effect management) directives. Significantly, managers were allowed to be members of the unions – as everyone was technically a 'worker' – and they were frequently 'elected' by the rank and file to head the enterprise-level trade union. Given the peculiarities of the Soviet system, workers and managers could perhaps find a basis for alliance to extract more resources from the state, but this meant that workers and their unions were less integrated into the system at the macro level (e.g.

loyalty to the Party-state) than at the enterprise level (Kubicek 2004: 24). Such reasoning helps explain why workers did not abandon their 'repressive' unions after the collapse of communism, why the collapse of the 'Soviet social contract' did not lead to massive de-unionisation, and why workers in some sectors – where unions controlled sizeable resources – were less prone to protest and form 'alternative' unions than in sectors without such resources (Crowley 1995, 1997).

Ukrainian trade unions did not deviate from this general Soviet model. Because of the Soviet Union's federal structure and the peculiarities of the branch and geographic sub-organisations of the Soviet All-Union Central Council of Trade Unions, there were actually two 'official' trade union federations in Ukraine during Soviet rule. One was the Ukrainian Republican Trade Union Council, which united nineteen unions from enterprises under nominal republican (Ukrainian) ownership. The other, larger organisation, was the Ukrainian branch of the All-Union Central Trade Unions Council, which included forty-four branch-specific unions from plants under central (Soviet) control (Pankow and Kopatko 2001: 184). This distinction, however, made little difference as union structures functioned similarly and all were ultimately responsible to dictates from Moscow. Both were further divided into smaller geographically defined subunits (e.g. *oblast* [regional] and municipal unions) as well as branch unions for specific economic sectors. Technically, union members elected their leaders and lower level organisations elected the leadership of higher-ranking bodies, but, like the Soviet elections, there was often only one candidate for a given post, reflecting the fact that union 'elections' were designed to affirm choices that had already been made higher up in the union or Party organisation.

The largest concentration of union members was in the more heavily industrialised regions of eastern and southern Ukraine, which had long been under imperial Russian and later Soviet rule. Parts of Western Ukraine, which had been part of Austro-Hungarian Empire and later independent Poland, Czechoslovakia, and Romania, were incorporated into the Soviet Union during World War II and were less industrialised, but the general Soviet model was quickly imposed in this region after the war.

Virtually all workers – ranging from coal miners to those in food processing to university lecturers – were expected to join the appropriate branch level trade union. One per cent of their wage was automatically deducted as union dues, meaning that Ukrainian workers did not actively choose to belong to a union. Ukrainian trade unions were ordered not only to tow the general pro-communist line but also work to promote Soviet solidarity, meaning that expressions of Ukrainian nationalism were not tolerated. It is thus important to remember that Ukrainian unions under Soviet times were subjugated both to the ideological demands of communism and to federal Soviet authority in Moscow.

Despite efforts by the Party and by management to control the unions, there were some signs of dissent. Although Ukraine did not experience a large workers' uprising like that which occurred in Russian city of Novocherkassk in 1962 – this was precipitated by cuts in wages, increases in food prices, and inadequate housing – some Ukrainian worker activists did campaign against communist and Russian rule. There were sporadic strikes, particularly among dockworkers in Odessa. There was, however, no fundamental change in Ukrainian labour relations, and by the 1970s new leadership in the Ukrainian Communist Party cracked down harder on dissent.

Nonetheless, by the end of the 1970s, there were both signs of worker discontent and renewed worker activism. For example, in 1978 two coal miners in the Donbass region in eastern Ukraine, Vladimir Klebanov and Aleksei Nikitin, established the Free Trade Union of the Soviet Working People. They emphasised that this organisation was not anti-communist or anti-Russian; instead, it was designed to uphold existing law by protecting worker rights and improving unsafe working conditions. Nonetheless, both men were threatened by local Partry authorities, were eventually arrested, and finally incarcerated in psychiatric hospitals. Some political dissidents praised Poland's Solidarity movement and argued that the Soviet Union was ripe for the foundation of independent unions. The communist authorities and the 'official' unions, however, had the resources to prevent the emergence of an independent workers' movement. According to one report from the Ukrainian Donbass region

> The bosses had absolute power to fire, reprimand, dock pay, deny vacation or mete out any combination of punishment they chose. In theory the workers enjoyed full rights to petition through their trade unions for redressing unfair treatment. In practice, workers usually agreed with their bosses. They were afraid to challenge them because they could only lose (Kuzio and Wilson 1994: 61).

3. Ukrainian Worker Mobilisation, The Drive for Independence, and the End of the USSR

Mikhail Gorbachev, the last leader of the Soviet Union (1985–91), launched a series of political and economic reforms which he intended to rescue the Soviet Union from a crisis of economic stagnation, geopolitical failures, and declining popular legitimacy. While increasing freedom of speech, allowing non-communist organisations to form, and decentralizing the economy, his reforms did not produce what he anticipated. Instead, the economy deteriorated, nationalist organisations emerged, and the Communist Party itself split into more pro-reform and conservative factions. In Ukraine, the cultural intelligentsia took the lead in campaigning for human rights, democracy, and the protection of Ukrainian language and culture.

Worker activism emerged in Ukraine in 1989, when the Soviet Union was affected by the largest wave of strike activity since the 1920s. The leaders in Ukraine were the coal miners in the Donbass region, who had always occupied a privileged position among the working class. The Donbass miners, along with miners in Russia and other parts of the Soviet Union, were not demanding national independence. Instead, they were protesting the failure of the Communist Party to deliver on its economic promises and the country's deteriorating economic conditions. Workers demanded better pay, more holidays, and better supply of consumer goods, including soap. As the strike spread, miners in more nationalist-oriented western Ukraine voiced more political demands, including democratic elections and the removal of the local communist leadership (Kuzio and Wilson 1994: 105–6).

The striking workers gradually began to organise themselves and broke with the 'official' union structures. Their separate strike committees formed into regional unions of strike committees. In the fall of 1989, a constituent assembly of the Free Trade Unions (*Vilni Profspilky Ukrainy*) of Ukraine was held in Donetsk, the leading mining centre. Similar organisations sprang up in other cities, and in February and March of 1990 independent workers groups formed, respectively, the Unity (*Iednist*) union in Kharkiv and the Solidarity union in Kiev. Other workers joined all-Union organisations that had branches throughout the Soviet Union. Many of these Ukrainian groups became cooperating with national-democratic organisations, human rights groups, and student organisations.

The mood among the public and the workers became more radical in 1990, when another wave of strikes, again spearheaded by the Donbass miners, shook Ukraine. This time, the demands of the miners were both economic and political, demanding the resignation of the Ukrainian government and nationalisation of communist property. Strike leaders also voiced support for Ukrainian sovereignty, noting that Ukraine had rich potential and would be better off if it was economically separate from the rest of the country. The government authorities strived to improve the workers' economic demands and voted in favour of a declaration of sovereignty.

By 1991 Ukrainian society was highly mobilised, with many new parties challenging the rule of the communist party and various civic organisations, including trade unions, demanding more and faster political and economic reform. In March 1991 miners again walked off the job, demanding the resignation of Gorbachev and strengthening Ukrainian sovereignty. In June 1991 union leaders and members of the national-democratic opposition met at the founding congress of the All-Ukrainian Union of Workers' Solidarity, but many felt that this organisation, which had its strongest local organisations in western Ukraine, represented the most radical wings of the worker's movement and the anti-communist opposition. Other worker groups, such as the Donbass branches of the all-Union Independent Miners Union, kept their distance, reflecting divides among Ukrainian workers and deeper divides in Ukrainian society. Gradually, however, as rule from Moscow weakened and other Soviet republics declared their independence, the Ukrainian communist party itself became dominated by 'national communists', who, after the ill-fated coup against Gorbachev in August 1991, voted in the Ukrainian parliament to declare Ukraine an independent country.

4. Trade Union Organisations in Post-Soviet Ukraine

On 1 December 1991, after Ukrainian voters overwhelmingly approved a referendum on independence, Ukraine officially became an independent country. While the rule of Communist Party had largely disintegrated and independent trade unions were a significant part of the pro-independence movement, labour relations did not radically change in the immediate post-Soviet period. The largest labour organisation in Ukraine was the Federation of Ukrainian Trade Unions (FPU, *Federatsiia Profspilok Ukrainy*), which was the Ukrainian successor to the communist-dominated union structures. The leadership of the FPU did not significantly change, it held onto the property in its possession under Soviet times, and by default it retained its membership.

Given this inheritance, it was very difficult for the FPU to emerge as a strong, independent voice for Ukrainian workers. The FPU itself is composed of 44 branch union federations in various industrial sectors (e.g. auto manufacturing, military-industrial complex, mining, metallurgy), and for the most part they are the same ones that existed under Soviet times. The FPU also has 26 regional (*oblast*) organisations in each of Ukraine's regions. With workers losing jobs, many moving to non-union sectors, and elimination of the automatic check-off for union membership, the FPU has steadily lost members. Whereas FPU affiliates had over 25 million members in 1990, by 2006 its membership had dwindled to 11 million. Unions attribute most of the membership loss to downsizing of industries, and indeed in most industrial sectors unions officially continue to represent over 90 per cent of the workforce. Thus, in comparison with other post-communist countries and with nations worldwide, union density in Ukraine (approximately 50 per cent of workers) remains quite high.

Most observers (Crowley 1997; Simon, 2000; Davis 2001; Kubicek 2000, 2002, 2004) argue that Ukrainian unions are quite weak. Given high levels of membership, on what basis can one conclude that post-Soviet Ukrainian unions are weak? Part of the answer is that workers do not have much confidence in trade unions. According to a 2000 survey of 8,200 Ukrainians, only 11 per cent thought that unions could help resolve the problem of wage arrears (arguably the most serious workplace issue at the time), 25 per cent thought unions would be useful in the case of unfair dismissals, and only 14 per cent expressed full or some confidence in the FPU unions. Only 43 per cent of the employed respondents in the survey claimed membership in a trade union, even though at the time the FPU claimed to represent 94 per cent of Ukrainian workers.[1] Much of the problem is that workers believe these unions have not shed their communist past and are still essentially allies of management and the state machinery, unwilling to stand up for worker interests by engaging in action against employers or the government. Membership in trade unions is thus exaggerated or a result of habit, unsanctioned use of automatic membership, and/or the desire of workers to be eligible to receive social benefits (e.g. access to vacation resorts) as they did under Soviet times. Indeed, the FPU has fought hard for control of recreation facilities and social insurance monies in order to provide a rationale for workers to join trade unions. Critics accuse the FPU of becoming little more than a commercial organisation, with most of its income allegedly coming from lease and sale of property and not from union dues.

The FPU has made concerted efforts to maintain unity among its various branch and regional unions. However, there have been schisms within the FPU, across sectors (e.g. between those sectors that depend

1 Data from ILO and State Committee on Statistics of Ukraine, 'Personal, Social, and Economic Safety', 2001. A survey by Democratic Initiatives in 1997 found that 88 per cent of Ukrainians claimed membership in no civic organisation, even when trade unions were on the list of available choices. See Kubicek 2004: 231, n.14.

on public subsidies and those that do not), across regions (e.g. between more Western-oriented, pro-reform union leaders in western Ukraine and more conservative leaders in eastern Ukraine), and for control over union resources. The FPU has emphasized that the union organism is like a cloth, in that little rips in it would soon mean no cloth at all (Kubicek 2004: 163). At the same time, however, individual FPU unions will accuse others of 'pulling the blanket over themselves', meaning that they seek select benefits for themselves without regard to the FPU as a whole.

In part because of disappointment with FPU unions and deteriorating economic conditions, new, 'independent' unions exist in a variety of sectors. Most, but not all, are holdovers from the late 1980s. These unions struggled to survive throughout the 1990s, forming various unstable confederations. By the end of 2003, 31 of these unions came together in the Confederation of Free Trade Unions of Ukraine (KVPU, *Konfederatsiia Vilnykh Profspilok Ukrainy*). The largest and most active of these unions has been the Independent Miners' Union (NPGU, *Nezalezhnaia Profspilka Gornykiv Ukrainy*), which emerged in the late 190s and by 2004 claimed 60,000 members, which is still only about one-tenth of the workers that belong to the FPU coal miners' union. There are also smaller, 'independent' unions among skilled workers such as air traffic controllers, locomotive drivers, dock workers, and airline pilots, all of whom have strike power because of the difficulty in finding replacement workers, as well as some isolated, enterprise-specific unions. By 2005 non-FPU unions still had fewer than one million members (precise figures are notoriously difficult to obtain), with the KVPU claiming only 240,000. Union leaders from the KVPU stress that they are 'true' trade unions as they are not compromised by ties to management or by a discreditable Soviet-era heritage, and in the 1990s these unions won the support of foreign labour organisations such as the AFL-CIO, the International Confederation of Free Trade Unions, and Poland's Solidarity trade union.

However, they have yet to break the dominance of the FPU among Ukrainian workers for several reasons. First, these unions do not have access to the same fringe benefits as the FPU, and many workers feared the loss of pensions and other perks if they left the FPU (Crowley 1995, 1997; Kubicek 2000, 2004). Secondly, because these unions threaten vested interests and have been more assertive against management and the state, non-FPU leaders have been subjected to various forms of intimidation, including death threats and assaults. Third, a widespread feeling of alienation and powerlessness among Ukrainians has complicated the efforts of new unions to win members. Because new unions have not (for the most part) demonstrated a systemic ability to protect workers in the harsh post-communist environment, they have had difficulty in persuading workers to take the risk of joining them or of establishing new unions on their own.

5. Post-Soviet Ukrainian Trade Unions and the Search for Social Partnership

Labour organisations in Ukraine operate in a political environment that, on paper at any rate, is much supportive of trade unions than that which existed under Soviet times. Unions have the right to organise, all trade unions have equal status, workers have the right to strikes, and no government permission is required to establish a trade union. The Law on Citizens' Organisations (which includes trade unions) stipulates non-interference by public authorities in the activities of these organisations, which have the right to establish and join federations on a voluntary basis. Unions are also empowered, unlike the case during Soviet rule, to conclude collective agreements at the branch or enterprise level.

In reality, however, the political environment has consistently favoured the FPU unions over their nascent rivals. As noted above, unions in the KVPU complain of harassment from the state and from management. Until 2002 unions were required to register with the state, and state authorities were known to deny registration to new unions. Moreover, to register as a national union, a union must either have branches in more than half of the administrative regions or have branches in more than half of the administrative regions where the enterprises of this sector are located. By definition, this requirement works against smaller unions, especially those located at a single enterprise, and thus non-FPU unions have had a difficult time competing with FPU unions for a seat at the table in national and branch-level collective bargaining. The Ukrainian Ombudsman for Human Rights reported that from 1998 to 2001 there were over 50,000 violations of workers' rights, including thousands of cases of violating workers' rights to organise unions for their protection.

Not surprisingly, the FPU has been viewed by many as a pro-government organisation. Its initial (1991–2004) head, Oleksandr Stoian, was an adviser to Leonid Kravchuk before he became president of the country (1991–4). FPU unions have been reluctant to engage in protests or strikes, despite a steady deterioration in conditions for Ukrainian workers. While one could argue that part of the problem is an engrained habit of passivity from Soviet times, another explanation would be that the state holds a very strong hand over the FPU, especially on the issue of union property, which the FPU is desperate not to lose. The threat to take away property or control over social insurance funds has been very useful for the government, and as a result the FPU has engaged in little more than symbolic protest against the government. In the words of Yurii Krivenko, an FPU official in Lviv in western Ukraine: 'Unions still exist only because they don't bother anyone' (Kubicek 2004: 166). Even amidst widespread public protests in 2001 over corruption and allegations of murder by President Kuchma, the FPU refrained from calling for strikes lest they be used for political purposes.

While many would accuse the FPU of being part of the 'party of power', it tried to establish itself as a more independent political actor, spearheading the formation of a Ukrainian Workers' Party. This group, however, failed to win parliamentary representation in 1998, 2002 and 2006 elections, although a handful of FPU officials (including Stoian) were elected to parliament as independent candidates. These representatives, however, either toed the government line on most issues or made common cause with the Communist Party, and pointedly did not align themselves with the national-democratic opposition.

FPU officials, while acknowledging many of their weaknesses in the political arena, prefer to emphasise attempts to forge social partnership with the government and employers. Indeed, Ukraine has established tripartite bodies such as the National Social Partnership Committee, created in 1993. This body includes 22 representatives from trade unions, ten of which come from the FPU, the remainder made of smaller union organisations. While some might take the existence of corporatist institutions – explicitly modelled on West European bodies – as proof of union strength, the fact is that these bodies have not worked well. They are responsible for concluding general agreements among the parties, but these agreements are routinely violated, often to labour's disadvantage. The fact is that two of the sides in the Committee – the state and the employers – are in a much stronger economic and political position, and throughout the 1990s the unions were unable to resolve problems of wage arrears and an average wage that was below the government-defined poverty level. Moreover, because of rivalries among the various unions, it was very difficult for Ukrainian trade unions to present a united front against employers or the state (Kubicek 2000).

Collective agreements are also concluded at the branch and enterprise level. Non-FPU union leaders would complain, however, of management efforts to avoid including them in enterprise-level negotiations, and until 2001 only one national union (almost always an FPU union) was recognised to conclude branch level agreements, a clear violation of ILO conventions. While collective agreements were regularly concluded and were often hailed by FPU leaders as significant accomplishments, they arguably meant little as wage arrears mounted (reaching $1.2 billion by 2000), demonstrating that unions had little power to defend the most basic right of workers: to be paid for their labour. In 2001, the FPU itself reported that violations of the labour code by national, regional, and local governments and employers that affected over two million workers, which makes any claim about the utility of collective agreements and social partnership ring hollow (Kubicek 2004: 168).

Many within the FPU recognise these problems, but the larger question is what can be done to make social partnership meaningful? Prior to the Orange Revolution in 2004, which increased hopes for democratic, accountable government, few had a solid answer. Serhei Donkriuk of the FPU acknowledged that there were few options, as protest and strikes were unlikely to produce positive results. Thus, the FPU continues to work for the 'middle ground of social partnership', because, in his words, 'what else can we do?' (Kubicek 2004: 169).

The unions of the VKPU, especially the NPGU, have taken a more confrontational position. While they obtained several seats on the Committee for Social Partnership, these unions are disillusioned by talk of social partnership. In part because they enjoy the confidence of their members, the unions have been more willing to engage in strikes and political protests. The largest wave of worker activism in post-Soviet Ukraine occurred in 1993, largely among coal miners in eastern Ukraine from the NPGU and more independent elements from the FPU's miners' union (Simon 2000: 150–9). Workers put forward both economic demands (e.g. higher wages indexed to inflation) as well as explicitly political demands (e.g. referendum of confidence in state authorities). The strikers, however, failed to turn it into a national strike or to make effective alliances with the national-democratic opposition in western Ukraine, as some in the Ukrainian-speaking regions of western Ukraine argued that the strikes in the Russified regions of eastern Ukraine were a Russian provocation. While the miners did 'win' with this strike, receiving higher wages and promises of a referendum (modified to become elections in 1994), future rounds of worker activism in the 1990s fared less well. An NPGU-led strike in 1996 led to the arrest and imprisonment of union leaders. By the end of the 1990s, strikes were far more isolated, typically restricted to a particular enterprise or locality. Many believed that strike activity was encouraged by management to win concessions from the state.

On the political front, efforts by independent unions to forge alliances had gone nowhere, as union heads accused all political parties of using the unions like prostitutes. In 2001, the NPGU was active in the 'Ukraine without Kuchma' movement, which was suppressed by the government. Most unions, however, both FPU and non-FPU, refused to join in such political action, believing it was unlikely to lead to success. Mikhail Volnyets, head of the NPGU, argued that political engagement was necessary, and in 2002 he was elected to parliament and allied himself with the opposition figure Yulia Tymoshenko, who would later become one of the leaders of the 2004 'Orange Revolution'.

6. Ukrainian Trade Unions and Economic Reforms

Throughout the 1990s, Ukraine suffered from a variety of economic problems: high inflation, declining growth, and wage arrears for workers. Official unemployment figures remained low (averaging six per cent), but many workers were forced to work part-time or received goods in lieu of a salary, if they were paid at all. Deteriorating economic conditions, combined with unions' ability to produce positive changes, led to a decline in confidence in trade unions and led many workers to look for new, often non-unionised jobs. At the same time, unions had to adapt to changing economic circumstances, including the introduction of private ownership and moves to integrate Ukraine into the global economy.

Of all of the economic reforms in the post-Soviet period, arguably the most significant one from the unions' perspective was privatisation. Under Soviet times, the vast majority of property was owned by the state. Movement to a free market system meant that the state would divest itself of these holdings. A central question, however, was who would inherit the property of the Soviet state.

Workers obviously had a stake in this debate. Millions of workers who had worked for years at state enterprises felt attached to their enterprise and believed that they should benefit from privatisation, perhaps by becoming the new legal owners. In the first years of independence, privatisation and other reform questions were largely delayed in Ukraine, which was a reform laggard. Lacking clear laws on privatisation or a comprehensive national program, buyers' associations were free to choose when an enterprise would be privatized. In practice, this meant that directors of enterprises were able to control the privatisation process to their own advantage.

In 1995 a voucher privatisation programme began in earnest, in which workers would be given vouchers, which they could then use to invest in firms of their choice. However, inflation had eaten away at the value of these certificates (which would be worth approximately $4). As in Russia, these vouchers were to be used for only a fraction of the purchase value of the firm, and in the end multiple means of privatisation (including auctions, insider purchasing, renting with buy-out options) were employed. By 1999 over half of the economy was in the non-state sector, and over 61,000 enterprises (mostly small firms) were privatized.

While workers had opportunity to buy shares in their firms, they ended up gaining little in the process. Lacking extra cash (thanks in part to wage arrears) and possessing only measly vouchers, they could buy few shares, even when they could buy them at a discount. On the other hand, enterprise directors – treated under the law as workers since they were technically employees – did have the resources on hand to buy shares, as well as the ability to buy (or coerce) shares from normal workers. Moreover, after 1998 voucher privatisation ended, with the remaining firms (including many of Ukraine's largest and potentially most profitable) sold through auctions in which workers had no wherewithal, economic or political, to participate.

Where were unions in this process? According to one FPU official, while unions were very interested, 'from the beginning they were pushed away from the process' (Kubicek 2004: 174). Unions had no legally defined role; instead, worker collectives (another Soviet-era artefact) were empowered to make decisions for the workers. Lacking solid information and experience and subject to manipulation from management, these bodies could do little to advocate for the workers. Union leaders from the FPU and their rivals could all agree that privatisation gave workers very little, although critics of the unions asserted that they should have been far more involved in the process and learned from the experiences of Ukraine's neighbours, such as Russia, were workers were similarly left with few benefits from privatisation.

By 2000 union leaders were resigned to the fact that privatisation had occurred and the process, however disadvantageous to workers, could not be re-done. The question thus became how unions would fare in an environment dominated by private ownership. In short, the answer is that privatisation has presented serious challenges to trade unions. Of course, workers in Ukraine faced a series of problems: a weak legal system, a bankrupt state, chronic corruption, and employee dependence upon management. One effect of privatisation, ironically, was to create widespread confusion. Whereas privatisation was ostensibly designed to establish lines of ownership and responsibility, it initially led to more ambiguity, as workers were unsure who or what is to blame for their predicament. Management, for example, would deflect protest by blaming the state for the enterprise's woes, and would attempt to enlist unions in their battles to win subsidies or contracts from the state. Privatisation has also exacerbated rifts among trade unions, as workers in the public sector with low salaries (e.g. teachers), workers in declining industrial sectors (e.g. mining, defence industries), and workers in more profitable branches (e.g. oil and gas) have very different interests and priorities. Privatisation has also led to the break-up of large firms into smaller ones (especially true in textiles and light industry), which has also hampered union organisation and solidarity.

An overarching question, however, is whether private ownership – or, more precisely, owners – has harmed trade unions. Certainly this is a widespread claim in numerous countries, but in the Ukrainian case the evidence is rather mixed. Some union leaders mention hostility toward unions, with management attempting to dismantle unions or (more commonly) maintaining a 'paternalist firm' by allowing unions to administer social programs while ignoring them on issues such as wages and work safety. Conversely, the fact that some private owners have moved to trim fringe benefits (e.g. by selling enterprise-owned resorts) has put some unions on the defensive. Others note that many owners in Ukraine are corrupt and have political connections that allow them to violate labour law with relative impunity. Meanwhile, there has been little effort to unionise workers in new, typically smaller firms (e.g. in construction, in financial services), where wages typically are higher and workers see few advantages to unionisation.

Some union leaders, however, report a more positive experience. Workers in the oil and gas sectors enjoy higher wages and benefits, a result (in part) of privatisation and the introduction of market forces. Others note that new private owners, less burdened with a Soviet past, are willing to work with unions as partners. Volnyets of the NPGU notes that he gets along well with some (not all) private owners, which is not that surprising given the NPGU's relationship with state authorities (Kubicek 2004). Moreover, it is important to note that workers in the state sector have not fared well: salaries are low, payment may be delayed, and management at state firms may also enjoy dubious ties to local governments, allowing them to skirt the law. Notably, both the FPU and KVPU unions throughout the 1990s favoured privatisation in principle, although neither was happy with the way it was carried out. In short, given how difficult circumstances were for unions under state ownership, many unions at least hoped that privatisation would open up new opportunities for themselves and for their members.

The pressures of globalisation have also been a challenge both to Ukraine and its trade unions. Ukraine, however, is a relative newcomer to the global economy, and in the first decade of its independence it lagged far behind both its immediate western neighbours and Russia in attracting foreign investment and engaging in foreign trade. For example, from 1992 to 2000 Ukraine attracted a mere $70 per capita in foreign investment, compared to $518 in Poland and $1,764 for Hungary (Kubicek 2004: 181). Part of the problem was geography and lack of natural resources, but rapacious bureaucrats, unstable legislation, economic collapse, poor infrastructure, and lack of laws protecting property hampered the country's ability to attract the attention of investors or boost its export capacity.

That said, there has been some foreign investment in certain sectors (e.g. auto production, oil, food processing, and construction), allowing one to draw some tentative conclusions about its impact on trade unions. What is interesting is that in Ukraine one encounters a generally favourable view of foreign investment and globalisation. Much of this is understandable: the state needs investment, workers need good jobs, and foreign firms may be more responsible and law-abiding than those owned by Ukrainians. Union leaders recognise that this position puts them at odds with Western trade unions, which are more fearful of globalisation. However, Ukraine, as an underdeveloped country, is in a different position, and, as leader of the Autoworkers Union explained in 2001, 'If a factory is closed, and people are not working, and an investor comes in and puts in money, creates jobs, and production increases, how can we complain?' Even in Lviv, the western Ukrainian city often characterised as the 'hotbed' of Ukrainian nationalism, union leaders supported Russian efforts to buy the moribund Lviv Bus Factory because this would preserve jobs (Kubicek 2004: 182). By and large, foreign investors who have purchased Ukrainian firms have been willing to work with Ukrainian unions, and many unions report that they are treated better by foreign ownership.

The situation is different at 'greenfield investments', new companies started by foreigners. In these cases, where there is no 'inherited' union, it has been difficult to establish trade unions, often due to the hostility of management. Until 2004, such firms were relatively rare, as foreign companies preferred to put money into existing infrastructure and have a Ukrainian partner to navigate the labyrinth of bureaucratic requirements. Ironically, as Ukraine charts a more democratic, Western-oriented path and receives more foreign investment in new enterprises, Ukrainian unions (like their counterparts in other post-communist countries, such as Poland) are likely to find globalisation a less benign influence, with workers to take the risk of joining them or of establishing new unions on their own.

7. Trade Unions and the Ukrainian Orange Revolution

Until 2004 Ukraine was saddled with an increasingly authoritarian state that created a difficult environment for trade unions, as well as other actors in civil society. At the end of 2004, the 'Orange Revolution' brought the pro-reform, pro-Western Viktor Yushchenko to the Ukrainian presidency. This event, which occurred with the participation of millions of Ukrainians who clamoured for democratic rights, was hailed as a victory of civil society. While numerous organisations took part in the protests that helped bring Yushchenko to power, the most visible were political-human rights organisations (e.g. the youth movement *Pora*). Among trade unions, the ever-politicized NPGU played a significant role, with Volnyets helping to organise the mass picketing of government buildings. On the other hand, Stoian of the FPU, steadfastly against the 'Orange' forces, called on Kuchma to impose a state of emergency to deal with the demonstrators.

Ultimately, Volnyets and the demonstrators prevailed, and the 'Orange Revolution' created prospects for a more democratic Ukraine that would respect political and civic freedoms. Political pressure on the 'independent' unions has thus largely evaporated (at least at the national level), although many still feel the pinch from employers or FPU unions. Meanwhile, the FPU must adjust to a different political reality. Stoian, discredited by his association with the old regime, was replaced by Oleksandr Yurkin, who was previously the head of the FPU-affiliated Union of Nuclear Power Industry Workers, was considered a reformer within FPU circles, and was loosely aligned with the 'Orange' forces. However, many other top, more conservative figures in the FPU are ensconced in their positions, and there is little reason to believe that the FPU leadership will be able to instill confidence in its ostensible members. In addition, as of 2007, splits within the Orange coalition and continued problems of political corruption have left the political future of the country very uncertain.

At the same time, however, assuming that Ukraine continues with pro-market reforms and opening itself up to global markets, the economic environment for trade unions may become worse. Membership will likely as shrink as workers continue to abandon Soviet-era industries for more prospective employment. Greenfield investments, either Ukrainian or foreign, will not inherit unions and may be hostile to their creation. Pressures to remain competitive on global markets may restrict manoeuvring on collective bargaining as well as dismantle aspects of the paternalist firm and thereby strip unions of some of their assets. Privatisation and diversification will continue to fracture any union movement, making worker solidarity across branches and firms more difficult. Such changes may help produce growth in the Ukrainian economy, but it is clear that Ukrainian trade unions will have to overcome both negative aspects of their heritage as well as the formidable challenges of the new political economy if they hope to become important economic and political actors.

Suggested Reading

Clarke, S., Fairbrother, P. and Borisov, V. (1995) *The Workers' Movement in Russia*, Aldershot: Edward Elgar.

Conquest, R. (1967) *Industrial Workers in the U.S.S.R.*, New York NY: Praeger.

Cook, L. (1993) *The Soviet Social Contract and Why It Failed: Welfare Policy and Workers' Politics from Brezhnev to Yeltsin*, Cambridge MA: Harvard University Press.

Crowley, S. (1995) 'Between Class and Nation: Worker Politics in the New Ukraine', *Communist and Post-Communist Studies* 28: 43–69.

——(1997) *Hot Coal, Cold Steel: Russian and Ukrainian Workers from the End of the Soviet Union to Postcommunist Transitions*, Ann Arbor MI: University of Michigan Press.

Davis, Sue (2001) *Trade Unions in Russia and Ukraine, 1985–1995*, New York NY: Palgrave.

Hough, J. (1979) 'Policy-Making and the Worker' in Kahan, A. and Ruble, B. (eds) *Industrial Labor in the USSR*, New York NY: Pergamon Press.

International Labour Organisation (ILO) and Ukrainian Academy of Labour and Social Relations (2000) *Suchasnyi profspilkovyi rukh v Ukraini ta problemy yoho konsolidatsii* (Contemporary Labour Movement in Ukraine and Problems of Its Consolidation), Kyiv: ILO.

Kubicek, P. (1996) 'Variations on a Corporatist Theme: Interest Associations in Post-Soviet Ukraine and Russia', *Europe-Asia Studies* 48: 27–46.

——(2000) *Unbroken Ties: The State, Interest Associations, and Corporatism in Post-Soviet Ukraine*, Ann Arbor MI: University of Michigan Press.

——(2002) 'Civil Society, Trade Unions, and Post-Soviet Democratisation: Evidence from Russia and Ukraine', *Europe-Asia Studies* 54: 603–24.

——(2004) *Organized Labor in Postcommunist States: From Solidarity to Infirmity*, Pittsburgh PA: University of Pittsburgh Press.

Kuzio, T. and Wilson, A. (1994) *Ukraine: Perestroika to Independence*, New York NY: St. Martin's.
Mandel, D. (2004) *Labour after Soviet Socialism: Autoworkers and Their Unions in Russia, Ukraine, and Belarus*, Montreal: Black Rose Books.
Pankow, W. and Kopatko, E. (2001) 'Workers and Unions in Postcommunist Ukraine' in Crowley, S. and Ost, D. (eds) *Workers after Workers' States: Labor and Politics in Postcommunist Eastern Europe*, Lanham MD: Rowman and Littlefield.
Ruble, B. (1981) *Soviet Trade Unions: Their Development in the 1970s*, Cambridge: Cambridge University Press.
Simon, Rick (2000) *Labour and Political Transformation in Russia and Ukraine*, Aldershot: Ashgate.

Africa and Middle East

The History of Trade Unionism in Cameroon

PIET KONINGS

1. Introduction

Surprisingly little research has been done on the history of trade unionism in Cameroon even though it appears to be quite unique in Africa. It is also complex because the country was partitioned in two separate parts after the German colonial era (1884–1916) until independence and reunification in 1961: one part, by far the largest, came under French rule and the other under British rule. As a result, two different systems of industrial relations and trade union models developed in the country, largely influenced by the Mandate and Trusteeship Authorities and the metropolitan trade unions.

Despite various differences in union organisation and ideology, trade unions in both parts of the country enjoyed a considerable measure of autonomy with regard to the state in the pre-independence and reunification era. Many trade unionists still consider this period as the Golden Age of trade unionism in Cameroon since the unions were able to play a significant role in the defence of their members' interests and also in the nationalist struggles, sometimes in close alliance with the newly created nationalist parties.

Following the establishment of a one-party state after independence and reunification, the new African leaders increasingly intervened in industrial relations. They urged the various central labour organisations to unite and transformed the colonial model of relative union autonomy into a new model of state-controlled trade unionism, allegedly for the sake of national unity and national development. Moreover, they were determined to harmonise the different systems of industrial relations and labour legislation then existing in Francophone and Anglophone Cameroon.

It was not until political liberalisation in the early 1990s that the trade union movement in Cameroon gradually began to reassert its autonomy, which it perceived as a necessary precondition to the improvement of members' living and working conditions that had deteriorated severely during the economic crisis and economic liberalisation. However, there were a number of obstacles that prevented union revitalisation, including the failure of union leaders to sever their ties with the state, their persistent struggle for power which led to growing fragmentation, and their diminished bargaining strength during economic liberalisation.

Strikingly, workers have never resigned themselves to their fate, even when faced with their leaders' blatant neglect of the defence of their interests in the post-colonial state. On the contrary, they have continued to simply bypass their leadership and organise collective actions independently, regularly resorting to illegal strike action. In addition, some sections of the working classes have recently been able to create autonomous and militant trade unions outside the existing union framework in spite of severe state repression.

2. Trade Unionism in the French and British Mandate and Trust Era, 1922–61

The partitioning of the erstwhile German Kamerun Protectorate (1884–1916) after World War I into French and British mandate and trust territories had an enormous impact on socio-economic and cultural developments in the area, notably in the field of industrial relations and trade unionism (Konings and Nyamnjoh 2003). While trade unionism emerged in both territories at almost the same time (around the end of World War II), important differences can be observed in the models introduced in the different parts of the country in terms of structure and organisation, ideology, and links with the metropolitan central labour organisations and the newly created nationalist parties. It is interesting that one major common preoccupation of both the French and the British Administering Authorities was to prevent unions from reinforcing the nationalist movement. Nevertheless, they did play a significant role in the anti-colonial struggles in both territories, either directly or indirectly, and served as the training ground for the country's future political leaders.

The French Mandate and Trust Territory

There were several reported attempts by workers in French Cameroon from the 1920s onwards to organise trade unions but these were bound to fail due to the French Administering Authority's fierce opposition and tactics of repression (Moumé-Étia 1991; Eyinga 1985). It was not until August 1944 in the aftermath of resolutions passed by French colonial governors at the Brazzaville Conference on the future of the French colonies in Africa (Joseph 1977) that trade unionism was legalised in French Cameroon.

Governor Pleven's decree of 7 August 1944 marked the start of determined efforts to organise workers in French Cameroon, a task made easier by further legislation in 1946 that abolished the *indigenat* and other forms of forced labour as well as the humiliating status of *sujet* (Kaptue 1986). The new unions naturally needed a model, and the obvious one was that of France. Thus trade unions in French Cameroon, as elsewhere in the French African colonies, came to closely follow the patterns of trade union organisation that prevailed in the mother country. In fact, they became organically linked to the metropolitan central labour organisations and, from their very inception, were split along the same political and ideological alignments of the metropolitan unions.

The first attempt to organise French Cameroonian workers was undertaken by the *Confédération Générale du Travail* (CGT), which was communist-dominated and the largest central labour organisation in France. The CGT championed class struggle and urged direct action when negotiations failed to improve workers' living and working conditions. Militant CGT trade unionists had been active in the territory for some time, having been involved in the organisation of white employees, and they now started to devote their time and energy to the setting up of local CGT branches and a central labour organisation affiliated to the CGT. Organising was focused on employees in the administration sector and commercial enterprises.

Trade union study circles founded by CGT militants in Douala and Yaoundé exposed aspiring local trade unionists to a radical critique of the economic and political aspects of colonialism. And on 18 December 1944, the *Union des Syndicats Confédérés du Cameroun* (USCC) was created under the leadership of one of the greatest French CGT militants, Gaston Donat (Joseph 1977). Among the first French Cameroonian leaders of the USCC were Ruben Um Nyobe, who was to become a key figure in the nationalist movement, Charles Assalé, a future prime minister in the Francophone part of the Federal Republic of Cameroon, and Jacques N'Gom, the third secretary-general of the USCC. These three, in turn, attended courses at the CGT headquarters in Paris and, when the USCC was offered a seat on the Economic Council in Paris, it was Assalé who represented the organisation (Moumé-Étia 1991). Um Nyobe was elected secretary-general of the USCC at the Ngaoundere Annual Congress in 1947 and he resigned from his job as court registrar to dedicate himself full-time to trade union matters (Verdzekov 1969: 345). It is important to point out here that in the French system of industrial relations, central labour organisations played a vital role in union policies and strategies as well as in negotiations with the state and employers about conditions of service. Trade union organisation at the local level thus tended to be weak.

From the very start, the USCC became a target of suspicion and attack by the administration and the Catholic mission. Neither was opposed to trade unionism *per se* but the administration became deeply concerned when the nascent trade union movement appeared to combine the pledge to improve the lot of workers with the voicing of general anti-colonial and nationalist sentiments. The Catholic mission accused the USCC of communist leanings. One of their main strategies to weaken the USCC was the encouragement of rival central labour organisations. The most vehement opposition to the USCC, however, came from the white settlers, the so-called *colons*. Unlike the administration and the Catholic mission, they continued to resist the introduction of trade unionism, which they saw as a grave threat to their control of labour in the territory. They deeply resented the abolition of all forms of forced labour and demanded a return to the old days of *laissez faire* (Joseph 1974). When the USCC began to protest against workers' deplorable living and working conditions and demanded higher wages, it was met with indifference and hostility by white employers. It soon became evident that many of the *colons*, annoyed by steady union growth and demands for higher wages, were prepared for a confrontation that would put an end to the unions once and for all.

Such a confrontation did occur on 21 December 1945 when a wildcat strike broke out on the Douala railways. This was reportedly organised outside the USCC, whose leadership feared that any strike would give the *colons* and the authorities an excuse to clamp down on the strikers and the unions (Moumé-Étia 1991; Kendrick 1979; Joseph 1974). At first the strike was orderly until a band of so-called 'sand-sand' boys, composed of the unemployed, poorly paid casual workers and criminal elements among the sub-proletariat, emerged from the immigrant slums of New Bell in Douala and joined the strikers. The strike then quickly turned into a riot. The activities of this band, armed chiefly with sticks, involved the destruction of property, pillaging and attacks on black workers. There was considerable suspicion among observers that the group was directly incited to violence by the *colons* who wanted to hold trade union leaders responsible for the disorder. As the union leaders expected, the riot gave rise to severe repression. The white settlers were armed with rifles and their actions during the disorder included the massacre of Cameroonians, the attempted assassination of trade union leaders and a rebellion against the colonial administration. To appease the settlers, the union leaders were imprisoned while an investigation was undertaken. In early 1946 the French CGT militants in the territory, whether or not they had been involved in the incidents, were repatriated to France.

The USCC leaders seemed not to be intimidated by their opponents and gradually resumed the fight for an improvement in workers' conditions of service. In the decade between 1945 and 1955, one of the overriding concerns of the USCC was the campaign to have the French government establish a more advanced labour code. As early as July 1945, the USCC was one of the territorial unions in French Africa that criticised the inadequacies of the 18 June 1945 Labour Code. In cooperation with the French CGT and other CGT affiliates in French Africa, the campaign was intensified until 15 December 1952 when the French Assembly finally approved a more progressive bill.

One of the most significant events in French Cameroon was the launching of a new party on 10 April 1948 by a number of USCC leaders such as Ruben Um Nyobe, Felix Moumie, Ernest Quandie and Abel Kingue. Um Nyobe was elected as its first secretary-general, and was later replaced at the head of the USCC by Jacques N'Gom. The birth of the *Union des Populations du Cameroun* (UPC) marked the beginning of a new era of radical and militant nationalism. The party's main goals were immediate independence and the reunification of French and British Cameroon (Joseph 1977; Konings and Nyamnjoh 2003). Within a year of its foundation, the UPC became the best-organised political party in French Cameroon thanks to its union base. Close collaboration between the UPC and the USCC was apparent at least between 1948 and 1956 when the political and socio-economic struggles of both organisations against colonial rule overlapped and complemented each other.

The USCC was soon confronted by rival central labour organisations. The Catholic mission, which had persistently urged its members to steer clear of the communist-inspired USCC, was determined to create a Christian trade union. In this endeavour, it sought the assistance of Dr Louis-Paul Aujoulat, a French doctor who had played a leading role in the launch of several Catholic action movements in French Cameroon and, in 1951, of a Catholic-dominated party, the *Bloc Démocratique Camerounais* (BDC), that aimed to counteract the nationalist left (Bayart 1979). In 1946 he approached one of the members of his extensive social network in France, Mr de Gaillarde, about setting up a Cameroonian section of the *Confédération Française de Travailleurs Chrétiens* (CFTC), with the help of Cameroonian collaborators including James Moukoko, Ernest Mongory and Benoît Mbangue (Mongory 1976–7; Verdzekov 1969). To found this Christian trade union movement on a firm footing, Aujoulat invited another French friend of his, Joseph Dumas, the then secretary-general of CFTC and a future deputy in the French National Assembly, to visit French Cameroon and take charge of union organisation. Dumas set about his task with zeal but had such radical and virulent opinions on social justice, wage levels and freedom of the press that the Catholic missionaries at the time took him for an imprudent agitator and only accorded him support with some reserve and circumspection (Verdzekov 1969). Most Protestant workers, however, refused to join the Catholic-dominated CFTC and preferred membership in the USCC. In 1952 the CFTC's seat was transferred from Douala to Yaoundé with its large Catholic population. Although most Catholic workers tended to support the conservative Catholic-dominated nationalist party, the BDC, the CFTC never established any formal link with the party.

In September 1947 a split occurred in the CGT in France, and the non-communist elements formed the *CGT-Force Ouvrière* (FO). The split was supported and even encouraged by the French government. From its inception the FO was closely connected to the *Section Française de l'Internationale Ouvrière* (SFIO), the French socialist party. It engaged in systematic anti-communist activities and its members were principally civil servants. The split in the metropolitan CGT had immediate repercussions in French Cameroon, leading to a split in the USCC. The FO was formally launched in April 1948 and in 1949 André Soucadaux was named High Commissioner in French Cameroon, remaining there till 1954. Soucadaux had SFIO sympathies and his secretary-general, Georges Spénale, was a staunch socialist. Both men set about encouraging the local branch of the FO in much the same way as the government was doing in France. They clearly wanted to offset the influence of the USCC, which they saw as the force behind the recently created radical nationalist party, the UPC. Charles Assalé, one of the founding members of the USCC, was asked to lead the FO. However, he soon resigned to launch a central labour organisation of his own, the *Union des Syndicats Autonomes du Cameroun* (USAC). Again, it did not take long for him to leave the USAC and enter politics, being elected to the territorial assembly. By the time of independence, the USAC had virtually disappeared. Despite its strong support from the Administering Authority, the FO remained a relatively small organisation and, as in France, it recruited its membership predominantly among civil servants.

The various attempts by the administration, the *colons* and the Catholic mission to weaken the USCC and create rival central labour organisations met with only limited success The USCC was able to achieve a much larger following than any of its rivals and its active role in pressing for independence certainly added to the popularity of its leaders. The officially reported union membership in French Cameroon grew from 14,000 in 1947 to some 30,000 in 1957 when unions claimed to represent over a quarter of the wage labour force. In spite of the competition, the USCC, with an estimated membership of 15,000 in 1957 (most probably a conservative estimate), still counted more workers than the FO, the CFTC and the USAC whose combined membership in the same year did not exceed 11,000 (Kendrick 1979; Joseph 1977). Considerable animosity existed between the USCC and the other union federations, evidenced by the mutual complaints received by the UN mission to the territory in 1950. USCC organisers complained that the French administration was trying to sabotage its efforts by violating its right to strike and persecuting militants, while they claimed that the Catholic clergy were openly fighting the USCC. The other federations, in turn, lamented that they were receiving insufficient support from the administration, which was said to be intimidated by the USCC (Verdzekov 1969).

In the late 1950s two new trade union developments became manifest in French Cameroon. The first was the search for autonomy from the French central labour organisations, which can be explained by the territory's growing nationalist feelings. At its 1956 congress the USCC severed its links with the CGT and renamed itself the *Confédération Générale Kamerunaise du Travail* (CGKT). Just a year before the CFTC had taken the decision to encourage Africans to set up their own autonomous central labour organisations, and workers in French Cameroon were actually the first to create such an autonomous confederation, christened the *Confédération Camerounaise des Syndicats Croyants* (CCSC). Faithful to the earlier policy of all the French central labour organisations, the FO continued to oppose the setting up of autonomous African central labour organisations and it was not until 1958 that it finally agreed to the creation of the *Confédération Africaine des Syndicats Libres* (CASL).

The second development was emerging dissent among the union leadership over policies and strategies. To this tension was added certain personal rivalries. As a result, federations tended to split into factions, often leading to further fragmentation of the labour movement. Following the start of guerrilla war by the UPC in 1955, there was growing dissent between the main leaders of the CGKT (the former USCC), Jacques N'Gom and Mayoa Beck. In addition to personal rivalries, there were differences of opinion about the union's policy and strategy. N'Gom tended to condemn UPC violence during guerrilla war and appeared to be increasingly willing to cooperate with the administration, while Beck remained loyal to the UPC. In 1957 the CGKT split into a N'Gom faction and a Beck faction but in early 1959 they reunited to form the *Union Générale Kamerunaise du Travail* (UGKT), although by July that year N'Gom had expelled the pro-Beck elements from the union. Similar developments occurred in other labour federations.

The British Mandate and Trust Territory

While French Cameroon was incorporated into the French colonial empire as a distinct administrative unit, British Cameroon was instead administered as an integral part of Nigeria during the mandate and trust era (Konings and Nyamnjoh 2003). Consequently, union development in the territory took place within the framework of industrial relations and trade unionism existing in Nigeria. And many of the unions functioning in the so-called Southern Cameroons were actually branches of trade unions based in Nigeria. Trade unions in British Cameroon, therefore, had much in common with Nigerian unions and should be studied with the Nigerian context in mind.

Remarkably it was as early as 1938 that the Colonial Office legalised trade union formation in Nigeria, although the actual implementation of this legalisation was postponed for some time because of vehement resistance on the part of some administrators and employers. It could be asked why the Colonial Office was so eager to promote the establishment and legalisation of trade unions in Nigeria and other British colonies (Davies 1966). The principal reason seems to have been the gradual awareness of the important intermediary role that trade unions were able to play in the control of labour, provided that the union leadership was guided along sound lines (Konings 1993). 'Sound' unionism in the British colonies was generally equated with:

- *Autonomous unionism.* Trade unionists were constantly advised to stay away from politics, particularly in the sense of preserving union autonomy with regard to the emergent nationalist movements and parties, and to restrict themselves to economic and industrial demands. In his 1930 dispatch to all colonial governors, the Secretary of State Lord Passfield (Sydney Webb) already sensed the threat of political unionism to colonial hegemony and stressed the need for continuous state supervision and the indoctrination of the emerging unions in the colonies (Millen 1963). He also recommended the compulsory registration of trade unions in the colonies, a recommendation that constituted an important departure from practices in the mother country, and was later incorporated in the 1938 Nigerian Trade Union Ordinance. Compulsory registration, of course, enabled the colonial administration to refuse legal recognition to any politically suspect organisation.
- *Responsible unionism.* Trade unionists were constantly advised to resolve their conflicts with employers in a cordial manner, i.e. through negotiation and collective bargaining, rather than through strikes. The freedom to use the strike weapon could only be resorted to if all other means of settling disputes, including conciliation and arbitration, had failed.

The propagation of this model of 'free but responsible trade unionism' was entrusted to the Labour Department, which was established in Nigeria in 1942. A special trade union division was added in 1946 but it was only in 1948 that a resident labour officer was stationed in Buea, the capital of the Southern Cameroons. He was responsible to the Labour Officer (Trade Unions) at Enugu in Eastern Nigeria for matters pertaining to trade unions. Staffed with professional trade unionists seconded from the British TUC, the Labour Department was to assist in the formation of new unions, advise existing unions on administrative problems, conduct union education programmes and promote harmonious industrial relations (Roper 1958: 66).

After the start of World War II, workers in Nigeria and the Southern Cameroons became increasingly discontented due to sharp cost of living increases (Ananaba 1969). They engaged in a series of strike actions and began organising into trade unions, a move that was facilitated by the colonial administration's enactment of the Nigerian Trade Union Ordinance in 1938. Most of the newly created unions were 'house' or 'company' unions, which made the local workplace the focus of union activities. In marked contrast to French Cameroon, central labour organisations tended to be either weak or non-existent. Despite efforts to establish a central labour organisation in British Cameroon during the mandate and trust era, no such organisation ever came into existence. Nor was any effort made by the British TUC labour officers to affiliate the newly created trade unions in British Cameroon with the metropolitan central labour organisation.

Unlike other parts of West Africa, the Southern Cameroons was characterised by a plantation economy that had been established during German colonial rule and has remained ever since as a dominant feature of the regional economy (Konings 1993). It is therefore not surprising that the plantations became the centre of trade union activities in the territory. Warmington (1960: 26) noted that the pioneer trade union in the Southern Cameroons emerged in 1944 on the Ndian Estate, one of the Unilever Pamol estates in Eastern Nigeria and the Southern Cameroons, but that by 1948 it had already been dissolved. As the Administering Authority reported in 1950, the three largest unions operating in the territory at that time were the Cameroon Development Corporation Workers' Union (CDCWU), the Likomba (Elders and Fyffes) Plantation Workers' Union, and the Pamol (UAC) Limited African Workers' Union, all of which were organisations for plantation workers (Konings 1993, 1998). The CDCWU, founded in 1947, was actually one of the largest trade unions in West Africa with a reported membership of 19,700 in 1952. It became generally regarded as one of the better-organised unions, and it more or less dominated the industrial relations scene in the Southern Cameroons during that period (Konings 1993).

The Labour Department on the whole succeeded in persuading trade union leaders in the Southern Cameroons that union autonomy was a cardinal principle of sound trade unionism. The CDCWU leadership, for example, strictly adhered to this principle, except for the years 1949–53 when it was affiliated to the Cameroon National Federation (CNF), a congress-type political organisation founded in May 1949 in Kumba. However, it would appear that the CNF's impact on the rank and file was only marginal, and it instead served the advancement of the political careers of Dr E.M.L. Endeley and Mr N.N. Mbile who combined CDCWU leadership with CNF leadership. Both were what Millen (1963) called 'outside' leaders in the union: they had had professional and political careers outside the plantations before being appointed as the first full-time officials within the union. Evidently they regarded union leadership as a stepping-stone to political leadership (Konings 1993). With this notable exception, union leaders in the Southern Cameroons tended to be conscious of the need to preserve a power base independent of the nationalist movement even where they agreed with common anti-colonialist objectives. They often perceived trade union autonomy not only as a guarantee for the representation and defence of their members' interests but also as a means of preventing political conflict and division within the unions themselves.

The Labour Department was less successful in turning the unions in British Cameroon into 'responsible' unions during this period. Several factors account for this relative failure, including the recalcitrant attitudes of government authorities and managers, the inadequacy of the negotiating machinery and, above all, the constant pressure by the rank and file on the generally more moderate union leadership to use the strike weapon to 'bring management and government to their knees'. A considerable number of labour disputes occurred during this period, some of them leading to major strikes called by the unions (Verdzekov 1969; Konings 1993, 1995, 1998). Despite the fact that unions were able to maintain a large measure of autonomy during decolonisation, their strike actions, though primarily 'economist' in motivation, were usually perceived as 'political' and 'anti-colonial' by others, especially the Administering Authority.

Like their French Cameroonian counterparts who sought autonomy from the metropolitan central labour organisations, British Cameroonian trade unions also strove for a larger degree of autonomy from the Nigerian trade unions, with the growth of nationalist feelings and the Southern Cameroons' achievement of full regional status within the Nigerian

Federation in 1958 (Konings and Nyamnjoh 2003). For instance, the Southern Cameroons Union of Teachers (SCUT) came into existence in 1959 after separating from the Nigerian Union of Teachers (NUT). It was to become one of the most important trade unions outside the plantation sector in British Cameroon, claiming in its heyday a membership of over 3,500 out of a total of about 5,000 teachers (Konings 2006a).

3. Trade Unionism in the Post-Colonial One-Party State Era, 1961–90

Following independence and reunification in 1961, the new African leaders had to come to terms with the role trade unions were to play in the newly created Federal Republic of Cameroon. Gradually, President Ahmadou Ahidjo (1961–82) began to express his views on the unions' post-colonial role: they were to make a constructive contribution to what he perceived as the major requirements for nation-building, namely national unity and national development (Ahidjo 1964).

In July 1962 he made an urgent appeal in Ebolowa to the internally divided trade union movement in the federated state of East Cameroon (the former French Cameroon) to unite for the sake of national unity. Following the establishment of a one-party state in the whole Federal Republic in September 1966, he selected the first congress of the *Union Nationale Camerounaise* (UNC) in March 1969 to renew his call for trade union unity in the Federal Republic and to spell out, with great precision, the role of trade unionism in the national development effort and its relationship with the party (Kendrick 1969; Konings 1993). He claimed on that occasion that in a country like Cameroon, 'where class conflict does not exist' and the state seeks to ensure social justice, the role of the unions should be constructive rather than contentious. Labour could only make demands in the light of the possibilities available in the economy where progress depended on mutual sacrifice by all strata of the population. He went on to attribute a fourfold role to trade unionism: (1) to apply the labour laws in the workplace and to enhance labour discipline and productivity; (2) to contribute to the professional training of its members and their education in development matters; (3) to mobilise the masses for the task of nation-building; and (4) to assist government efforts to improve workers' living standards.

To execute their new mission efficiently, Ahidjo exhorted union leaders to create one central labour organisation, cut their ties with foreign labour movements and replace 'irrelevant' ideologies with UNC principles. Evidently, the president's appeal was aimed at the establishment of state control over the relatively autonomous trade unions. This would be the next step in what Bayart (1979) called Ahidjo's 'hegemonic project': the creation of a one-party system to be followed by the merger of all existing trade union organisations into a single body subordinate to the party. Implementation of Ahidjo's project regarding trade unionism turned out to be more difficult in the federated state of West Cameroon (the former Southern Cameroons) than in East Cameroon.

In East Cameroon, where a one-party system had been virtually established by 1963, a considerable degree of trade union unity developed. A *Fédération des Syndicats du Cameroun* (FSC) was formed by the two rival factions of the UGKT (the former CGT-USCC) and the CASL (the former CGT-FO) after their disaffiliation from the World Federation of Trade Unions (WFTU) and the International Confederation of Free Trade Unions (ICFTU) respectively. The *Union des Syndicats Croyants du Cameroun* (USCC), the successor of the CCSC which had split and then reformed, at first seemed interested in the unification of the labour front in East Cameroon but finally opted to maintain its ties with regional and international labour federations. The new federation, the FSC, then represented all unionised workers in East Cameroon except those of the USCC (with its estimated 16 per cent of unionised workers).

The federated state of West Cameroon was one of the few African states where the political elite took over the colonial model of 'free but responsible trade unionism' and tried to maintain it. This must be attributed not only to the Anglophone political elite's strong attachment to the values and institutions introduced by the British Trusteeship Authority but also to trade union pressure; the union leadership constantly assured the West Cameroonian government that the unions were ready to play a constructive role in the national development effort on condition that existing trade union autonomy was not infringed upon by the government. The most important champion of trade union autonomy became Mr G.B. Fogam, the secretary-general of both the CDCWU and the West Cameroon Trades Union Congress (WCTUC). Fogam had been instrumental in the creation of the WCTUC on 20 January 1962, and his leading role in the newly created central labour organisation did justice to the dominant position of the CDCWU in the WCTUC. While the WCTUC insisted on the preservation of trade union autonomy from the state, it established close links with the British TUC and the ICFTU from the very start in the hope of obtaining financial and technical support as well as a number of trade union scholarships from these organisations (Konings 1993).

The period between 1966 and 1972 was a period of transition in West Cameroon from the creation of a one-party state in 1966 to that of a unitary state in 1972. The tightening grip of the federal state on the federated state of West Cameroon during this period was soon followed by an attempt by the federal state to establish control over the autonomous trade unions. For a better understanding of trade union developments in West Cameroon, it is important to note that Gabriel Fogam, the secretary-general of the CDCWU and the WCTUC, tended to support Ahidjo's pursuit of trade union unity in the country but was strongly opposed to state control over the unions.

Fogam attended the UNC Garoua Congress in 1969 in his capacity as secretary-general of the WCTUC. With the approval of other WCTUC leaders, he then took the initiative to establish the 'unity move' requested by President Ahidjo, which he thought could strengthen the bargaining power of the labour movement. He organised a meeting between the WCTUC and the two central labour organisations in East Cameroon in Limbe on 28 September 1969, at which the three parties agreed in principle to form one single trade union centre in the Federal Republic and discussed further steps towards trade union unity. The three central labour organisations also agreed to sever links with regional and international labour organisations. However, when it became increasingly evident that the federal state was aiming to integrate the unified trade union movement into the single party, WCTUC leaders resisted. The party and the Provincial Delegation of Labour (the former Labour Department) applied considerable pressure on the WCTUC to force it to abandon its claims of union autonomy (Konings 1993: 136).

Following a number of preparatory meetings, the three existing central labour organisations were dissolved in the autumn of 1971. After their dissolution, the *Union Nationale des Travailleurs du Cameroun* (UNTC) came into existence and on 10 February 1972 it elected a Confederal Bureau to manage its affairs. The president of the UNTC became a member of the Central Committee of the UNC.

A close look at the UNTC Statutes reveals its total subordination to the party. Article 3 declares categorically that 'The UNTC shall carry out its activities within the scope of political options prescribed by the UNC.' The organisational set-up of the UNTC was similar to that of the party. Moreover, the party's Political Bureau was represented in all the principal organs of the UNTC, to the extent that no UNTC decision could be taken without the Political Bureau's approval.

Article 9 of the Statutes clearly reflects Ahidjo's proposals at the 1969 UNC Garoua Congress by assigning a fourfold role to the UNTC in national development:

- to strive for the implementation of labour laws in the enterprises;
- to ensure discipline among its workers and to organise the systematic pursuit of an increased output so that Cameroon workers could become efficient labour producers and citizens conscious of development problems;
- to broaden and strengthen dialogue between employers and workers with a view to the peaceful settlement of labour disputes; and
- to cooperate closely with the government within the framework of options prescribed by the party for the attainment of national objectives of social and economic development.

The party hoped that this new trade union model would achieve what the colonial model of relative trade union autonomy had failed: the transformation of trade unions into instruments of labour control and responsible partners in national development. Following the creation of the UNTC, the union leadership was co-opted into the labour control structure apparatus, albeit in a subordinated position. It was supposed to play a major role in national development, especially by educating the workers in the virtues of increased production and constant dialogue with employers, rather than defending and protecting workers' interests.

The unions' controlling capacity was enhanced by the 1967 Federal Labour Code, which aimed to bring about a harmonisation of labour legislation in the Federal Republic. One of its most important regulations was the virtual outlawing of strikes. In matters of collective disputes, this Labour Code required that all peaceful channels available – principally the conciliatory efforts of the Labour Inspector and arbitration – be exhausted before a strike was called. Illegal strike action could be punished with the termination of the strikers' employment contracts.

However, it would appear that even the first Confederal Bureau of the UNTC was not always faithful to its primary responsibility of labour control. It was suddenly dissolved by the government on 1–2 August 1975 under the pretext that it had not been functioning properly because of internal conflict and mismanagement. In trade union circles, however, it is believed that the real reason for this drastic government intervention was the fact that the first president of the Confederal Bureau, Mr Moïse Satouglé Défith, continued to defend workers during conflicts with employers and to condone a considerable number of illegal strikes.

Almost no research has been done on workers' reactions to state-controlled trade unionism. In my own studies on plantation labour in Anglophone Cameroon (Konings 1993, 1995, 1998), I have demonstrated that the rank and file quickly lost confidence in the union leadership and rebelled against its control through regular illegal strikes. Illegal strike action became not only one of the most significant expressions of labour resistance against the state, management and union control but also one of the most effective labour strategies – many workers would argue the only effective strategy – of bringing long-standing grievances to the attention of those in positions of power in the Cameroonian post-colonial state.

The close relationship between the state and trade unions continued under Ahidjo's successor, Paul Biya. At the 1985 Bamenda Congress, Biya changed the name of the single party from UNC to *Rassemblement Démocratique du Peuple Camerounais* (RDPC) and commended the central labour organisation for its constructive role. The UNTC, in turn, immediately changed its name to *Organisation Syndicale des Travailleurs du Cameroun* (OSTC) and its then president, Mr J.-E. Abondo, 'thanked President Paul Biya a thousand times for all that he had done for the workers' (Foundation Friedrich-Ebert 1994). Soon afterwards, Abondo was appointed Minister of Defence, a reward for his services to the regime.

4. Trade Unionism in the Political Liberalisation Era, 1990 to the Present

Unlike several trade union movements elsewhere on the African continent (Konings 2000; Beckman and Sachikonye 2001), trade unions in Cameroon have played little role in the introduction of neo-liberal political reforms. Given the close ties between the post-colonial state and civil society, this is not altogether surprising. Although the corrupt and authoritarian Biya regime swiftly lost its legitimacy during the severe economic and political crisis in the late 1980s, OSTC continued to support the regime. Like the ruling RDPC party, it strongly condemned the increasing calls by civil society for political liberalisation and the introduction of a multiparty system. When the first opposition party, the Social Democratic Front (SDF), was formed in Anglophone Cameroon in May 1990, the then OSTC president, Mr D. Fouda Sima, expressed, as did other RDPC loyalists, 'his total rejection of what the Head of State has called political models imported from abroad' (Konings 2000: 179). Together with other OSTC leaders, he subsequently participated in anti-democracy marches organised by the regime.

When the Biya government, under considerable pressure from the Bretton Woods institutions and western donors (notably France), was compelled to introduce a multi-party system and increased freedom of speech and association in December 1990 (Konings 1996), growing dissatisfaction was felt among the rank and file with OSTC's performance and its continuing alliance with the ruling RDPC party. Many workers participated in the protracted 1991 'Ghost Town' campaign – essentially a civil disobedience action aimed at bringing the economy to a complete standstill and called by the radical opposition to force the Biya regime to hold a sovereign national conference (Takougang and Krieger 1998: 126–31). Even OSTC regional and local leaders began to call for union autonomy as a necessary precondition for the defence of its members' interests (Mehler 1997). Under mounting pressure, the OSTC leadership finally recognised, on 2 April 1991, its members' rights to join the political party of their choice. Eventually, the new Labour Code of 1992 guaranteed a large measure of union autonomy from the state. It also abolished the existing practice of trade union monolithism, allowing a group of at least twenty workers to form a union outside OSTC, and reintroduced the possibility of trade union affiliation with regional and international labour organisations (Republic of Cameroon 1992). To mark a new beginning, the central labour organisation then changed its name again to *Confédération Syndicale des Travailleurs du Cameroun* (CSTC).

The government devised a number of strategies to allow it to keep a close eye on union activities. Firstly, the 1992 Labour Code maintained one of the key instruments of labour control laid down in the former 1967 and 1974 Labour Codes, namely the compulsory registration of newly formed unions. Secondly, the government continued to intervene in existing unions by supporting trade union leaders loyal to the regime and harassing those engaged in opposition actions. And thirdly, it helped create rival trade union centres led by RDPC loyalists. For example, in April 1995, it sponsored the formation of the *Union des Syndicats Libres du Cameroun* (USLC) (Konings 2006b, 2007).

The trade union scene worsened from 1997 onwards when the CSTC leadership split into two factions, both claiming leadership. Their internal power struggle appears to have been motivated primarily by personal ambition and material interests rather than by pronounced differences in union policy and strategy. The leadership struggle almost completely paralysed union activities in defence of their members' interests. It sparked numerous court cases, the organisation of unity conferences held under the auspices of the ILO and international labour organisations, and renewed government intervention in the CSTC. The leadership wrangling was not resolved until 2002 when the government-aligned faction of Maximilien Ntone Diboté seized power with the support of the Minister of Labour and was subsequently recognised by the government. The defeated faction led by Benoît Essiga then broke away from the CSTC and launched another central labour organisation, the *Confédération Générale des Travailleurs-Liberté* (CGTL).

After 2000 the trade union movement became further fragmented (see Table 1). Three other central labour organisations were formed by new and old leaders in their search for power, namely the *Union Générale des Travailleurs du Cameroun* (UGTC), the *Confédération des Syndicats Indépendants du Cameroun* (CSIC) and the *Centrale Syndicale du Secteur Public* (CSP). And perhaps more importantly for the future of trade unionism in Cameroon, a new split occurred in the CSTC in 2005. Two of its most outstanding leaders, Louis Sombès and Cornelius Vewessee, renowned in Cameroon for their persistent championing of autonomous and militant trade unionism, created yet another central labour organisation, the *Confédération des Syndicats Autonomes du Cameroun* (CSAC), which attracted 65 per cent of the CSTC membership (Konings 2007). Obviously, increasing fragmentation of trade unionism in the country tends to thwart any united action. Generally speaking, the various central labour organisations are inclined to fight each other rather than form a common front against employers and the state.

Table 1. Central Labour Organisations in Cameroon

Name	% of trade union membership
Confédération des Syndicats Autonomes du Cameroun (CSAC)	38
Confédération Syndicale des Travailleurs du Cameroun (CSTC)	17
Union des Syndicats Libres du Cameroun (USLC)	15
Confédération Générale des Travailleurs-Liberté (CGTL)	11
Centrale Syndicale du Secteur Public (CSP)	10
Union Générale des Travailleurs du Cameroun (UGTC)	7.5
Confédération des Syndicats Indépendants du Cameroun (CSIC)	1.5
Total	100.0
N	270,000

Source: Compiled from various files in the Ministry of Labour and Social Security in Yaoundé.

The growing fragmentation of trade unionism was one reason for the weakened political and bargaining power during political and economic liberalisation. A second reason was the dramatic decline in membership. Many workers have resigned from the unions, disillusioned by their leaders' performance. The situation is compounded by the severe economic crisis and structural adjustment. Public- and private-sector retrenchments have led to heavy losses in union membership. Many workers are now forced to seek alternative survival strategies in the informal sector but no attempts have been made by the unions to organise them. It has been estimated that trade union membership has fallen from around 50 per cent of the labour force during the one-party state when there was considerable pressure put on workers by the state and the union leadership to be both party and union members, to approximately 25 to 30 per cent of the labour force during political and economic liberalisation. A third reason for the decline in union bargaining strength is the country's high rate of unemployment. Recent surveys have revealed that no less than 39 per cent of the labour force is either unemployed or underemployed (International Labour Organisation 2004). Such a large labour reserve puts enormous pressure on the labour market and wage levels. And finally, there is the neo-liberal demand for a deregulation of labour laws, which aims to create flexibility in the labour market. While the 1967 and 1974 Labour Codes introduced during the one-party state were generally seen as being labour friendly, the 1992 Labour Code enhanced management's position when it came to hiring, firing and remunerating workers. Rules governing employment security and minimum wages (Kendrick 1979; Konings 1993), for instance, were deregulated, withdrawing the protective safeguards and rights achieved by the union movement in the pre-adjustment era. Employers are now increasingly resorting to casualisation, outsourcing and temporary employment contracts, which enable them to cut labour costs and increase their control over labour.

In sharp contrast to the one-party state era, there has been a remarkable absence of any form of regular consultation between the government, employers and trade unions during the era of political and economic liberalisation. The channels for dialogue provided by the 1992 Labour Code, such as the National Consultative Commission on Labour and the National Commission for Health and Security at Work, no longer function. Last but not least, the unions themselves have never been able, with other civil society organisations, to devise an alternative to neo-liberal economic reforms that is less harmful to the interests of their members and other subaltern groups in society.

Given the blatant neglect of their interests by the existing unions, workers have either started to organise themselves into autonomous trade unions or to resort to independent militant strike actions. One hopeful development has been the emergence of several autonomous trade unions in the civil and public services, especially in the educational sector (Konings 2004, 2005). Their emergence has been all the more significant because civil servants are prohibited by law from forming trade unions, and the Biya government has ignored repeated ILO demands that civil servants be given the right to unionise in conformity with Convention 87 signed by Cameroon. Their leaders, who soon became victims of severe state repression, strongly condemned the inactivity of state-controlled trade unionism and pledged to contribute to the building of militant trade unionism in the country and to serve as a countervailing power to the ruling regime. Due to apparent government insensitivity to the plight of teachers, their trade unions have undertaken a variety of militant actions that have paralysed the educational system for a number of years, including demonstrations, the regular boycotting of examinations and intermittent strikes.

Other workers have displayed a growing militancy in the defence of their interests during the neo-liberal economic reforms. Several protracted strike actions against the current privatisation of public enterprises have been reported. In a recent article (Konings 2008), I give a detailed description of the workers' militant actions against the 2002 privatisation of the Cameroon Development Corporation's (CDC) tea estates in Anglophone Cameroon, the largest agro-industrial parastatal in the country. Confronted with unbearable living and working conditions after privatisation, the workers gradually lost interest in keeping their jobs at any cost and resumed informal and collective actions. Determined to receive all their accrued benefits before resigning, they engaged in protracted strike action that brought work on the tea estates to a standstill throughout 2006.

5. Conclusion

The history of trade unionism in Cameroon shows the unions' deepening crisis in the post-colonial state after a promising start in the pre-independence and reunification period. Legislation at the end of World War II led to an era of rapid growth of relatively autonomous trade unions in both the French and British mandate and trust territories that were able to play a significant role not only in the defence of their members' interests but also in the struggle against colonialism. The trade union models introduced by the Administering Authorities and metropolitan trade unions largely account for the fact that trade unions in French Cameroon were inclined to participate in nationalist struggles more directly than those in British Cameroon. Unlike in British Cameroon, however, conflicts emerged regarding the direction the nationalist movement and workers' defence should take. The trade union movement in French Cameroon became further fragmented in the mid 1950s as a result of personal rivalries and power struggles within the leadership of each of the existing central labour organisations.

The consolidation of political forces into a single party after independence and reunification in 1961 for the sake of national unity and national development eventually led to the transformation of a divided labour movement, which until then had been largely independent of the government in power, into a united front under the aegis of the party. This post-colonial model of labour control, however, has never been entirely successful, mainly because it failed to recognise the strength of the rank and file's militancy and solidarity which has been manifested in an unexpected number of illegal strikes.

For various reasons mentioned in this study, neo-liberal political and economic reforms appear to have weakened rather than strengthened the political power and bargaining strength of organised labour after many years of subordination to the state. This has given rise to widespread disillusion among the rank and file who have shown a growing militancy in their attempts to improve members' deteriorating living and working conditions. However, the central labour organisations' renewed pursuit of trade union autonomy and the current emergence of autonomous and militant trade unions in the civil and public sector provide grounds for optimism that the Cameroonian trade union movement will eventually succeed in loosening the controls of the corporatist state machine and become more meaningful to its members once again.

Suggested Reading

Ahidjo, A. (1964) *Contribution à la Construction Nationale*, Paris: Présence Africaine.

Ananaba, W. (1969) *The Trade Union Movement in Nigeria*, Benin City: Ethiope Publishing Corporation.

Bayart, J.-F. (1979) *L'État au Cameroun*, Paris: Presses de la Fondation Nationale des Sciences Politiques.

Beckman, B. and Sachikonye, L.M. (eds) (2001) *Labour Regimes and Liberalization: The Restructuring of State-Society Relations in Africa*, Harare: University of Zimbabwe Publications.

Davies, I. (1966) *African Trade Unions*, Harmondsworth: Penguin.

Eyinga, A. (1985) *Démocratie de Yaoundé: Syndicalisme d'abord, 1944–1946*, Paris: L'Harmattan.

Foundation Friedrich-Ebert (1994) *Le Syndicalisme dans le Processus de Démocratisation*, Yaoundé: Imprimerie Saint John.

International Labour Organisation (2004) *Les Statistiques sur l'Emploi et le Marché du Travail au Cameroun*, Yaoundé: Bureau International du Travail.

Joseph, R.A. (1974) 'Settlers, Strikers and *Sans-Travail:* The Douala Riots of September 1945', *Journal of African History* 15 (4): 669–87.

——(1977) *Radical Nationalism in Cameroun: Social Origins of the U.P.C. Rebellion*, Oxford: Oxford University Press.

Kaptue, L. (1986) *Travail et Main-d'Oeuvre au Cameroun sous Régime Français 1916–1952*, Paris: L'Harmattan.

Kendrick, R. (1979) 'Survey of Industrial Relations in Cameroon' in Damachi, U.G., Seibel, H.D. and Trachtman, L. (eds) *Industrial Relations in Africa*, London: Macmillan.

Kester, G. and Sidibé, O.O. (eds) (1997) *Trade Unions and Sustainable Democracy in Africa*, Aldershot: Avebury.

Konings, P. (1993) *Labour Resistance in Cameroon*, London: James Currey.

—— (1995) *Gender and Class in the Tea Estates of Cameroon*, Aldershot: Avebury.
—— (1996) 'The Post-Colonial State and Economic and Political Reforms in Cameroon' in Fernández Jilberto, A.E. and Mommen, A. (eds) *Liberalisation in the Developing World: Institutional and Economic Changes in Latin America, Africa and Asia*, London: Routledge.
—— (1998) *Unilever Estates in Crisis and the Power of Organizations in Cameroon*, Hamburg: LIT Verlag.
—— (2000) 'Trade Unions and Democratisation in Africa' in Konings, P., van Binsbergen, B. and Hesseling, G. (eds), *Trajectoires de Libération en Afrique Contemporaine*, Paris: Karthala.
—— (2004) 'Trade Union Activism among University Teachers during Cameroon's Political Liberalisation', *Nordic Journal of African Studies* 13 (3): 289–301.
—— (2005) 'Assessing the Power of Newly Created Teachers' Organisations during Cameroon's Political Liberalisation', *Journal of Higher Education in Africa* 3 (2): 130–54.
—— (2006a) 'Assessing the Role of Autonomous Teachers' Trade Unions in Anglophone Cameroon, 1959–1972', *Journal of African History* 47 (3): 415–36.
—— (2006b) 'African Trade Unions and the Challenge of Globalisation: A Comparative Study of Ghana and Cameroon' in Phelan, C. (ed.) *The Future of Organised Labour: Global Perspectives*, Oxford and Bern: Peter Lang.
—— (2007) 'Trade Unionism in Cameroon: From Crisis to Revitalisation?' in Phelan, C. (ed.) *Trade Union Revitalisation: Trends and Prospects in 34 Countries*, Oxford and Bern: Peter Lang.
—— (2008) 'Privatisation and Labour Militancy: The Case of Cameroon's Tea Estates', *Journal of Contemporary African Studies* 26 (1): 51–70.
Konings, P. and Nyamnjoh, F.B. (2003) *Negotiating an Anglophone Identity: A Study of the Politics of Recognition and Representation in Cameroon*, Leiden: Brill.
Mehler, A. (1997) 'Cameroun: une transition qui n'a pas eu lieu' in Daloz, J.-F. and Quantin, P. (eds) *Transitions Démocratiques Africaines: Dynamiques et Contraintes (1990–1994)*, Paris: Karthala.

Millen, B.H. (1963) *The Political Role of Labor in Developing Countries*, Washington: The Brookings Institution.
Mongory, J. (1976–7) 'Genèse et Contradiction du Syndicalisme Camerounais', *Revue Française d'Études Politiques Africaines* 132: 74–89 (Part I); 133: 56–83 (Part II); 134: 90–118 (Part III).
Moumé-Étia, L. (1991) *Cameroun: Les Années Ardentes: Aux Origines de la Vie Syndicale et Politique*, Paris: Jalivres.
Republic of Cameroon (1992) *Labour Code (Law No 92–007 of 14 August 1992)*, Yaoundé: National Printing Press.
Roper, J.I. (1958) *Labour Problems in West Africa*, Harmondsworth: Penguin.
Takougang, J. and Krieger, M. (1998) *African State and Society in the 1990s: Cameroon's Political Crossroads*, Boulder CO: Westview Press.
Verdzekov, P.B. (1969) 'The Relationship between Trade Unions and Political Parties in West Cameroon', PhD thesis, Pontifical University Gregoriana, Rome.
Warmington, W.A. (1960) *A West African Trade Union*, London: Oxford University Press.

Trade Unionism in Israel since 1945: Its Origins and Functions

ITZHAK HARPAZ

1. Background and Nature of the Histadrut

Organised labour in Israel consists of several trade unions, of which the largest, most prominent, and noteworthy is the Histadrut (Hebrew for 'association' or 'federation'). Other unions are much less significant or influential. Accordingly the present chapter solely concentrates on the Histadrut.

Several events occurring around turn of the twentieth century led to the birth of the Histadrut, 'The General Federation of Hebrew Workers in the Land of Israel'. According to Shirom (1983), among the foremost were the spread of communist and socialist ideologies and the awakening of national aspirations in East European countries with relatively large Jewish populations. In addition, anti-Semitism and pogroms against Jews in Tsarist Russia gave rise to the establishment of socialist-Zionist parties. These were guided by a major goal: immigration to Israel (then Palestine) and tilling its land (Shirom 1983). The Histadrut was founded in 1920 by labour Zionist political parties. The latter, consisting mainly of Russian Jewish immigrants arriving in Palestine at the beginning of the twentieth century, were genuinely influenced by the Russian-Jewish socialist tradition, and instilled its character into the new union and its charter.

The Histadrut's major goals, in the spirit of socialism and Zionism, may be discerned from the first resolution adopted at its inaugural conference: 'The general federation unites all workers and labourers of the land who live by the sweat of their brow without exploiting the toil of others, to promote land settlement, to involve itself in all economic and cultural issues affecting all labourers in Palestine, and to build a Hebrew workers' society in the land of Israel' (Israeli Labour Movement 2008). In its early years the Histadrut allowed membership of Jews only, but in 1943 it became involved in organising the rights of Arab workers as well. This was also reflected by dropping the phrase 'Hebrew' (workers) from its title in the 1960s.

Israel is perhaps one of the few states in the world in which in extensive labour and trade union activities existed prior to its establishment in 1948. The Histadrut played a major role in the development of the state of Israel, with responsibility for generating much of the nation's infrastructure and economy. It assumed roles usually fulfilled by a state, and nation building was among its foremost goals. Therefore, in addition to its traditional union functions it was uniquely involved in several other areas, such as economic, social and cultural activities. The next two sections outline these latter roles, after which the focus turns to the Histadrut's trade union function.

Economic Role

In the first decade of its existence the Histadrut established economic enterprises in such areas as agriculture, industry, holding companies, building and construction, transportation, and banking. From 1923 all these organisations and economic activities were managed and controlled by its Hevrat Ha'ovdim ('society of workers'). The Histadrut possessed and operated a number of enterprises, including the country's largest industrial conglomerates as well as the country's largest bank, Bank Hapoalim ('the workers' bank'). Most agricultural produce and dairy products were processed and supplied through Tnuva ('produce' or 'yield'), an organisation owned and operated by all agriculture settlements (kibbutzim and moshavim) in Israel (Tnuva was sold to private investors in 2008). In 1948 (the year Israel was established) the Histadrut controlled 25 per cent of the national economy (Sternhell 1998). In 1980 the Histadrut was the employer of approximately 250,000 workers (22 per cent of the Israeli civilian labour force).

Overall, Hevrat Ha'ovdim employees enjoyed better employment conditions, very stable industrial relations, and generally earned up to 15 per cent higher wages than their counterparts in similar occupations or industries. Another unique feature of employment in Histadrut enterprises was the fact that many of its organisations were initially established on Israel's periphery to provide employment for new immigrants. In many cases a Histadrut organisation was the major or sole employer for hundreds of families. Economic considerations, or profit making, were often overlooked by the Histadrut. For many years it also initiated a system of 'joint liability' or guarantee system between its organisations, where less profitable or even failing organisational bodies were supported by more successful ones. All these measures arose from ideological reasons; nevertheless, a non-official or latent goal of the Histadrut was recruitment of new members, and possibly making them supporters of Mapai, the leading political labour party.

Social, Cultural and Other Actvities

Over the years the Histadrut provided elaborate and diverse social, cultural and educational services. It established assorted social institutions, including a network of efficient social care organisations, such as child day-care centres, elderly care and old-age facilities. The Histadrut initiated an educational system of schools, colleges and vocational training institutions.

The Histadrut operated several publishing houses, and a daily newspaper, *Davar,* appeared from 1925 to 1996. For many years it was involved in and supported professional and a variety of competitive sports, as well as amateur and popular sports.

The Histadrut also provided a comprehensive health care system. One of the most important functions offered to its members was health services and health insurance through Kupat Holim Clalit ('general sick fund'). The fund's numerous clinics and hospitals across the country, and health insurance, also served as a most potent stimulus for Histadrut membership (Haberfeld 1995). Owing to lack of significant health care alternatives, Kupat Holim developed into the main organisation providing health care to the majority of Israel's population: 75 to 85 per cent of all households at various times (Shirom 1983). Approximately one third of the Histadrut's finances were generated from the health fund revenues. The comment in the previous section about the Histadrut's organisational and employment practices on Israel's periphery may also hold for its health provision practices to the masses. While these services were provided for ideological reasons, in offering them the Histadrut sought new members – again, with their potential for becoming eventual supporters of Mapai labour party. The inclusion of the health fund in the overall operating budget became vital for the functioning of organisational and trade union activities of the federation.

At the height of its power in the 1970s the Histadrut controlled about 30 per cent of the nation's economy, and about 80 per cent of the work force (1.5 million workers) were Histadrut members. For these reasons, as well as its political influence, the Histadrut was often referred to as 'a state within a state'. One example of its political power is the fact that almost every Histadrut chairman, or its leaders, served as Member of Knesset (Parliament) or held a ministerial role. Moreover, David Ben-Gurion, the Histadrut's first chairman (1921–35), was elected as Israel's first prime minister. Several other prime ministers (among them Levi Eshkol and Golda Meir), as well as some of Israel's early presidents, had held various important roles in the Histadrut prior to assuming their national positions.

Nature of Union Roles

The majority of trade unions in Israel belong to the Histadrut, consisting currently of approximately 700,000 members (http://www.histadrut.org.il). It is estimated that of Israel's workforce, consisting of 2.7 million workers, roughly 40 per cent are unionised (including members of unions not included in the Histadrut). This figure is in accord with that of an independent study conducted by Tel Aviv University researchers (Cohen et al. 2003). About 26 per cent belong to the New Histadrut, approximately 11 per cent to the National Workers' Organization, and some 3 per cent to the rest.

The Histadrut's labour union activities take place at several levels. On the level of the work place or plant (in unionised organisations), employees directly elect their representatives, forming a 'local union board' or committee. However, local boards have practically no power to make decisions with regard to labour conflicts, strike declaration, or signing collective agreements. They mainly represent individual members before the employer only on issues such as grievances, welfare, and so forth.

The second level is regional; currently the country is divided into 23 regions (there were 77 regions prior to the 1995 restructuring of the Histadrut). All industrial relations issues in a region (organisational, occupational, or professional) are handled by a region. This includes the right to make decisions on labour conflicts and strike declarations.

The third level is composed of national unions organised by industrial sector, large employers, or specific trades. In 1995 there were 44 national unions; nevertheless, the number of national unions changes from time to time, mainly because of frequent mergers.

The Histadrut's most important arm is its Trade Union Department; it is highly centralised and is responsible for all the professional operations of all its unions. Since the 1980s, with the waning of the Histadrut, power has steadily shifted towards unions within the Histadrut strategically situated in the public sector or elsewhere in the economy. These include unions of clerical workers and government employees, engineers, and nurses, as well as workers in monopolies such as the Electricity Company, Bezeq Telephone Company, the Aircraft Industry, and the Port Authority, among others. All these unions can, and often do, call (wildcat) strikes without the authorisation of the Trade Union Department. In recent years the Teachers' Organisation, Senior University Professors' Association, and the Israeli Medical Association, all non-Histadrut-affiliated unions, have also been involved in various lengthy industrial disputes with the government, mainly over wages and working conditions.

2. Societal Changes and Their Impact on the Histadrut

The first years of the new state entailed remarkable changes. By 1952 its population had doubled (from 870,000 in 1948) and by the early 1960s had tripled (2,430,000) (Statistical Abstracts of Israel 2005, 2007). The state had to allocate all its recourses to infrastructure, housing, equipment, establishing employment places, training, social services, health, and education. During this epoch Histadrut's activities may be characterised as driven by Israel's national priorities. These included advancing national goals such as the absorption of new immigrants, development of the national economy, placement of individuals (mainly immigrants) in new towns on the periphery, and agricultural settlements. It had all the organisational means to do so through its control of powerful industrial conglomerates, public construction and housing, transportation, banking credit and borrowing, pension funds, and supply and distribution of produce. It dominated health care provision throughout the entire state, incorporating most new immigrants into its ranks. During this era, lasting until the mid-1970s, the Histadrut was at its zenith.

Several social, political, and economic transformations have taken place in Israel, particularly in the last three decades, which proved detrimental to the status of the Histadrut. From pre-statehood, Israel rested on a centralistic economic and collectivistic ideological orientation. This was the direction taken by every ruling coalition, which comprised various forms of workers' or labour parties. This pursuit exercised a significant influence on lifestyle, educational system, economy, and work values in Israel. A new era began in 1977, with the replacement of the succession of labour-oriented socialist governments by a coalition of parties headed by the Likud party. The latter emphasised a more liberal ideology, and a philosophy that supported a free market economy as well as a more individualistic orientation. The first buds of decentralisation and pluralism started to appear. Social legitimisation of the importance of individual rights, rather than national collective needs, coincided with infiltration into Israeli society of modern Western norms. A rise in the standard of living strengthened the trend to material values, and at the same time weakened the ideology of cooperation, mutual assurance, and aid for feeble sectors of society. During the 1980s and 1990s Israel experienced an accelerated process of globalisation through increasing exposure to Western culture and lifestyle.

Government involvement in the market diminished, as did subsidies, thus allowing market forces to operate. Israel underwent a gradual move from a relatively centralised economy to a capitalistic market economy (Horowitz and Lissak 1990). In this regard, all Likud-headed governments since 1977 gradually restricted their financial support and subsidisation of the Histadrut's health-provision services, namely Kupat Holim Clalit. Government's main goal was to sever its relationship with the Histadrut, and either nationalise or privatise health services. By 1992 Kupat Holim health services were in a grave financial crisis with a debt of more than NIS 2 billion (more than $600 million).

Since the mid-1980s privatisation of state-run institutions has intensified, affecting many large organisations in various industries. At present the general tendency in Israel toward a more individualistic orientation is stronger than ever. Israel is rapidly changing from a centralised to a decentralised society. From domination by state institutions and a leadership that supported collectivism and solidarity, it is becoming a more divided, pluralistic, and individualistic society, like most industrialised nations.

A major transition occurred in the balance of power in the labour market and industrial relations system. Particularly noteworthy was the breakdown of a large part of the Histradrut's industrial and cooperative sectors. Owing to heavy financial losses, political pressure, and value changes, the omnipotent Histadrut was compelled to divest its economic enterprises (Hevrat Ha'ovdim), either by selling them to private investors or by simply shutting them down. Consequently, this powerful sector, which employed more than one-quarter of Israel's labour force in the 1970s, has practically vanished. The economic crises, which resulted in mass redundancies initiated by the large conglomerates, in addition to privatisation of state-controlled concerns, have likewise led to the almost complete termination of the sacred institution of 'tenure at work'. They have also generated a double digit unemployment rate, which has caused great financial uncertainty in the labour force (Samuel and Harpaz 2004). Another notable phenomenon taking place in this period was a shift of approximately 40 per cent of the Israeli labour force from collective bargaining agreements to personal contracts (Zosman 1995). Consequently the Histadrut experienced an overall reduction in its influence as a trade union, especially regarding wage determination.

A major shift of power took place within the Histadrut in 1994 when the Labour party lost its leadership and governing role of the union for the first time since its founding in 1920. Assuming control was a new party consisting of individuals who had left the Labour party because of power struggles, mainly based on ideological differences. The new party (RAM) restructured the Histadrut, selling or eliminating all its remaining non-trade union assets or activities. It changed its name to the New Histadrut, declaring that its foremost goal was to function mainly as a trade union. A detrimental blow to the Histadrut's activities occurred in January 1995, when Israel's National Compulsory Health Insurance Law, which secures medical coverage for all citisens, went into effect. The Histadrut could no longer sustain Kupat Holim Clalit, its health-provision function, and the bond between the health fund and Histadrut membership was broken. One of the most dramatic falls in union participation rate in history occurred in Israel. According to Histadrut chairman Amir Peretz, membership dropped almost instantaneously from 1.8 million (about 80 per cent of the work force) to 200,000 (Rubin 1996). The Histadrut's influence in the Israeli economy and politics has drastically declined. As a result of losing the income generated from its health services, and membership dues, its resources significantly shrunk. The labour union faced total collapse and bankruptcy. To survive, it underwent an immense restructuring and mass redundancies of its machinery. Presently it retains about 300 individuals on its payroll throughout the country (compared to about 3,000 in the 1980s). It was also compelled to sell many of its valuable real estate assets strategically located in urban centres.

Since 1995 the Histadrut has greatly declined in strength, and it is practically non-existent in the private sector. Currently it remains a major force in wage and employment issues, predominantly in the public sector.

3. Histadrut's Role in Collective Bargaining

Collective bargaining in Israel is administered by the Collective Agreement Law, 1957. It lays down minimal broad rules regarding industrial relations and collective agreements pertaining to employees' rights, terms of employment, and entitlements and obligations of the parties to the agreement. The law distinguishes two categories of collective agreements: a general collective agreement, which covers an industry or the entire workforce, and a special collective agreement, concerning only one employer or workplace. Collective bargaining is primarily applicable in the organised workforce, although non-unionised individuals frequently enjoy some of its provisions. This may occur since the Minister of Industry, Trade and Labour is authorised to extend a collective agreement, applying it to the whole labour market or a particular industry.

Until the early 1990s collective bargaining and collective agreements played a fundamental role in the Israeli industrial relations system. These agreements fixed work practices and also covered general wage increases and working conditions, as well as procedural matters pertaining to industrial relations. Throughout this era collective agreements were negotiated and signed on three levels: national, industry, and plant. At each level employees could frequently receive additional benefits. Bargaining usually began at the national level (termed the 'framework agreement') and produced pay increases for all union members, as well as often expanding to encompass the entire workforce by an 'extension order'. Next, industry bargaining took place in the main industrial or service sectors, resulting in a collective agreement with additional benefits and provisions particular to that industry. Such agreements likewise were often expanded to the entire industry. Subsequent to the national and industry agreements many workplaces negotiated plant agreements, yielding benefits and wage increases specific to that organisation. The upshot of this scheme was often a huge number of collective agreements, forcing employers constantly to negotiate with different union units or workers' committees, often causing numerous labour disputes. While this structure afforded workers security and improved working conditions, it generally gave employers ample flexibility to move workers from one job to another.

Over the years the Histadrut endorsed the negotiation of general collective agreements, which reflected the power of its Trade Union Department to obtain benefits for its members. In recent years collective bargaining has shifted towards decentralisation. The focus of negotiations has moved down to industrial sector, occupational groups, and mostly the plant level. The gap left by the Histadrut's Trade Union Department's loss of power has been filled by its strong, sometimes militant trade unions (e.g. Port Authority or Electricity Company employees) or powerful shop committees of local plants.

The deterioration of the Histadrut has been accompanied by a significant decrease in its communication and co-operation with employers. A major indication of this is that no 'framework agreement' at the national level has been signed since 1995. Since then, relations may be described as 'cool', with minimal contacts between the two sides. From the workers' perspective, especially in frail sectors in the economy, the absence of collective bargaining has eroded some of the protection they need (Davidov 2004). In March 2006 the Histadrut and the Coordination Bureau of Economic Organisations (representing the leading industrial and economic organisations in Israel) initiated a resumption of talks, aimed at reaching a new 'framework agreement'. Some of this change may be attributed to the new leadership (perhaps more judicious) that took office in both organisations. Furthermore, the two sides perceive government attempts in recent years to intervene in the industrial relations system through legislation as a real threat to their flexible and independent operations in the labour market. Prior to their deliberations concerning a new general collective 'framework agreement' for the whole industrial sector, the Coordination Council of Economic Organisations and the Histadrut signed a new agreement. It states, for the first time, that industrial relations in Israel are to be arranged by means of deliberations, negotiations, and the signing of collective agreements, and not by legislation. They hope that this agreement will stymie any unilateral government legislation in the realm of industrial relations in Israel.

A notable recent example of the 'honeymoon' between the Histadrut and the Coordination Council of Economic Organisations is their collective agreement signed in mid-2007. It provides a pension plan for all employees in the labour force who did not enjoy such a benefit. Despite the government's objections to this particular plan, the Minister of Industry, Trade and Labour had to issue an extension order of the pension plan. Accordingly, as of January 2008 all employers have been obliged to allot part of their employees' salaries to pension funds.

4. Present State of the Histadrut

The last quarter century has found the Histadrut in a constant struggle for survival, variously ignoring, or being unwilling or unable to face the fact that Israeli society has undergone some major structural transformations. Like great empires of the past falling from grace, the Histadrut refuses to accept the new reality. Moreover, with the turn to an individualistic orientation in Israel, the Histadrut generally does not enjoy wide support from the public or the media. Consequently, some major impediments block the growth of trade unionism in Israel.

One obvious factor is the steady decline in the number of blue-collar workers employed in construction and the industrial sector, who traditionally were a major source of union membership. According to the Statistical Abstracts of Israel (2007), their share fell from 32.3 per cent of the labour force in 1955 to about 18 per cent in 2006.

Another important aspect is that many gains or social benefits previously achieved through collective agreements between the Histadrut and employers or the government evolved down the years into laws legislated by the Knesset. This has made traditional services or protection provided by the Histadrut obsolete or redundant. Among others, these include laws concerning minimum wage, working hours, vacations, and equal employment opportunities. Paradoxically, the Histadrut was often a major partner or even the catalyst for the passing of these laws.

Some additional problems potentially hampering trade union growth and perhaps survival in its present form, to be discussed below, are attitudes and values of the new breed of workers, knowledge and professional workers, temporary workers, and the government's position against the Histadrut.

Attitudes and Values of the New Breed of Workers

During Israel's pre-state era, and throughout the early years of its independent existence, most of the population developed a heavy dependence on the Histadrut for most aspects of their lives. Yet the generation born in Israel in the 1960s and 1970s cultivated immense resentment towards it. The characteristics of young people entering the labour market today differ markedly from those of their parents. The Israeli labour force has become more individualistic and materialistic, and less collectively oriented, as personal instrumental achievements and self-indulgence outweigh contributions to society (Harpaz 1999). Young workers are much better educated, highly career- and achievement-oriented, and less involved or motivated by class struggle and workers' solidarity. They perceive Histadrut as an archaic bureaucracy, a dinosaur which at most might hamper their individual achievements and goals. In their study of union determinates, Harel Tzafrir and Bamberger (2000) found that Histadrut membership in the 1980s (in contrast to that after 1995) consisted of individuals who were more ideologically committed – a trait hard to find in the new breed of workers. This group perhaps best mirrors the changing attitudes to trade unions and their current status in Israeli society. Closely related to the category of young workers objecting to unionisation is that of other highly educated groups.

Knowledge and Professional Workers

This category includes workers employed mainly in the high-technology industry ('golden-collar workers') and various professionals, such as lawyers, accountants, insurance agents, and other specialists. All these occupations are typified by very long and hard working hours, which, considering the efforts, are perhaps not fairly compensated. The Histadrut considered making an effort to recruit high-technology workers in recent years, but all such attempts were to no avail. Even during the burst of the high-tech 'bubble' in the early 2000s, when masses of workers were unemployed and desperate, the Histadrut failed to attract them. Similarly, other professional workers, particularly at early stages of their careers, do not seek the succour of unions to improve their sometimes paltry pay and inadequate working conditions.

Temporary Workers

A widespread phenomenon in the Israeli labour market is the employment of temporary workers, hired through temporary employment agencies. This practice, prevalent in both the private and public sector, is mainly applied to allow 'management flexibility'. In effect it is a pervasive strategy for hiring individuals where no regular positions are available, or to avoid the need to grant tenure in the public sector, to pay the minimum wage, or to establish a formal employment relationship. In fact, it has created one of the most exploited groups in the Israeli labour market, often experiencing adverse working conditions, or being (illegally) paid below minimum wage. There are approximately 250,000 temporary workers in Israel (9 per cent of the labour force) who should serve as fertile ground for unionisation efforts. Conversely, temporary workers are a complex group for trade unions to organise as they are poorly educated, unaware of their rights, highly mobile between work places, widely spread geographically, and perhaps too timid to seek organisation. In recent years the National Workers' Organisation and the New Histadrut have negotiated collective agreements on behalf of these workers with temporary employment agencies. While such agreements include a clause concerning transfer of dues to the Histadrut from non-members (agency dues of 0.07 per cent of one's pay), most of these workers reject unionisation.

Government Antagonism towards the Histadrut

In recent years the Histadrut has been locked in bitter adversarial conflicts with Israel's governments, particularly those headed by the Likud party. The organisation was explicitly perceived as a major obstacle to the state accomplishing its neo-liberal plans. In 2003 the Finance Ministry under Benjamin Netanyahu proclaimed that its greatest achievement was the breaking of organised labour. In late 2005 the Histadrut suffered a blow when the Knesset passed a law prohibiting the chairperson of a labour union to serve simultaneously in two roles: Member of Knesset and union chairperson. In the early the 2000s, when negotiations between the two sides did not progress rapidly, or in a direction favouring the government's position, the latter undertook to strip the Histadrut of its bargaining power, or right to strike, by means of legislation. Another example of the government's attitude to labour occurred in 2005 during the longest strike in Israel's history. Drivers at a small private bus company struck, demanding better working conditions and wages. When negotiations failed the Ministry of Transport interfered, breaking the strike by allowing an alternative bus company to operate in lieu of the striking workers. This was the first occurrence in Israel's history of such an episode in its industrial relations system. This case may also serve as a good illustration of the current state of the unions in Israel. Government's attempts to publicly de-legitimise the Histadrut and distort its image create additional obstacles in its efforts at survival and growth.

At present the relations between the Histadrut and the government appear to have rather better prospects. The coalition formed by a new government in 2006 includes the Labour party as a major partner, leaving the Likud party in the opposition.

5. Histadrut's Measures to Secure its Future

In the past few decades unions worldwide have grown weaker, with plummeting membership. Everywhere they seem to face similar issues. Various plans intended to change the situation are not particularly successful. Only in countries where unions offer some essential services to their members or society at large, which no other body provides, do they still enjoy favourable status and a substantial membership. Such is the case in most Scandinavian countries, where unions are also responsible for administering unemployment benefits. It was the case with the Histadrut prior to 1995, when it was the dominant health provider in Israel.

The New Histadrut has launched several recruiting campaigns in recent years. They mainly targeted some of the groups mentioned above: young individuals just entering the labour market, temporary workers, professionals, and women. In addition to the obvious and objective obstacles faced by the Histadrut, making it appealing to new members is an extremely complex task. The Histadrut cannot grant the range of benefits it provided prior to 1995, so its main efforts emphasise making new collective agreements or broadening existing ones. The Histadrut also provides individual legal counselling and assistance, some of it through its web site. (Note: since early 2008 and until the time of writing at the end of May, the web site has been under construction.)

With the pervasiveness of privatisation in the Israeli economy, the Histadrut has been involved in struggles to defend workers' rights in many cases of privatisation and transfer of ownership, as well as in cases where restructuring or 'efficiency measures', as they are often termed by management, jeopardise workers' rights. The Histadrut seems still to maintain somewhat the view that a trade union should not remain one-dimensional in its activities (Zilony 2001). Accordingly, it also gives a great deal of publicity to its involvement in various non-trade union activities, related to unjust treatment of workers in Israel. Such was its joining socially active independent organisations (NGOs) in their nationwide struggle against poverty. Another recent activity is the effort to improve adverse working conditions, such as those of department and retail store cashiers who are required to provide services standing on their feet all day long, being forbidden to sit down. The Histadrut's consumerism branch is also active, publishing surveys of employers' and organisations' non-compliance with the law, such as not displaying price tags on various products. And as an act aimed at potential young members, the Histadrut has on several occasions expressed sympathy for university students struggling for a reduction in tuition fees.

In recent years the Histadrut has faced some 'competition' from NGOs which specifically attempt to protect employees' rights or even assist them in their unionisation efforts. These NGOs operate among populations notably absent from the Histadrut roster: young employees in the hospitality services. Obviously the Histadrut is not pleased by such 'intervention', and tries to play down such efforts and the relative success that they have had.

Although the Histadrut is taking some positive steps in its attempt to improve its image through such activities, most of the public seem unaware of these endeavours, or do not credit them to the Histadrut. The effectiveness of these efforts is unknown; nevertheless, it has managed to enlarge its membership from a rock bottom of 200,000 in 1995 to a current 700,000 members.

6. Conclusion

The Histadrut, like other labour unions, came into being to protect workers' rights and interests, which individuals could not achieve on their own. This is the unions' main function and the reason they are still needed today. Attempts to break down the unions, or make them an illegitimate partner in the industrial relations system (consisting of employers, government, and labour), do not contribute to the stability of that fragile system in Israel. Unilateral actions by the government in the labour market, disregarding labour, have proved highly destructive for the Israeli economy in recent years. The tripartite model is still considered the most effective way to manage industrial relation systems in the modern world.

Today the Histadrut is in a downward spiral, where declining membership and waning political power feed off each other. One way for the Histadrut to pull out of this dive is to regain the moral high ground and reconstitute itself as a broad movement dedicated to social and economic justice. It needs to shed its image of a stronghold for several powerful unions, determined to protect their privileged status in critical public sector industries (e.g. energy, ports). The Histadrut has to utilise more effectively the little sympathy that Israelis may still have for poorly paid workers and their growing anxiety about their own pensions, health care, and job security. This conceivably may be achieved by giving support to the least protected elements in the labour market, such as unorganised exploited workers in a range of service branches (e.g. retailing and food, personnel services, and hospitality industries) and migrant workers. These groups are often treated by their employers extremely badly, sometimes inhumanly.

Since the 1990s the Histadrut has failed to reach out to constituents who traditionally join unions or need their protection: low-income blue-collar and service-sector (not public-sector) employees, women, and Israeli Arab workers. One domain from which the Histadrut has been glaringly absent is its backing of migrant workers. This without doubt is the most exploited category of workers in the labour market. Numerous Israeli labour laws are apparently broken by many employers of migrant workers, without any genuine attempt at enforcement by the authorities. The case of migrant workers deserves particular consideration. At present they constitute more than 8 per cent of the total labour force (Statistical Abstracts of Israel 2005), which is apparently the highest proportion of migrant workers in any country. Many of them, possibly about equal in number to legal workers, are illegally based in Israel. Many employers have taken advantage of the situation; they pay them significantly below the legal minimum wage, disregard health and social benefits, and more. Several NGOs, principally 'Kav-Laoved', voluntarily provide support for exploited workers, but most official bodies in Israel hardly intervene to alleviate their situation. This state of affairs could serve the Histadrut as an excellent opportunity to take a stand. The Israeli unions seem to be missing the enormous opportunity that this situation provides, from a humanitarian perspective as well as for their prospective growth. According to Histadrut's bylaws, migrant or foreign workers cannot become members; however, it could make a firm commitment in this regard. It could negotiate collective agreements that apply to this group (collecting agency dues) or take concrete steps to protect migrant workers or recruit them into its ranks.

One example of the path the Histadrut has to forge was demonstrated recently. It initiated legislation intended to force employers to grant tenure to workers supplied via temporary employment agencies after nine months of employment. Another example is the Histadrut's joining in protecting the rights of workers experiencing adverse working conditions, and its participation in legislation to introduce measures against such circumstances in the workplace.

A major obstacle to the Histadrut's enhancement of its status continues to be its negative image in Israeli public opinion. This seems to be an organisation that everybody loves to hate. It needs to conduct a very thorough and candid examination of its inability to convince the public, including masses of workers, that it is a viable and important force in Israeli society. Without such a move, including attempts to take corrective and perhaps even some painful actions, its future seems to remain uncertain.

Suggested Reading

Cohen, Y., Haberfeld, Y., Mundlak, G. and Saporta, I. (2003) 'Unpacking Union Density: Union Membership and Coverage in the Transformation of the Israeli Industrial Relations System', *Industrial Relations* 42: 692–712.

Davidov, G. (2004) 'The Actors of Collective Bargaining: Israel', *Bulletin of Comparative Labour Relations*: 171–82.

Haberfeld, Y. (1995) 'Why Do Workers Join Unions? The Case of Israel', *Industrial and Labour Relations Review* 48: 656–70.

Harel, G.H., Tzafrir, S. and Bamberger, P. (2000) 'Institutional Change and Union Membership: A Longitudinal Analysis of Union Membership Determinants in Israel', *Industrial Relations* 39: 460–85.

Harpaz, I. (1999) 'Work Values in Israel: Stability and Change Over Time', *Monthly Labor Review* 122: 46–50.

——(2002) 'Expressing a Wish to Continue or Stop Working as Related to the Meaning of Work', *European Journal of Work and Organizational Psychology* 11: 177–98.

Horowitz, D., and Lissak, M. (1990) *Distress in Utopia: Israel, Society in Overload.* Tel Aviv: Am Oved (Hebrew).

Rubin, D. (1996) 'Taking Histadrut out of Debt, Officials See Twin Mission: Trade Unions, Social Services', *Metro West Jewish News*, 2 May.

Samuel, Y. and Harpaz, I. (2004) 'Trends and Developments in Work and Organizations in Israel' in Samuel, Y. and Harpaz, I. (eds) *Work and Organizations in Israel: Studies of Israeli Society*, London: Transaction.

Statistical Abstracts of Israel (2006) http://www1.cbs.gov.il

Zilony, E. (2001) 'Industrial Relations System in Israel for the 2000s', *Human Resources* [*Mashabei Enosh*], January: 34–8 (Hebrew).

Zosman, T. (1995) 'From Collective Agreements to Individual Contracts: Wage, Industrial Relations, and the Histadrut', *Economics Quarterly* [*Riv'on LeKalkala*] 42: 17–35 (Hebrew).

Trade Unions in Nigeria since 1945

IFEANYI P. ONYEONORU AND JIMI O. ADESINA

1. Introduction

In this chapter, we review the evolution and experience of trade unions in Nigeria since 1945. The cycle of political developments in the country – from colonialism to post-colonial civil rule, military rule, military dictatorship and civil rule under the regime of neo-liberalism – have been significant in shaping the experience of the unions in Nigeria. Following the 1939 trade union ordinance, which provided formal recognition for union and modes of registration, trade unions have grown exponentially. Particularly in the past 30 years, Nigerian unions have witnessed periods of resurgence and repression. While particularly severe under periods of military dictatorships, repression has not been limited to such periods, and the last nine years of 'civilian democratic' rule has seen a return to state-organised attacks on the trade union movement. A defining aspect of state repression – including repression through legislative institutions of liberal-democracy – in the post-1998 period is the neo-liberal framework of economic policy, which reinforces the repressive nature of the state vis-à-vis the unions. It is, important, however, to keep in mind that the labour movement is only one of the organisational expressions of civil society that has experienced such repression. The post-1999 period has witnessed a distinct reinvention of the unions, and a return to a tradition of active engagement of the labour movement in national economic and political struggles.

This chapter examines the experience and nature of unions (especially in their relationship with the state) in four distinct periods. First is the period between 1945 and 1978, a period that saw a shift from union fragmentation to restructuring, mainly at the level of the central labour organisations in Nigeria. Second, we examine unionism in the years between 1978 and 1998, which involved significant changes in the forms of the expressions of the state: from the military regime of 1975 to 1979, to the civilian government of 1979 to 1983, and the different shades of military regimes thereafter. The latter culminated in the extremely repressive regime of Sani Abacha between 1993 and 1998. Third, we examine the experience and resurgence of national-level union activism in the period of civil rule after 1998. In the face of repression and cooptation, we witnessed the Nigerian trade union movement in its many dimensions. While the 'ideology of developmentalism' defined the state–union experience between 1971 and 1979, the experience since 1985 has been shaped by neo-liberalism, which reinforced the repressive nature of the state interaction with unions.

2. From Fragmentation to Restructuring: Nigerian Trade Unions, 1945 and 1978

Between 1945 and 1975, the Nigerian trade union movement represented a plethora of micro-unions affiliated to rancorous and divisive labour centres, which were themselves heavily dependent on external support and funding. By 1976 when unions were reorganised there were 896 organisations, according to the Registrar of Trade Unions, with a total membership of 724,697 people. This represented an increase from 14 in 1940 with a total membership of 4,337.

By 1974 the Nigerian central labour organisations had coalesced into four: the United Labour Congress, the Nigerian Trade Union Congress, Labour Unity Front, and the Nigerian Workers' Council. Between them, the first two labour centres accounted for over 75 per cent of the affiliated unions.

Table 1. Unions and Union Membership in Nigeria, 1940–76

Years	Number of Unions	Total Membership
1940	14	4,337
1950–1	144	144,358
1960–1	360	274,126
1970–1	751	705,712
1975–6	936	772,751
1976	896	724,697

Source: Ministry of Labour records.

While it is true that many of the organisations on the register were not trade unions in the proper sense, and a number of those that should have been on the register were not (Cohen 1974), these years were nonetheless characterised by the proliferation of unions, rampant union schism and short-lived unity, and considerable influence by labour international centres in the organisation of the national labour centres (Ananaba 1969; Cohen 1974; Otobo 1986).

Cohen (1974: 112–18) identified seven factors that shaped union structure at this time and defined the nature of fragmentation and disunity. First, the 'legal provisions for the registration of new unions' were extremely permissive. Any five persons could come together and form a union. Second, the lines of demarcation within the public service – life style, income, orientation, and so forth – made it difficult to organise blue-collar and white-collar workers in the same union. Third, the diffusion of industrial (employing) establishments across the country promoted micro-unions. Fourth, ethnic and regional considerations promoted factionalism in the trade union movement. Fifth, regional pressures and considerations encouraged regionally based unions. This was further accentuated by the division of the country into regions, each with its own governments and employing units. Sixth, employers themselves, especially in the organised private sector, permitted only 'house' unions which became the pattern with the large private sector employers. Seventh, the prevailing types of union leadership also contributed to the factionalism and micro-unionism: 'the aggregate income that the general secretaries can expect to receive from organising several small unions is greater than the income they would receive from an amalgamated union'.

A further factor, identified by Cohen and elaborated by Otobo (1986), is the impact of international labour affiliation. In a classical case of donor dirigisme, not only were leaders of the labour centres addicted to donor funds, but their dependency created a narcotic effect on trade unionism at the level of the central labour organisations. Indeed, in spite of claims of ideological factionalism, the so-called communist/anti-communist orientation is generally a poor guide to understanding shop-floor activism. Both in its immanent and definite forms, affiliation to international labour centres made merger of labour centres difficult. It is, however, naïve to think that the ideological division within the labour movement was purely instrumental. The key question was the degree to which such division actually percolated on the shop floor.

Cohen also identified another important factor: the hostility of the Registrar of Trade Unions to merger efforts (Cohen 1974: 118). Indeed the Registrar opposed the first effort in 1974 by two trade union centres to merge (Ohiorhenuan and Adesina 1989). The refusal of the Murtala Regime[1] to recognise the merger of *all* the labour centres in December 1975 is equally important in this regard. Justified on the grounds of ending the Cold War-inspired foreign influence on the Nigerian trade union movement, the objection of the military regime was opportunistic. A class agenda was dressed up in nationalist garb: ridding Nigeria of 'foreign ideologies', and part of a wider campaign against 'corruption' and foreign influence.

1 The military regime of General Murtala Muhammed came to power in July 1975 following the *coup d'état* against General Yakubu Gowon's regime. Muhammed's second in command was General Olusegun Obasanjo, who became Head of State following the 13 February 1976 assassination of Muhammed by a group of dissident army officers.

3. Trade Unions in the Context of a 'Capitalist Development' Agenda

The effort by the trade union centres to merge was initiated in September 1974 at the funeral of J.A. Oduleye, the national treasurer of one of the four labour centres at the time;[2] a merger process that was completed by mid-1975 (Otobo 1988: 119; Ohiorhenuan and Adesina 1989: 156). The merger led to the formation of one central labour organisation, the Nigerian Labour Congress (NLC), with an inaugural conference slated for 18 December 1975. A set of middle-ranking trade unionists that lost out in the allocation of positions which accompanied the merger sought to sabotage the event. Five days before the inaugural conference they denounced the new labour centre in the media and asked the new military regime not to recognise the NLC. This plea came a week after the federal minister of Labour had announced that the government would adopt a policy of 'limited government intervention' and 'guided democracy' (Ohiorhenuan and Adesina 1989: 156). Not only did the military regime refuse to recognise the merger, but a day before the inaugural conference state security personnel raided the offices of the labour centres, and briefly detained some of the union leaders.

On 12 February 1976 the regime set up the Adebiyi Panel to investigate the trade unions and their leaders. An Administrator was later appointed to re-organise the trade unions, leading to the setting up of 42 unions, 19 staff associations and 9 employers' associations. On 28 February 1978 the Nigeria Labour Congress (NLC) was launched with Hassan Sumonu as its first elected president. The show-trial of the trade union leaders by the Adebiyi Panel (with government officials and appointees as prosecutor, judge and jury) was of course an attempt to discredit the unionists. The process of re-organisation of the trade unions, apart from violating ILO Conventions Nos 87 and 98, was designed to oust professional trade unionists

2 This is generally referred to as the *Apena Declaration*; the name referring to the major public cemetery in Lagos.

from the emergent unions. It took a concerted effort by the trade unionists themselves to defeat the agenda; they had organised themselves under the umbrella of the National Association of Professional Trade Unionists of Nigeria (Ohiorhenuan and Adesina 1989: 158). It was this formation that made the emergence of Hassan Sumonu as the first president of the NLC possible.

The restructuring exercise took place in the context of what Hutchful (1986: 16) among others, referred to as the 'the ideology of developmentalism'; the regime's agenda for capitalist development. In addition to the setting up of 'responsible unions' (Otobo 1981: 67), the military regime enacted decrees overhauling the national grievance machinery. The decrees were meant to arrest worker militancy. In 1976 and 1977 three main statutes on industrial disputes were enacted: the 1976 Trade Disputes Decree, the 1976 Trade Disputes (Essential Services) Decree, and the 1977 Petroleum Production and Distribution (Anti-Sabotage) Decree, as well as 1977 amendments to each of the above 1976 decrees (Ohiorhenuan and Adesina 1989).

The 1976 Trade Disputes Decree No.7,[3] which replaced a 1968 decree,[4] created a permanent Industrial Arbitration Panel (IAP) and a National Industrial Court (NIC).[5] It provided for a mediation process with a mediator appointed by the parties themselves, and a conciliator appointed by the Ministry of Labour for situations when mediation failed. If conciliation also failed, the dispute was referred to the arbitration panel. The NIC was a court of final jurisdiction on disputes. Although at each stage there was a provision for appeal, the Federal Commissioner (a cabinet level minister)

3 Decrees passed under the military were adopted by the civilian legislature and called 'Acts'. To avoid confusion on the origin of the statutes we refer to them as 'Decrees'.

4 This is the Trade Disputes (Emergency Provision) Decree No. 21 of 1968, subsequently amended in Decrees No. 2 of 1969 and No. 36 of 1973. The arbitration body was then called the Industrial Arbitration Tribunal.

5 IAP has 12 members; a Chairman, a Vice-Chairman and ten other members. Two each are appointed on the recommendation of NLC and NECA. The NIC has five members, including a president. All are appointed by the Commissioner.

had power to confirm or reject an IAP or NIC ruling. Collective agreements were deemed valid only after the Commissioner's approval. The intent of this and other laws at the time was to limit the disruption of production activities. Another 1976 decree prohibited any form of industrial action that would disrupt establishments providing 'essential services'.[6] The head of the military government assumed the power to proscribe any union[7] violating the dispute procedure outlined in Decree 7. The power of indefinite detention, first promulgated in the 1969 amendment, was also reinstated. The courts were barred from inquiring into the decrees. Further amendments to Decree 7 in 1977 strengthened the power of the Commissioner to suspend disputes, confirm or reject IAP rulings, increased the penalty for violating the procedure to six months jail term for unionists and a fine for employers, and removed the power of employers, the IAP or NIC to grant wage increases. For the first time, the principle of 'No Work, No Pay' was put on the statute books. A more sinister use of state power came in the form of the 1977 Petroleum Anti-Sabotage Decree, which prescribed the death penalty or a 23-year jail term for disrupting or attempting to disrupt the production or distribution of petroleum products. The decree was what a senior union official calls 'the Damocles sword hanging over our heads'. The draconian decrees came from General Olusegun Obasanjo, who had replaced Murtala Mohammed as the head of the military regime following a failed coup attempt in February 1976 and the assassination of Mohammed.

The various statutes reinforced existing mechanisms for the repression of worker activists, ostensibly within the framework of grievance handling. To mention just a few examples: in October 1977 two Shell-British Petroleum unions were proscribed by the regime for initiating industrial action; in 1978, the union leaders in the Peugeot plant in Kaduna were jailed for

6 The 1976 Trade Disputes (Essential Services) Decree (No. 23). 'Essential services' cover the public sector, electricity, water, fuel, medical services provision, all forms of transportation, air and sea ports, electronic media, communications medium, supplies of materials for the Armed Forces, and others.

7 A proscribed union would have its property seized by the State and failure to hand over union property would result in a five-year jail sentence.

three months for 'contempt' of the Arbitration Panel. Nor did violent police reaction to worker protest diminish. In 1978, 1982 and 1985, industrial actions by workers at the Volkswagen plant (VON), outside Lagos, led to fatalities committed by the police.

4. Democracy, Adjustment and Dictatorship, 1978–98

Relations between the various regimes and the NLC since 1978 have been anything but cordial. In the face of the failure of the right-wing elements within the trade union movement to secure control of the NLC, the military regime responded by withholding payment of the NLC's subvention, which the regime had promised before the NLC's inauguration in 1978. The regime did provide the Congress with a headquarters, yet it was, in the words of the first Congress president, 'perforated with listening devices'[8] planted by the state security agency.

The NLC campaigned on a wide range of broad social and specific work issues while reviving the tradition of the workers' organisations and speaking on behalf of other subordinate classes in society. This resurgence in union activism brought the Congress into collision with the different regimes since 1979. The campaign which the Congress shelved in 1979 – because of the transition to civil rule – was revived in 1980.[9] On 1 October 1979 the military regime handed power to an elected government. At the federal level the government was formed by a coalition of the National Party of Nigeria (NPN) and the Nigerian People's Party (NPP), led by an executive president, Shehu Shagari of the NPN.

Within a few months, the trade unions revived the campaign for a national minimum wage, among other things; a campaign that led to the

8 Hassan Sunmonu, the Congress President, in 1982, speaking at the University of Ibadan's Industrial Relations programme seminar.

9 See NLC's *The Workers' Charter*, 1980.

General Strike of 1980 (Otobo 1981). Over the following two years, the federal government responded with attempts to break the Congress, by promoting a self-styled 'anti-communist' group within the movement. Partly as a result of the resolute fight put up by the Congress, and the warning from the security service of the threat to 'national security' which the existence of multiple labour centres would cause; the federal government abandoned its crackdown while continuing to sponsor the right-wing group (Otobo 1988).

On 31 December 1983 civilian rule was terminated by a *coup d'état*. It came on the heels of three years of outrageous profligacy on the part of the NPN government and a rigged general election earlier in 1983. The military regime was headed by General Muhammadu Buhari. While the space to mobilise and defend workers' rights had improved under the civilian government, it shrank severely under subsequent military regimes, and it was under the post-1983 military regimes that the trade union movement would face the most virulent attacks. The aircraft pilots and engineers union, the medical doctors and resident officers unions were, in 1984, the first to feel the wrath of a hostile and repressive state. The unions were not only banned, but many of their officials were incarcerated for extended periods. The attack on unions, which was part of a wider attack on various dissenting civic bodies and organisations, heightened under the military regime of Ibrahim Babangida (1985–93) and the Structural Adjustment Programme. In July 1985 Babangida had led the ousting of Buhari and his deputy (General Tunde Idiagbon) in a palace coup. Beyond personality clashes, at stake was the economic future of the country and the country's relationship with the Bretton Woods institutions. In spite of the Babangida regime's claim of crafting a home-grown economic reform programme, the regime entered into an orthodox structural adjustment programme arrangement with the World Bank and the International Monetary Fund in 1986. In the build-up to this, the labour movement led the campaign against the adoption of the neo-liberal policy framework, and subsequently became a focal point of resistance against the programme. While adjustment did not create state repression, it altered the terms of engagement between unions and the state and provided international support (or at least acquiescence) for the repression (Adesina 1998); it was normatively justified by casting unions as part of an urban coalition and a special interest group with a stake in maintaining an allegedly pervasive system of rent seeking (Adesina 1994).

A dramatic example of state repression against the labour movement came in May 1986, when a student demonstration in Zaria was attacked by armed police and over 20 people were killed.[10] The Nigeria Labour Congress (NLC), the Academic Staff Union of Universities (ASUU) and the National Association of Nigerian Students (NANS) responded with a plan for a nation-wide protest demonstration on 4 June. The Babangida regime not only had all the leaders of the various bodies arrested on the eve of the demonstration, but also placed the armed forces on full alert. The NLC headquarters in Lagos was placed under police occupation. Naval warships were stationed off Lagos harbour and Air Force helicopter gunships kept vigil over Lagos. The para-military and the armed forces were ordered to shoot demonstrators on sight (Mohammed 1986).

A month later, a new decree was enacted, making it illegal for 'senior staff' associations to affiliate with the NLC and revoking the automatic dues check-off provision of 1978 for these unions. The decree was to organisationally disengage militant senior staff unions like ASUU from the NLC, given their assumed radicalising influence on the latter. Secondly, revoking the automatic check-off of dues, it was felt, might weaken these unions by making their financing more difficult and by increasing the non-unionised segment of senior staff workers. It should be noted that the militant senior staff unions, since 1984, have been the main focus of opposition to the regime. In the period between then and 1993, the trade union movement was subjected to sustained attacks culminating in ousting of elected union officials in 1998 and the installation of a government-appointed administrator to run the NLC (Otobo 1992; Adesina 1998, 2003). This led to the disruption of union activities and a significant downturn in labour activism and militancy on the shop floor (Adesina 1998, 2003), although resistance

10 There had been an earlier demonstration against various aspects of the regime's policies; the IMF policies, retrenchment of workers, pay-cut and the underfunding of education.

against the regime shifted to white-collar unions like ASUU and professional civic organisations (Adewumi and Adesina 1999).

On the wider political scene, the transition to civil rule, despite intense pressure from civic organisations, was aborted by the annulment of presidential elections scheduled for 12 June 1993. The upheaval that the annulment unleashed led to the replacement of Babangida with an interim government, nominally headed by a civilian. When the court declared the interim government illegal, Nigeria reverted in November 1993 to a military regime led by General Sani Abacha. Abacha had for the better part of two years been the second most powerful person in the Babangida regime and the *de-facto* head of the interim government.

The labour policy of the Abacha regime can best be understood as part of its need for total control of the political landscape, with three distinct phases: a tentative phase of trying to garner legitimacy (November 1993 to May 1994); a second phase from June 1994 to March 1996 marked by extreme repression; and a third phase from March 1996 to May 1998 that combined repression with the construction of a hegemonic project (Adesina 2003). The trade union movement was particularly hard hit during the second phase.

Resistance against the annulment of the June 1993 election and the refusal of the Abacha regime to reverse the annulment widened in 1994. Among the leading civil society organisations involved in the demand for release of the election results and declaration of the winner, Bashorun MKO Abiola, were factions of the trade union movement. While NLC and many unions had folded under the weight of government repression, the oil workers' unions complemented the wider civil resistance through strike actions in July and August 1994. In response, the regime arrested the union leaders and seized control of the headquarters of the two oil workers unions, in addition to those of the NLC which had briefly reverted to elected unions officials in 1992. Evidence from the national labour statistics suggests, however, that in spite of the extensive repression at the national level and the silencing of national union leaders, resistance remained strong at the workplace level (Adesina 2003). Strike propensity and average striker days rose dramatically between 1993 and 1998. Average striker days rose from 7.03 in 1993 to 152.35 in 1994. While it fell to 125.61 days in 1997, it rose again to 138.42 days in 1998. Strike propensity, the chance that a dispute will lead to a strike action, rose from 0.5 in 1992 to 0.92 in 1997, the highest figure for more than twenty years, before declining slightly to 0.87 in 1998 (Adesina 2003). While workplace union actions after 1994 were expressed in terms of employment disputes, most were clearly driven by the wider political resistance against the regime; most prominent of these were the actions embarked upon by white collar unions such as ASUU.

The resistance of 1993 and 1994 at the national level was increasingly met with repression and co-optation, even as the oil workers leaders like Ovie Kokori were languishing in jail (Adesina 1997, 2003). Among the main legal instruments of coercion were the Trade Union (Amendment) Decree 1996 (No. 4 of 5 January), Trade Disputes (Essential Services Deregulation, Proscription and Prohibition from Participation in Trade Union Activities) Decree 1996 (No. 24 of 21 August), Trade Unions (Amendment) (No. 2) Decree 1996 (No. 26 of 16 October), and the Trade Unions (International Affiliation) Decree 1996 (No. 29 of 23 October).

While Decree 4 gave legal backing to the restructuring of the 41 labour unions to 29 through merger, it went beyond this. In contrast with earlier laws, union merger only required 'a resolution... signed by the President or the secretary of the merging unions' (S.27 (1)(a)), which would come into effect once approved by the Registrar of Trade Unions. However, if the regime was 'lending' the rump of union leaders who chose collusion with the regime over resistance, there was to be a sting in the tail. A new sub-section 7 was inserted into S.33 of the original Act barring 'non-members' of unions from contesting any elective office of the NLC. That section defined general secretaries and other paid officials of unions as 'non-members'; in other words the same general-secretaries who worked with the regime's Minister of Labour in drafting the law. Co-optation, it would seem, is limited by how far the regime felt it could trust the unionists outside its jails. A 'no-strike' clause was now mandatory for all Collective Agreement (amended S.16A).

Decree 29, ostensibly signed into law on 23 October 1996, was not made public until April 1997. It barred all trade unions and the labour centre from affiliation with international labour organisation, unless 'a specific application' requesting such affiliation received 'approval [from] the Provisional

Ruling Council' (S.3 (1c)). The decree exempted the Organisation of African Trade Union Unity (OATUU) and the so-called Organisation of Trade Unions for West Africa from its otherwise blanket ban. Contravention of the decree meant a heavy fine or a five-year jail sentence, or both, and the union's licence was to be revoked. While not new in its general provisions, it was distinct in listing the International Labour Organisation among the organisations from which trade unions were barred from affiliating!

Decree 24, signed into law on 21 August, was the regime's response to the industrial action by members of the Academic Staff Union of Universities (ASUU), in effect proscribing the party in which it was engaged in an industrial dispute. The union responded by asking the courts to re-affirm its members' rights to organise under the African Charter of Human and Peoples' Rights. The courts' interpretation hinged on the specifics of Decree 24, which a High Court ruled did not specifically prohibit union organisation at the level of each campus. In a separate case, an Appeal Court ruled that while the government could suspend the constitution in Nigeria, it could not vitiate its obligations under the African Charter, which included the right to form trade unions, although not indicating at which level.

While the attacks on trade unions had a chilling effect at the level of the central labour organisation, there is little evidence that it succeeded in ensuring 'behaviour modification' at the level of the workplace 'and the reason is quite clear. In the context of worsening economic conditions, tightening labour market, declining purchasing power and increased poverty, as was the case Nigeria, shopfloor resistance increased' (Adesina 2003: 17).

5. Neo-Liberalism, Civil Rule and Union Activism, 1999–2006

The death of Sani Abacha on 8 June 1998 shifted the political trajectory in the direction of a handover of power to an elected civilian government in 1999. The option of a return of the mandate to Bashorun Abiola was foreclosed following his death in government custody shortly after the death of Abacha. The period between June 1998 and April 1999 marked a shift away from repression. Political prisoners, including union leaders such as Ovie Kokori, were released and union officials regained control of their organisations. The ban on many unions was also lifted, along with the normalisation of political activities, as part of the transition to civilian rule. In May 1999, Olusegun Obasanjo of the People's Democratic Party took office as an elected president.

Under the democratic experiment that began in 1999, organised labour, inspired by the possibilities afforded by the return to civil rule, became actively involved in policy contestations within the framework of 'social movement unionism'. In February 1999 Adams Oshiomole was elected president of the NLC. Many within the labour movement spoke of a 'new beginning' in which unions would be alive to their 'vanguardist' role in Nigeria's process of democratisation. At a rally in Abuja on 18 November 1999 organised by the Congress to commemorate the fiftieth anniversary of the Iva Valley massacre of coalmine workers in Nigeria, the NLC President made clear that he understood that the 'civil governance expects trade unions to defend democracy in future'. Such an expectation was realistic 'because so far, the trade unions are still the only Pan-Nigerian organization with the organization, orientation, and vision to defend democracy in the event of future military incursion or the emergence of dictatorship' (Oshiomhole 1999: 2). Committing labour to a broad based agenda typical of 'social movement unions', the NLC President pledged a strategy of building alliances with other civil society organisations with which it shares identical perspectives (Oshiomhole 1999). In this, the Nigerian labour centre stands in sharp contrast to its South African counterpart.

The NLC's new spirit was illustrated when it challenged the government's unilateral price deregulation of the down stream sector of the oil industry. During the Fourth Republic (1999–2007) the Obasanjo administration adjusted the price of petroleum products ten times; it reflected a wider hold of the Bretton Woods institutions and the neo-liberal agenda on Nigeria's macro-economic management. The first of the price adjustments took place on 1 June 2000 without prior public notice. The government justified the price increases with arguments that had been popular with military governments in Nigeria: the need to reduce the burden of subsidy and to eliminate the smuggling of the petroleum products to neighbouring countries. Similar arguments had led to dramatic price increases during the military era. The NLC leadership reacted promptly to the increases in a press statement widely published in Nigerian dailies, indicating its objection to the absence of negotiations in the determination of prices. The NLC understood the inflationary effects of price increases, and their deleterious impact on the cost of living. On 3 June the Central Working Committee of the Congress formally demanded the reversal of the increases and issued a strike notice. The government's refusal to negotiate the issue led to the general strike called by the NLC, which began on 8 June 2000. Labour collaborated with Nigerian students who joined the protests through their organisation, the National Association of Nigerian Students (NANS). The protests were widespread and effective as public sector and some private sector organisations joined in response to the NLC call for action. The government was finally compelled to negotiate with the leadership of the NLC which resulted in reductions in the price of the products. The NLC had shown itself capable of mobilising not only the Nigerian workers but also other elements of the civil society. Some state and federal legislators as well as officials of the ruling Peoples Democratic Party (PDP) supported the position of the Congress.

The price adjustment proposed by the government in February 2001, was stalled by a similar protest by the NLC that involved pamphleteering, marches, rallies, picketing and media propaganda. The Congress, for instance, organised national rallies and marches in Lagos, Abuja and all states of the federation between 21 and 27 March 2001. The marches and rallies were reported peaceful, while critical pamphlets were distributed widely to members of the public. Several state governors identified with the position of the NLC during the workers' protests, in Oyo State and Kwara State for instance. The action of the NLC resulted in a public hearing on the matter organised by the National Assembly and public debates at various levels of the Nigerian public arena, after which the Senate President publicly distanced himself and the senate from the planned 'deregulation' of petroleum product prices.

Increases in the prices of petroleum products were, nevertheless, implemented on 1 January 2002, again without prior notice. The decision of the Obasanjo administration to implement the increases during the New Year's holiday was strategic. Workers were on vacation, making mobilisation more difficult. The NLC, however, conducted a belated strike on 16 January 2002. The government thereupon took the NLC to court, winning a judicial victory as the strike was declared illegal. The NLC president and other officials of the union, as well as the President of ASUU, were arrested and charged with breaching public order. The strike was officially called off on 17 January 2002, by the Central Working Committee (CWC) of the NLC, following a ruling of the Abuja High Court. The unionists were released on bail while the House Committee on Petroleum met with stakeholders in the petroleum industry on 23 January 2002 to seek a resolution of the crisis. Yet the union action had an impact; on 19 March 2002 the senate overwhelmingly rejected a government-sponsored bill seeking to confer the power to increase the prices of petroleum products on a government agency, the Petroleum Product Pricing Regulatory Agency (PPPRA). The senate also cautioned the government against further increases of the products (*The Monitor*, 20 March 2002). The NLC strike had sensitised legislators to deregulation and its impact on the citizenry. It is noteworthy that the national assembly is dominated by the PDP.

Perhaps the most momentous struggle by the NLC against deregulation took place in the wake the 20 June 2003 price adjustment that represented a 52 per cent increase in the price of petroleum products. The NLC as usual led the opposition to the price hike along with several civil society organisations. These include, the Academic Staff Union of Universities (ASUU), Manufactures Association of Nigeria (MAN), Nigerian Bar Association (NBA), Committee for the Defence of Human Rights

(CDHR), religious organisations such as the Pentecostal Fellowship of Nigeria (PEN), National Prayer Movement, National Association of Nigerian Students (NANS) Association of Market Women and Men, Alliance for Democracy (AD), United Action for Democracy and Organized Private Sector (OPS). In this instance, the Manufacturers Association of Nigeria (MAN), Nigerian Association of Chambers of Commerce, Industry, Mines and Agriculture (NACCIMA) and the Nigeria Employers Consultative Association (NECA) also opposed the increases. The opposition of these organisations demonstrated the hollowness of the Bretton Woods institution's claims that their neo-liberal agenda is in the interest of the productive fractions of national capital.

Taking the initiative, the federal government obtained an injunction from Justice Ade Alabi of Ikeja High Court in Lagos restraining Oshiomhole and all 29 NLC affiliates from going ahead with a strike planned for 30 June 2003. According to Justice Alabi, the restraining order was necessary in view of the likely difficulty in enforcing any mandatory order directing the numerous public and private sector workers that make up the Congress to return to work once the strike commenced. The injunction was later to be at the centre of a contempt case instituted by the Government against trade union centre. The NLC President described it as a 'black market injunction', 'frivolous', and an 'abuse of the court process'. (*Sunday Punch*, 29 June 2003). The Committee for the Defence of Human Rights (CDHR) similarly condemned the 'frequent and obscure use of court process and procedures' which was the hallmark of the Obasanjo administration. It emphasised that in light of government's deliberate undermining of the independence of the judiciary through its disregard for the rule of law, it lacked the moral basis to use a court injunction to restrain the NLC.

The National Economic Intelligence Committee (NEIC) also expressed fears that the new rates would impact negatively on inflation in the country. In a widely publicised report the Committee observed that 'the inflation rate would rise to 11.64 per cent up from the previously projected rate of 9.45 per cent' (*The Punch*, 2 July 2003). Recognising that the government's action was based on a pressures from the World Bank and the IMF, the statement asked why the government ignored allegations of massive smuggling of crude oil and corruption surrounding the management of crude meant for domestic consumption, even though ending smuggling and corruption would generate more funds for development than any fuel tax imposed on Nigerians.

In an NLC press release of 29 June 2003, signed by its President, the labour centre explained that the struggle against high oil product prices was a public interest issue rather than typical trade dispute. The labour movement was playing its traditional vanguardist role. The NLC in this regard emphasised the democratic significance of the protest; more than the reversal of price increases in the prices of the oil products, the planned protest was aimed at combating the growing authoritarianism of President Obasanjo's second term in office. Hence, the real challenge was to ensure that Nigerian workers and did not loose their right to protest under a democratic constitution.

The federal government for its part also used the news media, threatening workers with the 'no work on pay' clause. The NLC, however, proceeded with the nationwide protest as planned. The senior staff union in the oil sector, the Petroleum and Natural Gas Senior Staff Association (PENGASSAN), stated the union's unflinching support for the NLC action and threatened to shut down oil operations if the government hesitated to reach an agreement with organised labour.

Police brutality against protesters led to widespread casualties, especially in the capital Abuja, in the country's commercial capital Lagos, and in the oil city of Port Harcourt. At the end of the strike the death toll was estimated at 21 and scores of protesters sustained severe injuries sustained. At the Abuja Federal Secretariat, for instance, armed police invaded and condoned off the national headquarters of the NLC, precipitating skirmishes and a stampede, and several intense conflicts elsewhere in the capital city. In a statement signed by the NLC President, Adams Oshiomohole, the Congress made particular reference to police shooting of 'four innocent and unarmed protesters' at Maraba and Nyanya Abuja, and described it as 'a virtual throwback to the dark ages of military rule, when police became an instrument for suppressing peaceful agitation, pickets and protests'. The statement regretted the massive and indiscriminate use of live ammunition and tear gas by the police which were reported in various parts of the country, especially Lagos and Abuja. Oshiomhole told reporters that he was 'manhandled and tear gassed at the Federal Secretariat, in the midst of what was a peaceful picket' (*The Guardian*, 2 July 2003). The police also savagely beat up the Labour Editor of *Vanguard* newspaper, Mrs. Funmi Komolafe, Mr. Rotime Ajai of Abuja bureau of the same paper, George Oshodi of the Associated Press, and Mrs. Huawa Mustapha of the NLC's Research Department. At least three persons were reported killed in Port Harcourt as a result of clashes between policemen and protesters who were mainly students (*The Guardian*, 3 July 2003). Amidst brutality and a rising death toll, the NLC called off its strike on 8 July 2003, with price increases going into effect. There could hardly be a more stark evidence of the threat that Neo-liberalism poses for democratic governance.

When President Obasanjo announced yet further price increases on 1 October 2003, the NLC threatened to disrupt the All-Africa Games, which Nigeria was then hosting. The planned strike was averted through mediation involving the 36 state governors in Nigeria. President Obasanjo, in a dramatic national broadcast in which he was physically shaking with fury, accused the NLC of misleading the populace on the deregulation issue and of being involved in a destabilisation project as well as running a parallel government. This was to mark the beginning of the President's resolve to deal decisively with the trade union movement. Thereafter, NLC officials were arrested and detained for picketing those who defied the status quo agreement brokered by the governors. President Obasanjo sponsored the Trade Union Amendment Bill at the National Assembly. The rhetoric behind the bill spoke of promoting the democratisation of labour and enhancing choice for all Nigerian workers in the true spirit of the Constitution, but the bill contained numerous authoritarian provisions:

1. Conferring upon the Minister discretionary powers in deciding whether or not members of trade unions employed in different trades, occupations or industries can form or join a single federation of trades unions.
2. Inserting a no-strike clause in the collective bargaining agreement as a condition for remittance of union dues by employers.
3. Requiring a two-thirds majority vote of all members before trade unions or registered federations could conduct a strike.

4. De-registering the Nigeria Labour Congress (NLC) as the only legally recognised central labour organisation.
5. Imposing six months jail term for picketing.

ILO Director Cornelus Dzakpasu urged the government to reconsider and fashion a law that would be acceptable to all stakeholders in the industrial relations sector, stressing the need for observance of social dialogue as enshrined in its Convention 144 on tripartism in the process leading to reforms of labour laws (*This Day*, 8, 19, 26 August 2004). Intensive lobbying by the NLC and a public hearing on the bill on 25 August led the Senate Committee to make several modifications in the bill, including the removal of the no-strike clause in collective bargaining agreements. The National Assembly passed the amended bill into law on 23 March 2005, spurred by the government's resolve to ride roughshod over civil society in the implementation of its neo-liberal 'reform' agenda. The cycle of increases in petroleum products, and labour led struggles against them, continued until the last days of the Obasanjo government in May 2007. A final increase two days before his departure brought the total increase in the pump price in the period 1999–2007 to 275 per cent.

6. Conclusion

A central claim of President Obasanjo in justifying the use of state power (coercive and legislative) against the NLC has been that unions have no business in political activism. It is noteworthy that a 'democratic' dispensation, in the context of neo-liberalism, would seek to deny unions a widely accepted right (Flanders 1975: 30). Social life, generally, and employment relations, specifically, are shot through with power relations (Adesina 1992), and this makes industrial relations essentially political. This fact is universal while the specific nature and manifestation of the political factor in unionism may depend on such conditioning factors as the character of the state (Onyeonoru 2001) and the strategy of employers as well as the nature of power relations between these and labour. The political dynamics of trade unions are an integral part of the wider national and international political process.

The unique position of unions in the social system, their membership base and associated resources are often used directly by the official union leadership for explicitly political purposes in the larger society, and indirectly by governments and political parties in alliance with this leadership. In this sense, social movement unionism (Waterman 1991), represents resistance to the unbridled structure of exploitation and related injustices premised on the notion of self-interest which remains the organising principle of neo-liberalism and its state manifestation. The movement approach adopted by the NLC becomes inevitable given the authoritarian tendency associated with the implementation of neo-liberal reforms, even under the conditions of 'democracy' (Onyeonoru 2004). The continuity of labelling union activism as 'political unionism' from the colonial to different shades of post-colonial regimes in Nigeria received a boost under the neo-liberal conditions in Nigeria even under a 'democratic' government after 1998.

While the Nigerian trade union movement has a long track record of active engagement in defending workers rights, specifically, and wider citizens' rights generally, this is neither uniform nor consistently so. The progressive role of the labour movement has been subjected to persistent repression and state violence, whether in the context of colonial or post-colonial states, civil or military. This is, however, not to discount the relative space that a wider 'democratic' political environment offers for unions. In spite of the significant upsurge in workplace or shopfloor activism in the period before 1994 relative to the weakening of national-level activism, the post-1999 period provided a relatively wider berth for union revival. However, while the imperial/class expression of state power may shift in different periods, there is nothing in the return to 'democracy' that necessarily protects the workers and their organisations from state repression. Under conditions of neo-liberalism, democratic civil rule combines with class-greed and 'primitive accumulation' to undermine general well-being of citizens. Unions, as an expression of popular will, will have to form alliances with other popular forces in society in defeating this manifestation of state power.

Suggested Reading

Adesina, J.O. (1992) 'Towards the Reconstruction of Industrial Relations Theory' in Otobo, D. (ed.), *Further Readings in Nigerian Industrial Relations*, Ibadan: Malthouse.

——(1994) *Labour in the Explanation of an African Crisis*, Dakar: Codesria Books.

——(1997) *Trade Union Structure and Effectiveness*, Lagos: Frederich Ebert Foundation.

——(1998) 'Structural Adjustment and the Transformation of Labour Identities: What's New and Does it Matter?' in Jega, A. (ed.) *The Transformation of Popular Identities under Adjustment*, Uppsala: Nordic African Institute.

——(2003) 'The Labour Policy of a Neo-Führer State: The Nigeria Case', *Annals of the Social Science Academy of Nigeria* 14.

Adewumi, F. and Adesina, J. (1999) 'Occupational Groups', in Oyediran, O. and Agbaje, A. (eds) *Nigeria: Politics of Transition and Governance, 1986–1996*, Dakar: Codesria Books.

Ananaba, W. (1969) *Trade Union Movement in Nigeria*, Benin: Ethiope Publishing Company.

Cohen, R. (1974) *Labour and Politics in Nigeria*, Heinemann: London.

Farnham, O. and Pimlott, J. (1990) *Understanding Industrial Relations*, 4th edition, Eastbourne: Cassell.

Flanders, A. (1975) 'The Nature of Collective Bargaining' in Flanders, A. (ed.) *Collective Bargaining*, Harmondworth: Penguin.

Hutchful, E. (1986) 'The Modern State and Violence: The Peripheral Situation', *International Journal of the Sociology of Law* 14 (2).

Hyman, R. (1984) *Strikes*, 3rd edition, London: Fontana.

Ohiorhenuan, J.F.E. and Adesina, J.O. (1989) 'The State and Control of Labour' in Ohiorhenuan, J.F.E. (ed.) *Capital and the State in Nigeria*, Westport CT: Greenwood Press.

Onyeonoru, I. (2000) 'The Political Question in Trade Unionism', *African Journal for the Psychological Study of Social Issues* 5 (1): 110–26.

—(2004) 'Collective Bargaining in an Emerging Nigerian Democracy' in Agbaje, A., Diamond, L. and Onwudiwe, E. (eds) *Nigeria's Struggle for Development and Good Governance: Festschrift For Oyeleye Oyediran*, Ibadan: Ibadan University Press.

—(2006) 'Globalization and Trade Union Resistance' *African Journal for the Psychological Study of Social Issues* 7 (1): 71–98.

Oshiomhole, A. (1999) 'Being Text of an Address Presented by Mr Adams Oshiomhole, President, Nigeria Labour Congress at the Workers Rally Organized to Commemorate the 50th Anniversary of Iva Valley Massacre on November 18'.

Otobo, D. (1981) 'The Nigerian General Strike of 1981', *Review of African Political Economy* 22: 65–81.

—(1986) *Foreign Interests and Nigerian Trade Unions*, Ibadan: Heinemann Educational.

—(1992) *Further Readings in Nigerian Industrial Relations*, Lagos: Malthouse Press.

—(1988) *State and Industrial Relations in Nigeria*, Lagos: Malthouse Press.

Waterman, P. (1991) 'Social Movement Unionism: A New Model for A New World', Institute of Social Studies, The Hague, Working Paper Series, No. 110.

Workers Divided, Workers Uniting: South African Unions since 1945

SAKHELA BUHLUNGU AND EDWARD WEBSTER

1. Introduction

The process of industrialisation in South Africa was characterised by the creation of a bifurcated labour market which accorded differential status and material rewards to different sections of the emerging working class. This division has remained a key feature of the country's industrial relations system and has left an indelible mark on the form and character of trade unionism.

This chapter traces the emergence of two broad traditions in the South African labour movement, a predominantly white labourist tradition, and a fragile non-racial tradition rooted in the African working class and influenced by the communist party. Both of these traditions experienced a serious set-back and defeat with the capturing of state power by a virulently white supremacist Afrikaner Nationalist Party in 1948. This led to a realignment of the labour movement with the non-racial tradition forming the South African Congress of Trade Unions (SACTU), aligning itself to the increasingly militant African Nationalist movement, and the white labourist tradition forming the Trade Union Council of South Africa (TUCSA). The rapidly expanding economy of the 1960s opened up new opportunities in the 1970s for a united trade union movement. This emerged in part in 1985 with the formation of the Congress of South African Trade Unions (COSATU). In the last part of this chapter we examine the role of COSATU in the struggle for democracy and conclude by outlining the challenges facing a divided working class and its elusive search for unity.

2. Origins of Trade Unions in South Africa

White workers formed craft unions based predominantly on the English experience of skilled workers of trade unionism to protect their occupational interests. Industrial unionism for white workers later emerged in the 1920s amongst the growing class of industrial workers. These two forms of unionism tended to coincide with ethnic cleavages within the white community, English-speaking workers in the craft unions and Afrikaner workers in the emerging industrial unions. A single federation for white unions, the Trades and Labour Council (T&LC) was established in the 1920s and this federation continued until the 1950s. Similar to several British settler colonies such as Australia, a labourist tradition emerged with the formation of a Labour Party aligned with the T&LC.

However, unlike Australia, the labourist tradition in South Africa faced three challenges. The first was the rise of an ethnic-based Afrikaner nationalism which shrewdly targeted white workers and their trade unions, as a constituency, ultimately winning power with their support in 1948. As O'Meara (1978) has shown, it was the Afrikaner working class constituencies that were decisive in the victory of Afrikaner nationalism in 1948. The second challenge was how the T&LC would relate to the small but significant intermediate group of workers, namely the coloured in the Cape and Indian workers in Natal, who were 'insiders' in relation to the labour legislation and could therefore belong to trade unions, but were 'outsiders' in terms of their racial 'non-white' status (see for example, Freund 1995). Importantly their outsider status excluded them from certain key artisanal skills and education and training opportunities.

The third challenge facing the labourist tradition was how to relate to those workers who were excluded altogether from the industrial relations system and were subject to a specific regime of labour control such as pass laws and denial of residential rights in the city, namely African workers. As a result, the bulk of them were confined to a system of oscillating migrancy between the rural Bantustans and the cities. A small but significant section of the T&LC, many of whom were members of the

Communist Party of South Africa, argued that the real working class were the African workers and that the priority should be to organise them. It was this latter political current, which we refer to as the non-racial tradition in the labour movement that came to play a decisive role in African unionism in the post-World War II period. This non-racial tradition was associated with communists as they preferred to treat black workers as a class and therefore argued for non-racialism.

What complicates the labour history of South Africa is the fact that the process of industrialisation did not simply create a proletarian class that was entirely dependent on wage labour. Colonial dispossession and proletarianisation of the indigenous population had created a large stratum of agricultural labourers, sharecroppers, home workers, self-employed workers, an impoverished peasant class and a small petty bourgeoisie of teachers, clerks and other semi-professionals. The boundaries between these strata were fluid and this shaped the form that early trade unionism amongst African workers took. The first attempt at the unionisation of black workers, in the 1920s, the Industrial and Commercial Workers (ICU), was highly successful precisely because it responded to these hybrid forms of labour. Indeed, within a few years of its formation, the ICU experienced phenomenal growth to 100,000 members nationwide, capturing popular imagination by successfully challenging current racial practices such as the dipping of Africans in disinfectant in Durban in the 1920s (Bradford 1987).

However this upsurge of labour organisation among African workers rapidly disintegrated towards the end of the decade, in part because of strategic differences over where organisational energies should be concentrated. On the one hand, there were the architects of the ICU who believed that the notion of unionism needed to be expanded beyond the classic wage earner to include the hybrid forms of labour that were emerging in the context of industrialisation in the periphery. For them a general union was more appropriate than a craft or industrial one. On the other hand, there were the liberals and communists who believed that a trade union should be based on workers in the industrial sector who are fully dependent on wage labour.

By the mid-1940s there were two dominant traditions in the South African labour movement. On the one hand, there was a dominant labourist tradition which incorporated the Afrikaner and English groupings as well as the intermediate stratum of Indian and coloured workers. On the other hand there was an emerging non-racial tradition that was rooted in the rapidly growing urban industrial working class. In 1941 the Council of Non-European Trade Unions (CNETU) was formed and, taking advantage of African advancement during World War II, became a powerful voice for these workers. A key union in CNETU was the newly formed African Mineworkers Union whose emergence marked a turning point in South African labour history as it was the first successful attempt to organise core workers at the centre of the economy, the ultra-exploited African miners.

3. State Reaction and Setbacks to Unionism, 1945–50

Faced by rapid urbanisation and worker militancy during the war, white South Africa responded in contradictory ways. On the one hand there were those who argued for controlled urbanisation through the acceptance of a stable urban African working class. This view was shared amongst business people in the manufacturing and retail sectors. On the other hand there were a growing number of whites who were deeply threatened by the prospect of a loss of control and power by the white community. These anxieties were fuelled by the significant growth of communism internationally and amongst the growing African working class. This racist reaction was strongest amongst the white working class, particularly Afrikaners, and the farming community who were losing sections of their workforce to higher paying employers in the towns. The discontent was captured by an emerging Afrikaner petty bourgeoisie who, drawing on Afrikaner nationalist sentiment, campaigned around the slogan of 'apartheid', a more systematic form of racial segregation than had existed in the past (O'Meara 1978).

This attempt to roll back the forces of urbanisation and economic integration was consolidated by a series of defeats for the emerging African labour movement. The first setback came in the form of the brutal crushing of the historic mineworkers' strike in August 1946. Following an impressive display of worker solidarity over a strike demanding improved wages, the mobilisation was met with employer intransigence and police brutality. The defeat led to the collapse of the AMU and forced a rethink on how the rights of black workers could be successfully achieved.

In the aftermath of the African mineworkers' strike white political parties began to openly mobilise against African advancement, emphasising instead white protection and white solidarity. Thus in 1948 the National Party came into power specifically on a programme of racial social engineering in all spheres – the workplace, residential areas, the cities, educational institutions, churches, cultural and interpersonal relations. In the sphere of work, legislation was enacted consolidating the monopoly of skills in white hands, including legislation outlawing racially mixed unions and forcing registered unions with white, Indian and coloured members to introduce racially separate branches and to have whites-only national executive structures. This attempt at racial social engineering took on ludicrous forms such as racially separate toilets and eating facilities at the workplace and even racially segregated work spaces. In one instance employers were forced by the government to paint a yellow line around the white worker to separate him from his fellow black worker working on the same machine as they were not able to build a physical wall between them (Webster 1985: 165).

The most significant attack on the emerging African trade union movement was the euphemistically named Suppression of Communism Act of 1950. Ostensibly designed to curb the activities of members of the Communist Party, its effect was to clamp down on all forms of union organisation and to restrict the activities of key union organisers through the draconian system of banning, an order that restricted the banned person to their home and prevented from communicating with more than one person at a time. Thus to all intents and purposes, by 1950 all attempts at the organisation of African workers and more generally the non-racial tradition had been defeated. Those unions that survived, such as the Food and Canning Workers Union, were forced to retreat into a narrow and ineffectual form of collective bargaining.

4. Realignment, the 1950s and 1960s

Ironically, by attempting to separate the trade unionists from members of the Communist Party of South Africa (later renamed the South African Communist Party), the government pushed the non-racial tradition of the trade union movement closer to the nationalist movement. The suppression of communists and unionists coincided with the a dramatic revitalisation of the African National Congress, first through the establishment of the ANC Youth League with a new generation of leaders such as Nelson Mandela, Walter Sisulu and Oliver Tambo, and the launching in 1952 of a campaign of defiance against unjust laws. This shift in the centre of gravity in popular mobilisation is illustrated best by the launching of the first stayaway led by the ANC in June 1950. This emerging alliance between unions and the ANC gained further momentum during the 1952 defiance campaign and culminated in the formation of the South African Congress of Trade Unions (SACTU) in March 1955.

The formation of SACTU brought together two distinct traditions of mobilisation, namely, the non-racial tradition, which included a significant number of coloured and Indian unions and a few white sympathisers, and the growing nationalist political movement. This new alliance brought into being a new form of unionism, best described as political unionism. Political unionism involves a relationship between unions and a political movement, where the trade unions accept a subordinate role within the alliance. SACTU's participation in the Congress alliance facilitated a rapid increase in trade union membership in certain regions (Lambert 1988). This was achieved through mobilising the oppressed across class and race lines around key campaigns led by the nationalist movement. In particular, the federation gained new members and increased its profile by participating in the campaign to solicit ideas and draw up the Freedom Charter in 1955. Another good example of the synergy between SACTU and the ANC was the successful stayaway in 1958 over a pound-a-day campaign. However, political unionism also brought SACTU into direct conflict with the apartheid state and the organisation felt the full force of state repression in the 1960s after the banning of the ANC and its turn to armed struggle. Many union organisers were recruited by the armed wing of the ANC, Umkhonto Wesizwe, and were arrested and served long terms of imprisonment, and others were sent to the gallows. By 1964 SACTU had ceased public activities in South Africa and a few of its leaders had regrouped in exile where they actively lobbied for sanctions against South Africa. This brought to an end yet another cycle of trade union militancy and popular mobilisation that was only to re-emerge a decade later.

In response to the shift to a new centre of gravity located in SACTU's alliance with the ANC, the T&LC was forced to re-align. This realignment had begun with the formation of the South African Confederation of Labour (SACL) which was essentially the Afrikaner trade union arm of the ruling Nationalist Party. At the same time, a segment of T&LC unions had joined SACTU. However, the bulk of the T&LC continued the white labourist tradition, reconstituting the federation into the Trades Union Council of South Africa (TUCSA). The fact that TUCSA was the leading voice in the key industrial relations institutions allowed it to continue well into the 1970s as the dominant trade union presence in South Africa (Ensor 1978). Its longevity derived from its ability to practice apolitical business unionism, which provided ongoing services around wages and basic conditions of service for its members. The apartheid system provided considerable protection and benefit for white workers and to a lesser extent, coloured and Indian workers. Indeed, white workers continued to enjoy their status as a labour aristocracy. This status was legitimised by the fact that TUCSA continued well into the 1970s as the only South African affiliate of the ICFTU and the only representative of labour for South Africa at the ILO.

However, the challenges that had confronted white workers from the beginning of industrialisation remained, albeit in a more pressing form. On the one hand, coloured and Indian workers were experiencing the repressive effects of apartheid and were resisting the attempts to subordinate them within TUCSA. On the other hand, white workers had to respond to the growing numerically preponderant, but rightless and voiceless African workforce. The strategy with regard to the latter was that of parallel unions. Parallel unions were introduced both to defend the existing position of white workers in the labour market, by extending organisational rights to black workers, and at the same time to extend control over them by bringing them under the wing of white unions. For example the established TUCSA Garment Workers' Union established a separate parallel union for African workers, the National Union of Clothing Workers. Similarly, the coloured union, the National Automobile and Allied Workers Union established a parallel union, the National Union of Motor Assembly and Rubber Workers Union of South Africa (NUMARWOSA). Not surprisingly these racially paternalistic arrangements were fraught with tensions and were seen for what they were: a strategy to prevent the emergence of independent African unions.

In order to provide African workers with a voice, TUCSA had set up an African Affairs department in 1966 as an alternative to bringing parallel unions in as independent affiliates. TUCSA employed Eric Tyacke, an active member of the Young Christian Workers, and Loet Douwes-Dekker, an experienced industrial relations practitioner, to run the department. A motion was tabled at the 1969 conference of TUCSA to open its doors to black unions. The motion was lost and Tyacke and Douwes-Dekker resigned and formed the Urban Training Project, a labour service organisation designed to provide educational, organisational and strategic support to workers and, later, the emerging unions (Lowry 1999).

Underlying the tensions around the formation of the African labour movement was a deep ideological cleavage reflecting the sharp Cold War divisions within world politics at the time. The West was deeply suspicious of the central role of the reconstituted Soviet-aligned South African Communist Party (SACP), within the Congress alliance. In an abortive attempt to establish a rival to SACTU, TUCSA and conservative elements within the International Confederation of Free Trade Unions (ICFTU) sponsored the launch of the Federation of Free African Trade Unions of South African (Lodge 1983; Friedman 1987). Coincidentally, at the time a group of Africanists had just broken away from the ANC expressing similar concerns regarding the dominant role played by communists within the alliance. In the event, this initiative failed to take root.

5. Workers Uniting, 1972–94

The early 1970s opened a new phase of union mobilisation which was to culminate in 1985 in the creation of the first representative nationwide federation, the Congress of South African Trade Unions (COSATU). The decisive moment was the wave of strikes in January– February 1973 in the Durban–Pinetown area. This led to the development of an alternative political tradition in the union movement. While it continued the non-racial tradition of SACTU, it eschewed political action outside production. These shopfloor unions believed that it was important to avoid aligning themselves with the nationalist movement. They, particularly those affiliated to the Federation of South African Trade Unions (FOSATU) which was formed in 1979, emphasised instead the building of democratic strictures around the principles of accountability and the mandating of worker representatives. They saw this as the basis for developing a working class leadership in the factories. These unions argued that this strategy provided the best means of survival in the face of state repression, and of building strong industrial unions, democratically controlled by workers. Some within this political tradition supported the creation of a mass-based working class party as an alternative to the SACP.

In the late 1970s the 'national-democratic' tradition re-emerged in the labour movement with the advent of general unions, particularly the South African Allied Workers Union, which followed in the tradition of SACTU. These 'community unions' argued that workers' struggle in factories and townships was indivisible, and that unions had an obligation to take up community issues. They were critical of what they branded 'economism' and 'workerism' which sought to restrict worker mobilisation to factory struggles.

This 'national-democratic' tradition involved a view that South Africa could not be understood in simple class terms. Social reality was based on a 'colonialism of a special type' necessitating national-democratic rather that class struggle as the appropriate strategic response. This meant a multi-class alliance under the leadership of the ANC, drawing all the sectors of the oppressed black masses and sympathetic whites, and aiming to establish a 'national democracy'. Supporters of this view differed over whether it was necessary to pass through a national-democratic stage before a socialist stage (the two-stage notion of revolution), or whether national and class struggle could take place conterminously.

The picture of unions and politics in South Africa has often been incomplete through neglect of a third political tradition, that of black consciousness. Its origins lie partly in the Africanist ideology articulated by the Pan-African Congress (PAC), which broke away from the ANC in 1959 because of the latter's 'multi-racial' definition of the nation. Black consciousness has similarities to the national-democratic position, in that it holds that racial oppression is a manifestation of national oppression. However, its emphasis on racial structures and identities virtually excludes class relations from its analysis. This has often given rise to voluntaristic and romantic forms of organisation and mobilisation.

The formation of COSATU in December 1985 brought together unions from all three political traditions: the well-organised industrial unions drawn from the shop floor tradition; the general unions drawn from the national-democratic tradition; and the National Union of Mineworkers (NUM), having recently broken from the black consciousness tradition.

Responding to the euphoric mood, a COSATU delegation visited Lusaka in February 1986 to speak to the exiled ANC. A joint communiqué was issued in which the independence of COSATU was acknowledged, while the federation committed itself to the struggle for a non-racial South Africa under the leadership of the ANC. This clear identification with the national-democratic tradition brought the legacy of division in the labour movement to the surface again.

Critics within the shop floor tradition believed that the COSATU leadership had acted without a proper mandate in visiting Lusaka and should have made it clearer that COSATU would struggle 'independently under its own leadership' within the broad alliance. By implying that COSATU was 'operating under the leadership of the ANC', critics argued, a spirit of sectarianism could develop towards alternative political traditions. Some within the shop floor tradition went further and argued that the national-democratic tradition stood in absolute contradiction to working-class politics. Organisational style and political content were such, it was argued, that any involvement of the working class in such politics must lead to the surrendering of trade union independence and with it the abandonment of working-class politics.

The political differences that divided COSATU in its first 18 months of existence narrowed and in some cases were buried in the face of the state onslaught during 1987 and 1988. The necessity for unity forced a tactical and strategic compromise, but it had not removed the differences underlying the competing political traditions. Implicit in this broad-front strategy was the view that class contradictions are secondary to the national-democratic struggle (Fine and Webster 1989).

In 1989 the reformist F.W. de Klerk replaced P.W. Botha as president and signalled his intention to reform apartheid. In February 1990 he announced the unbanning of the ANC, PAC and the SACP, and he freed Nelson Mandela. Over the next 12 months the ANC, COSATU and the SACP forged a formal alliance that cautiously began to distance itself from the armed struggle and insurrectionist elements in its ranks.

It has become conventional wisdom that South Africa had a 'bloodless' transition from apartheid to democracy. This was not the case. More people were killed in the civil war that ravaged KwaZulu-Natal and parts of the former Transvaal from 1990 to 1994 than all the years before that. It began in 1986 in Natal when COSATU members were killed at the Dunlop tyre factory in Howick. Much of this conflict was fuelled by agents from the security establishment of the apartheid state and vigilante groups linked to Inkatha, the Zulu nationalist group and its associated formations. This had a profound impact on KwaZulu-Natal, in polarising civil society between 'comrades' and 'sell-outs'. Trade unions played a key role in negotiating the peace accord signed in 1991, creating a framework for peace to be negotiated at the local level and in bringing about reconciliation within communities. This assisted in keeping negotiations over the transition to democracy at a national level on track.

During this period of transition white unions had become increasingly marginal and irrelevant to the broader struggles undertaken by workers. TUCSA's strategy of parallel unions had failed and in 1979 when black workers were given the right to belong to registered union, these unions became irrelevant. In the face of these changes a few of the TUCSA unions attempted to reform from above by recruiting black workers but maintaining separate racial branches. This opened up a fierce battle between the new independent black unions in FOSATU (and later COSATU) and the established unions over who was to represent the black worker. The established unions had control over the centralised bargaining forums, the Industrial Councils, and over the decades had accumulated substantial funds and won significant benefits such as medical aid, pension funds and housing allowances. Their position was entrenched by the closed shop agreements that they had won and their access to artisanal skills that their members had acquired during the apartheid era. However, they failed to make significant inroads into the black workforce because they faced a credibility gap and because the new unions had established a more democratic and community oriented style of unionism, what has been described as social movement unionism (Webster 1988). As the political struggle intensified during the 1980s this new form of unionism came sharply to the fore. However, divisions between black and white workers made the principle of non-racialism rather shallow. Even though there were leading white officials in COSATU unions, the social distance between them and the workers remained (Buhlungu 2006a).

By the early 1980s TUCSA was a spent force and it formally disbanded in 1986. Most of its affiliates remained non-aligned until the early 1990s when they regrouped under the banner of a new national centre, the Federation of South African Labour (FEDSAL), later to become FEDUSA in 1996. As the class basis of Afrikaner nationalism changed, those Afrikaner unions that were linked to the early National Party found themselves in limbo. This is clearest in the case of the Mynwerkers Unie that had been central to the National Party victory in 1948 and now found itself abandoned by the ruling party as it began to dismantle the job colour bar. Faced by this threat to their privileged position, Afrikaner unions aligned themselves to a rightwing breakaway from the National Party, the Herstigte Nasionale Party of Dr Andries Treurnicht. In 1994 when race discrimination was outlawed they were forced to open their membership to all workers. The Mynwerkers Unie reinvented itself as the militant champion of those workers threatened by Affirmation Action and embarked, under the new name of Solidarity, on imaginative entrepreneurial activities to service this broader constituency.

In the meantime many of the Indian and coloured workers who occupied the intermediate position in the workforce had been drawn into the non-racial tradition of FOSATU, and later COSATU. Indeed many of their unions such as the coloured NAAWU and the Western Province Motor Assembly Workers' Union went on to lay the foundations of the new non-racial unions. Importantly the first general secretary of COSATU, Jay Naidoo, was an Indian South African.

6. Unions and the Transition to Democracy: The Case of COSATU

At the beginning of the 1990s COSATU had become the largest trade union federation in South Africa's history and pivotal in the struggle for democracy. In addition to its role in the peace movement, five interventions by COSATU during this period helped to shape the democratic transition and the nature of the alliance: the combination of mass action with negotiation helped to break the deadlocks at important moments; its involvement in economic policy-making generated new institutions, such as the National Economic Development and Labour Council (NEDLAC) and research into new industrial policies; it contributed to the new constitution, which included the right to strike; it was a central political actor, mobilising support for the ANC during the 1994 election; and it initiated and advocated the Reconstruction and Development Programme (RDP). The RDP originated in an attempt by labour to produce an accord that would tie a newly elected ANC government to a labour-driven development programme. In its final formulation, the RDP envisioned as a first priority 'beginning to meet the basic needs of people: jobs, land, housing, water, electricity, telecommunications, transport, a clean and healthy environment, nutrition, health care and welfare' (ANC 1994).

But class contradictions began to come to the fore as the newly unbanned ANC leadership came under a set of local and international pressures to change its economic thinking. From the 1950s, the ANC was publicly committed to a state-interventionist redistributive strategy, as articulated in its central policy document, the Freedom Charter. This policy was publicly reconfirmed by Nelson Mandela on his release from prison in February 1990. If, however, Mandela had entered prison at a time when nationalisation was an article of faith, he was released into a world where self-regulating markets had become the mantra.

From 1990, there were a series of economic policy reversals through which the ANC leadership came to adopt positions increasingly consistent with the neoliberal orthodoxy. By late 1993 the ANC had made a number of concessions on macro-economic policy which were to culminate in 1996 in the Growth, Employment and Redistribution (GEAR) strategy (Webster and Adler 1999: 363–71). GEAR aimed to achieve growth through fiscal-deficit reduction, gradual relaxation of exchange controls, reduction in tariffs, tax reductions to encourage the private sector (and especially direct foreign) investment, and privatisation. While maintaining in public discourse that GEAR was an extension of the RDP, and even on some occasions the Freedom Charter, these assurances rang increasingly hollow.

When GEAR was released the alliance partners were angered both by the content, which they then saw for the first time, and because the government asserted that it was 'non-negotiable'. The then COSATU general-secretary Sam Shilowa publicly criticised GEAR and indicated that these policies could never have emerged from the ANC before the 1994 elections. Agreement could not be reached inside COSATU on how to react to GEAR: some believed that the policy should be given a chance and the government should not be attacked during a currency crisis; others wanted openly to oppose the policy. The issue threatened to be divisive both within and between the alliance partners and, in the words of a leading alliance figure, the 'people walked away from it' (Webster and Adler 1999: 368). Thus, with painful irony, what began as an accord to bind an ANC government to a left-wing development programme ended up ensnaring both COSATU and the SACP in a neoliberal-inspired macro-economic policy (Webster and Adler 1999: 368).

The failure of GEAR to perform anywhere close to its own expectations for growth and job creation led to growing tension between the ANC and COSATU. In 1998 both President Mandela and Deputy-President Mbeki used high-profile speeches to COSATU's Central Committee and the SACP's congress to rebuke both organisations for questioning the government's economic policy. Mandela accused trade unions of being 'selfish' and 'sectoral', bent on protecting their interests at the expense of the nation (Bramdaw and Louw 2000). Compared to the mass of unemployed living below subsistence, workers organised in trade unions were being regarded in certain government circles as a privileged labour aristocracy.

As the implementation of the new economic policy began to impact on COSATU members, union leaders became increasingly vocal in their criticisms of government economic policy. For the first time COSATU affiliates publicly discussed an alternative to the ANC to lead the alliance. At the annual congress in August 2000 of the National Union of Metal Workers of South Africa (NUMSA) a resolution was tabled for the SACP to replace the ANC as leader of the Alliance. After considerable debate the congress rejected this resolution and committed itself to 'the strategic relevance of the ANC-led alliance in the current context of the national democratic revolution' (Bramdaw and Louw 2000). At the same time the South African Municipal Workers' Union (SAMWU) resolved at its annual congress 'that the process of beginning a discussion on an alternative to the alliance should begin' (Gumede 2005). Increasingly, the alliance seemed to be no more than an electoral machine that came to life at election time. 'Since the adoption of GEAR by the ruling party', Blade Nzimande, general secretary of the SACP remarked at the SAMWU congress, 'there has been a reluctance within the alliance to meet' (Bramdaw and Louw 2000).

The impact of the ideology of self-regulating markets has not only led to tensions within the alliance; it has also led to an erosion of the organisational base of the union movement through retrenchment and the growing use of various forms of casual employment. This has segmented the labour market into three roughly equal zones: a core of relatively protected workers, a non-core of vulnerable part-time, temporary and contract workers, and a periphery of informal and unemployed workers (Webster and von Holdt 2005).

The organisational terrain of informal work is very different from that facing traditional trade unionism, and workers began turning to alternative forms of organisation for support (Buhlungu 2006b). Religion plays a central role in community based organisations, as do relationships between households where food and care-work is shared. This could explain the support for controversial, populist ANC leader, Jacob Zuma. As argued elsewhere:

> Their support for Zuma indicated their sense that the trade union movement has been increasingly marginalized within the Alliance, and that its concerns – notably over jobs – have been sidelined in the formation of government policy. From this perspective, Zuma – who since his dismissal (as deputy-president of the country in 2005 for facing corruption charges; subsequently he also faced a rape charge) has been presenting himself as the victim of a conspiracy by shadowy and politically reactionary forces – was adopted by the left-wing of the Alliance as a unifying symbol for the downtrodden, the oppressed and the excluded. He was adept at cultivating this image, which was well-received among a workforce increasingly vulnerable to the insecurities of casualization (Southall, Webster and Buhlungu 2006: 221).

New social movements, such as the Treatment Action Campaign (TAC) and the Anti-Privatization Forum (APF), emerged as a powerful voice of these marginalised groups, but whether they will form links with the labour movement and whether, in turn, the labour movement will establish links with them, remains to be seen (Webster and Buhlungu 2004). However, there is a sense in which union leaders are realising the limitations of their current responses to this new wave of social activism and are searching for new responses. As Willie Madisha, former president of COSATU, argued:

> COSATU must find ways of pulling new social movements close to COSATU. It must find ways of working closely with them. COSATU, the ANC and the SACP were involved in the formation of the APF, the TAC and the LPM [Landless People's Movement]. Now they have abandoned them and see them as an enemy (quoted in Webster and Buhlungu 2004).

On the other hand, labour's central role in the struggle for liberation and the institutionalised voice it has acquired within the policy-making process, enabled it to persuade the Department of Trade and Industry (DTI) in late 2006 to win a temporary reprieve of three years on the importation of clothing and textiles from China. The creation of NEDLAC, as well as its alliance with the governing party, gives labour opportunities to influence policy at the national level in spite of the erosion of its shop floor power base. The result of this weakening at the base and influence at the top is a class stalemate where the forces challenging market liberalisation 'do not have the capacity to impose their alternative ideas on either the state or domestic and international capital. Nor is the government and capital able to satisfy the economic demands of this constituency through GEAR. Neither can they crush the opposition' (Webster and Adler 1999: 371).

7. Structure of the Contemporary Union Movement

The structure of the labour movement continues to mirror the past. The first aspect is the large number of unions and union federations. In 2002 there were 16 union federations registered with the Department of Labour (Department of Labour 2002). Indeed, as Table 1 shows, over seven years the number of registered unions nearly doubled, from 248 in 1995 to 485 in 2002. Importantly, many of these unions are small and are struggling to survive. Those that are large tend to be a result of mergers that have taken place over a relatively long period of time.

Table 1. Unionised Workers and Registered Unions, 1995–2002

Year	Registered Unions	Members
1995	248	2,690,727
1996	334	3,016,933
1997	417	3,412,645
1998	463	3,801,388
1999	499	3,359,497
2000	464	3,500,000
2001	485	3,900,000
2002	485	3,600,000

A second feature of union structure is that the majority of unionised workers are concentrated in a few unions in three federations, as Table 2 illustrates. In the case of COSATU there are 10 affiliates with more than 100,000 members each. By contrast, none of NACTU's 22 affiliates has more than 50,000 members, with many claiming less than 5,000 members.

Table 2. Membership of the Largest Federations

Federation	Membership
COSATU	1,864,121
FEDUSA	527,628
NACTU	300,000

Thirdly, in spite of the growing concentration and coordination of union activities through such institutions as NEDLAC where there is a common labour caucus, the labour movement remains highly fragmented, racially, occupationally, politically, and by organisational style as illustrated by Diagram 1 below.

Diagram 1. Fragmentation of Labour

	COSATU	NACTU	FEDUSA
Race	Predominantly black	Black	Majority non-black
Occupational categories	Predominantly blue collar	Blue collar	White collar
Politics	Aligned to ANC/SACP	Origins in Pan-Africanism and Black Consciousness but non-aligned	Non-Aligned
Organisational Style	Mobilisation	Lobbying	Lobbying

As Diagram 1 shows, COSATU, the largest federation, remains predominantly black, blue collar, politically aligned to the ANC and the SACP and relies on militant mobilisation in the workplace and on the streets using traditional tactics such as strikes and stayaways. By contrast, and in spite of its attempts to distance itself from its white staff association image of the past, FEDUSA continues to draw its membership from the upper end of the labour market, which is predominantly white, coloured and Indian, and white collar. It is non-aligned politically and relies heavily on lobbying to influence the political process. It also emphasises the individual provision of services and benefits for its members. NACTU, the smallest of the three represents distinct political traditions, Pan-Africanism and Black Consciousness, which have not yet found an effective voice in the new South Africa. To some extent their constituency is similar to COSATU's but its organisational style relies on influencing informal political networks. According to former NACTU general secretary, Cunningham Ngcukana, the federation sees its role as a 'partnership in transformation' (interview by the authors, 11 August 2002) rather than as an oppositional social force.

However, largely as a result of a drop in foreign funding, NACTU has seen a steady erosion of its membership and has been forced to close down most of its provincial offices and retrench staff (interview by the authors with Ngcukana, 14 August 2003). The formation of Solidarity (previously

MWU-Solidarity) in 1997 and the Confederation of South African Workers Unions (CONSAWU) in 2002 mirrors and deepens these divisions.

The fourth feature of union structure is that the federations are driven by their affiliates and therefore exhibit a high degree of decentralisation. The majority of federation structures have limited organisational resources and decision-making lies with affiliates, thus diminishing the capacity of federations to mobilise workers or to exercise any control and monitor the activities of workers. FEDUSA has a small head office staffed by ten full-time officials funded from an annual budget of about R4 million. It has no regional offices or staff. NACTU also has a small head office of 16 officials and two regional offices in Durban and Cape Town. It also means that it is difficult to coordinate and articulate a coherent set of common economic and political policies. A good example is the failure of the federations to develop a common investment arm and their failure to prevent affiliates to develop their own or control their activities.

The final aspect of union structure is the strikingly uneven distribution of resources between and within federations. This results in uneven participation in the new labour market institutions that have been created since 1994 such as NEDLAC, the National Skills Authority, and the South African Qualifications Authority, as well as the traditional collective bargaining structures such as bargaining councils. On the one hand, these unions and federations have relatively large head offices and regional offices. COSATU's 19 affiliates have a combined total of 1831 full-time officials, with 275 of these belonging to one union alone, the National Union of Metalworkers (NUMSA) (COSATU 2003). They have regular newspapers or journals, use e-mail for communication and have up-to-date websites. Some of them also have specialised departments focusing on research and union education (see Diagram 2 below). COSATU, in particular through the establishment of NALEDI in 1992 has access to in-house research expertise. NALEDI employs 13 full-time research staff providing union leadership with up-to-date information on issues such as labour market and economic trends for processes such as the job summits and the NEDLAC policy processes. By contrast neither NACTU nor FEDUSA has a dedicated research department and both are forced to 'outsource' their research to consultants and labour service organisations such as FAFO, a research NGO. As a consequence these federations often struggle to keep up with the constant demand for inputs on policy on a range of fronts with employers and the state.

A similar inequality exists in the field of union education and training. Only COSATU and most of its affiliates have specialised education departments and full-time education officers. COSATU affiliates have a total of seventy full time educators at national and regional level (COSATU 2003). In addition, both COSATU and FEDUSA created in 1997 a joint labour education institute, the Development Institute for Training, Support and Education for Labour (DITSELA), dedicated to the design and delivery of trade union education and training programmes. From March 2002 to March 2003 DITSELA trained 3,076 'learners' in a variety of education activities including short courses and advanced courses in organising, labour law, union educators and a leadership course for women. Currently the institute employs 17 full-time staff members and has a budget of nearly R5 million (DITSELA, 2003).

Diagram 2. Distribution of Resources

	COSATU	FEDUSA	NACTU
Education Department	Yes Participates in Ditsela	No Participates in Ditsela	No
Research Department	Yes Internal policy unit and Naledi	No	No
Internet Usage	Yes	Limited	No
Media (e.g. Newspaper)	Yes	Yes	Came out once, discontinued
E-mail	Yes	Partial and fax	Fax
Mergers	Many	Some	Few

8. Conclusion

We have suggested that the legacy of past divisions and organisational practices continues to shape the structure of the contemporary labour movement. Is it possible for labour to break from this legacy of fragmentation and potential marginalisation and overcome these divisions? Elsewhere we have identified six initiatives being undertaken to revitalise labour (Webster and Buhlungu 2007). In this chapter we have traced the different forms of unionism that have emerged over the last century in the South African labour movement, namely craft, industrial and general unionism as well as political unionism, business unionism and social movement unionism. This variety of forms of unionism reflects the hybrid nature of the labour market. Unlike the traditional narrative of proletarianising workers becoming full-time wage earners in the city, the South African workforce consists of a variety of forms of proletarian and semi-proletarian forms of labouring activities. These include workers retaining close links with the countryside, growing forms of self-employment, domestic work, agricultural labour and a growing unemployed workforce. Any attempt to build a strong and united labour movement will have to be grounded in the reality of this labour market. This may necessitate a rethink of the appropriateness of existing forms of unionism and their relationship to political parties, communities, small businesses, the unemployed and the growing number of immigrant workers. This is all the more important because in the absence of a comprehensive social security system the individual wage earner is deeply embedded in a household which is a site dependent on multiple sources of wage and non-wage incomes and is therefore a site of stability for a larger group of people than the traditional nuclear family. A crucial point of departure then for worker unity is not simply a focus on the needs of individual workers, but there is a need to extend union activities to their households and to their communities.

Suggested Reading

ANC (1994) *The Reconstruction and Development Programme*, Johannesburg: Umanyano Publications.

Adler, G.M. (1994) '"The Factory Belongs to All Who Work in It": Race, Class and Collective Action in the South African Motor Industry, 1967–1986', PhD thesis, Columbia University.

Bradford, H. (1987) *A Taste of Freedom: The ICU in Rural South Africa, 1924–1930*, New Haven CT: Yale University Press.

Bramdaw, N. and Louw, I. (2000) 'ANC Alliance has trouble meeting', *Business Day*, 28 April.

Buhlungu, S. (2006a) 'Rebels without a Cause of Their Own? The Contradictory Location of White Officials in Black Unions in South Africa, 1973–1994', *Current Sociology* 54 (3): 427–51.

—— (2006b) 'Upstarts or Bearers of Tradition? The Anti-Privatisation Forum of Gauteng' in Ballard, R., Habib, A. and Valodia, I. (eds) *Globalisation, Marginalisation and New Social Movements in Post-Apartheid South Africa*, Durban: University of KwaZulu-Natal Press.

COSATU (2003) *Organisational Review*, Johannesburg: COSATU.

Department of Labour (2002) *Annual Report*, Pretoria: Government Printer.

DITSELA (2002) *Annual Report*, Ditsela: Johannesburg.

Ensor, L. (1978) 'TUCSA's Relationship with African Trade Unions: Attempt at Control 1954–1962' in Webster, E. (ed.) *Essays in Southern African Labour History*, Johannesburg: Ravan Press.

Fine, A. and Webster, E. (1989) 'Transcending Traditions: Trade Unions and Political Unity', in Moss, G. and Obery, I. (eds) *South African Review* 5, Johannesburg: Ravan Press.

Freund, B. (1995) *Insiders and Outsiders: The Indian Working Class of Durban 1910–1990*, Portsmouth NH: Heinemann; Pietermaritzburg: University of Natal Press; London: James Currey.

Friedman, S. (1987) *Building Tomorrow Today: African Workers in Trade Unions, 1970–1984*, Johannesburg: Ravan Press.
Gumede, W.M. (2005) *Thabo Mbeki and the Battle for the Soul of the ANC*, Cape Town: Zebra.
Lambert, R.V. (1988) 'Political Unionism in South Africa: The South African Congress of Trade Unions, 1955–1965', PhD thesis, University of the Witwatersrand, Johannesburg.
Lodge, T. (1983) *Black Politics in South Africa since 1945*, Johannesburg: Ravan Press.
Lowry, D. (1999) *20 Years in the Labour Movement: The Urban Training Project and Change in South Africa, 1971–1991*, Johannesburg: Wadmore.
O'Meara, D. (1978) 'White Trade Unionism, Political Power and Afrikaner Nationalism' in Webster, E. (ed.) *Essays in Southern African Labour History*. Johannesburg: Ravan Press.
Sithole, J. and Ndlovu, S. (2006) 'The Revival of the Labour Movement, 1970–1980' in *The Road to Democracy in South Africa, Vol. 2, 1970–1980*, Pretoria: UNISA.
Southall, R., Webster, E. and Buhlungu, S. (2006) 'Afterword', in Buhlungu, S. (ed.) *Trade Unions and Democracy: COSATU Workers' Political Attitudes in South Africa*, Cape Town: HSRC Press.
Webster, E. (1985) *Cast in a Racial Mould: Labour Process and Trade Unionism in the Foundries*, Johannesburg: Ravan.
——(1988) 'The Rise of Social Movement Unionism; The Two Faces of the Black Trade Union Movement in South Africa' in Frankel, P., Pines, N. and Swilling, M. (eds) *State, Resistance and Change in South Africa*, North Ryde NY: Croom Helm.
Webster, E. and Adler, E. (1999) 'Towards a Class Compromise in South Africa's Double Transition: Bargained Liberalization and the Consolidation of Democracy', *Politics and Society* 27 (2).
Webster, E. and Buhlungu, S. (2004) 'Between Marginalization and Revitalisation: The State of Trade Unionism in South Africa', *Review of African Political Economy* 100 (31): 229–45.

——(2007) 'The State of Trade Unionism in South Africa' in Phelan, C. (ed.) *Trade Union Revitalisation: Trends and Prospects in 34 Countries*, Oxford and Bern: Peter Lang.

Von Holdt, K. and Webster, E. (2005) 'Work Restructuring and the Crisis of Social Reproduction: A Southern Perspective' in Webster, E. and von Holdt, K. (eds) *Beyond the Apartheid Workplace: Studies in Transition.* Scottsville: University of Natal Press.

Zimbabwe Congress of Trade Unions

FREEK SCHIPHORST

1. Introduction

The Zimbabwe Congress of Trade Unions (ZCTU) was created on 28 February 1981, some ten months after Zimbabwe gained its independence. In those ten months ZANU(PF) – the party that won the first general election in March 1980 – made certain that this new organisation toed the party line. Indeed, until 1989 the ZCTU was in varying degrees subservient to the ruling party. Thereafter the ZCTU was revamped, and with a rejuvenated leadership it managed to chart an independent course which culminated in the leading role it played in the formation of the Movement for Democratic Change (MDC), the first opposition party that seriously challenges the rule of ZANU-PF and its leader, Robert Mugabe. This chapter will first look at the industrial relations climate and the position of organised labour therein prior to independence, starting in 1948. Then the first decade of the ZCTU (1980–9) will be examined, and finally the period up to 1999, the year in which the ZCTU launched the MDC.

2. Labour before Independence, 1948–80

In the 1940s mounting nationalist aspirations combined with growing dissatisfaction among African workers with appallingly poor living and working conditions. Inadequate wages and housing provisions led black labour to migrate to the urban centres. A number of Commissions of Inquiry were set up, all recommending drastic changes, none of which were implemented. This led to a period of labour unrest, including a significant strike of African railway workers in 1945, which finally culminated in a country-wide general strike in 1948. During this strike, Sir Godfrey Huggins, Prime Minister of Southern Rhodesia, declared in the Legislative Assembly in Salisbury that 'We are witnessing the emergence of the proletariat and in this country it happens to be black' (Schiphorst 2001: 142).

The colonial government recognised that a continuation of this black worker unrest in the urban centres was undesirable for further capitalist development. In the early 1950s the white establishment discussed legislation which would cater to the growing black aspirations for legitimate trade unions. A strike at the Wankie coal mine in 1954 acted as a catalyst. Garfield Todd, the then Prime Minister, later recalled that 'The men had grievances and no adequate machinery to let them be known' (Schiphorst 2001: 144). The absence of formally recognised unions prevented the airing of grievances, and it also inhibited government control of African labour. Hardwicke Holderness, at the time a white Member of Parliament in Salisbury, wrote in his memoirs:

> [T]he thinking which had been developing in government official circles [...] was that something would have to be done about some form of legal recognition and control (especially control) of specifically African trade unions. [T]he existence of African unions would obviate the kind of difficulty that had been encountered during the Wankie strike – the problem of not knowing what leaders the authorities could deal with. There had been a steady growth in the number of unofficial organisations in existence and the number of African workers belonging to them, and there was a need for a law to control them (Schiphorst 2001: 145).

White society had to take the new urban proletariat into account in such a way that would satisfy some of its demands yet at the same time would not intensify African nationalism. The early attempts of white political leadership were often thwarted by opposition from white trade unions representing skilled workers, fearful that in a multi-racial union, unskilled black workers would outvote them.

The interest of the white business community and white labour were reflected in the Industrial Conciliation Act (ICA) of 1959. For the first time black African workers were allowed to form or join trade unions for the purpose of engaging in collective bargaining in National Industrial Councils. Not all black workers were covered: farm workers and domestic servants were excluded from its jurisdiction.[1] Black trade unions could be registered if they did not compete with an existing (white) trade union; and if they were considered 'representative' and 'non-political' (Wood 1982: 55). The Act's intention was to chart the African nationalist leadership that was also active in the trade union movement. This was openly admitted by the Minister of Labour when he introduced the Bill in Parliament: 'It could be argued that to provide for these associations is nothing more than a control measure and let me be perfectly frank, it is' (Schiphorst 2001: 40).

The 1958 annual report of the Ministry of Labour listed 27 African trade unions. With the introduction of the ICA 1959, African unions were slow to register: from 2 in 1960, to 6 in 1962 and then to 26 in 1964 (Brand 1971: 95, 101). This later increase can be explained by the decision taken in 1961 by the Southern Rhodesia Trades Union Congress to recognise the new industrial legislation and its urging of affiliates to register. One of the union leaders later recalled that 'the consensus of opinion then seemed to be that we were going to work within the Industrial Conciliation Act on condition that we were going to be recognised' (Schiphorst 2001: 41).

Rather than racial segregation, the ICA 1959 allowed trade union fragmentation on the basis of skill. Skilled unions had mostly a white membership and leadership.[2] Unions of the unskilled often had a black membership and leadership. These latter were 'organisationally and financially weak, competitively disabled both by the hostility of the political power structure and the debilitating effects of the industrial negotiating machinery'. They were 'required to oppose not only organised employer groups, but also workers of a higher order of skill who view the develop-

1 Wood states that 51.6 per cent of black wage earners were covered by the Act (1982: 55).

2 Wood has calculated that there were between 13,000 and 17,000 black members of the white-dominated 'multi-racial' unions in 1979 (1987: 86).

ment of African trade unionism as a potential threat to the stability of the white working class' (Harris 1974: 68).

The black union movement was also divided along the lines that split the nationalist movement into ZANU and ZAPU in 1963. At the time of the Unilateral Declaration of Independence (UDI) in 1965, the two black national labour centres were the African Trade Union Congress (ATUC) associated with ZANU, and the National African Federation of Unions (NAFU) associated with ZAPU, a situation that persisted until 1974. Differences between the labour centres also hinged on issues of internal union democracy and accountability. Personality clashes as well as personal ambitions played a role too. Breakaways and the formation of new unions also resulted from dissatisfaction with corrupt practices.

Rifts and factions were one source of trade union weakness in this period. Another prominent source was the repressive nature of the state. The labour control provisions of the ICA 1959 were complimented by the police and security forces. Close police surveillance of union activities and meetings, harassment, arrests and detention of trade union leaders were commonplace. As a result union leaders sought, to the extent possible, to distance their organisations from the nationalist political parties, in part to evade police repression. Politics again played a role after 1975 when the final phase of the white regime had begun and unions were making themselves ready for a new era. Following the crisis in ZANU in 1976–7[3] three factions arose. A pro-Mugabe faction formed the Zimbabwe Trade Union Congress (ZTUC), led by Albert Mugabe, Robert Mugabe's younger (step) brother. Another faction supported Muzorewa's UANC and a smaller faction supported ZAPU.

In the late 1970s the discussions leading to the so-called 'internal settlement' in the political arena were replicated on the trade union front. In 1977 veteran trade unionist Reuben Jamela launched the Zimbabwe Federation of Labour (ZFL). Politically the ZFL leaned towards the United African

3 See Martin and Johnson (1981: 191–214), for details of this crisis which led to the ousting of Ndabaningi Sithole as president of ZANU and the appointment of Robert Mugabe as his successor.

National Council led by Bishop Muzorewa (Shadur 1994: 69). Black trade union leaders from the African Trade Union Congress (ATUC) – supporting Ndabaningi Sithole's ZANU party – and the Zimbabwe Federation of Labour (ZFL) began merger talks with the white-led Trades Union Congress of Rhodesia (TUCR). ATUC's Phineas Sithole and TUCR's Howard Bloomfield succeeded, and in 1979 the Muzorewa government recognised the interim committee of the United Trade Unions of Zimbabwe (UTUZ), although this organisation had mainly a paper existence.

In 1980 there were 40 registered trade unions with a total membership of 79,310, representing 8 per cent of the formally employed (Riddell 1981: 243, 256). In addition there were 71 known but unregistered trade unions with an estimated membership of some 30,000 members. Including the organised employees in the public sector, there were some 200,000 organised employees, or a density of 20 per cent (Riddell 1981: 260).[4]

Some two months after independence, veteran white trade unionists attempted to form one single national centre and to revamp the United Trade Unions of Zimbabwe (UTUZ). Also involved were Elphegio Soko and Phineas Sithole from the United Textile Workers' Union and Abisha Kupfuma from the Hotel and Catering Workers Union (Republic of Zimbabwe 1987: 23). The Ministry of Labour strongly objected to this move. The Zimbabwe Trade Union Congress (ZTUC) re-emerged, led by Albert Mugabe. Before independence this centre only had two small affiliates and it had been predominantly active as a recruiting agency for ZANU(PF)'s guerrilla army (Wood 1987: 65). After independence trade union leaders-cum-politicians rapidly switched their allegiances from the Muzorewa-Sithole camp, and the associated UTUZ, to the one federation openly backed by ZANU(PF), the ZTUC (Wood 1987: 65). Abisha Kupfuma and Elphegio Soko were the most prominent among the camp-switchers.

The new Minister of Labour appointed a committee to create a single national labour centre. Although members were drawn from different

4 Wood is more cautious: he gives a total trade union membership of 101,305 (Wood 1988: 295). At the eve of independence at least seven trade union umbrella organisations had developed (Schiphorst 2001:49).

national trade unions and held opposing political views, the committee had a strong ZANU(PF) bias. There were other ways in which the creation of a union centre favourable to ZANU(PF) was ensured. Unions (and their centres) associated with ZAPU were kept under close surveillance, and the formation of spurious rival unions was encouraged. When the Congress to create the single national centre was held, the state of affairs at it was chaotic. 210 delegates representing 52 different unions claimed entrance rights. Declared membership strengths were not verified. As one union leader remarked later, 'There was no check made as to whether delegates attending the congress had been elected by their union, appointed by some other "king-maker" or self-imposed (e.g. A.G. Mugabe attended and got elected when he had lost a vote of confidence in his union)' (Republic of Zimbabwe 1987: 50). When the Congress was over, out of the 52 attending unions only 32 could 'be verified as actually existing; the remaining had disappeared into air' (Mitchell 1987: 114).

The chaos at the Congress sheds light on the undemocratic nature of many trade unions at the time. Trade union leaders often considered 'their' unions almost as their own property. Any decision regarding the union could be taken without consulting the membership. Issues of affiliation, mergers or breakaways were often dealt with by one person. Riddell reports instances of union leaders who could not recall ever having been voted in power (1981: 244). This posture of the trade union leadership would severely affect trade unionism in Zimbabwe during its first decade, as we will see. Likewise, problems related to the lack of a tradition of internal democracy and accountability bedevilled the trade union movement in an independent Zimbabwe. For the ruling party this was not a primary concern. What mattered to the politicians was how to ensure that the trade union movement would toe the party line.

3. A Captive Labour Movement, 1980–9

Formed at an 'all-comers' congress which was organised by an interim committee described as 'a puppet of ZANU(PF)' (Shadur 1994: 102), it was no surprise that pro ZANU(PF) union leaders found their way into the first executive of the Zimbabwe Congress of Trade Unions (ZCTU). After the still unresolved death of the first Secretary General, Albert Mugabe, in 1981, a 'gang of four' took effective control of the ZCTU and ran the national labour centre as a leadership clique: Makwarimba, Kupfuma, Moyo and Mashavira, with the support of Soko, Njekesa and Ndawana. All seven were staunch ZANU(PF) members. The union base of some of these trade union leaders was dubious. Mitchell argues that the 'first four years of the ZCTU's existence were nothing sort of disastrous. The image presented to the public was that of individuals and cliques quarrelling among themselves, united only in their subservience to the Ministry of Labour' (1987: 116).

Serving the party was paramount. With weak power bases of their own, these men were loyal to the source of power that had given them their places: Minister of Labour Kumbirai Kangai and ZANU(PF). There was an unquestioning acceptance of the submission of the labour centre to party and its government. The first leadership of the ZCTU gave the party and its government the full and uncritical initiative in all labour matters, and they continued the strategy of undermining the position of those union leaders whom they considered non ZANU. A number of these latter were from the long-established unions who had in the colonial past decided to refrain from close ties with any political party. Now, these older unions were viewed as 'sell-outs to imperialism' (Shadur 1994: 106).

ZCTU executives encouraged or supported splinter unions. Between 1981 and 1984 the number of (known) unregistered unions almost doubled, while membership of these unions almost tripled (Republic of Zimbabwe 1987: 38). Indeed, the encouragement of splinter unions was not only a way in which the ruling political party sought to side-track potential recruitment bases for ZAPU. It was also a tested means of securing or extending support by the new leadership of the ZCTU against rivals in the organisation.

The ruling clique did not consult or inform affiliated unions on every issue. The Trade Union Survey 1984 reports that affiliated unions complained about lack of information regarding the drafts of the new Labour Bill and other essential matters (Republic of Zimbabwe 1987: 54–5). In a meeting of trade union leaders the Secretary General of the ZCTU cut short a discussion on the lack involvement of unions in the wage setting process by announcing that 'This is a matter between the government, ruling party and the leadership of the ZCTU. This is not a matter for public discussion' (Shadur 1994: 107).

However, as early as July 1982 newspaper stories appeared on the ZCTU's 'maladministration, mismanagement of organisation funds, possible theft by conversion and misappropriation of income from international organisations' (Wood 1987: 74). Criticism of this sort fell on deaf ears as long as Kumbirai Kangai remained Minister of Labour. With the arrival of his replacement, Frederick Shava, in January 1984, attacks in the press intensified. Articles detailed numerous instances of corruption and criticised the ruling clique for failing to hold a national congress in contravention of the ZCTU's provisional constitution.

The beleaguered clique responded to the attacks in a time-tested way: they accused their critics of supporting the opposition party, ZAPU. But the ruling party did intervene to put an end to union corruption. The most plausible reason for this is that corruption had opened the way for a leadership challenge from within the labour movement. This challenge came from the long-established trade unions, many of which were associated to Bulawayo, the stronghold of rival political party ZAPU. When the ZCTU was created by ZANU(PF) in 1981, two political adversaries were identified: the white trade unions, representing settler interest, and John Nkomo's ZAPU. And whereas by 1984 white opposition had lost most of its vigour, ZAPU was still a force to reckon with in the political arena. The government was in danger of loosing its grip on the labour movement by supporting the very men it had put at its helm. Damage control was required, and a team of four administrators was appointed clean up the mess at ZCTU headquarters (*Herald*, 22 October 1984). In March 1985 an

Interim Committee was formed, headed by the President of the Associated Mineworkers Unions, Jeffrey Mutandare, to prepare for the long-awaited second Congress in July 1985.

This Congress was quick to pledge itself to 'scientific socialism', the ideology of the ruling party, but at the same time it ousted those at the forefront of infighting and corruption: the gang of four. Jeffrey Mutandare became the new ZCTU President. He represented a form a trade unionism which was not overtly dominated by party political alliances. Formed in 1938, the mineworkers union was a well-established organisation. It had become multiracial after the ICA of 1959, was run along professional lines and, after bringing into its fold a splinter union which claimed to be closer to ZANU(PF), and the white-collar mining union, in 1982, it was by far the largest union in the country. The new Secretary General, Anselm Chitehwe, was a staunch ZANU(PF) supporter.

Although the Congress now had a new leadership, its way of operating did not change. The leadership style of Chitehwe differed little from that of his predecessor. He too operated as if the ZCTU was his personal property, and he too succumbed to the temptations of office. Amidst allegations of embezzlement of funds he and four other officials were forced to resign in 1986. The ZCTU's President, Jeffrey Mutandare, being also the president of the mineworkers union, had neither time nor energy to run the ZCTU office. Thus the ZCTU headquarters ceased to operate effectively. Not until 1988 did Mutandare convene an extraordinary Congress to elect a new Secretary General.

Black labour welcomed independence with a wave of strikes. The period 1980–1 saw a total of almost two hundred strikes, an unprecedented number even in the colonial days. Generally, the outbreak of these strikes was attributed to a crisis of expectations: black workers seemed to want too much, too quickly. The new regime instituted a minimum wage, and proceeded with the creation of institutions to regulate industrial relations. Realising that the presence of trade unions at the shop floor was weak the government created a machinery to improve communications between management and workers: the workers' committee, which was independent of the trade unions.

In September 1980 the Commission of Inquiry into Incomes, Prices and Conditions of Service (known as the Riddell Commission after its chairman) investigated the collective bargaining machinery. The ICA 1959 had created two routes: industrial councils for sectors where both a union and an employer organisation would be present, and an industrial board for those sectors where either of the two was absent and where therefore the Minister of Labour had to play an important role. The Commission came out strongly in favour of the further development of the Industrial Council system and against the continuation of the Industrial Boards (Riddell 1981: 263). The long-awaited Labour Relations Act of 1985 (LRA 1985) recreated institutions for collective bargaining: Employment Councils and Employment Boards, replacing the Industrial Councils and Boards which existed under the ICA 1959.

Initially, however, collective bargaining had a strong governmental input. Minimum wages were announced by the government usually at the May Day rally in Harare's main stadium. At the same time, the government also indicated maximum wage increases. These minima and maxima became known as the government defined parameters within which unions and employers were allowed to bargain. Throughout the 1980s, employers and unions alike criticised this 'fettered bargaining'. However, slowly, tri-partite collective bargaining with governmental parameters was to give way to bi-partite negotiations. And indeed, from 1990 onwards, parameters were no longer announced and bargaining was left completely to the two sides in the Employment Councils.

Not surprisingly this bargaining in Employment Councils found a willing reception with employers. In the chaotic years after independence employers felt unable to influence governmental wage setting but the Councils allowed the determination of much more 'realistic' wages in line with employers' ability to pay. As a result, after 1990 the number of Employment Councils grew steadily while the number of Boards, and Ministerial interference rapidly decreased. Or, in the words of the ZCTU Secretary General in 1992: 'as far as industrial relations are concerned we have pushed the state to a point where it no longer is having a role in determining what happens on the factory floor' (Sachikonye 1997: 124).

At the end of this first decade trade unions were weak: they lacked a strong base on the shop floor, and their organisational and financial strength was poorly developed. After the first four disastrous years the ZCTU slowly began to develop its own bureaucracy and to create functioning departments, e.g. Education, Women's Desk, and the Research and Economics Department, although staffing was plagued by a high turnover. As a result little support could be given in this period to the affiliated unions in their bargaining efforts. New and relatively weak as these trade unions were, they could do little but stay close to the prevailing power of that time: the ruling political party ZANU(PF).

The ruling party and its government moved slowly in its labour policies. At independence immediate 'corrective measures' were taken to remove racist clauses from the Industrial Conciliation Act 1959, after which legislative work for a longer-term, more structural settlement regarding organised labour could start. The introduction of worker committees and Works Councils at each and every enterprise would serve to create channels of communication that would help to soothe emotions after decades of apartheid-like industrial rule and ease relations between management and workers. A number of writers have characterised the relationship between the state and organised labour in this period as 'corporatist' (Shadur 1994: 13). Certainly some of the more obvious features of corporatism such as concentration of interest representation and control over the leadership were prevalent in Zimbabwe, but the essential ingredient of the corporatist arrangement is absent: the meaningful involvement of organised labour in decision-making as a *quid pro quo* for a restrained position.

At the end of the decade, the ZCTU had become critical of some of the government's policies but the legitimacy of ZANU(PF)'s rule was not questioned. ZANU(PF) could be content; for a predominantly rural-based political party that had never had shown much attention to urban labour, it had done remarkable well in the urban areas. The initial waves of strikes following independence had not become politically dangerous and the most important policy intervention, the introduction of the new Labour Relations Act, had been successfully concluded.

The developments until 1989 can best be labelled as a form of benign labour control rather than a corporatist arrangement. Trade unions and their national centre received paternalistic support from ZANU(PF). Party control did not involve a form of interest mediation or interest representation. The ZCTU was never seriously involved in any decision regarding labour policy. The annual adjustment of the minimum wage was not part of a consultation process between the Ministry of Labour and the ZCTU. The very marginal way in which the ZCTU was involved in drafting the new labour legislation in the early 1980s as well as the absence of meaningful consultation on the economic policy in this first decade also illustrates this point.

4. Becoming a Force of Opposition, 1989–99

At the extraordinary Congress of the ZCTU in 1989 its President was re-elected and a new General-Secretary appeared on the scene: Morgan Tsvangirai. His candidature was a surprise move by the group of trade union leaders of long standing who wanted the Congress to adopt professional standards in its administration (Schiphorst 2001: 96–8). ZANU(PF) was moving in the other direction. After the signing of the Unity Accord between ZAPU and ZANU(PF) in 1987, moves were made to introduce a one-party state. The constitution of Zimbabwe was amended, and an Executive Presidency was created with Robert Mugabe as its first incumbent with far-reaching powers. However, the merger of the two political parties also ended a tense period heralding greater press freedom and freedom of speech.[5] It created the political space to be critical of party politics again. It is against this background that one must assess the slow but gradual moves by the ZCTU to severe its close ties with ZANU(PF).

5 Since 1982 the army's Fifth Brigade had been deployed in Matabeleland to forcefully deal with the so-called dissident problem. Tens of thousands lost their lives. See Catholic Commission (1977) for details.

During the late 1980s the government embarked on a major economic restructuring programme without consulting the ZCTU. The ruling party did not think it could gain anything by consulting labour. Moreover, the political assessment was that organised labour was not able to muster any resistance. And indeed, ZANU(PF)'s assessment proved them initially right; restructuring and the subsequent economic structural adjustment programme (ESAP) were introduced without major resistance. This confirmed to ZANU(PF) once more that organised labour was weak.

Under the leadership of Tsvangirai, however, the ZCTU began to fight back. His first task was to bring sound administrative principles and a sense of professionalism to the head-office of the ZCTU. And then he moved to establish, stronger than ever before, principles of democracy and accountability. Morgan Tsvangirai also personified the new forces within the movement that sought a broader base for the ZCTU. Attempts were made to open regional and district offices of the ZCTU; formal alliances and alliances of solidarity were sought with other groups and organisations in society, such as the organisations of employees in the public sector, but also the organisation of co-operatives and student organisations.

In voicing the concern of the labour movement it also became apparent that the ZCTU was not following a very narrow or parochial course. Not only did the ZCTU criticise wage freezes and price increases but it also urged a boycott of increases in council rates. It organised meetings in residential areas in Harare to discuss community needs regarding housing, transport, education and health services. In criticising the city council, the ZCTU quite specifically set itself up as the voice of the 'unemployed, illiterate, homeless and sick people in residential areas whose needs the city council should also be concerned about' (*Herald*, 2 February 1989).

The ZCTU also challenged the government's new policy on attracting foreign investment. The ZCTU called the proposed investment code 'an intention to entrench capitalism which exploits the workers' (*Herald*, 16 February 1989) and labelled its adoption a 'capitalist victory' (*Financial Gazette*, 18 February 1989). The widely publicised revelations in the 'Willowgate' scandal, involving several (former) ministers and high-ranking party members, did the party no good either. Union leaders blasted politicians who violated their own Leadership Code, and the ZCTU slowly positioned itself in public as the organisation that cared not only about the plight of the wage-workers but also that of the masses. Whereas ZANU(PF) liked to pose as the champion of the *povo* (i.e. the ordinary man/woman) the ZCTU criticised ZANU(PF) leaders for enriching themselves while failing to hold up to their promises. The ZCTU, using the same idiom (of socialism) which hitherto had seemed to be the prerogative of ZANU(PF), posed itself time and again as an alternative, rather than an extension of the party. It was this spectre, more than the maladministration of the national centre, the unrest on the industrial front, or even more than the corruption scandals within its own ranks that worried the party and necessitated action.

In the following years the party endeavoured to undermine the ZCTU. The first move was the widely publicised arrest in 1989 of its President, Jeffrey Mutandare, on allegations of corruption. These allegations proved to be true; apparently Mutandare had fallen into a trap set by the CIO (Schiphorst 2001: 103–4). Soon after Morgan Tsvangirai was arrested; his support for student demonstrations criticising ZANU(PF) led to charges that he was a South African infiltrator. However, the next year, at the Third National Congress, Tsvangirai was re-elected unopposed, and Gibson Sibanda (from the Railways Unions) was elected to replace Mutandare as President. ZANU(PF) had been unable to place its henchmen in prominent places. Subsequently, ZANU(PF) sought to erode the leadership base from within, using the few remaining supporters it had on the General Council of the ZCTU. Disgruntled leaders of six unions called upon the leadership of the ZCTU to resign because of supposed incompetence, maladministration and fraud. The six held caucus meetings and were allowed access to the state-controlled media. Since the allegations had no factual basis they had little impact, and the ZCTU continued to criticise the economic policy of liberalisation and price de-controls of the government.

The government responded by ignoring the ZCTU and introducing important pieces of legislation. In 1991 a structural adjustment programme (ESAP) was announced, and a year later important amendments were made to the Labour Relations Act. Although on the latter some consultation had taken place, the version that was rushed through parliament shocked the trade union movement. The Act effectively ended the era of 'one union – one industry' and increased the power of the Works Councils by diminishing those of the trade unions; an agreement between a Works Council and management now overrode a National Collective Agreement. Ministerial powers were increased, strike action made more difficult, and the system of employment security for workers was deregulated.

Angered by the new laws and the deteriorating economy, the trade unions took to the streets in protest. The ZCTU boycotted a meeting with the Minister of Labour. The government controlled media sought to depict the ZCTU as a body defending the parochial, sectional interests of a small group, a body with obvious party political objectives that was preparing to enter the political arena for the 1995 general elections. However, in the three years leading up to 1995, the ZCTU did not form a party. On the contrary, it stuck firmly to its position that it was a labour movement. As such it was a political force, but not a political party.

The ZCTU did become increasingly active. It formed regional structures, revamped its office in Bulawayo and opened new offices in Mutare and Gweru. New departments were added to existing ones (e.g. Organising, Information, Projects, Legal, Occupational Health and Safety, and later, Employment Creation). Projects were started to reach out to workers on issues of labour law, and training was extended to worker representatives. Public meetings were organised throughout the country where people could air their grievances with economic life. Cooperation with the university led to proper studies to prepare for collective bargaining. Its own decision-making culture was also professionalised. Morgan Tsvangirai re-instated the General Council of the ZCTU as the prime decision-making body. The strategies, tactics and direction that the ZCTU adopted were no longer decided upon by one man (as had often happened in the past), but were all the result of deliberations and decisions by the General Council. This made the ZCTU stronger. This kind of leadership differed from the leadership that characterised the previous generation of union leaders who, more often than not, saw the union as their personal tool. The younger generation of trade union leaders (who were members of the General Council) were now involved in the decision-making process, thus creating a broad foundation for the ZCTU in the labour movement.

When the protests against ESAP failed, the ZCTU changed course from obstruction to constructive co-operation through social partnership. In a position paper on Industrial Relations given in 1994, Morgan Tsvangirai declared that the labour movement had always realised the need for adjustment of the economy, but that 'If social partners could sit together to address some of these problems, we are sure ESAP would be turned into a pill less bitter to swallow than is currently the case' (Tsvangirai 1994: 31). He subsequently argued that relations between employers and unions had been constructive over the past two years and he called for the establishment of a similar productive relationship between 'civic organisation and the state' (Tsvangirai 1994: 34). He argued that:

> Certain fundamental principles have to be genuinely considered and applied, [and] these primarily include 1) the acceptance and full recognition of each other as social partners, 2) the objective regard to issues and an amicable resolution of differences without unnecessary antagonism, 3) constant dialogue [...] 4) transparency and good faith in all negotiations at a tripartite level (Tsvangirai 1994: 38).

The ZCTU had come full circle. After a painful process in which the ZCTU managed to free itself from close links with the political party, it now sought 'rapprochement'. However, the difference was that this time, the ZCTU did so based on autonomous strength. This was certainly recognised by the political leadership who responded to the ZCTU moves by a series of friendly gestures. Government most certainly was pleased that with the help and strong support from the ZCTU the National Social Security Scheme survived early hiccups, caused by corruption and public dissatisfaction by the compulsory dues. But when the ZCTU insisted on a more meaningful inclusion in policy-making, it found that the door was still closed. Being on speaking terms was not the same as having a social partnership.

In 1995 the fourth national ZCTU congress was convened. This was the first time that a Secretary General of the ZCTU had served a full term, a remarkable feat in the Zimbabwean context. Even more remarkable was that ZCTU Economics Department, guided by Godfrey Kanyenze, had prepared a well-researched document for this Congress, which not only severely criticised the government's economic policy but also outlined an alternative to it, called 'Beyond ESAP: Framework for a Long-Term Development Strategy in Zimbabwe Beyond the Economic Structural Adjustment Programme (ESAP)' (ZCTU 1995).

In it, the ZCTU presented itself as an organisation with a broad concern; not only would the national centre defend the interests of workers but now it also seriously addressed alternative policies for national economic development. The study reviewed, in addition to industry and the labour market, land distribution and trade policies. By this time the effects on ESAP were clearly felt. Retrenchments in public but especially the private sectors (textile and clothing, engineering) had hit hard and tens of thousands had lost their jobs. Inflation was rising, prices were no longer controlled and living standards eroded.

After its 1995 National Congress, the ZCTU set out to create a wider impact for the principles and policies outlined in the Beyond ESAP study. This 'Educational and Advocacy Programme' aimed to educate 'workers and the Zimbabwean population at large on what was wrong with ESAP, and what the ZCTU is proposing as an alternative strategy for development' (Kanyenze 1996: 11). To this end, cooperation was sought with the NGO community in Zimbabwe, and affiliated unions were to be strengthened through training on how to cope with the adverse effects of ESAP (Kanyenze 1996: 11–12). Also, discussions were started with 'national stakeholders'. In December 1995 the ZCTU organised a national conference 'to develop national strategies for the development of Zimbabwe' (ZCTU 1995: 1). Bringing together representatives from various government ministries, employers' associations, and NGOs, the conference recommended the creation of a 'representative consultative body along the lines of NEDLAC in South Africa to ensure that divergent views are captured for national policy making' (ZCTU 1995: 2).

In 1996 the ZCTU pursued yet another strategy to strengthen the labour movement: building alliances with other worker associations, notably those in the public sector. Initial moves in this direction were taken as far back as 1990, when the ZCTU supported, both publicly and behind the scenes, strikes of nurses and teachers. This resulted in the first serious contacts especially between the ZCTU and ZIMTA, the teachers' organisation. Over the years the ZCTU advocated labour legislation that would not differentiate between private sector and public sector workers, a 'harmonised' labour bill. In 1993 a team of technical experts from the ILO drafted such a bill, but little progress was made. And whereas the overtures to the ZIMTA faltered, rapprochement with the Public Service Association (PSA) was more successful. In August 1996 the PSA affiliated with the ZCTU (Behind 1996: 4, 17).[6]

The public sector strikes that broke out in August 1996 proved to be a turning point. Over 150,000 civil servants all over the country stayed away from work in September 1996. One month later, health workers struck in Harare and Bulawayo. In both these strikes the ZCTU played some role in acting as a broker between the associations and the ministries as well as serving as a communication channel to members in the regions. In the health workers' strike in particular, the ZCTU leadership negotiated with the Minister of Labour in which he agreed to re-instate the striking nurses if the ZCTU could persuade them to go back to work (Behind 1996: 10; Morgan Tsvangirai, interview 2001). When soon thereafter the Minister reneged on this promise and issued dismissal notices to all strikers, all confidence in the government as a negotiating partner was lost. Amidst quite some confusion, the ZCTU issued a call for a General Strike to take place 12–14 November 1996. According to Tsvangirai the strike call itself 'flopped' but in retrospect, he believed that ZCTU's role as broker in the preceding sectional strikes had been positive. 'The ZCTU came out strongly because it showed we looked after the interests of all workers, even though they were not affiliated, as the nurses were then not with the ZCTU' (Morgan Tsvangirai, interview 2001).

Following the failure of the general strike call, the ZCTU commissioned a study to analyse the events. Among the issues discussed, it was noted that the stumbling block for the introduction of the harmonised labour bill was the constitution itself (Tsvangirai, interview data 2001). This conclusion led to a greater involvement of the ZCTU in the discussion on

6 The affiliation boosted ZCTU membership by 47,000. However a year later this increase dropped to 20,000 and in 2003 the PSA was disaffiliated for not paying its dues to the ZCTU.

constitutional amendment, discussions that were initiated by the churches and other parts of civic society. In May 1997 the National Constitutional Assembly was formed and Tsvangirai became its chair. Although the initial interest of the ZCTU was labour legislation, this was now broadened to 'include democracy itself: the electoral laws, the position of rural workers, in short broad issues around governance' (Tsvangirai, interview 2001). In other words, the public sector strikes and the failed general strike drove the ZCTU into the constitutional debate, a debate that would fundamentally challenge the political legitimacy of the incumbent regime.

ZCTU lobbying throughout 1997 for the harmonised labour bill and a new economic policy met with little success. However, the ZCTU did believe that progress was being made on its old idea of a tri-partite consultative forum, along the lines of an institution recently created in South Africa (NEDLAC). This idea, first launched in connection with the 'Beyond ESAP' study in 1995, was further developed in extensive discussions with the business community as well as with the Ministry of Labour. In October 1996 the ZCTU organised a tri-partite study visit to South Africa. Consequently, the ZCTU concluded that the body should be composed of national stakeholders, i.e. organised labour, organised business, organised civic society, academia and government. When the institution was launched, however, the ZCTU discovered that government wanted a Malaysia-type body, where members were appointed on individual merit to advise the President. Thereupon the ZCTU withdrew it co-operation.

The ZCTU was also disappointed when in 1997 the government announced that war veterans would receive free education and health care, a lump sum payment and a pension, to be financed by a five per cent levy on all wages. This levy came on the heels of an increase in the sales tax and new taxes on petrol. After months of strikes and demonstrations for higher wages, this new wage levy for veterans, imposed without consultation, soured relations even further. The ZCTU leadership realised that the government was unwilling to engage in regularised industrial relations (Saunders 2001: 158). Henceforth the ZCTU viewed all proposals from ZANU-PF and its government for social partnership with utmost suspicion. The ZCTU called for a National Demonstration in December 1997, which was well attended.

Prices continued to rise, however, leading to food riots in January 1998, and the government called for a meeting of the consultative forum. The ZCTU declined in the invitation. Instead, the General Council ordered a 'National Stay-Away' in March 1998. On 3 and 4 March the country virtually came to a standstill in what was the biggest general strike since 1948. The nation-wide success of this Stay-Away can be attributed to a number of factors. The deteriorating economic situation aggravated by the unbudgeted expenditure of ZIM$4 billion for war veterans made poverty (61 per cent of the population was below the poverty line) both deeper and acute (ECA 2001: 109–10). The growing organisational strength of the ZCTU and its affiliates also accounts for the success of the worker protests. From 150,581 in 1985, the membership of ZCTU affiliates grew to 197,487 in 1995 (in 2004 it stood at 219,418).

ZANU(PF) sought to counter the growing strength of ZCTU by creating a rival national labour federation in 1998: the Zimbabwe Federation of Trade Unions (ZFTU). The ZFTU was led by Alfred Makwarimba, member of the infamous 'gang of four' and ousted in 1985 from the ZCTU, and Joseph Chinatomba, the Harare leader of the war veterans, who served as its vice-president and principal spokesperson. Funded by the party, the ZFTU sought to recruit members by force and intimidation, but by this time the ZCTU had established a strong presence among working people. In late 1998 the ZCTU stepped up its efforts to organise meetings throughout the country, in peri-urban areas and so-called growth points in rural areas. In well attended public hearings the ZCTU leadership received a mandate to move ahead with a political programme (Kondo 2000). A National Working People's Convention was convened in February 1999, followed by an extraordinary ZCTU Congress in August 1999 to 'resolve whether or not to coordinate and facilitate the process leading to the establishment of a vigorous Political Movement for Change in Zimbabwe' (Kondo 2000: 16). On 11 September 1999 the Movement for Democratic Change (MDC) was launched, which in January 2000 elected Morgan Tsvangirai as its President. In February 2001, as the MDC grew, Tsvangirai gave up his role as ZCTU Secretary General; Wellington Chibebe was elected as the new ZCTU Secretary General and Lovemore Matombo became President. Labour relations had been politicised to such an extent that only a political solution could resolve the crisis (see also Saunders 2001: 158).

7. Conclusion

In the years after 1989 the ZCTU was transformed from a captive ZANU(PF) organisation to a major oppositional force with political aspirations. In a time of severe economic dislocation and one-party rule the trade union movement assumed broader responsibilities and ambitions. It now catered for the waged worker in the formal sector, but also for the retrenched worker, the unemployed and those working in the informal economy. Labour in the communal lands again served as dumping ground for those who could no longer afford to live in the urban areas. If this were labelled a widening of the constituency 'downwards' there was also a widening 'upwards' to include the semi-professionals in defiance of the government's moves to divide and rule the labour movement. The ZCTU widened its traditional constituency by stretching out to the people employed by the government (such as nurses and teachers) and struck alliances with other groups, notably the students, human rights organisations and churches.

At the same time the ZCTU strengthened its base on the shop floor by extending its organisation to regional and district levels. The trade unions sought to represent the interests of workers and the communities in which they lived through collective bargaining, through enterprise forms of worker representation and through addressing those issues at fora that hitherto had not existed at district, regional and national levels. Between 1992 and 1997, the ZCTU sought to capitalise on this new image of the trade union movement as a broad social movement. It aspired to become a viable social partner, capable of engaging in serious social dialogue on national issues. In line with its new role as the voice of the people it demanded inclusion in policy making. But neither ZANU(FP), nor its government was capable of sharing political authority.

As a party with a limited urban programme ZANU(PF) had to create for itself a foothold in organised labour at independence. It did so by sidelining existing structures in which it played no role and creating a new national centre with party loyalists in leadership positions. When their actions became too embarrassing the party found itself without strong allies in the labour movement to impose its will. ZANU(PF) remained content as long as the national labour centre was too weak to influence events. Yet the ZCTU took advantage of the relative neglect and had started to strengthen its organisation and its links to civic society. ZANU(PF) countered with media campaigns, the arrest of labour leaders and attempts to create divisions within the ZCTU. When this policy failed ZANU(PF) turned more repressive, combating legal demonstrations through strong police intervention and arrest. The tactic of creating splinter unions was revived by funding allies and the creation of a competing national centre. When this too proved insufficient, harsh repression, continuous intimidation, arrests and the outlawing of meetings became increasingly commonplace. However, neither terror nor the total bankruptcy of the economy eradicated the ZCTU. The organisation has shown a remarkable resilience that could well be a promising harbinger for a new era in Zimbabwe, a new era that no doubt will arrive.

Suggested Reading

Brand, C.M. (1971) 'Politics and African Trade Unionism in Rhodesia since Federation', *Rhodesian History* 2: 89–110.

Catholic Commission for Justice and Peace in Zimbabwe (1997) *Breaking the Silence: A Report on the Disturbances in Matabeleland and the Midlands 1980–1987*, Harare: CCJP and the Legal Resource Foundation.

Cooper, F. (1996) *Decolonization and African Society: The Labor Question in French and British Africa*, Cambridge: Cambridge University Press.

Davies, R. (1975) 'Leadership and Unity in Rhodesian Black Trade Unions', *South African Labour Bulletin* 1 (9): 12–28.
ECA (Economic Commission for Africa) (2001) *Economic Report on Africa*, Addis Ababa: United Nations Commission on Africa.
Harris, P. (1974) 'Industrial Relations in Rhodesia', *South African Journal of Economics* 42: 65–84.
Kanyenze, G. (1996) 'Beyond the Economic Structural Adjustment Programme (ESAP)' in *Zimbabwe: An Overview of the ZCTU Project*, Harare: Economics Department, ZCTU, mimeo.
Kondo, T. (2002) *The 'Workers' Driven' and 'Peoples-Centred' Development Process For Zimbabwe: June 1996 to February 2000: Comprehensive Report for the Advocacy Programme Beyond ESAP Phase 1*, Harare: Zimbabwe Congress of Trade Unions.
Martin, D. and Johnson, P. (1981) *The Struggle for Zimbabwe: The Chimurenga War*, London: Faber; Harare: Zimbabwe Publishing House.
Mitchell, B. (1987) 'The State and the Workers Movement in Zimbabwe', *South African Labour Bulletin* 12 (6/7): 104–22.
Raftopoulos, B. (1995) 'Nationalism and Labour in Salisbury, 1953–1965', *Journal of Southern African Studies* 21: 79–93.
Republic of Zimbabwe (1987) *Labour and Economy: Report of the National Trade Unions Survey, Zimbabwe, 1984, Volume I*, Harare: Ministry of Labour, Manpower Planning and Social Welfare, Department of Research and Planning.
Riddell, R.C. (1981) *Report of the Commission of Inquiry into Incomes, Prices and Conditions of Service under the Chairmanship of Roger C. Riddell*, Harare: Government Printer.
Sachikonye, L.M. (1986) 'State, Capital and Trade Unions' in Mandaza, I. (ed.) *Zimbabwe: The Political Economy of Transition 1980–1986*, Dakar: CODESRIA.
—— (1997) 'Trade Unions: Economic and Political Development in Zimbabwe since Independence in 1980' in Raftopoulos, B. and Phimister, I. (eds) *Keep on Knocking: A History of the Labour Movement in Zimbabwe 1900–1997*, Harare: Baobab Books.

Saunders, R. (2001) 'Striking Ahead: Industrial Action and Labour Movement Development in Zimbabwe' in Raftopoulos, B. and Sachikonye, I. (eds) *Striking Back: The Labour Movement and the Post-Colonial State in Zimbabwe 1980–2000*, Harare: Weaver Press.

Schiphorst, F.B. (2001) 'Strength and Weakness: The Rise of the Zimbabwe Congress of Trade Unions (ZCTU) and the Development of Labour Relations 1980–1995', PhD thesis, University of Leiden, Leiden.

Shadur, M.A. (1994) *Labour Relations in a Developing Country: A Case Study on Zimbabwe*, Aldershot: Avebury.

Tsvangirai, M. (1994) 'Position Paper on Industrial Relations in Zimbabwe' in Sibanda, A. (ed.): *Report on the Symposium and Inaugural Congress of the Zimbabwe Industrial Relations Association (ZIRA), held at the Monomatapa Hotel, Harare 14 July 1994*, Harare: Institute of Development Studies, University of Zimbabwe.

Wood, B. (1982) 'Background Profile of the Zimbabwean Labour Movement, 1890–1959', abridged by David Mandel, in Boyd, R. (ed.) *Changing Patterns of Worker Relations in Zimbabwe: Conference Report*, Montreal: McGill University.

—— (1987) 'Roots of Trade Union Weakness in Post-Independence Zimbabwe', *South African Labour Bulletin* 12 (6/7): 47–92.

—— (1988) 'Trade Union-Organization and the Working Class' in Stoneman, C. (ed.) *Zimbabwe's Prospects: Issues of Race, Class, State, and Capital in Southern Africa*, Basingstoke: Macmillan.

ZCTU (1995) *Beyond the Economic Structural Adjustment Programme (ESAP): A Framework for a Long-Term Development Strategy in Zimbabwe: Interim Report, August 1985*, Harare: Zimbabwe Congress of Trade Unions.

Notes on Contributors

JIMI ADESINA, PhD is Professor of Sociology at Rhodes University, South Africa. He received his undergraduate and master's training at the University of Ibadan (Nigeria), and his doctorate degree training at the University of Warwick (UK). His research interests are in the field of Social Theory, Labour and Development Studies, and Social Policy. He has published extensively in these areas. His recent works include *Africa's Development Challenges in the New Millennium* (London: Zed Books, 2006) and *Social Policy in Sub-Saharan African Context* (Basingstoke: Palgrave Macmillan, 2007).

SAKHELA BUHLUNGU is Professor of Sociology at the University of Johannesburg, South Africa. His work experience includes time as a union education officer and assistant general secretary and as a writer for COSATU's magazine *The Shopsteward*. He has published widely on the South African labour movement. His latest publication is *Trade Unions and Democracy: COSATU Workers' Political Attitudes in South Africa* (ed.) (Cape Town: HSRC Press, 2006).

GUY GROUX is Research Director at CNRS (National Centre of Scientific Research) and Sciences Po-Paris. He teaches at Sciences Po-Paris and ESCP-EAP (European School of Management), and he is the author of numerous books and articles about trade unions in France and Europe. His most recent book is *La Grève* (with Jean-Marie-Pernot) (Paris: Presses de Sciences Po, 2008).

KERSTIN HAMANN (PhD Washington University, St Louis) is Professor of Political Science at the University of Central Florida with a research concentration on Spanish politics, comparative political economy, and the scholarship of teaching and learning. Her recent publications include

Democracy and Institutional Development: Spain in Comparative Theoretical Perspective (co-edited with Bonnie Field; Basingstoke: Palgrave Macmillan, 2009) and *Assessment in Political Science* (co-edited with Michelle Deardorff and John Ishiyama; Washington. DC: American Political Science Association, 2008).

ITZHAK HARPAZ is Director of the Centre for the Study of Organisations and Human Resource Management, and a Professor at the Graduate School of Management, University of Haifa, Israel. He is the author or co-author of numerous scientific publications, and six books. His main areas of expertise include: industrial relations, organisational behaviour, human resource management, and cross-cultural comparative management.

ANDERS KJELLBERG is Associate Professor in the Department of Sociology, Lund University, Sweden. His research projects in progress are: 'Union Density in Global Perspective' and 'Cultures and Strategies of Employers' Associations'.

PIET KONINGS is a senior researcher at the African Studies Centre, University of Leiden, the Netherlands. He has carried out extensive research on labour, trade unionism and economic and political developments in Ghana and Cameroon, and he has published widely on these topics. His latest books include *Negotiating an Anglophone Identity: A Study of the Politics of Recognition and Representation in Cameroon* (Leiden: Brill, 2003) and *Crisis and Creativity: Exploring the Wealth of the African Neighbourhood* (Leiden: Brill, 2006).

PAUL KUBICEK is Professor and Chair of the Political Science Department at Oakland University in Rochester Michigan. He has published extensively on post-communist politics, particularly on developments in Ukraine. He is the author of *Organized Labor in Postcommunist States: From Solidarity to Infirmity* (Pittsburgh: University of Pittsburgh Press, 2004).

KEITH LAYBOURN is Professor of History at the University of Huddersfield and editor of the *Annual Bulletin of Historical Literature*. He has written prolifically on British Labour Party history, producing more than 42 books and 75 articles. He wrote *Britain's First Labour Government* (Basingstoke: Palgrave Macmillan, 2006) with John Shepherd, and his most recent book is *Working-Class Gambling in Britain* c. *1906–1960s* (Lewiston, NY: Edwin Mellen, 2007).

MIGUEL MARTÍNEZ LUCIO is Professor at the University of Manchester (Manchester Business School). He has written on industrial relations, employment studies and economic regulation. The focus of his work is the transformation of regulation within employment relations and the impact of globalisation and new forms of competition at work. He is also working on the changing nature of trade union identity and strategy in countries such as Spain, the United Kingdom, and Europe more generally.

LÁSZLÓ NEUMANN (PhD in Sociology) is senior research fellow at the Institute for Social Policy and Labour (formerly Research Institute of Labour) and at the Centre for European Employment Studies of the Institute for Political Science, HAS. Once an adviser to an independent union federation (LIGA), he lectures in industrial relations at the Corvinus University, Budapest.

IFEANYI P. ONYEONORU, PhD is Reader in Sociology at the University of Ibadan (Nigeria). He received his undergraduate training at the Imo State University (Nigeria) and his MSc and PhD at the University of Ibadan. His research interest is in the field of Labour Studies, and has published widely in this area.

DAVID OST, Professor of Political Science at Hobart and William Smith Colleges in Geneva, New York, has written on political economy, labour, and democratisation in eastern Europe for a wide variety of publications, and is on the editorial board of *Politics and Society* and *Studie Socjologiczne*. His most recent book, *The Defeat of Solidarity* (Ithaca, NY: Cornell University Press, 2005), won the 2006 award for the best book in the political economy of postsocialism, and its publication in a 2007 translation elicited wide critical discussion in Poland.

PATRICK PASTURE is Associate Professor of History at the Katholieke Universiteit Leuven, where he co-ordinates the RU Modernity & Society 1800–2000. His research focuses on European labour history and the long term social history of religion in Europe and the US.

CRAIG PHELAN is editor of the journal *Labor History*. He is Professor of Modern History at Kingston University London. Most recently he has edited *The Future of Organised Labour: Global Perspectives* (Oxford and Bern: Peter Lang, 2006) and *Trade Union Revitalisation: Trends and Prospects in 34 Countries* (Oxford and Bern, Peter Lang, 2007).

VALERIA PULIGNANO is Professor in Sociology of Labour and Industrial Relations at the Katholieke Universiteit in Leuven (Belgium) and Associate Fellow at IRRU-IROB – University of Warwick (UK).

FREEK SCHIPHORST is Senior Lecturer at the Institute of Social Studies in The Hague, The Netherlands, in the Work, Employment and Globalisation Programme. In the 1980s and 1990s he was responsible for the Zimbabwe part of a project of international trade union co-operation on workers' participation. More recently, his research and teaching has focused on work in the informal economy and the possibilities of trade unions in organising workers therein.

STEPHEN J. SILVIA is an Associate Professor and Director of Doctoral Studies at the School of International Service, American University, Washington DC. He has been a visiting scholar at Harvard University, the Freie Universität Berlin and the Wirtschafts- und Sozialwissenschaftliches Institut des Deutschen Gewerkschaftsbundes. He specializes in comparative labour markets and comparative industrial relations, with a focus on Germany and the European Union. He has published in *Comparative Politics*, *German Politics*, *German Studies Review*, *Gewerkschaftliche Monatshefte*, *Industrial and Labor Relations Review*, *International Journal of Political Economy*, *Journal of Public Policy*, *New German Critique* and *West European Politics*.

EDWARD WEBSTER is Professor of Sociology and co-director of the Sociology of Work Unit (SWOP) at the University of the Witwatersrand. He has published widely on work and labour in South Africa and was president of the labour movements research committee (RC44) of the International Sociological Association.

MICHAL WENZEL, who received his PhD in Sociology from the Polish Academy of Sciences, has been a visiting scholar at the University of Michigan and the Max Planck Institute for the Study of Societies in Cologne. He currently works as a researcher at the CBOS Public Opinion Research Centre in Warsaw, where he specialises in labour relations, minority rights, and new technologies. He also teaches social research methodology at Warsaw University, and has written numerous articles and research reports about trade unions in Poland.

Index

American Federation of Labor–Congress of Industrial Organizations (AFL–CIO) 249, 285
Attlee, Clement 66, 200, 201
Austria x, 231
Australia 212, 388

Belgium xi, 139
- Automobile industry 29–30
- Belgian Labour Party 3–4
- Collective bargaining 14, 17, 18–19, 22, 28
- Communists 8–9, 10
- *Confédération des Syndicats Chrétiens* 7
- *Fédération Générale du Travail de Belgique* (FGTB) 9, 13, 16, 18
- Free rider problem 19
- Labour law 14–15, 17, 19, 24–5, 27–8
- *Mouvement Syndical Unifié* (MSU) 7
- New social movements 21–2, 29–30, 31
- Social insurance 11–13
- Social pact 8, 11–12, 23, 26, 27–8
- Strikes 17–18, 20–1, 28
- Unemployment 22, 23, 27
- Union membership 3, 25
- Union pluralism 3–5, 6, 8–9, 19–20, 23–4, 25, 30, 31
- Union political autonomy 10
- *Union des Travailleurs Manuels et Intellectuels* (UTMA) 7
- Women 21, 29
- Works councils 14–15

Beveridge, William 11
Blair, Tony 215, 216, 217
Böckler, Hans 68

Cameroon
- British mandate 323–7, 337–8
- Cameroon Development Corporation Workers' Union (CDCWU) 325–6
- Collective bargaining 324
- Colonial rule 315, 316–17
- *Confédération Générale Kamerunaise du Travail* (CGKT) 322–3
- *Confédération des Syndicats Autonomes du Cameroun* (CSAC) 334, 335
- *Confédération Syndicale des Travailleurs du Cameroun* (CSTC) 333, 335
- French mandate 317–23, 337–8
- Informal sector 335
- Labour law 331, 333
- Neo-liberalism 336, 337
- *Rassemblement Démocratique du Peuple Camerounais* (RDPC) 332, 333
- One-party state 315–16, 327–32, 333, 338
- Strikes 319, 326, 331
- Structural adjustment 335
- Unemployment 335–6
- Union density 335
- *Union Générale Kamerunaise du Travail* (UGKT) 323

Union Nationale des Travailleurs du Cameroun (UNTC) 330–2
Union des Syndicats Confédérés du Cameroun (USCC) 318–22, 328
Union fragmentation 333–4
Canada 212
Catholic Church 11, 38, 67, 106, 318–19
China xiii
Chirac, Jacques 48
Churchill, Winston 202
Cold War 9–10, 38, 366, 394
Comisiones Obreras (CCOO) (Spain) 122, 127, 128–9, 130–2, 133, 137–9, 141, 142, 144
Communism x, xiii–xiv, 8–9, 10, 38, 39, 63, 66, 67, 68, 106, 123, 127, 128, 163, 232, 235–7, 262–70, 291–6, 317, 321, 366, 387, 392–5
Confederación Nacional de Trabajadores (CNT) (Spain) 123, 142–3
Confédération Générale du Travail (CGT) (France) 38, 39, 44, 54–6, 59, 62, 63, 317–18
Confédération Française Démocratique du Travail (CFDT) (France) 38, 54–6, 58, 62–3
Confédération Française des Travailleurs Chrétiens (CFTC) (France) 38–9, 54, 56, 62, 320–1, 322
Confédération Générale des Cadres (CGC) (France) 54, 56, 63
Confédération Syndicale des Travailleurs du Cameroun (CSTC) 333, 335
Confédération des Syndicats Autonomes du Cameroun (CSAC) 334, 335
Confédération des Syndicats Chrétiens (Belgium) 7
Confederazione Generale Italiana del Lavoro (CGIL) (Italy) 105–6, 107–11, 113, 114, 115–18
Confederazione Italiana Sindacati Lavoratori (CISL) (Italy) 106–7, 108–11, 113, 115–18
Congress of South African Trade Unions (COSATU) 275–6, 387, 395, 396–7, 398, 399, 400, 401, 402, 404, 405, 406, 407

Da Silva, Luiz Inacio Lula xii
Denmark 161, 162, 164, 189
Deutsche Angestellten–Gewerkschaft (DAG) (Germany) 70–1
Deutschen Gewerkschaftsbund (DGB) (Germany) 68, 71, 76, 77, 78, 79, 80, 81–4

Eisenhower, Dwight 126
European Trade Union Confederation (ETUC) 138
European Union (EU) xiii, 28, 53, 82–3, 98, 134, 156–7, 159, 187, 201, 223, 257, 258, 283, 286

Fabius, Laurent 46, 48, 49
Fascism 97, 99, 104, 105, 107, 123, 232
Fédération Générale du Travail de Belgique (FGTB) (Belgium) 9, 13, 16, 18
Federation of Unions of South Africa (FEDUSA) 398, 405, 406, 407
Federatsiia Profspilok Ukrainy (FPU) (Ukraine) 298–301, 302–4, 306, 309–10
Finland 189
Force ouvrière (FO) (France) 38, 54–6, 62, 322
Fordism ix, x, xi, 16, 27, 47–8, 53, 121, 125, 126
France x, 7, 21, 66, 67, 101, 123
Collective bargaining 37, 41, 43–4, 46–8, 49, 50–2, 60

Company elections 55–6, 58
Confédération Générale du Travail (CGT) 38, 39, 44, 54–6, 59, 62, 63
Confédération Française Démocratique du Travail (CFDT) 38, 54–6, 58, 62–3
Confédération Française des Travailleurs Chrétiens (CFTC) 38–9, 54, 56, 62, 320–1, 322
Confédération Générale des Cadres (CGC) 54, 56, 63
Conseil National de la Résistance (CNR) 39–40, 41
Force ouvrière (FO) 38, 54–6, 62, 322
Immigrants 58
Labour law 37, 40, 41–2, 48–52
May 1968 44, 55
Membership loss 54–5, 59
Nationalisation of industries 42–5, 48
Parti communist français (PCF) 38, 63
Private sector 46–8, 59
Public sector 42–5, 48, 59
Strikes 44, 47, 56–8
Unemployment 47
Union fragmentation 59–60
Union membership 38–9, 54–5, 59
Women 49, 58
Franco, Francisco 121, 128

De Gaulle, Charles 39, 40, 52
Germany x, 54, 139, 231
Collective bargaining 71, 73, 76, 85–8
Deutsche Angestellten–Gewerkschaft (DAG) 70–1
Deutschen Gewerkschaftsbund (DGB) 68, 71, 76, 77, 78, 79, 80, 81–4
Einheitsgewerkschaft 67–8, 70
Employers' associations 85–7
Freier Deutscher Gewerkschaftsbund (FDGB) 66
German unification 76–8, 84
Industrial unionism 69–70
Industriegewerkschaft Metall (IG Metall) 69, 78, 83, 85, 87–8
Kommunistische Partei Deutschlands (KPD) 66, 67
Labour laws 74
Labour share of national income 75, 91
Mitbestimmung (codetermination) 71–2
Social movement unionism 85
Sozialdemokratische Partei Deutschlands (SPD) 66, 67, 68, 74, 75
Sozialistische Einheitspartei (SED) 66
Strikes 75, 84, 90
Unemployment 74–5, 76, 84, 90
Union finances 80–1
Union membership 73, 74, 75, 77–8, 88, 91
Union mergers 79–80
Union organising 85
Union structure 68–70
Women 81
Works councils 71–2
Giscard d'Estaing, Valéry 43
Globalisation 78, 89, 135, 308–9
Gorbachev, Mikhail 291, 296, 297
Gramsci, Antonio 97, 145

Histadrut (Israel) 343–60
Hitler, Adolf 65, 67
Hungary 308
Austerity measures 253–4
Collective bargaining 231, 244, 248

Communist party (MKP) 232
Democratic League of Independent Trade Unions (LIGA) 246, 247, 249, 252, 253, 259
Greater Budapest Central Workers' Council (KMT) 239
Hungarian Workers' Party (MSZMP) 234, 236, 246, 250
Interest Reconciliation Council (ÉT) 248, 253, 255, 256–7
Labour law 232, 250–1, 255, 257–8
National Association of Hungarian Trade Unions (MSZOSZ) 247–8, 249
National Centre of Hungarian Trade Unions 233–4
National Council of Trade Unions (SZOT) 235–6, 238, 239, 242, 243, 244–5, 247, 250, 251, 252–3
Privatisation 254
Revolution of 1956 237–40
Social Democratic Party (MSZDP) 231
Stalinist dictatorship 235–7
Strikes 231, 239, 245, 257
Union elections 251–2
Union fragmentation 249–53
Union membership 231, 232, 244
Union pluralism 244–9
Work competitions 236
Hyman, Richard 97–8, 105, 106, 148

International Confederation of Free Trade Unions (ICFTU) 62, 253, 328, 393, 394
International Labour Organisation (ILO) 334, 336, 375, 382, 393
Industriegewerkschaft Metall (IG Metall) (Germany) 69, 78, 83, 85, 87–8
International Monetary Fund (IMF) xii, 205, 371, 379–80
Israel
Collective bargaining 349–50, 351–3
Coordination Council of Economic Organisations 352–3
Decentralisation and pluralism 348–9
Health provision 348, 349, 350, 357
Histadrut background and goals 343–4
Histadrut economic role 344–5
Histadrut social and cultural function 345–6
Histadrut Trade Union Department 346–7, 352
Immigrants 348
Labour force composition 354–6
Labour law 351, 353–4
Labour-state relations 356, 358–9
Migrant workers 359–60
Privatisation 349, 357
Public sector 350, 359
Public opinion 360
Temporary work 355–6
Unemployment 349
Union membership 346, 358
Unions and professional workers 355, 357
Unions and young workers 354, 357, 358
Women 357, 359
Italy x, 54, 125, 212, 232
Agriculture 100–1
Associazioni Cristiana e dei Lavoratori Italiani (ACLI) 106
Collective bargaining 114–16
Confederazione Generale Italiana del Lavoro (CGIL) 105–6, 107–11, 113, 114, 115–18
Confederazione Italiana Sindacati Lavoratori (CISL) 106–7, 108–11, 113, 115–18

Autunno caldo (Hot Autumn 1969) 108–11
Factory councils 108–9
Fascism 97, 99, 104, 105, 107
Industrial development 100
Labour laws 112, 116
Libera Confederazione Generale Italiana del Lavoro (LCGIL) 106
Pact of Rome (1944) 98, 105, 110
Partito Comunista Italiano (PCI) 106, 108
Rerum Novarum 102
Social concertation 112–14, 115–16
Strikes 106
Union centralisation 113
Union membership 113
Union pluralism 98, 99, 102–4, 116–18
Unione Italiana del Lavoro (UIL) 107, 108, 109–11, 113, 115–18

Japan x
Jospin, Lionel 48

Keynesianism ix, x–xi, 11, 18, 22, 45, 46, 137
Kohl, Helmut 74
Khrushchev, Nikita 265, 266

Leopold III, King (Belgium) 10–11
LO (Swedish Confederation of Trade Unions) 157, 158, 159, 161, 162–5, 167–9, 170–1, 172, 173, 174, 177, 178, 181–2, 184, 185, 186, 187, 188, 189, 195

Maastricht Treaty (1992) 24
Major, John 210
Mandela, Nelson 392, 401
Mexico 123
Mills, C. Wright 148
Mitterrand, François 43, 52
Monks, John 217–18, 225
Mouvement Syndical Unifié (MSU) (Belgium) 7
Movement for Democratic Change (MDC) (Zimbabwe) xii
Mugabe, Robert xii
Mussolini, Benito 97

Nagy, Imre 239
National Association of Hungarian Trade Unions (MSZOSZ) 247–8, 249
National Council of Trade Unions (SZOT) (Hungary) 235–6, 238, 239, 242, 243, 244–5, 247, 250, 251, 252–3
National Council of Trade Unions (*Ogólnopolska Porozumienie Związków Zawodowych*, OPZZ) (Poland) 276–8, 279, 280, 281, 283, 286
National Council of Trade Unions (NACTU) (South Africa) 404, 405, 406, 407
Nationalsozialistische Deutsche Arbeiterpartei (Nazi Party) 6, 65, 66, 67
Netherlands 20
Nezalezhnaia Profspilka Gornykiv Ukrainy (NPGU) (Ukraine) 300, 304, 307, 309
Neo-liberalism 25, 98, 336, 337, 363, 382–4
Nigeria 323, 324, 325
Colonial rule 363–4, 383
International labour affiliations 366
Labour law 365, 368–70, 374–5, 381–2
Military rule 363, 364, 367, 368, 371, 373, 383
National Association of Nigerian Students (NANS) 372, 377, 379

Neo-liberalism 363, 364, 376, 377, 382–4
Nigerian Labour Congress (NLC) 367–8, 372, 373, 376–82, 383
State repression of unions 371–2, 375, 379–81, 382, 383
Strikes 369–71, 373–4, 375, 377–8, 379–81
Structural adjustment programme 371
Union fragmentation and disunity 364–6
Union membership 364, 365
Union mergers 367–8
Nigerian Labour Congress (NLC) 367–8, 372, 373, 376–82, 383
Non-governmental organisations (NGO) 357–8, 359, 429
Norway 161, 162, 164, 189

Obasanjo, Olusegun 369, 376, 377, 381, 382

Parti communist français (PCF) 38, 63
Perón, Juan xii
Pétain, Philippe 39
Poland 308, 309
Central Council of Trade Unions (CRZZ) 264, 266–7, 268, 270
Labour law 267
Martial law 273, 274
National Council of Trade Unions (*Ogólnopolska Porozumienie Związków Zawodowych*, OPZZ) 276–8, 279, 280, 281, 283, 286
Solidarity 261, 262, 268–9, 272–5, 277–82, 283–4, 285, 286
Stalinism 261
Statist industrial relations 263
Strikes 261–2, 266, 270, 273
Unemployment 280
Union membership 279, 282–4
White collar workers 285–6
Women 272
Workers' attitudes toward unions 271–2
Workers' Defence Committee (KOR) 269
Workplace councils 264, 267

Roosevelt, Franklin D. 11

SACO (Swedish Confederation of Professional Associations) 177–9, 188, 195
Sarkozy, Nicolas 52
Schmidt, Helmut 75
Social movement unionism 85, 376, 383, 408, 433
Solidarity (Poland) 245, 261, 262, 268–9, 272–5, 277–82, 283–4, 285, 286
South Africa xii, 376, 431
African National Congress (ANC) 392–3, 394, 395–7, 399–400, 401, 402
Apartheid 390, 391, 392–3, 398
Congress of South African Trade Unions (COSATU) 275–6, 387, 395, 396–7, 398, 399, 400, 401, 402, 404, 405, 406, 407
Federation of Unions of South Africa (FEDUSA) 398, 405, 406, 407
Labour force 389–90, 408
National Council of Trade Unions (NACTU) 404, 405, 406, 407
Neo-liberalism 400
National Economic Development and Labour Council (NEDLAC) 399, 403, 431
Parallel unions 393–4
Religion 402

Segmented labour market 401
South African Congress of Trade Unions (SACTU) 387, 392–3, 394, 395
South African Communist Party (SACP) 389, 391, 392, 394, 395, 400
State repression 391, 393, 395
Strikes 391, 395
Trade Union Council of South Africa (TUCSA) 387, 393–4, 397–8
Trades and Labour Council (T&LC) 388, 393
Union membership 392, 404
Union structure 403–7

Soviet Union xiii, 66, 232, 233, 265, 291, 292–5

Spain 54
Collective bargaining 132, 138–9
Comisiones Obreras (CCOO) 122, 127, 128–9, 130–2, 133, 137–9, 141, 142, 144
Confederación Nacional de Trabajadores (CNT) 123, 142–3
Immigrants 142
Industrial relations under Franco 123–8, 135
Labour laws 124, 131–3
Neo-corporatism 135–7
Organización Sindical Española (OSE) 124, 127
Secret police 123
Social pacts 132, 135–7
Strikes 126, 132
Training and lifelong learning 139–40
Unemployment 135
Union elections 133, 141–2, 144
Unión General de Trabajadores (UGT) 122, 123–4, 127, 128–9, 130–2, 133, 137–9, 142, 144
Union identity 121, 122, 145, 148
Union membership 129–30
Union unity versus pluralism 131, 144
Women 142, 143

Stalin, Josef 236, 265, 266

Structural adjustment programmes (SAPs) xiii, 371

Sweden x, xi, 54
Basic Agreement (1938) 157–9, 162, 167, 171
Collective bargaining 155–6, 162–5, 167–9, 175–6, 183–6, 194
Industry Agreement (1997) 156, 171, 183–6, 194
Labour law 156, 172–6, 183–4
LO (Swedish Confederation of Trade Unions) 157, 158, 159, 161, 162–5, 167–9, 170–1, 172, 173, 174, 177, 178, 181–2, 184, 185, 186, 187, 188, 189, 195
Role of state in industrial relations 166–7, 183–4
SAF (Swedish Employers' Federation) 157–9, 160–2, 164, 165, 166, 167–9, 171, 172, 173, 174, 181–2, 183–6, 195
SN (Confederation of Swedish Enterprise) 159, 183, 186, 188–9, 194, 195
SACO (Swedish Confederation of Professional Associations) 177–9, 188, 195
Solidaristic wage policy 170–1
Strikes and lockouts 158, 160–1, 162, 163, 166, 87
TCO (Swedish Confederation of Professional Employees) 177–9, 181, 182, 187, 188, 195
Unemployment insurance 189–93
Union centralisation 161, 162–5, 174–7
Union density 156, 158–9, 162, 189–93

White-collar unions 156, 177–81
Women 179–81

TCO (Swedish Confederation of Professional Employees) 177–9, 181, 182, 187, 188, 195
Thatcher, Margaret 54, 200
Trades Union Congress (TUC) (UK) 54, 62, 200, 201, 202, 203, 209, 212, 213–18, 219, 220, 222, 225, 324
Truman, Harry S. 66–7
Tsvangirai, Morgan 424, 425, 426, 427, 428, 430, 431, 432

Ukraine
Federatsiia Profspilok Ukrainy (FPU) 298–301, 302–4, 306, 309–10
Globalisation 308–9
Konfederatsiia Vilnykh Profspilok Ukrainy (KVPU) 300, 301
Nezalezhnaia Profspilka Gornykiv Ukrainy (NPGU) 300, 304, 307, 309
Orange Revolution 291, 303, 304, 309–10
Privatisation 305–8, 310
Strikes 295, 296–7, 303, 304
Tripartite bodies 302–3
Ukrainian Workers' party 304
Under Soviet rule 291, 292–6
Union elections 294
Union membership 298–9, 300
Union politics 304
Workers' rights violations 302
Unión General de Trabajadores (UGT) (Spain) 122, 123–4, 127, 128–9, 130–2, 133, 137–9, 142, 144
Union des Travailleurs Manuels et Intellectuels (UTMA) (Belgium) 7
Unione Italiana del Lavoro (UIL) (Italy) 107, 108, 109–11, 113, 115–18
United Kingdom x, 11, 44, 54, 66–7, 68, 69, 109, 123, 144
Collective bargaining 201, 202, 203, 205, 206–7
Conservative Party 202, 203, 206, 208–11
Donovan Report 206–7
Full employment 202, 208
Labour laws 202, 204, 205, 206–8, 209–11
Labour Party 200, 201–2, 203, 207–8, 214, 215, 216, 217, 225
National Economic Development Council 203, 208, 215
Partnership agreements 201, 216, 219, 222–3
Strikes 201, 204, 205, 207, 209, 211–12
Thatcherism and unions 208–13, 214
Trades Union Congress (TUC) 54, 62, 200, 201, 202, 203, 209, 212, 213–18, 219, 220, 222, 225, 324
Unions and ethnicity 220–1
Union membership 200, 212–13, 216, 219
Union organising 223–4
White collar workers 213
Women 220–1
United States x, 8, 11, 53, 62, 66–7, 68, 69, 106, 156, 167, 201, 212

Verhofstadt, Guy 25

Walesa, Lech 278–9
Webb, Sydney 323
Wilson, Harold 203–5, 206
Woodcock, George 203
World Bank xii, 371, 379–80
World Federation of Trade Unions (WFTU) 62, 238, 253, 328

World War I 101, 231, 316
World War II ix, xi, xiv, 4, 6, 8, 10, 37, 45, 55, 84, 88, 89, 99, 104, 123, 158, 168, 200, 201, 261, 325, 390

Yushchenko, Victor 309

Zapatero, José Luis Rodríguez 123
Zimbabwe xii
  African Trade Union Congress (ATUC) 416
  Colonial rule 413–18
  Collective bargaining 422
  Labour laws 414–15, 423, 424, 426–7
  Movement for Democratic Change (MDC) xii, 413, 432
  National African Federation of Unions (NAFU) 416
  Political repression 426–7, 434
  Public sector 429–30
  Rival unions 419–20, 432, 434
  Strikes 414, 421, 430, 431, 432
  Structural adjustment programme 425, 426–7, 428, 429
  Union dependence on ruling party 423–4
  Union fragmentation 415–18
  Union membership 417
  Union mismanagement 420–1
  Works councils 423
  Zimbabwe Congress of Trade Unions (ZCTU) 413, 419–21, 422, 423, 424–34
Zimbabwe Congress of Trade Unions (ZCTU) 413, 419–21, 422, 423, 424–34

Trade Unions Past, Present and Future

Edited by Craig Phelan

This series publishes monographs and edited collections on the history, present condition and possible future role of organised labour around the world. Multi-disciplinary in approach, geographically and chronologically diverse, this series is dedicated to the study of trade unionism and the undeniably significant role it has played in modern society. Topics include the historical development of organised labour in a variety of national and regional settings; the political, economic and legal contexts in which trade unionism functions; trade union internationalism past and present; comparative and cross-border studies; trade unions' role in promoting economic equality and social justice; and trade union revitalisation and future prospects. The aims of the series are to promote an appreciation of the diversity of trade union experience worldwide and to provide an international forum for lively debate on all aspects of the subject.

Volume 1 Craig Phelan (ed.): Trade Unionism since 1945: Towards a Global History. Volume 1: Western Europe, Eastern Europe, Africa and the Middle East.
467 pages. 2009. ISBN 978-3-03911-410-8